Comparative Plant Succession amo
Biomes of the World

Despite more than a century of study by ecologists, recovery following disturbances (succession) is not fully understood. This book provides the first global synthesis that compares plant succession in all major terrestrial biomes and after all major terrestrial disturbances. It asks critical questions such as: Does succession follow general patterns across biomes and disturbance types? Do factors that control succession differ from biome to biome? If common drivers exist, what are they? Are they abiotic or biotic, or both? The authors provide insights on broad, generalizable patterns that go beyond site-specific studies, and present discussions on factors such as varying temporal dynamics, latitudinal differences, human-caused versus natural disturbances, and the role of invasive alien species. This book is a must-read for researchers and students in ecology, plant ecology, restoration ecology, and conservation biology. It also provides a valuable framework to aid land managers attempting to manipulate successional recovery following increasingly intense and widespread human-made disturbances.

KAREL PRACH is Professor of Botany in the Faculty of Science, University of South Bohemia, and Senior Research Scientist at the Institute of Botany, Czech Academy of Science, Czech Republic. He has published extensively in the areas of succession, restoration, river floodplains, and ecology of alien plants. He is the current president of the Czech Botanical Society.

LAWRENCE R. WALKER is Professor Emeritus in the School of Life Sciences, University of Nevada, Las Vegas. His research focuses on succession, disturbance ecology, and restoration. He taught ecology, conservation biology, and scientific writing for 30 years. He has published ten previous books, is an ISI Highly Cited Researcher, and held the Wilder Chair in Botany at the University of Hawaii (2009–2010).

ECOLOGY, BIODIVERSITY, AND CONSERVATION

The world's biological diversity faces unprecedented threats. The urgent challenge facing the concerned biologist is to understand ecological processes well enough to maintain their functioning in the face of the pressures resulting from human population growth. Those concerned with the conservation of biodiversity and with restoration also need to be acquainted with the political, social, historical, economic and legal frameworks within which ecological and conservation practice must be developed. The new Ecology, Biodiversity, and Conservation series will present balanced, comprehensive, up-to-date, and critical reviews of selected topics within the sciences of ecology and conservation biology, both botanical and zoological, and both 'pure' and 'applied'. It is aimed at advanced final-year undergraduates, graduate students, researchers, and university teachers, as well as ecologists and conservationists in industry, government and the voluntary sectors. The series encompasses a wide range of approaches and scales (spatial, temporal, and taxonomic), including quantitative, theoretical, population, community, ecosystem, landscape, historical, experimental, behavioural and evolutionary studies. The emphasis is on science related to the real world of plants and animals rather than on purely theoretical abstractions and mathematical models. Books in this series consider issues from a broad perspective. Some books challenge existing paradigms and present new ecological concepts, empirical or theoretical models, and testable hypotheses. Other books explore new approaches and present syntheses on topics of ecological importance.

Ecology and Control of Introduced Plants
Judith H. Myers and Dawn Bazely

Invertebrate Conservation and Agricultural Ecosystems
T. R. New

Comparative Plant Succession among Terrestrial Biomes of the World

KAREL PRACH

University of South Bohemia

LAWRENCE R. WALKER

University of Nevada

CAMBRIDGE
UNIVERSITY PRESS

CAMBRIDGE
UNIVERSITY PRESS

University Printing House, Cambridge CB2 8BS, United Kingdom

One Liberty Plaza, 20th Floor, New York, NY 10006, USA

477 Williamstown Road, Port Melbourne, VIC 3207, Australia

314–321, 3rd Floor, Plot 3, Splendor Forum, Jasola District Centre, New Delhi – 110025, India

79 Anson Road, #06–04/06, Singapore 079906

Cambridge University Press is part of the University of Cambridge.

It furthers the University's mission by disseminating knowledge in the pursuit of education, learning, and research at the highest international levels of excellence.

www.cambridge.org
Information on this title: www.cambridge.org/9781108472760
DOI: 10.1017/9781108561167

First published 2020

Printed in the United Kingdom by TJ International Ltd, Padstow Cornwall

A catalogue record for this publication is available from the British Library.

Library of Congress Cataloging-in-Publication Data
Names: Prach, Karel, 1953– author. | Walker, Lawrence R., author.
Title: Comparative plant succession among terrestrial biomes of the world / Karel Prach, Lawrence R. Walker.
Description: Cambridge ; New York, NY : Cambridge University Press, 2020. | Series: Ecology, biodiversity and conservation | Includes bibliographical references and index.
Identifiers: LCCN 2019035838 (print) | LCCN 2019035839 (ebook) | ISBN 9781108472760 (hardback) | ISBN 9781108460248 (paperback) | ISBN 9781108561167 (ebook)
Subjects: LCSH: Plant succession. | Plant communities. | Ecological disturbances.
Classification: LCC QK910 .P73 2020 (print) | LCC QK910 (ebook) | DDC 581.7/18–dc23
LC record available at lccn.loc.gov/2019035838
LC ebook record available at lccn.loc.gov/2019035839

ISBN 978-1-108-47276-0 Hardback
ISBN 978-1-108-46024-8 Paperback

Contents

Color plates can be found between pages 244 and 245.

Preface

This book emerged from sharing a sticky, cinnamon-covered funnel cake while sitting on the grass in a park in Boulder City, Nevada. We, Karel and Lawrence, were scheming about new ways to work together and we agreed that a long-standing challenge in succession research was the lack of generalization at broader spatial scales. What if we could find a few basic ways to compare enough studies from many disturbances and biomes? Would that help unwind the numerous threads of successional research that, like the strings of our funnel cake, seemed hopelessly tangled? With the enthusiastic support of our wives, we decided to tackle the challenge to search for possible patterns among the thousands of studies of succession. We were encouraged by our recent paper (Prach & Walker, 2019) that showed clear latitudinal trends, following mining and abandoned fields, in what we call the success of succession, or the return to a study's local potential natural vegetation. Were such patterns the first glimpses to a more robust generalization? This book thus represents both the first comprehensive survey of plant succession in nearly two decades as well as the first attempt at global comparisons of terrestrial succession among all major disturbances and biomes. We encourage you to dip into it to see how we fared.

Plant succession is a central theme in ecology that focuses on temporal dynamics. Yet, despite the large number of site-specific studies, there is a lack of comparative studies on succession that consider broad geographical scales. In our research careers, we have attempted to address this imbalance.

Another aspect of succession that concerns us both is its applicability to practical issues of conservation and restoration. We see restoration as the deliberate manipulation of succession to a desired goal. We also have found that often well-intentioned manipulations are counterproductive to achieving a desirable endpoint, particularly if principles of ecological succession are not understood. Thus we hope that this book will be useful not only to academic ecologists but also to practically oriented people including conservationists and restorationists.

We have many people who helped this book come to fruition. First, of course, are our wives, who deserve much thanks for their patience, not only when we wrote in our own homes but when we were visiting each other. Karel thanks his home institutions, the Faculty of Science USB in České Budějovice (especially his Restoration Ecology Working Group) and the Institute of Botany, Czech Academy of Science for support, and funding for the project from Grant no. 17-09979S and partly from Grant no. 20-06065S from the Czech National Science Foundation. Lawrence thanks his institution, the University of Nevada, Las Vegas, for logistical and financial support. We both thank the staff of Cambridge University Press, particularly Dominic Lewis and Michael Usher, the series editor, for their encouragement and support of this project and the external reviews of the prospectus that they provided. Petra Pospíšilová diligently made many of our figures, Luboš Tichý and Petra Janečková helped with statistics, and Petra Janečková also was very helpful in searching the literature for suitable studies. We are indebted to our many colleagues whose detailed and insightful comments greatly improved the book. Reviewers included Richard Bardgett, Sandor Bartha, Peter Bellingham, Phil Burton, Ray Callaway, Bruce Clarkson, Roger del Moral, Ned Fetcher, Fred Landau, Scott Meiners, Ondřej Mudrák, Martin Prach, Marcel Rejmánek, Joanne Sharpe, and Aaron Shiels. We also thank our colleagues Ivana Jongepierová, Iveta Kadlecová, Jitka Klimešová, Jan Š. Lepš, Anička Müllerová, Klára Řehounková, and Martina Vašutová for additional support. Photos were kindly shared by Grizelle Gonzalez, Lenka Oplatková, Elizabeth Powell, Lenka Šebelíková, and Zuzana Veverková (see figure legends for credits).

1 · *Introduction*

Plant succession is the replacement of plant species and communities over time in response to a disturbance of either natural or human origin. It is a unifying concept of ecology, integrating temporal and spatial scales, abiotic and biotic disturbances, plant-soil and plant-animal interactions, plant life histories, biodiversity patterns, species interactions, and other fundamental ecological principles across a heterogeneous landscape. While we have a simple, intuitive grasp that plant communities change (e.g., abandoned pastures change to forests; vegetation recovers following damaged by fire), the actual drivers of such change are not fully understood, even after more than a century of formal study (Clements, 1916; Glenn-Lewin *et al.*, 1992; Meiners *et al.*, 2015a). One of the challenges is that most work on plant succession (henceforth "succession" because of the preponderance of plant-focused studies; but see heterotrophic succession, Walker & del Moral, 2003) has been specific to a given site or type of disturbance. Yet progress has been made in identifying certain ecological principles that are likely to be important in succession. In this book, we explore global-scale patterns of several key aspects of plant succession to discern at what level generalizations about succession are possible. For the first time, we systematically compare terrestrial successional processes following all major disturbances among all the world's biomes. This synthesis also provides a framework for aiding land managers attempting to manipulate succession through restoration (Prach & Walker, 2011).

The incomplete understanding of successional drivers is clearly a function of the complexity of interacting and continuously changing variables. For example, on a recent lava flow, there are many unpredictable factors, each with successional consequences. These variables include the stochastic nature of seed dispersal and germination; abiotic influences such as climate fluctuations, surface chemistry, and nutrient status; presence or absence of competing plants or hungry animals; and sequential colonists and plant communities that reinforce, displace, or have no effect on the first plant colonists. These series of stochastic events therefore accumulate uncertainty over time. Moreover, humans change the whole surrounding landscape, including with the introduction of invasive alien species that can be particularly good invaders of new disturbances (e.g., on the lava flows in Hawaii; Vitousek *et al.*, 1987). Predicting detailed future plant communities on that patch of lava therefore becomes as complex as predicting the weather years in advance. And even when local successional patterns are discernible, how broadly they apply is still unclear. Despite these hesitations, we are convinced that certain successional traits can be predicted.

Three topics of successional studies became the basis for our global comparison of succession, in part because of their importance to understanding succession and in part because they were commonly measured and therefore provided a basis for comparison among studies. First, the focus of many successional studies has been on trajectories and rates of change. For example, if succession is directional, which community represents the final or relatively stable endpoint and how long and how many intermediate communities are needed to get there? Are there multiple pathways to the same endpoint or are their multiple endpoints? And to what degree does any eventual endpoint resemble the predisturbance or surrounding vegetation? These questions have important implications for establishing and achieving restoration goals. We used two aspects of this area of research in our comparisons: 1) the success of a sere (successional sequence) in achieving a resemblance to the natural vegetation, and 2) whether the trajectories in a given study were convergent, divergent, or neither.

A second area of inquiry in ecology has been on patterns and causes of biodiversity. This interest stems from both a theoretical interest in how species evolve in dynamic environments and a practical interest in conserving species in the face of natural and human disturbances. One factor affecting biodiversity is species interactions (among plants and among trophic levels). In succession, much effort has been focused on determining when positive (facilitative) or negative (competitive) interactions are most likely to drive succession. In our comparative studies, we examined patterns of change in species richness (an aspect of species diversity) during succession.

A third topic in ecology is the increasingly urgent concern about the influence of invasive alien species, introduced directly or indirectly by humans. The rapid spread of plant species around the world has resulted in many new communities with profound consequences for ecosystem function and successional dynamics. Unfortunately, these consequences are poorly understood. We compared the degree to which invasive alien species affected succession in different biomes and after different disturbances.

Because of the great heterogeneity of data presented in studies on succession, and the frequent absence of primary data, we used only simple ordinal or categorical evaluations of the trends in successional trajectories, species richness, and importance of alien invasive species. This simplification enabled us to compare more studies than would have been possible with a more analytical and quantitative approach.

We wrote this book for several reasons. First, it was time for a global update on the steady output of successional studies. Recent book-length reviews addressing succession have tended to be more site-specific (Meiners et al., 2015b), disturbance-specific (Cramer & Hobbs, 2007); or focused on disturbance (Johnson & Miyanishi, 2007; Walker, 2012; Wohlgemuth et al., 2019) or restoration (Walker et al., 2007) more than on succession. Second, the accumulation of site-specific studies challenges us to ask: Are we ready to make broad generalizations about succession, and if so, at what spatial scale? Third, although biomes and disturbances are a fundamental aspect of vegetation studies, no one has yet explicitly contrasted succession among biomes within a disturbance type or among disturbance types. Fourth, any theoretical implications from such comprehensive comparisons could potentially advance our still incomplete understanding of successional principles. Finally, practical implications will help guide managers who are trying to conserve still relatively pristine natural areas or to restore damaged lands. Generalizations, where possible, will help those in poorly studied biomes or disturbances glean strategies appropriate for their use.

One previous attempt to summarize succession by habitat (Burrows, 1990), and the most recent comprehensive book on succession in general (Walker & del Moral, 2003) are several decades old. Therefore, we hope that this book, with its comparative approach to studying succession by biomes and disturbance types, helps further our general understanding of temporal dynamics. We are encouraged by several recent papers (e.g., Peltzer et al., 2010; Meiners et al., 2015a) and a special feature (Chang & Turner, 2019) that focus on novel findings and future directions for successional research.

Our book is organized into three sections. Part I (Chapters 1–3) continues with an overview of how humans have interacted with and studied succession and an overview of the terrestrial biomes of the world.

Part II (Chapters 4–15) examines succession by disturbance type and includes 1) a description of the disturbance, 2) abiotic and biotic variables that affect succession following each disturbance, and the results of our comparative analyses, and 3) theoretical and practical implications of our findings. Details on how we chose certain studies for comparison are found in Chapter 4. Part III presents a synthesis of several prominent themes that emerged from Part II and a conclusion with future challenges for studies of succession. At the end of the book is Appendix 1, a glossary, and Appendix 2 containing the literature and search phrases used in our comparative analyses.

Part I
Plant Succession and Biomes

2 · *Humans and Succession*

2.1 Introduction

Succession is a natural process of ecosystem development following a disturbance. In this chapter, we review basic theoretical concepts concerning succession and examine how humans have interacted with it. We document how human approaches to environmental change gradually became more formalized as a study of succession, a study that is now a dynamic tenet of ecology. We end the chapter with a discussion of how succession is currently studied.

Humans have long been aware that their environment changes over time (Clements, 1916). Hunters and gatherers needed to know how seasonal variables such as leaf cover and frost duration or longer-term changes such as forest encroachment on grasslands affected their prey. They probably used fire to intentionally manipulate the proportion of woody plants and herbs. Farmers understood the implications of their short-term manipulations of soil fertility on longer-term soil quality and crop success and the implications of cutting down trees on forest regrowth. The development of early human societies depended on successful, sustainable harvesting of natural resources, so the focus was largely on practical management concerns. Therefore, humans have long influenced the natural forces driving succession.

Throughout human history, we have consistently improved our ability to extract natural resources by clearing forests, draining wetlands, and mining raw materials. As humans became more efficient at resource extraction, these changes increased our role as manipulators of temporal dynamics. For example, the rapid expansion of humanity has intensified natural and anthropogenic disturbances; depleted populations of animals we hunt and fish; expanded and manipulated crops; facilitated the spread of nonnative plants; and created new plant communities better adapted to the changing environmental conditions (del Moral & Walker, 2007). Each of these manipulations altered succession, which now is clearly a process overwhelmingly dominated by human modifications. Here, to provide context, we review a history of successional concepts, describe the current conceptual framework, and present several methodological approaches to understanding succession.

2.2 History of Ideas

As early as 300 BC, Theophrastus documented changes of vegetation along a river floodplain. During the eighteenth century, naturalists recorded successional changes in vegetation on seashores, in bogs, in water-filled ditches, in abandoned fields, and on rocks (Walker & del Moral, 2003). Formal study of temporal vegetation dynamics began in the nineteenth century with observers of both generalized (Humboldt & Bonpland, 1807) and detailed (Thoreau, 1860) patterns of change. Clements (1928) reviews the earliest literature on succession, noting that the term "succession" was used from the early nineteenth century to describe how lakes convert to meadows and pools to mosses and how long-term changes altered landscapes. Thoreau (1860) coined the term "forest succession" to explain changes after logging. These and other observations culminated in the publication of *Oecology of Plants* by Warming (1895, 1909). This treatise is foundational to modern ecology and has succession as a fundamental theme. Warming perceived that change in plant communities (succession) came from a struggle among organisms and thought that external disturbances were frequent enough to minimize equilibrium conditions. By the early twentieth century, the concept of succession was well established, although with competing perspectives of holism, which emphasized emergent properties at the community level, and the reductionist view of a community as simply a sum of its parts (Smuts, 1926). Holism emphasized equilibrium between plants and their environment (Clements, 1916), and reductionism emphasized disequilibrium (Cowles, 1901; Gleason, 1926). Indeed, succession became a central concept in the newly emerging field of ecology (McIntosh, 1999) with holism and reductionism alternating in cycles of relative popularity until both merged into a more integrated view of successional dynamics by the end of the twentieth century.

Clements (1916, 1928, 1936) developed the holistic, equilibrium concept of plant community responses to disturbances. His perspective was at once dynamic and static, logical and dogmatic, and it dominated ecological thought until the late 1950s. Clements grounded his work in practical applications to agriculture, range management, and fire ecology, mostly in the American Midwest and West, but covered all types of natural disturbances, including volcanoes, dunes, melting glaciers, and floodplains. While recognizing the multiple, complex dynamics of plant responses to disturbances and community change through succession, Clements thought that change generally ended with equilibrium between plants and their environment. He called this equilibrium the climax stage of succession and considered it to be controlled primarily by climate: vegetation in a given climate would reach a predictable climatic climax. At broad geographical scales, the climatic climax concept resembles the concept of biomes (see Chapter 3), a term also introduced by Clements. Although Clements emphasized internal or autogenic responses as drivers of plant communities to a climax, he also addressed ongoing or new disturbances and the role of humans. Later in his career, he presented the ultimately rather unpopular analogy of plant community development to that of an organism, with the climax representing the final, dominant, adult stage. The eventual accumulation of examples of the absence of climax vegetation was explained through definitions of such modifiers as dis-climaxes, sub-climaxes, pre-climaxes, and numerous other alternatives, but these gradually weakened the strength of his initial logic. However, Clementsian views are rooted in our need for generalizations to explain complexity in our environment, and holism continues to be a factor in considerations of succession.

One Clementsian paradigm that continues to receive support is that organisms modify their environment; another is that positive (facilitative) and negative (competitive) interactions between species are key drivers of succession. A third view is that the development of plant communities is intrinsically tied to soil development (Moravec, 1969; Wardle et al., 2004; Peltzer et al., 2010). Several early ecology textbooks uncritically promoted the climax concept (Oosting, 1948; Odum, 1953), and Odum (1969) later suggested that during succession many ecosystem-level processes are predictable. The emerging subdiscipline of ecosystem ecology (especially as developed by the International Biological Program; McIntosh, 1999) often supported the Clementsian view that internal dynamics of an ecosystem become more important than external factors as ecosystem complexity increases (e.g., Margalef, 1968). Analogies were made between ecosystem function and the laws of thermodynamics (Odum & Pinkerton, 1955; Jørgenson, 1997). Ecosystem assembly, or the coalescing of groups of species into communities during succession

(Drake, 1990), is another approach with Clementsian roots. In this view, there are certain predictable rules that dictate the permissible combinations of species at a given site and stage. Much debate (see Wilson, 1994) ensued about the importance of competition (Diamond, 1975) versus chance (Connor & Simberloff, 1976) when Diamond proposed assembly rules for guilds of birds on newly disturbed islands in New Guinea. Connor and Simberloff vigorously debated the validity of such general rules. The search for generalizable rules continues with the focus shifting toward community rather than ecosystem assembly (Weiher *et al.*, 1998; Weiher & Keddy, 1999; Leibold & Chase, 2018). In a similar vein, keystone species (Paine, 1969; Ehrenfeld, 2000) are considered critical to both ecosystem assembly and succession and there is currently much interest in looking for general patterns of functional traits of species (Funk *et al.*, 2016).

The overarching concern of holists was that a top-down, deductive approach to succession was needed to provide a conceptual framework and avoid the accumulation of an incoherent morass of detailed observations (Walker & del Moral, 2003). This desire for a grand underlying scheme to explain succession will never fade, and provides a healthy antidote to the reductionist approach.

In contrast to Clements, others in his cohort of early ecologists emphasized an inductive approach and a reductionist disequilibrium view of succession, following Warming's lead. Cowles (1901), like Warming, studied succession on dunes and found no evidence of a predictable climax vegetation but frequent and largely stochastic disturbances instead, leading to the view that succession is a "variable approaching a variable" (Cowles, 1901). Gleason's (1926) reductionism took the form of what he called the individualistic concept, in that each species dispersed independently of other species across a landscape. Succession following dunes or on exposed rocks was not predictable in this worldview. Gleason did not see plant communities as more than the sum of their parts, focusing, in contrast to Clements, on individual species rather than community properties and pattern over process. His views were not supported at the time and he left ecology for that reason. Ironically, he was eventually recognized as an eminent ecologist in 1959 (Cain, 1959), an act that represented a paradigm shift from a half century of dominance of the holistic school of thought. Reductionism arguably remained the dominant approach to succession until the end of the twentieth century (Miles, 1979; Glenn-Lewin, 1980; Walker & del Moral, 2003), despite waves of neoholism represented by ecosystem ecology during the International

Biological Program in the 1960s and 1970s and the resurgence of an emphasis on positive interactions among plants in the 1990s (Callaway, 1995).

One feature of the reductionist approach in the last half of the twentieth century was an emphasis on the stochasticity of species establishment. Rather than a predictable sequence of arrival of new species based on site conditions and interactions with resident species, each species could arrive randomly. Alternatively, all major players in succession might be present in the early stages, sorting out over time due to differential longevities. Succession in this scenario (initial floristic composition; Egler, 1954) is merely the result of sequential conspicuousness of the plant species. Also important to reductionism was the set of species available to colonize a sere from the surrounding landscape (Zobel, 1997). The difference between the set of species in the region that can potentially inhabit a particular site and those that do establish has been called "dark diversity" (Pärtel et al., 2011; arguably useful to either holism or reductionism). Other more or less individualistic approaches to succession emphasized the distinct and sometimes conflicting role of plant parts (e.g., buds, leaves, stems, roots; Harper, 1977), individualistic responses to disturbance (Raup, 1971), and an evolutionary framework for succession (Pickett, 1976). Finally, a Gleasonian emphasis on spatial pattern led to the study of how species are distributed along environmental gradients. Continuous and overlapping distribution patterns of individual species suggest a lack of sharply defined plant communities. Ordination analysis was developed to measure such distributions and their change over time (Austin, 1985; Goodall, 1986). In contrast, sharp breaks in species distributions for multiple species at the same point along environmental gradients suggest a more Clementsian view of clearly defined communities of interacting species. Those species can also affect their environment. For example, Wilson and Agnew (1992) proposed that several types of vegetation mosaics and boundaries are logical outcomes of positive feedback switches, whereby a community, and not just individual species, can modify the environment to its own advantage.

Whittaker (1953) proposed a merger of the views of Gleason and Clements, where multiple climaxes were possible across landscape-scale gradients. An update of this concept is that a landscape is composed of an interacting set of patches in various stages of succession (patch dynamics; Naveh & Lieberman, 1984; Pickett & White, 1985; Amarasekare & Possingham, 2001). In the landscape context, a related concept useful to succession is the theory of island biogeography developed by MacArthur and Wilson (1967) for colonization of real islands. A disturbed site can be seen as a habitat island that is colonized by species from its surroundings. The landscape context also includes the concept of metapopulations (Levins, 1969; Hanski, 1999), or a network of interacting populations of a given species with other populations of the same species in the surrounding landscape. Thus, the structure and species composition of the surrounding landscape and the colonization ability of species occurring there (diaspore pressure) are considered in studies of succession.

The failure to develop an overarching conceptual generalization about succession coincided with a burgeoning interest in conceptual and numerical models based on experimental and observational data (Walker & del Moral, 2003). In the last several decades, students of succession have willingly entered into that morass of observations that Clements and his followers had worried about, but with new sampling and statistical tools to help organize and analyze the data. Successional models have largely focused on mechanisms of species change and rarely attempted to explain entire seres. Models can emphasize autogenic or allogenic processes as drivers of succession (Walker & del Moral, 2003). One much-cited conceptual model, which recognized both random and deterministic interactions among species, was contributed by Connell and Slatyer (1977). They combined several earlier concepts, including from Clements, and suggested that initial colonists could facilitate, inhibit, or have no effect on later colonists. This scenario for early successional interactions (or any addition of a new species to an existing plant community) was relatively straightforward. However, subsequent steps in their three successional pathways were less clear and appeared to variously require positive, negative, or neutral interactions among species (Pickett et al., 1987a; Walker & Chapin, 1987; but see Connell et al., 1987). A second conceptual model was presented by Grime (1977), whereby succession could be explained as a sequence of plants best adapted to disturbance, then competition, and finally stress. For example, Lepš et al. (1982) used this model to explain succession in plowed fields. A third conceptual model by Noble and Slatyer (1980) emphasized vital attributes, which included how a species arrived at or persisted on a site, how quickly it established, and how rapidly it reached reproductive maturity. They used this model to successfully predict forest succession in Australia. Various other conceptual models (e.g., Pickett et al., 1987b; Walker & Chapin, 1987; Tilman, 1988; Burrows, 1990; Matthews, 1992) emphasizing processes of arrival, establishment, growth, competition, and facilitation are summarized in Walker and del Moral (2003). None of these models has emerged as universally applicable but each helped to explain part of the complexity of succession.

Neither the holistic (Clementsian) nor the reductionist (Gleasonian) view of succession has prevailed, and elements of each have been discarded as untenable (e.g., Clement's organismal analogy and single climatic climax or Gleason's complete independence of plants). Today, traces of both schools of thought remain in the tendency to emphasize either a synthetic or an analytical approach, but the earlier strict dichotomy is now largely of historical interest. In the latter decades of the twentieth century, analysts of successional dynamics began to focus on the relative importance of these coexisting drivers, depending on environmental stress and successional stage (Walker & Chapin, 1987; Callaway & Walker, 1997), which has led to a more integrated view of successional drivers. In addition, other potential drivers of succession are being recognized, including allelopathy, predation and herbivory, mutualism, invasive species, and life-history characteristics (Pickett *et al.*, 1987b). The concept of predictable seres ending in a climax has given way to the idea of multiple pathways and multiple endpoints, but the search continues for just what is predictable and when (Lepš & Rejmánek, 1991; Glenn-Lewin *et al.*, 1992; Lindenmayer *et al.*, 2010). Next, we discuss some themes that currently engage students of succession and highlight challenges for succession research in the coming decades.

2.3 Current Conceptual Framework

A recent paper (Meiners *et al.*, 2015a) asked: "Is successional research nearing its climax?" In other words, have insights provided by the study of succession peaked in output and begun to decline in their usefulness to ecology and society? The authors argued to the contrary, suggesting several avenues of active and potential future research on succession with great utility to science and society. Here, we introduce our own list (with input from Meiners *et al.*, 2015a and Prach & Walker, 2011) of four twenty-first-century research themes in succession research: 1) the role of disturbance characteristics in driving succession (including invasive alien species and climate change), 2) how succession proceeds at various temporal and spatial scales, 3) community assembly and functional traits (including predictability of successional trajectories), and 4) management implications. These topics have their origins in the preceding century of successional research discussed in the previous section and are developed further in Parts II and III of this book.

The role of disturbance is a topic inherently tied to subsequent successional changes (Pickett *et al.*, 1987b; Walker, 1999a; Jentsch & White, 2019) because disturbances are the crucial events that initiate succession. Their type, severity, and frequency determine the onset of succession and subsequent disturbances continue to modify successional processes (Pickett & White, 1985; White & Jentsch, 2001, 2004) and alter some aspects of the stability of an ecosystem (Holling, 1973). Resilience, a component of ecosystem stability, and its counterpart, resistance, are current topics in research on succession (Buma, 2015). Resilience is the ability of an ecosystem to return to its pre-disturbance condition; resistance is the ability to persist unchanged in the face of a disturbance (Pimm, 1984). Rapid succession after disturbance to a pre-disturbance stage is a sign of resilience as well as an adaptive feature of an ecosystem to a changing environment. Land managers are interested in promoting both resilience and resistance, depending on successional status and restoration goals for a particular ecosystem. Another recent concern of land managers is the spread of invasive alien species, which are a pervasive type of biotic disturbance in succession (e.g., Mooney *et al.*, 2005). Participation of all alien species usually decreases during succession (Rejmánek, 1989) but some competitive invasive aliens can dominate late successional stages, representing undesirable outcomes of succession. A particular question, with both theoretical and practical consequences, is which successional stages are prone to invasions, that is, when is an invasion window open (Johnstone, 1986)? The link between succession and invasion could certainly be better exploited to help understand both important processes. In later chapters, we examine succession within (Part II) and among (Part III, Chapter 16) disturbance types. Invasive alien species are one of four focal topics in Part II but we do not examine in detail how their role changes during the course of succession, concentrating instead on their participation in late successional stages. More detailed comparative analyses are needed.

Succession is best considered at multiple temporal and spatial scales (Chang & Turner, 2019). Incorporating geographic variation into our studies of succession (Meiners *et al.*, 2015a) helps us link land-use change to successional dynamics and expand our ability to compare seres at larger scales (Prach *et al.*, 2014d; van Breugel et al., 2019). Including multiple temporal scales can help us better manipulate succession through restoration by understanding past management legacies and present global climate change (Bhaskar *et al.*, 2014; Walker & Wardle, 2014). Processes measured at small scales (e.g., plant-microbe interactions, nutrient uptake) occur rapidly, while processes relevant to larger scales (e.g., nutrient depletion, landscape eutrophication, plant migration, or changes in regional species pools) occur more slowly (McLauchlan *et al.*, 2014). What happens between plants and microbes, or plants and herbivores at micro and local scales helps drive successional dynamics (Cutler *et al.*, 2008; Turner *et al.*, 2019). Longer-term processes such as nutrient depletion, eutrophication, and erosion constrain the possible successional patterns (Pickett, 1976; Peltzer *et al.*, 2010; Teste & Laliberté, 2019). By expanding or contracting the lens at which we study succession, we learn to ask different questions and perceive succession as a process of intermediate scale influenced by, and perhaps connecting shorter and longer processes (Walker & Wardle, 2014). In Chapter 16, we further explore the importance of addressing both temporal and spatial scales in the study of succession.

Community assembly, particularly as explained by the functional traits of plants, is another topic that intrigues scientists studying succession (Weiher & Keddy, 1999). Predictability of community assembly (of a given suite of species) appears to be highest for ecosystem functions (e.g., productivity, nitrogen-fixing ability, flammability) with declining predictability of growth form or morphology (e.g., tree vs. herb, seed size, shade provider, or user), and biotic interactions (e.g., dispersal, herbivory, competition). The exact species composition appears to be the most difficult characteristic to predict. A similar ranking of predictability occurs within a successional framework where some simple functions recover before vegetation structure, and species composition recovering last. These rankings of predictability also affect restoration decisions, where restoration ecologists try to recreate and perhaps accelerate a natural sere (Luken, 1990). For example, it is much easier to observe (or restore) some simple ecosystem functions and vegetation of a certain desirable structure (e.g., continuous cover to decrease erosion) than it is to build a community of similar species composition to the original, pre-disturbance condition or to that of a reference ecosystem. Of course, additional, complex ecosystem functions and species interactions depend on that particular suite of species and are therefore slower to return (and harder to reconstruct). The successional implications of functional traits (Prach *et al.*, 1997; Kunstler *et al.*, 2016) and community assembly (Temperton *et al.*, 2004) are sometimes considered, but these two topics are also addressed in many other contexts (e.g., resource acquisition: Díaz *et al.*, 2004; evolution: Mittelbach & Schemske, 2015; species niches: Kraft *et al.*, 2015; agroecology: Faucon *et al.*, 2017). Indeed, predicting ecological processes from plant traits has been called the Holy Grail of ecology (Lavorel *et al.*, 2007; Funk *et al.*, 2016). We suggest that this predictability should be pursued not only for functional traits and communities of individual seres but also be applied to successional trajectories of multiple seres across a landscape. In Part II, we examine trajectories of succession by disturbance type (but without explicit links to species traits); in Chapter 16, we continue our examination of functional traits, community assembly, and the predictability of trajectories.

Our final topic is the strong link between studies of succession and land management. Clements sought better conditions for farmers in the central United States (McIntosh, 1985). Forest gap models of succession (Shugart & West, 1980) and watershed manipulations (Bormann & Likens, 1979) addressed consequences of various logging strategies. Conservation biologists and restoration ecologists are better able to manage critical ecosystems when links to plant interactions (Gomez-Aparicio, 2009) and succession (Bradshaw, 2000; Prach *et al.*, 2001; Walker *et al.*, 2007; Prach & Walker, 2011) are recognized. Conservation biologists ask how protected areas or particular plant communities will react to ongoing climate changes, large-scale eutrophication, changes in regional species pools (e.g., due to invasion of alien species), and changing management intensity. Restoration ecologists are interested in manipulating succession to generate a desired outcome (Hobbs & Suding, 2009). Restoration can be seen as an effort to initiate, accelerate, slow down, turn back, divert, or mimic succession (Prach & Walker, 2011). For example, will increased disturbances, introduction of alien species, or climate change result in persistence of early successional stages and higher participation of invasive alien species in succession? Will increased temperatures result in shifts in successional trajectories? Future work in succession must address community change in a dynamic and novel landscape, and consider how natural communities should be preserved or restored or left in their novel condition (Hobbs *et al.*, 2009). Consequently, better integration of research on succession and ecological restoration is highly desirable (Walker *et al.*, 2007). In Chapter 16, we expand on the links between succession and both conservation and restoration.

We end this chapter with some comments on how to study succession. Here we highlight certain areas of current research, not in an attempt to be comprehensive, but to emphasize various threads of active ecological research on succession.

2.4 Methodological Approaches

There are two principal ways to study succession and other ecological phenomena. The first is to conduct controlled experiments, the second is to describe existing patterns. Experiments address the direct causes of successional change but are limited for practical reasons by their relatively small size (typically $\ll 1$ km^2), short duration (typically <10 years), and minimal replication where costs or logistics are limiting. Thus, any extrapolation of results to broader temporal and spatial scales must be done with caution. Because of these limitations, experimental studies are uncommon. Even less common are repeated experiments conducted over a larger geographical scale (van der Putten et al., 2000; Fridley & Wright, 2012; Prach et al., 2014c). In contrast, a descriptive approach generally correlates vegetation characteristics with environmental factors in time and space, and can be conducted at larger temporal and spatial scales. Chronosequences allow time scales of centuries (Pickett, 1989). The descriptive approach tends to be more commonly used than the experimental one and usually exploits correlative statistics. However, correlation does not equate with causality, so conclusions are limited to descriptions of patterns.

The descriptive approach typically studies succession by following change in permanent plots or uses chronosequences where plots of different ages are assumed to represent a successional trajectory (space-for-time substitution; Pickett, 1989; Walker et al., 2010). One can also combine both approaches by observing a series of chronosequence plots over time. The disadvantage of the chronosequence approach is that we cannot be sure that the plots are really comparable for all decisive environmental parameters (Johnson & Miyanishi, 2008). Even if we measure the appropriate parameters, we cannot usually reconstruct the history of the plots from the onset of succession, including various idiosyncratic events that might substantially influence succession. By contrast, we can usually reconstruct much longer seres than by the permanent plot approach, though several long-term studies of permanent plots do exist in the United Kingdom (Oxford): 175 years (Perryman et al., 2018); Denmark: 170 years (Kollmann & Rasmussen, 2012); and the United States (New Jersey): 58 years (Meiners et al., 2002). The generally less reliable data from chronosequences, in comparison to direct observation of permanent plots over time, can be somewhat compensated by a high number of plots and stages ranging over large environmental gradients. Results from experimental studies, studies in permanent plots, and data from chronosequences have substantially contributed to our knowledge about the processes and patterns of ecological succession.

Recent computerized modeling approaches that simulate succession have the advantage that they can predict future successional trajectories (Lohier *et al.*, 2016). However, a common limitation of such models is verification of the outputs with real data. In addition to the quantitative data obtained by experiments, permanent plots, and chronosequences, there are various qualitative data on the course of succession that are often obtained only by field experience. Such information is typically available at larger scales than plot-based studies, but must be used with caution because it cannot be rigorously tested. Nevertheless, this observational information can be used to generate hypotheses for subsequent testing and verification as well as in the interpretation of the more rigorous, quantitative data from plots. Such information can also be used in expert systems predicting successional change (Prach *et al.*, 1999).

Comparative studies of either many seres or one sere over a large geographical scale are scarce. We found only a few studies where succession on more than two seres were compared, but recognize that further inquiry could result in more. These studies include Walker (1995), Fox *et al.* (1996), Timoney *et al.* (1997) and a number of studies by Prach and his team (e.g., Prach *et al.*, 1993, 1997, 2014d, 2016). There are more studies analyzing one type of succession over a larger geographical area ($>10^4$ km^2). They mostly concern harvested peatlands (e.g., Graf *et al.*, 2008; Konvalinková & Prach, 2010; Triisberg *et al.*, 2014), abandoned fields (Prach, 1985; Tulus *et al.*, 2013; Prach *et al.*, 2014a), and clearcutting (LaPage & Banner, 2014; Kusumoto *et al.*, 2015). Some studies did not reconstruct chronosequences but compared late successional forests across Europe (De Frenne *et al.*, 2011), eastern Australia (Sams *et al.*, 2017), or the eastern United States (Wright & Fridley, 2010). Other comparative work on succession examines functional groups of plant species (Pausas & Lavorel, 2003), soil parameters (e.g., Messer, 1988; Zarin & Johnson, 1995a, 1995b), or soil organisms (Schipper *et al.*, 2001).

Some recent studies have evaluated the effectiveness of spontaneous succession to reach late successional stages in a reasonable time, using meta-analyses across large areas of the globe (Crouzeilles *et al.*, 2016; Meli *et al.*, 2017). The comparative analyses that we used for comparing succession in abandoned fields and in mine sites among the world biomes (Prach & Walker, 2019) are extended to other disturbances in this book (see Chapter 4). We expect that with rapidly improving analytical and statistical tools, the number of comparative studies of succession across multiple gradients, biomes, and disturbance types will increase. We hope that this book helps promote such important comparisons.

3 · *Terrestrial Biomes*

In this chapter, we present an introductory description of the particular biomes, providing a background to the patterns of succession. Our primary sources for information about the world biomes were Archibold (1995) and Breckle (2002), and for North America, Barbour and Billings (2000). We use the term *biome* in a broad sense as a widely distributed ecosystem characterized by vegetation with similar life forms and with occurrence, structure, and functioning of the biome largely determined by macroclimate and seasonality. We consider the following nine biomes:

- Tropical rain forests (TR), including also cloud, montane, and subtropical rain forests
- Tropical dry forests (TD), including seasonal, semi-deciduous, or deciduous forests and savannas
- Aridlands (AR), including deserts, semideserts, sage brush and pinyon-juniper vegetation of North America, and juniper shrublands of Eurasia
- Mediterranean-type (ME), including maquis in Europe, chaparral in California, mattoral in Chile, fynbos and renosterveld in South Africa, and mallee, karri, and jarrah in southwestern Australia; henceforth simply "Mediterranean biome"
- Temperate grasslands (TG), including steppes, pampas, and prairies
- Temperate broadleaf forests (TB), including both evergreen and deciduous forests
- Coniferous forests (CF), including mostly boreal forests, plus coniferous forests in western North America, and coniferous forests occurring in mountains or other specific habitats in the temperate broadleaf forest zone
- Tundra (TU), including true tundra and subarctic shrublands
- Alpine (AL), including also páramo and puna in tropical and subtropical mountains

The last two biomes were usually combined into Arctic-alpine ecosystems (AA) due to the paucity of appropriate studies and their usual similarity. We did not separately consider wetlands because they occur in all biomes.

3.1 Causes of Present Distributions

Solar energy and its distribution across the globe is the decisive factor shaping biomes. The flux of solar energy to each site on the globe is determined by three main factors: 1) latitude, 2) season, and 3) shape of the surface.

Latitude determines the absolute amount of solar energy and how it is distributed throughout the year. The highest total input is at the Equator, the lowest at the poles. The ratio between input (radiation) and output (re-radiation) determines the net energy balance, which is positive at lower latitudes but negative at higher latitudes. This energy surplus at lower latitudes is redistributed across the globe through circulation of the atmosphere and oceans. The energy balance determines the patterns of temperature and precipitation, the most important factors influencing the biomes and, consequently, processes such as succession.

The solar energy input exhibits increasingly pronounced seasonality with increasing latitude. Seasonality is determined by the inclination of earth's axis relative to the axis of earth's orbit around the sun (about 23.5° from a perpendicular orientation). Without this inclination, there would not be any spring, summer, autumn, or winter. At the Equator, there is no seasonality; day and night have nearly the same length for the whole year. In contrast, at the poles, the polar night lasts half of the year and the polar day the other half of the year. Seasonality at mid-latitudes is midway between the two extremes. Organisms have had to develop various adaptations to this seasonality and the accompanying amounts of precipitation and temperature.

The shape of earth's surface is the third main factor that influences the solar energy balance. For example, a south-facing slope with 10° inclination in the Northern Hemisphere receives approximately the same solar energy as a flat surface 10° latitude farther south, and any nearby north-facing slope of the same 10° inclination receives the solar energy equal to 10° latitude farther north. Slope therefore modifies local climate and may also influence successional trajectories at a given site.

Differences in regional solar energy balance drive atmospheric circulation across the globe (Fig. 3.1) and determine the main distribution and dynamics of high and low atmospheric pressure systems. Warmer air is lighter and moves up, thus low pressure is formed, while cold air is

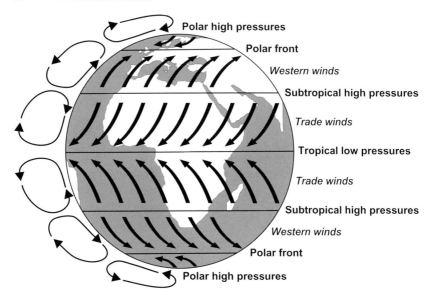

Figure 3.1 Global circulation of the atmosphere.

heavier, moves down to the surface, and creates conditions of high pressure. The whole system is very dynamic and unstable but one can observe certain regular patterns. The highest input of solar energy at the Equator warms up the air mass starting in the morning at the sun rises. Warm air moves upward, cooling at higher elevations above the surface, which triggers condensation of water vapor in the rain, typically in the afternoon. This circadian pattern is similar throughout the year in the tropics and moisture and temperature are highly stable. Because of ascending air, there is a belt of stable low pressures. The ascending air gets colder and turns partly to the north and partly to the south from the Equator. At about 30° N or S latitude, this air returns back to the surface as cold, dry air, forming a relatively stable belt of high pressure, and then returns back to the Equator in the form of rather regular trade winds. Because the globe rotates around its axis from west to east and because of the resultant Coriolis forces, the direction of the trade winds is from northeast to southwest in the Northern Hemisphere and from southeast to northwest in the Southern Hemisphere. At higher latitudes, westerly winds prevail, again due to earth's rotation. On both poles there is permanently cold air, which is comparably heavy, resulting in stable high pressure conditions. Driven by that high pressure at the poles, winds leaving either pole for lower latitudes can interfere with the westerlies.

The hemisphere experiencing summer is inclined more to the sun while winter is caused by less direct sunlight. Consequently, the global air mass circulation moves to the north or south following the seasonal position of the earth relative to the sun. This seasonal shift has important consequences for the biomes. For example, the expansion of the tropical low pressure belt to higher latitudes brings rain while subtropical high pressures bring hot and dry summers to the Mediterranean and comparable areas. In winter, when the belt of low pressure moves back to the Equator, a dry season ensues at about 5–20° latitude, and if subtropical high pressures move back to lower latitudes, westerly winds bring precipitation to the Mediterranean areas.

The global air circulation described in the preceding text is modified and sometimes nullified by unequal distribution of the continents and oceans. Land surfaces warm up faster than oceans from solar radiation, but they also cool faster. This difference means that in summer, continents are warmer than surrounding oceans, so warm air rises off the land and a low pressure system is formed. Consequently, the air descends over the oceans and blows back to the continent, usually bringing moist air to the continent. In winter, cold heavy air over the continent goes down to the surface, creating high atmospheric pressure conditions that usually lead to dry, cold winds that blow from the continent to the ocean. These different rates of warming and cooling of oceans and continents trigger monsoons. Because Eurasia forms the largest continent surrounded by large oceans, it is where monsoons are most intensive. In southeastern Asia, the Himalayas form a barrier to the movement of wet air masses, leading to particularly strong summer monsoons. The winter monsoon may bring, for example, very cold weather to western Europe, called a Siberian freeze. Although monsoons are most evident in Eurasia, the same principle operates at smaller scales, even on islands, and may modify the occurrence of low and high pressures and thus, local climate. The vertical structure of the earth's surface provides additional modifications to air circulation. Large and high mountain ranges differ in precipitation between windward (wet) and leeward (dry) slopes because winds cool and lose moisture as they rise on the windward side but descend as dry air on the leeward side, creating a rain shadow.

Given the variations in annual temperature (Fig. 3.2) and precipitation (Fig. 3.3) formed through the mechanisms described in the preceding text, climatic zones are formed (Breckle, 2002). These climatic zones include tropical equatorial, tropical seasonal, subtropical, transitional with winter rains and hot and dry summers, temperate, boreal, and polar. The

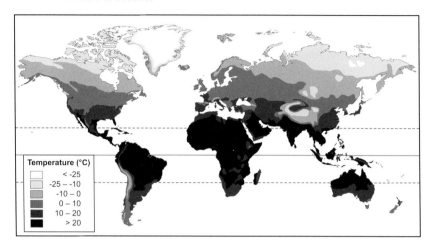

Figure 3.2 Global distribution of mean annual temperature (°C).

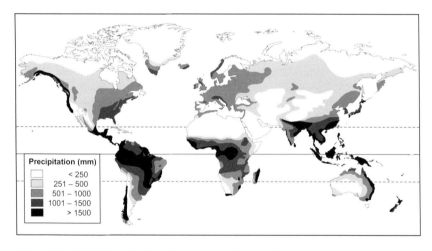

Figure 3.3 Global distribution of mean annual precipitation (mm).

biomes closely reflect these climatic zones. For the last three climatic zones, strong winter frosts are typical and organisms have adapted to this factor.

The climate and its seasonality at a particular site on the earth can be illustrated by a climatic diagram. Such diagrams nicely summarize the most relevant climatic characteristics changing over the year. Various versions of climatic diagrams exist, but for characterizing the biomes we used here a simplified version of the climatic diagrams originally

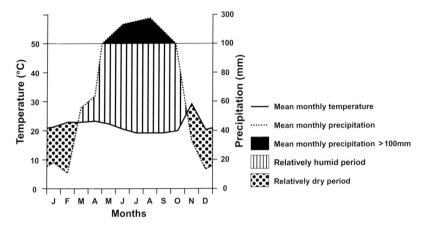

Figure 3.4 Simplified climate diagram: The horizontal axis represents months from January to December in the Northern Hemisphere (or alternatively from July to June in the Southern Hemisphere). The left vertical axis expresses the mean monthly temperature scaled by 10°C increments. The right vertical axis represents the mean monthly precipitation scaled by 20 mm increments. In the case of monthly precipitation over 100 mm, the scale is by 200 mm increments. The scaling is designed in such a way that in the case when the precipitation curve is below the temperature curve, it indicates a relatively dry period. In the case when the precipitation curve is above the temperature curve, there is a relatively humid period. This climatic diagram can be used as a guide to the inserted climate diagrams on subsequent biome distribution maps.

suggested by Walter (1970). We used them as insets in the distribution maps for all but the alpine biome, which is too variable for an insert (see Sections 3.2–3.9). The basic information in a climate diagram is explained in Fig. 3.4. Whittaker (1975) presented a scheme where the distribution of particular biomes is related to mean annual temperature and mean annual precipitation. A slightly adapted version of this diagram, to match biomes used in this book, is presented in Fig. 3.5. In Chapter 4, we placed particular studies on succession onto this diagram, demonstrating from which climate and which biomes the studies originated.

Plant biomass and species diversity are the ecosystem characteristics that have been most frequently considered within and across biomes and are also frequently investigated in studies of succession. The nearly universal emphasis on aboveground factors determined a similar focus for us, although we recognize the critical importance of belowground dynamics in driving succession (Bardgett & Wardle, 2010). Biomass reflects climatic conditions; it is highest in the wet tropics, followed by

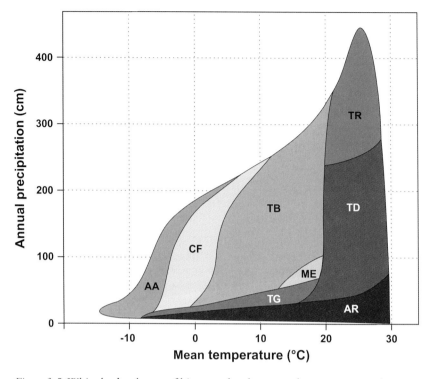

Figure 3.5 Whittaker's scheme of biomes related to annual temperature and precipitation, and adapted to correspond to the biomes used in this book. For biome abbreviations see p. 20.
Adapted from Whittaker (1975) and Ricklefs (2000), with permission from Pearsons

wet temperate forests, and is lowest in arid and cold areas (Breckle 2002). Diversity is influenced by the evolutionary history of a particular biome. Generally, plant richness is highest in the tropics (Fig. 3.6) and in several examples of the Mediterranean biome, including southwestern Australia and the southernmost tip of Africa (Cape Region). At these locations, vegetation has developed through a long-lasting, relatively uninterrupted history of geographical and ecological isolation (Lomolino *et al.*, 2006). Generally, the number of species of vascular plants decreases with latitude (Fig. 3.7; Kreft & Jetz, 2007), and we expect that the subset of species participating in succession also decreases with latitude.

The distributions of each biome, presented in Sections 3.2–3.10, concern only their idealized, potential area and disregard changes caused by humans, such as large-scale deforestation or desertification. In the past two decades, several studies have examined how the distribution of

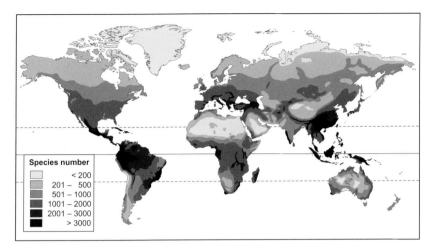

Figure 3.6 Global distribution of plant richness (species number per 10,000 km²). Adapted with permission from Barthlott *et al.* (1996), University of Bonn, Germany

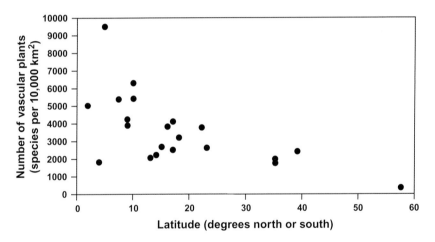

Figure 3.7 Decrease of plant species richness with latitude. See Reid and Miller (1989).

biomes will change due to global climate change. Although the predictions differ in details, they usually suggest a poleward shift in biome distribution, especially in the Northern Hemisphere, or desertification in arid regions. Fragmentation of some biomes also is predicted (Rizzo & Wiken, 1992). Such large-scale shifts in biome distributions and composition are perhaps the largest spatial scale at which succession can be studied. Gradual encroachment of woody vegetation into tundra was, for example, documented by Sturm *et al.* (2001). More information on biome shifts can be found, in Adams (2007), Schimel (2013), and Chapin *et al.* (2013).

3.2 Tropical Rain Forests

3.2.1 Description and Distribution

In addition to the typical tropical rain forests, we include montane and cloud forests in this category. There are three distinct geographic zones for tropical rain forests (Fig. 3.8), which largely differ in species composition; plant life forms and vegetation structure are generally similar among the zones. For further reading about tropical rain forests, see Whitmore (1998), Bermingham *et al.* (2005), and Carson and Schnitzer (2008).

3.2.2 Macroclimate and Its Seasonality

Climate is very stable annually, exhibiting little or no seasonality. Temperature and water availability are optimal for biota. Temperature fluctuates slightly around 25°C. Going to the north or south, seasonality appears at about 5° latitude, especially in precipitation (see Sections 3.1 and 3.3). As seasonality becomes more pronounced, the rain forests transition to seasonal tropical forests with alternating periods of drought or rain.

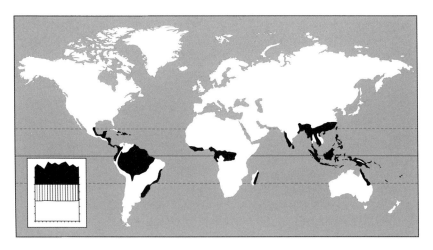

Figure 3.8 Distribution of tropical rain forests and the corresponding simplified climate diagram (see Fig. 3.4 for explanation).

3.2.3 Abiotic Conditions

Though macroclimates and mesoclimates are usually very stable and highly favorable for plants, microclimates can differ. At the top of the tree canopy, temperature and moisture fluctuate during the day, while inside the forest the microclimate is stable. Little light penetrates to the understory so most photosynthesis is in the canopy.

Soils are old and leached of most nutrients. The soils are generally acidic (low pH) and are usually red in color due to high levels of oxidized iron, which can form an impermeable lateritic crust. Remaining nutrients are mostly bound in organic matter, reducing their immediate availability (particularly nitrogen, phosphorus, and mobile ions such as potassium). But litter decays quickly in the wet and warm environment and nutrients are immediately used by plants; nutrient uptake is often facilitated by mycorrhizae. Some exceptions to low soil fertility include soils on young volcanic substrates and regularly flooded sites. When the soil is used for agriculture, it rapidly loses its fertility as the thin organic layer decomposes and nutrients are further leached.

3.2.4 Biota

This is the biome with the highest total number of species (>100,000, or more than one third of the world's flora). Species richness of trees is striking, reaching up to 400 species per hectare. Prevailing life forms are trees, epiphytes, and lianas (Plate 1). Ninety percent of the world's liana species occur in this biome. The high richness has developed due to a favorable environment and the long and relatively undisturbed evolutionary history (although the extent of the biome has fluctuated, particularly during periods of glaciation). Species richness is maintained by permanent, small-scale disturbances when individual trees or branches fall (gap dynamics; see Section 3.2.5). Second to the competition for nutrients is competition for light. Due to the low light levels at the ground layer, parasitic and saprophytic plants often occur there. Productivity and actual living biomass are highest among terrestrial biomes.

3.2.5 Natural Disturbances

The formation of gaps in the canopy enables light to penetrate deeper into the layers of vegetation, promoting colonization by other species and helping to maintain species richness. Although we generally do not cover such small-scale successional dynamics in this book, we briefly mention gap dynamics in Section 15.2. Cyclones impact many tropical rain forests, often initiating succession. Earthquakes, volcanic lava and tephra, and floods also disturb tropical rain forests.

3.2.6 Human Impact

Among those native tribes that practiced agriculture, shifting agriculture (also called "slash and burn") was the traditional approach to cultivate the land. This small-scale and short-term cultivation did usually not cause any substantial degradation of soil and vegetation. Modern agriculture, introduced to many areas of the rain forests, especially in the form of large-scale plantations (e.g., for palm oil), causes irreversible changes in soils and vegetation. Large-scale clearcutting for timber has similar negative effects. Previously undamaged tropical rain forests have been reduced worldwide to less than 30% of their original extent and large areas are now covered by secondary forests that often originate from secondary succession after clearcutting (Chazdon, 2014).

3.3 Tropical Dry Forests

3.3.1 Description and Distribution

With increasing seasonality of precipitation and decreasing total precipitation, there is a transition from evergreen dry forests, to semi-deciduous and deciduous forests (Plate 2), to typical savannas, to tropical grasslands with total dominance of grasses. A savanna is a mixed forest-grassland ecosystem characterized by continuous grass layer with a discontinuous tree canopy. This heterogeneous tropical dry biome surrounds tropical rain forests. There are four main zones: the largest and most continuous are found in Africa, Latin America (called *cerrado*), Australia, and the Indo-Malaysian region (Fig. 3.9). For further information, we recommend Huntly and Walker (1982), Mistry (2000), Dirzo *et al.* (2011), and Chazdon (2014).

3.3.2 Macroclimate and Its Seasonality

Going north or south from the Equator, seasonality increases as the result of global air circulation patterns and the seasonal tilt of the earth (see Section 3.1). Beginning at about 5° latitude, precipitation becomes more

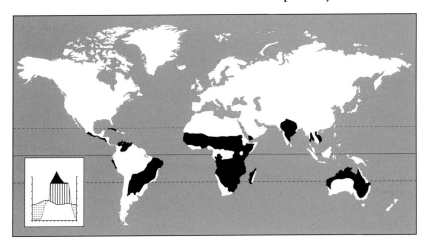

Figure 3.9 Distribution of tropical dry forests and savannas, and the corresponding simplified climate diagram (see Fig. 3.4 for explanation).

seasonal and decreases with increasing latitude. Wet and dry seasons alternate over the course of a year, from two rainy seasons to only one between approximately 15° and 25° latitude. Precipitation, in combination with substrate texture, topography, fire frequency, and biotic and human impacts, determines the physiognomy of the biome. At <500 mm of annual precipitation, an open woodland savanna usually occurs; <300 mm results in a shrubby savanna or a predominately grassy savanna (where woody species are concentrated only in favorable sites); at 200 mm there are usual transitions to a semi-desert. These figures are only tentative because of the interaction of the seasonality of precipitation with the many factors previously mentioned. Throughout this biome, the predominate physical feature is the pronounced seasonality of climate and the corresponding phenology of the organisms.

3.3.3 Abiotic Conditions

Canopies that are at least seasonally open allow light to penetrate to the ground, thus dry tropical forests usually have a rich herb layer composed mostly of grasses. Soils are old, with their origin during the Tertiary Period, and are similar to that of tropical rain forests, red in color, and with an impermeable lateritic crust. How deep the crust is located influences water availability and seasonal flooding at a site. When the roots of trees or shrubs penetrate the crust, they tap into additional water sources. The ratio between woody and herbaceous vegetation is often affected by the presence and permeability of the lateritic crust.

3.3.4 Biota

Deciduous leaves are adaptations to the dry period found in this biome (or to winter cold in temperate biomes). Woody species are generally more limited than grasses by drought because they cannot go completely dormant. But when rains start, grasses are capable of fast growth because they take in water and nutrients through their dense root system. This biome is famous for its high diversity of large herbivores, which influence physiognomy of vegetation (i.e., the proportion of trees to grasses). The co-evolution of trees and grasses with herbivores led to many adaptations, including the development of traits such as thorns on trees or the production of chemical compounds by plants to deter herbivores. Generally, grasses are well adapted to herbivory as they can quickly recover lost biomass.

3.3.5 Natural Disturbances

Plants in this biome are adapted to drought, grazing, and fire. Woody species are often protected against fire by thick bark. Grasses have buds close to the ground and are protected by dry standing biomass and litter that burn quickly before the growing meristems can be damaged. Local floods in the rainy season are another type of natural disturbance.

3.3.6 Human Impact

Influences of humans on this biome have been profound and long-lasting. Early humans originated in the African savannas. Such a long co-evolution with humans may explain why African savannas are less damaged by recent human activities such as excessive grazing, more frequent fires, or invasive alien species than are other savannas such as those in South America. In the Indo-Malaysian region, the biome was nearly completely converted to agriculture or deteriorated from other activities in this heavily populated part of the world. In Australia, this biome is better preserved due to its historically low human population density and the late introduction of agriculture. In many regions, humans reduced native herbivores and instead introduced livestock. The resulting overgrazing largely led to deterioration of the biome.

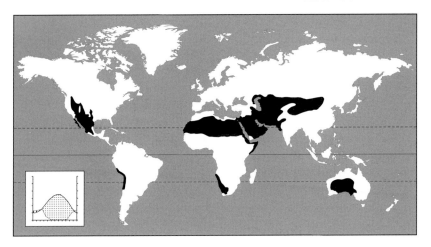

Figure 3.10 Distribution of aridlands and the corresponding simplified climate diagram (see Fig. 3.4 for explanation).

3.4 Aridlands

3.4.1 Description and Distribution

We consider here deserts, semi-deserts, and arid, open woodlands of low stature such as the pinyon-juniper vegetation in southwestern North America (Fig. 3.10). Deserts are characterized by discontinuous vegetation that occurs only on favorable sites; semi-deserts are characterized by widely spaced but continuous vegetation. Hot deserts occur in the tropics and subtropics (except at high elevation) where strong winter frosts do not occur; cold deserts occur at higher latitudes and elevations and have a cold winter season. Aridity has several interacting causes: a) stable high pressure zones around the tropics of Cancer (e.g., the Sahara and Arabian Deserts) and Capricorn (e.g., the Kalahari and Australian deserts); b) rain shadow on the leeward side of mountain ranges (e.g., the deserts in southwestern North America; Plate 3); c) in centers of continents least accessible to coastal rains (e.g., the Gobi Desert), and d) at the contacts of cold oceanic currents and hot continents (e.g., the Atacama and Namib Deserts). For further information, see Whitford (2002) and Ward (2016).

3.4.2 Macroclimate and Its Seasonality

Deserts usually occur if mean annual precipitation is <200 mm, but seasonal distribution of precipitation and other factors can vary. Even if higher amounts of precipitation fall in a short period then the rest of the year is without precipitation so a desert can occur. The type of rain is also important. With heavy, short-lasting rains, the water disappears quickly through run off, while gentle, long-lasting rains are more readily absorbed by the substrate, providing higher water availability for plants. There can be summer rains (e.g., in the southern Sahara when the low pressure belt from the Equator expands northward), or winter rains (e.g., in the northern Sahara, when wet westerlies move to the south), or both (e.g., in southwestern North America due to western winter winds and southern summer monsoons). There is large seasonal variation (especially in cold deserts) and diurnal variation of temperature. Clear, sunny days and dry air are responsible for intensive radiation and fast re-radiation in the night. The highest, officially recognized temperature ever measured is 56.7°C for Death Valley in the Mohave Desert in North America.

3.4.3 Abiotic Conditions

The limiting factors for biota are the lack of moisture and high temperatures. Substrate texture contributes to drought conditions. Clay-rich soils reduce rain water penetration and standing water readily evaporates, while coarser sand and rocky substrates allow deeper penetration of rain water and reduce evaporation. High evaporation is also associated with high salinity as ions accumulate at the substrate surface. Aridland soils (aridisols) are poorly developed and generally infertile. All these factors influence succession after a disturbance.

3.4.4 Biota

Prevailing life forms are therophytes (annuals), geophytes (perennials surviving the dry period in organs under the soil surface, e.g. as bulbs), low woody species, and succulents. The main effect of these life forms is to diminish water loss through transpiration in dry seasons. This goal is achieved by: 1) life cycle (dormant seeds of annuals, deciduous leaves when dry season starts); 2) various morphological adaptations such as the existence of small, sclerophylous leaves that have the ability to close their stomata; hairy or waxy coatings; formation of water storage tissues (succulents); or deep root systems (53 m deep was reported for *Prosopis* in Nevada); or 3) physiological adaptations such as CAM photosynthesis. Annuals often germinate from a long-dormant seed bank only in years of higher than usual precipitation. For perennials, it is convenient to spread vegetatively. Long-distance dispersal is not the primary adaptation but many species can be dispersed by animals or wind, which can be advantageous to colonize large, anthropogenic disturbances.

3.4.5 Natural Disturbances

Sudden onset drought can be a disturbance, even in an aridland where plants are well adapted to drought. Vegetation can be disturbed by blowing sand in open deserts and by fire, especially in semi-deserts with relatively higher biomass and more continuous vegetation cover than are found in deserts. Flash floods can also affect deserts. Fine materials (silts, clays) are prone to wind and occasionally to water erosion.

3.4.6 Human Impact

Humans contribute to desert formation (the desertification process), often by allowing the land to be overgrazed. In the case of the Sahara Desert, the initial desertification happened due to both human activities and climate change several thousand year ago; humans are still affecting desertification today, for example, in the Sahel region. Because of human introductions of invasive alien species, fire frequency has increased in some aridlands beyond the levels to which the biome was adapted. Some parts of deserts are convenient for agriculture, either with or without irrigation, and, when these areas are abandoned, succession may proceed. Similarly, succession occurs when various mining activities cease or settlements are abandoned.

3.5 Mediterranean

3.5.1 Description and Distribution

This biome is characterized by the dominance of small trees and shrubs that usually have small, evergreen leaves. It occurs around $40°$ latitude in five isolated locations: the European Mediterranean (vegetation mostly called maquis; Plate 4); California (chaparral), Chile (mattoral), the southern tip of Africa around Cape Town (fynbos, renosterveld), and southwestern Australia (mallee, karri, jarrah) (Fig. 3.11). The biome occurs on the western sides of the continents. Though it only covers 1.8% of the world's terrestrial surface, it harbors nearly 10% of all vascular

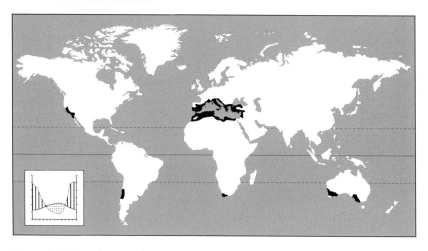

Figure 3.11 Distribution of Mediterranean ecosystems and the corresponding simplified climate diagram (see Fig. 3.4 for explanation).

plants in the world. For further information, see Arroyo *et al.* (1995), Blondel and Aronson (1999), and Esler *et al.* (2018).

3.5.2 Macroclimate and Its Seasonality

In this biome, the summers are dry and warm and the winters are wet and cool, but with little or no frost. The dry, warm summer is caused by high pressure systems moving from lower latitudes and bringing with them dry trade winds. On the east sides of continents the trade winds bring moisture from the oceans and evergreen broadleaf forests predominate. In winter, the zone of prevailing western winds moves to these zones from higher latitudes and brings rain. Summer rains can be occasional or more regular, as in the American chaparral where there are summer monsoons. There are usually two growing seasons, the main one in spring when water is still available from winter rains, and then one in late summer, either due to monsoons or when the winter rains start again and temperatures are not yet too low for plant growth.

3.5.3 Abiotic Conditions

Seasonal dynamics of soil moisture are the main factors shaping the Mediterranean biome and its transition to other biomes, such as semi-deserts, evergreen broadleaf forests, or deciduous temperate forests (in this case usually in interaction with lower winter temperatures). Evergreen leaves retard nutrient cycling by their slower decomposition, thereby reducing nutrient availability. Another important abiotic factor in this biome is fire (see Section 3.5.5).

3.5.4 Biota

The high species richness has several causes, including the mixing of temperate and tropical floristic elements, topographic diversity (especially in the Mediterranean region), extensive speciation (e.g., 600 species of the genus *Erica* in the South African fynbos), and isolation that led to high levels of endemism. Despite the wide range of species there is convergence of life forms. One adaptive trait is small, evergreen leaves that are adaptive in the hot, dry summers because they minimize transpiration. Transpiration is further decreased by leaf surfaces covered by trichomes and waxes, small stomata, and the production of volatile compounds that reduce water vapor on and near the leaf surface. A disadvantage of the small, evergreen leaves is lower photosynthetic rates compared to deciduous, mesophyllous leaves. Consequently, on wetter sites, such as north-facing slopes or floodplains, deciduous trees may outcompete the evergreens. Most plant species in this biome are capable of resprouting quickly after the frequent fires or cutting.

3.5.5 Natural Disturbances

Fires were always a natural component of the Mediterranean biome and the biota adapted to this type of disturbance. However, fires have become more frequent due to human activities in many parts of this biome. For example, the natural fire return interval for the Californian chaparral used to be about 100 years, but now is only 20–30 years. In addition to resprouting, some species have developed thick bark as fire protection (such as the well-known cork oak, *Quercus suber* in the Mediterranean). Other plants are stimulated to germinate by the high temperature or smoke from fire. Browsing and grazing by native herbivores are less frequent than in many other biomes because of the low palatability of the plants.

3.5.6 Human Impact

The European Mediterranean region has been influenced by intensive human activities for >10,000 years. These activities include tree cutting, grazing of livestock, and changing fire frequency. This history with humans may have led to its apparent resistance to invasion of alien species compared to other regions in the same biome that are more susceptible. One region, the American chaparral, is particularly prone to invasion by alien species (e.g., annual grasses). Likewise, the South African fynbos is threatened by the intentional planting of aliens such as *Pinus radiata* or *Acacia* species that then escape and spread. Both fire protection, often practiced in the past century, and too frequent fires may disrupt the ecosystem and change subsequent successional trajectories. Various restoration activities based on manipulation of fire frequency, intensity of livestock grazing, and control of invasive alien species are in progress.

3.6 Temperate Grasslands

3.6.1 Description and Distribution

Grasses dominate this biome but patches of trees or shrubs are typical in transition zones to deciduous temperate forests or coniferous forests (Fig. 3.12). In transitions to deserts and semi-deserts or in areas with high salinity, forbs (e.g., *Artemisia* and members of the Chenopodiaceae) may dominate. Temperate grasslands most commonly occur in the centers of continents where there is a lack of summer precipitation. There are three main regions: central Eurasia (steppes *sensu stricto*; Plate 5), central North

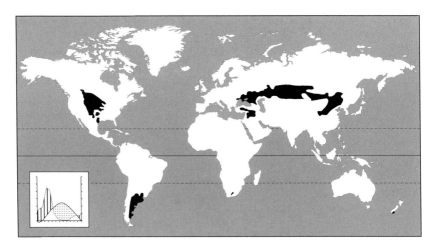

Figure 3.12 Distribution of temperate grasslands and the corresponding simplified climate diagram (see Fig. 3.4 for explanation).

America (prairies), and temperate South America (pampas). Smaller temperate grasslands are found in southeastern South Africa and in southeastern South Island, New Zealand. The original Russian term steppe is often used for the whole biome and is typically subdivided into tall grass and short grass steppes or prairies. For more information, see Knapp *et al.* (1998), Lauenroth and Burke (2008), and Wilsey (2018).

3.6.2 Macroclimate and Its Seasonality

Because this biome is located in the interior of continents in the temperate zone, there are cold winters with heavy frosts and some snow. Water from melting snow is available for plants in spring, which is the best growing season. Summer is hot and dry. High seasonal and diurnal temperature fluctuations are typical, due usually to dry, sunny days and clear nights (when the solar radiation absorbed during the day is re-radiated away from the ground).

3.6.3 Abiotic Conditions

Low soil moisture in summer inhibits establishment of woody species in temperate grasslands. The dryness is sometimes enforced by salinity where evapotranspiration markedly prevails over precipitation. However, there is usually a balance between evapotranspiration and precipitation, nutrients are not leached out, and pH is about neutral. Dense roots of grasses ensure by their turnover that there is soil organic matter throughout the soil profile. Annual aboveground biomass production usually decays each year, providing nutrients for the next growing season. Thus, soils are generally fertile. Chernozem is a typical soil type.

3.6.4 Biota

Some steppes can be species-rich at small spatial scales (up to 50 species m^2), unless they have been previously plowed. In addition to grasses, annuals and geophytes (with bulbs under the soil surface) are usually present. However, steppes under certain extreme site conditions (e.g., high elevation, stoniness, or isolated occurrence) can be species-poor, with strong dominance by a single species of grass. Competition between grasses and woody species follows similar principles as in the case of tropical savannas. Soil microbial activity is usually high, and there are many insect herbivores, while large herbivores have been mostly reduced by humans.

3.6.5 Natural Disturbances

Fires can occur during dry summers, triggered by lightning. Grazing by wild animals is the primary natural disturbance. Other natural disturbances are generally unimportant.

3.6.6 Human Impact

How temperate grasslands would look like now without the long-term effects of past human disturbances is difficult to know. Humans (particularly in Eurasia) have influenced this biome for thousands of years by cutting woody species in steppe-forests, increasing frequency of fires, hunting herbivores, and later converting large areas to arable land. Native herbivores were largely substituted by domestic ones, usually leading to overgrazing. (Somewhere between 30 and 70 million bison lived in North American prairies before European colonists arrived. Today there are only a few small, managed herds.) Colonists also introduced, either unintentionally or intentionally (to increase fodder production), many alien grasses and other species. The most influenced in this way were the South American pampas. Finally, large areas of most temperate grasslands have been converted to arable land and its abandonment leads to secondary succession. Today, there are some attempts to restore the original temperate grasslands.

3.7 Temperate Broadleaf Forests

3.7.1 Description and Distribution

We consider here both evergreen and deciduous forests where trees with large, photosynthetically active leaves dominate. The evergreen temperate forests occur especially in southeastern China, but elsewhere are either limited in extent or are atypical. The majority of temperate forests are deciduous with three main areas of occurrence: eastern North America, Europe (Plate 6), and eastern Asia (Fig. 3.13). These forests occur approximately between $40°$ and $50°$ latitude, but in Europe are shifted northward due to the warming influence of the Gulf Stream. In the Southern Hemisphere there is limited land at these latitudes, so this

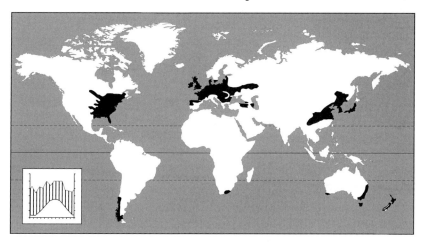

Figure 3.13 Distribution of temperate broadleaf forests and the corresponding simplified climate diagram (see Fig. 3.4 for explanation).

biome only covers small areas of southern Chile, southeastern Australia, and the South Island of New Zealand. For more information, see Davis (1996), Peterken (1996), and Frelich (2002).

3.7.2 Macroclimate and Its Seasonality

There is sufficient annual precipitation and favorable summer temperatures to support the growth of large trees. Winter frosts are typical and increase in severity with increasing distance from coastlines. Increasing continentality is also associated with longer summer dry periods and gradual transitions to steppes (prairies). Where the growing season is too short for this biome (<120 days with average daily temperature at least 10°C), boreal coniferous forests appear. Transitions to the Mediterranean biome appear when summer is too dry and hot, unless severe winter frosts occur.

3.7.3 Abiotic Conditions

Growth is not usually limited by either soil moisture or summer temperature, but occasional extremes may affect the biome. Soils are typically Cambisols, which have variable fertility depending on the bedrock. In an oceanic climate, leaching is common, resulting in generally more acidic and less fertile soils. Litter does not usually accumulate, but is mostly decomposed throughout the year, making nutrients available to plants.

3.7.4 Biota

Broad, usually mesophyllous leaves are very effective in assimilating carbon. An extensive herb layer usually grows in the forests just before the tree leaves expand in the spring. Evergreen trees can survive cold temperatures down to $-5°C$ to $-10°C$, while most deciduous trees in this biome can survive temperatures to ca. $-45°C$. Species diversity is lowest in Europe, highest in eastern Asia, and intermediate in North America, due to glacial–interglacial oscillations and topography. In Europe, species could not easily migrate south (and then return to the north) during glacial advances because of the east-west orientation of the mountains (Alps, Carpathians, Pyrenees). Plant migrations were easier in North America where the mountains are generally oriented north-south. Moreover, the Mediterranean Sea in Europe and to some degree the Caribbean Sea in North America added additional barriers to migration. In eastern Asia, there are no limiting montane or water barriers and Quaternary glaciations were mild, so species either survived *in situ* or more easily migrated south during glaciated periods and back north during warmer periods. Consequently, the total number of broadleaf trees in Asia is nearly 10 times higher than in Europe and all European genera also occur in Asia.

3.7.5 Natural Disturbances

Wind disturbance can form small to large gaps and heavy snow and ice can damage the forests. Fire occurs but is not typical and is usually of limited extent. Landslides and avalanches can occur in topographically diverse, mountainous landscapes.

3.7.6 Human Impact

Selective tree cutting or cutting in small patches is historically the main influence of humans on this biome, in addition to grazing and burning. Large-scale clearcutting has been a widespread practice for the last several hundred years and has often led to the conversion of the forests to monospecific plantations composed of alien species. Large areas have also been converted to arable land because of the fertile soils and proximity to large human populations. Fast expansion of settlements (and now urban areas) has further destroyed this biome. However, many restoration activities are currently underway. The majority of ecological studies, including those dealing with succession, originate from this biome.

3.8 Coniferous Forests

3.8.1 Description and Distribution

We consider here all forests dominated by conifers in late successional stages, except juniper-pinyon and similar woodlands, which we included in aridlands (see Section 3.4). This biome has a nearly continuous circumpolar distribution in Eurasia and North America at about 60° North latitude (Fig. 3.14). The northernmost occurrence is reported from Taymyr peninsula at 72° North latitude. In the Southern Hemisphere, there is almost no land at this latitude and this biome covers only a small area in southern Chile and Argentina. Forests in the northern belt are often called boreal forests or taiga (Plate 7). But coniferous forests may also occur azonally in other biomes (e.g., in mountains). We also consider here the distinct North American coniferous forests that are found in the Pacific Northwest from the boreal zone to northern California. There are transitions to tundra as the growing season becomes too short to support tree growth and to deciduous broadleaf forests as the

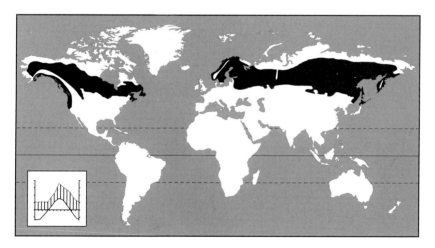

Figure 3.14 Distribution of coniferous forests and the corresponding simplified climate diagram (see Fig. 3.4 for explanation).

growing season becomes longer and precipitation is not limited. Transitions to temperate grasslands occur when summer dryness increases, or, in northern California to chaparral. For more information about this biome see Shugart *et al.* (1992) and Johnson (1995).

3.8.2 Macroclimate and Its Seasonality

There is a pronounced seasonality in temperature, due to the high latitude and continentality. The lowest air temperature ever measured outside Antarctica was −72°C in Omjakon, Siberia. Summer temperatures can be >30°C, again due to the continentality. In coastal regions of the continents the seasonal amplitude is smaller because of the moderating influence of the ocean. Snow is typical in winter and supplies water when it melts. Because precipitation often exceeds evapotranspiration, there can be a surplus of water in the soil, which has led to extensive peat formation; permafrost may also contribute to peat formation.

3.8.3 Abiotic Conditions

Prevalence of precipitation over evapotranspiration promotes the formation of podsols, with a prominent, light-gray leached soil horizon, that results in low nutrient availability and low pH. At higher latitudes, permafrost often occurs at 1–1.5 m depth. Much of the present distribution of this forest type was directly influenced by the extent of the most recent glaciation and the subsequent patterns of recolonization.

3.8.4 Biota

Species richness is generally the lowest among the forested biomes, partly due to glaciation. Exceptions include the high-diversity pockets of forests where the trees presumably survived in glacial refugia (e.g., along the Pacific coast of North American and eastern Asia). Species richness is also higher in so-called hemi-boreal forests, which represent an ecotone with deciduous broadleaf forests or temperate grasslands. Species with needles are generally better adapted than are broadleaf species to environmental conditions such as short growing seasons, low temperatures, a lack or surplus of water, lack of nutrients, fire, or browsing by herbivores. But decomposition of needles is usually slower, thus nutrient are not as easily recycled as in the case of broad leaves. Ectomycorrhizae help to overcome the lack of nutrients. Also, trees with evergreen needles do not need to invest in an annual renewal of leaf tissue, saving energy and nutrients. Deciduousness has developed among conifers (e.g., *Larix*) as an adaptation to extremely low temperature.

3.8.5 Natural Disturbances

Fire, especially in drier continental regions, and heavy snow in more oceanic areas represent the most common natural disturbances, but to which this biome is usually well adapted. Wind and occasional insect outbreaks are other disturbances. Fire helps to recycle nutrients and opens space for other species. Dominant, late successional species are usually adapted to fire by having a thick bark to survive, or having various adaptations to germinate immediately after fire. Mosaic disturbances (fire, wind, insect outbreaks) of natural frequency and intensity help to maintain species diversity on the landscape scale and should not be reduced. The distinct types of succession that follow fire, wind, and insect outbreaks have been frequently studied in this biome.

3.8.6 Human Impact

Historically, this biome has been the least influenced by humans among the forested biomes, due to fewer human residents. However, in the past two centuries, large-scale clearcutting or conversion to agricultural land in more favorable parts have caused extensive destruction, especially in newly populated parts of Siberia and Canada. Large areas have been converted to monospecific plantations; conifers are appropriate for industrial forestry because they tend to have predictably high seed production, are easy to cultivate in nurseries, and have high-quality timber. Fortunately, the regeneration ability of this biome is usually high. Coniferous trees originating in this biome are often planted into other biomes.

3.9 Tundra

3.9.1 Description and Distribution

We consider here treeless vegetation, mostly in the Arctic but with small patches in Antarctica (Fig. 3.15). In addition to the typical tundra (Plate 8), we also include the transitional subarctic zone where shrubs may dominate, such as *Betula tortuosa* in western, and *B. ermannii* in eastern Eurasia, or very small and scattered individuals of the dominant species of the boreal

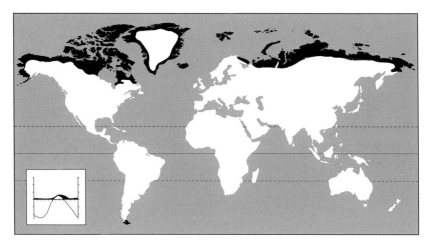

Figure 3.15 Distribution of tundra and the corresponding simplified climate diagram (see Fig. 3.4 for explanation).

coniferous zones (usually *Picea* species). Alpine tundra is included in alpine biomes (see Section 3.10). Tundra is circumpolar in distribution in the Northern Hemisphere. In the Southern Hemisphere it occurs only in the southernmost tip of South America, and on islands and in small "oases" on the Antarctic Peninsula. The term *tundra* originates from the Sami language and was later modified into its present form from the Russian language. For more information about this biome see Chapin *et al.* (1992), Chapin and Körner (1995), and Thomas *et al.* (2008). In most of our analyses we merged the tundra biome with arctic ecosystems into an Arctic-alpine category.

3.9.2 Macroclimate and Its Seasonality

The occurrence of this biome is not determined by low winter temperatures (see Section 3.8.2) but by a short growing season, due to the high latitudes. Tundra usually occurs if there are <30 days with average daily temperature at least $10°C$, but such average figures can be largely modified by local conditions, especially by topography (the contrast between south-facing and north-facing slopes is often distinct here). Summer often starts late (e.g., July in the Northern Hemisphere) because of the long-lasting and late melting of snow and frozen soil. The short summer is partly compensated by the fact that there is permanent summer day light. Because of low levels of evapotranspiration, low levels of precipitation do not usually limit plant growth.

3.9.3 Abiotic Conditions

Probably the most important factor that shapes the whole biome is the depth to which the frozen surface melts in summer. The deeper the melting of this layer, the richer the vegetation. Permafrost is everywhere. Due to generally low temperatures and a short growing season, productivity and decomposition rates are extremely low and nutrients often accumulate in a raw humus layer where the nutrients are of limited availability to plants. Species in the family Fabaceae, typical for the biome, have the advantage of fixing atmospheric nitrogen; species in the family Ericaceae benefit from their association with mycorrhizae. Soils are undeveloped and shallow.

3.9.4 Biota

There are many species or at least genera that are commonly found throughout the Northern Hemisphere distribution of this biome. Because large areas were glaciated, most species had to recolonize the vast area from their refugia, which were located mostly to the south of their present distributions. However, former glacial refugia inside the present biome have been proposed, such as far-northern Alaska. For the whole Arctic, about 900 species of vascular plants are reported (e.g., Alaska ca. 600, Greenland ca. 400, Svalbard ca. 160). Species in the Ericaceae, Vacciniaceae, or Cyperaceae families often dominate the biome, together with dwarf willows (*Salix* spp.) and birches (*Betula nana*). Annual species are uncommon because their fast growth is not possible in the extreme environment. Perennials capable of vegetative spread have an advantage because successful reproduction is often limited to rare favorable years. Vivipary is also advantageous. Prostrate or cushion growth forms exploit relatively high surface temperatures, better maintain moisture, heat, and nutrients, and are more resistant than more upright growth forms to abrasive forces such as wind and blowing ice crystals.

3.9.5 Natural Disturbances

Wind and blowing snow are widespread natural disturbances; avalanches, solifluction, floods, or landslides occur locally in unstable substrates (such as recently deglaciated terrain). With a drying climate, fire is now another disturbance in the tundra. As a natural disturbance, glaciation can be considered, and under present glacial retreat, primary succession is readily observed.

3.9.6 Human Impact

In the past, there was almost no visible human impact on this biome. More recently, mining and transport, especially by heavy machinery, have disturbed this biome. Because of its large extent, disturbances in the tundra are perhaps less urgent than disturbance levels in other biomes, though locally these activities can be very disturbing and spontaneous recovery is generally very slow. Besides these direct disturbances, however, the whole biome is being destabilized by ongoing climate change, with the largest temperature increases in the world. This impact probably represents the most serious threat for the future.

3.10 Alpine

3.10.1 Description and Distribution

We consider here all ecosystems above the tree line on mountains (Plate 9), or above shrubs or grasslands in dry regions without forests. The tree line is highest at about $30°$ latitude and then decreases toward the poles. In the Arctic, the tree line is not developed and the alpine zone, if not glaciated, is considered a part of the tundra. Alpine areas are remarkably extensive, with 6.7% of land above 2,000 m elevation and 4% above 3,000 m. Mountains provide a third dimension to the horizontal distribution of biomes; vertical zonation of vegetation in the mountains can resemble the horizontal distribution of biomes across various latitudes. Alpine vegetation can resemble tundra but this similarity decreases with decreasing latitude. Tropical alpine ecosystems are quite distinctive in climate and vegetation. For distribution of main mountain ranges see Fig. 3.16. For further information about alpine ecosystems see Wielgolaski (1997), Körner (2003), and Nagy and Grabherr (2009).

3.10.2 Macroclimate and Its Seasonality

Air temperature decreases on average about $0.6°C$ per 100 m of elevation and air gets thinner at higher elevations. In the thin air, surfaces rapidly heat up from intense solar radiation during the day and rapidly cool down at night from re-radiation of that energy to the atmosphere, resulting in abrupt changes in diurnal surface temperatures. Seasonality

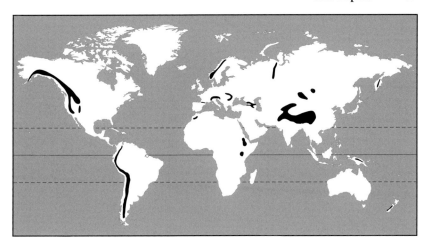

Figure 3.16 Distribution of main alpine ecosystems. No climatic diagram is presented because their climates are highly variable.

reflects the respective latitude. Precipitation is highly variable, even differing on windward and leeward slopes of the same mountain. Land at elevations above a typical cloud layer can be relatively dry, as can mountains located in the centers of continents or in the rain shadow of other mountain ranges. Microclimate and mesoclimate are generally more important than macroclimate. At high elevations, ultraviolet radiation may be important for organisms.

3.10.3 Abiotic Conditions

The distinct relief substantially modifies most abiotic factors, such as temperature, site moisture, soil depth, available nutrients, and erosion. Unequal distribution of snow and the rate of its melting determine the length of the growing season and the amount of moisture available for plants. Because the bedrock is often exposed, its chemistry (especially pH) influences the vegetation. Because of slow decomposition of litter, there is often a lack of available nutrients, but there are also comparatively fertile sites in the alpine zone, especially along streams.

3.10.4 Biota

Despite the decrease of species number with elevation, mountains represent important sources of biodiversity. Mountain ranges or individual summits can be seen as isolated islands, where speciation led to the high rate of endemism. Mountains also served as refugia for cold-adapted species in warmer parts of the Quaternary period. Species isolated in these refugia possibly evolved to become endemic species. Vascular plants grow to at least 6,200 m elevation in the Himalayas. To adapt, species developed traits similar to tundra species (see Section 3.9). Succulent forms often developed as an adaptation to the lack of water or its frozen state in the soil. Tropical alpine plants typical of páramo vegetation in the South American Andes, in Africa, and in New Guinea include plants with giant rosettes (*Espeletia*, *Senecio*, *Lobelia*) that can survive short-term, diurnal ground frosts due to their well-protected stems, but do not survive longer winter frosts. Consequently, this growth form occurs only in the tropics where there is no seasonality.

3.10.5 Natural Disturbances

Wind, blowing snow, avalanches, soil erosion, and landslides represent widespread natural disturbances, while volcanism and the local expansion of glaciers (currently rare) are also factors affecting alpine biomes. However, glacial retreats often expose new substrates.

3.10.6 Human Impact

Many mountains above the tree line were traditionally used as summer pastures, but also winter grazing of domestic animals has been reported from those mountains with little or no snow cover. Such extensive grazing had a generally positive impact on species diversity (cf. the Intermediate Disturbance Hypothesis) and its decline in past decades has often led to decreases in diversity. Other recent human interventions are usually destructive but they still occur in limited spots, such as mining, building ski resorts, and road construction. Alpine vegetation generally recovers slowly after such disturbances, which moreover trigger soil erosion, landslides, and avalanches. But various restoration projects are conducted in the mountains, including restoration of traditional grazing or mowing. Nearly everywhere in high mountains we can now observe glacial retreat and subsequent succession.

Part II
Succession by Disturbance Type

4 · *Comparative Approach*

In this chapter, we describe the structure for Part II, where we present a comparative analysis of succession triggered by 10 common types of disturbance in order of increasing human influence (Chapters 5–14): almost no influence (natural: volcanoes, glaciers, cyclones), some influence (intermediate: dunes, landslides, floods, fire), and complete influence (anthropogenic: clearcuts, plowed fields, mines) (Fig. 4.1). Within each disturbance type we cover four topics. First, we describe the disturbance, including what causes it, its spatial patterns, and subsequent disturbances that it might trigger. Second, we discuss the succession that follows that type of disturbance, including abiotic variables (substrate, light, nutrients), biotic variables (biological legacies, dispersal, species colonization and adaptations, the role of invasive alien species, plant–plant interactions, and trophic interactions), and the successional patterns that we found within and among biomes. These patterns resulted from our comparative analyses of multiple studies. Third, we outline several theoretical implications of our findings. Fourth, we address practical implications for management concerns. We end Part II with a brief overview of other anthropogenic disturbances that are not as widespread, frequent, or readily assessed from a successional perspective (Chapter 15).

Our comparative analyses of seres within and among biomes focused on an evaluation of the success of succession, or to what degree a sere progressed toward a desired stage. One measure of success can be when native species from undisturbed reference vegetation dominate, or what has been called potential natural vegetation (Loidi & Fernández-Gonzáles, 2012; Jackson, 2013). Such a successional stage is usually called a target by restoration ecologists (van Andel & Aronson, 2012). However, the potential natural vegetation cannot always be a target. Instead, some young successional stages, harboring rare, endangered, and often protected species and providing good ecosystem services, can represent a target (Řehounková et al., 2016). In addition, there can be multiple potential targets of potential natural vegetation, given particular site

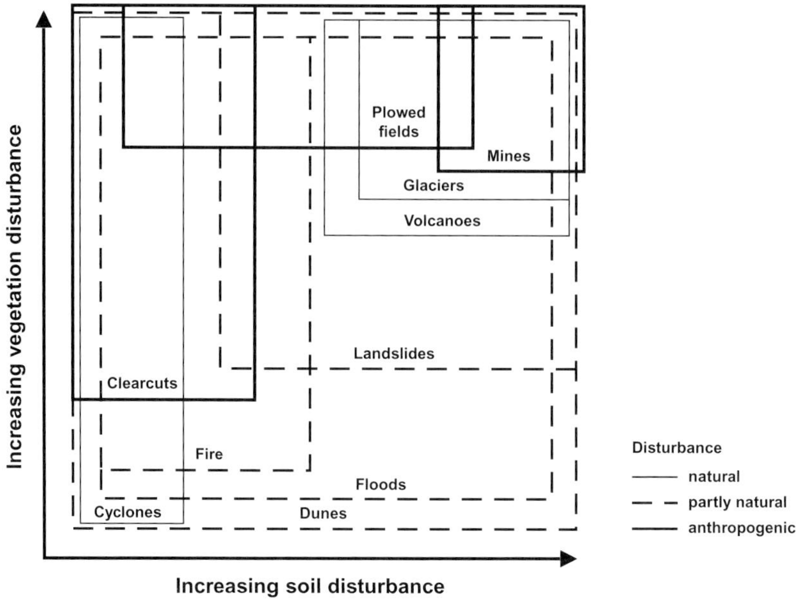

Figure 4.1 Ten types of disturbances considered in this book and their influence on soil and vegetation.

characteristics or irreversible environmental changes caused by human activities (Somodi *et al.*, 2017). In the following text, we speak about a target and evaluate if succession was successful in reaching it.

For our analyses, we searched for papers using appropriate combinations of keywords (Appendix 2) to select titles in the Web of Science to obtain a core collection of studies. We supplemented this source with other available literature of which we were aware, including our own studies and less accessible literature that we assembled. Despite our best efforts to include all readily available literature useful for our purposes, we recognize that at best we have assembled only a sample of all studies on succession. After the initial search, we excluded studies that obviously did not concern chronosequences or that dealt only with one species or a particular phenomenon. From the remaining studies, we selected only those that fit the following criteria:

1. The chosen papers described succession over a long enough period, usually more than two decades, to allow evaluation of potential success of succession. In some cases, when target species established sooner, it was possible to make the evaluation for shorter chronosequences. Alternatively, if invasive alien species or native ruderals established

and it was evident that they would arrest or divert succession for a long period, we also included such studies.

2. A sufficient number of comparable sites or stages (at least three) were analyzed. In a few cases, the evaluation was possible if only one site was repeatedly sampled or it was sufficiently old to decide if succession had been approaching the expected target or not.

3. Target vegetation (see preceding text) was explicitly described by the authors, or evident from the data or the context of the respective studies.

4. Species composition of both successional and target stages were sufficiently described.

5. Succession was clearly spontaneous with no or minimal additional disturbances or no post-disturbance human manipulations such as sowing, planting, or management.

The location of each study in the respective biome was assigned based on information provided in the study. We largely followed the designation of terrestrial world biomes by Archibold (1995) (see Chapter 3). Coordinates, mean annual temperature, and mean annual precipitation were recorded for each study. Values for large studies were averaged when necessary. When climate data were not available, we obtained them from LocClim (www.fao.org/nr/climpag/locclim). In a few papers, more than one sere was described, so the number of seres considered was sometimes higher than the number of studies (Fig. 4.2).

From each of the papers selected for the comparative analyses, we extracted, when possible, trends in: 1) success of succession (closeness of approach to a target, i.e. to potential natural vegetation or another desired state for restoration) (Table 4.1); see also Prach and Walker (2019); 2) successional trajectory (convergent, divergent, variable); 3) species richness (increasing, decreasing, variable); and 4) importance of invasive alien species in later successional stages in arresting, diverting, or otherwise altering succession (highly important, partly important, unimportant). If invasive aliens were dominant in early stages of succession (often weeds and ruderals in various anthropogenic seres) and then rapidly disappeared, we considered them unimportant. We evaluated success for every chosen study but were not always able to evaluate the other three categories due to insufficient information. In addition, our "variable" categories for trajectories and richness represented several patterns that did not fit into our broad categories. Trajectories that were unidirectional (with no subseres for comparison) or parallel could not be

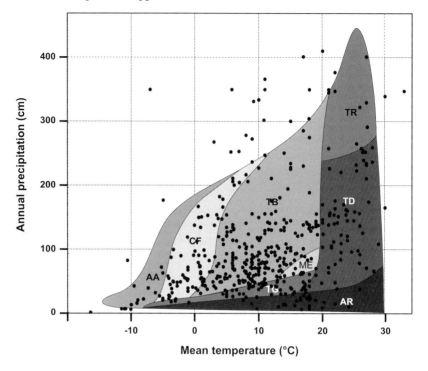

Figure 4.2 Distribution of all chosen studies by biome (each black dot represents a separate study; N = 530 studies). TR: temperate rain forests, TD: temperate dry forests, AR: aridlands, ME: Mediterranean, TG: temperate grasslands, TB: temperate broadleaf forests, CF: coniferous forests, AA: Arctic-alpine. Fig. 3.5 was used as a template.

considered convergent or divergent (see Walker *et al.*, 2010b for more on the relationship between trajectories and succession). We focused on richness patterns that increased or decreased, labeling as variable patterns that were U-shaped, inverted U-shaped, flat, or with substantial inter-annual fluctuations.

Other desirable comparisons of successional studies include such topics as biomass, rate of species exchange (turnover), or the roles of certain functional or species-specific traits. However, we were only able to discuss these additional topics in a general way because we lacked suffi-cient detailed and mutually comparable primary data to be able to make close comparisons. Table 4.2 summarizes the numbers of papers used for the comparative analysis for each disturbance type and biome. Appendix 2 lists the authors of those papers. Full citations are located in the

Table 4.1 *Criteria for success of succession, or spontaneous restoration of the potential natural vegetation or of another target stage desired for restoration*

Category	Criteria
Successful	Spontaneous recovery of a target, i.e. the potential natural vegetation (PNV) or another targeted state (e.g., one desirable for restoration). Presence of natural or semi-natural species composition and often with continuous vegetation cover. The target states or trends to reach them clearly evident not later than within several decades (≤ 100 years). The presence of weeds and/ or aliens unimportant in the late successional stages (as defined by passage of time and sequential replacements of vegetation).
Partly successful	Partial recovery of the target as defined in the preceding text. In addition to the desired target species, some weeds (ruderals) and/ or alien species are present in the late successional stages but do not dominate. Alternatively, recovery of target state is expected to take a long time ($\gg 100$ years).
Unsuccessful	Undesirable weeds (ruderals) and often aliens dominant in later-successional stages. Trends to recovery of a target stage not evident after several decades. Alternatively, sparse or no vegetation due to extreme site severity (usually low pH) or instability.

See Prach and Walker (2019).

references. When we had at least five studies in a biome, it was analyzed separately. However, for three disturbance types where we had fewer than five studies in tropical dry forests (volcanoes, cyclones, clearcuts) we merged them with the similarly vegetated tropical rain forests and once the reverse occurred (fewer than five studies in tropical rain forest for fire). Our Arctic-alpine category combined tundra and alpine biomes (based on similar vegetation; see Chapter 3) and was used throughout for all analyses except glaciers, where we had at least five studies in both tundra and alpine biomes. Some disturbances were logically confined to only certain biomes (clearcuts occur only in forests; glaciers occur only where it is sufficiently cold). Throughout the book, we present biomes in approximate order of increasing latitude (tropical rain forest to Arctic-alpine) and disturbances in approximate order of increasing human influence (volcanoes to mines).

Table 4.3 sorts biomes by climate and vegetative characteristics that we used in subsequent chapters: warm versus cold, dry versus wet, and

Table 4.2 *The numbers of titles reviewed from Web of Science and other sources, total studies used in our comparative analyses, and number of studies by biome listed by the 10 types of disturbance. Disturbances are listed in increasing order of human influence.*

Disturbance type	Titles	Studies used	Biome (no. of studies)							
			TR	TD	AR	ME	TG	TB	CF	AA
Volcanoes	496	36	12	1	0	3	0	10	7	3
Glaciers	185	25	0	0	0	0	0	1	6	18
Cyclones	154	21	10	1	0	0	0	8	2	0
Dunes	659	39	2	1	2	9	0	19	5	1
Landslides	194	46	13	0	1	2	0	16	8	6
Floods	965	48	3	1	4	1	2	17	16	4
Fire	1,937	83	1	8	7	23	6	9	27	2
Clearcuts	1,510	65	14	2	0	4	0	23	22	0
Plowed fields	445	93	10	8	7	14	21	25	5	3
Mines	376	74	7	6	1	7	4	35	12	2
Totals	6,921	530	72	28	22	63	33	163	110	39

Biome abbreviations: TR: tropical rain forests, TD: tropical dry forests, AR: aridlands, ME: Mediterranean, TG: temperate grasslands, TB: temperate broadleaf forests, CF: coniferous forests, AA: Arctic-alpine.

See Appendix 2 for search phrases used in Web of Science and lists of the chosen studies.

Table 4.3 *Sorting of biomes by climate and vegetation criteria*

	Criteria	TR	TD	AR	ME	TG	TB	CF	AA
Temperature	Warm	X	X	X	X				
	Cold					X	X	X	X
Humidity	Dry		X	X	X	X			
	Wet	X					X	X	X
Vegetation	Forested	X	X		X		X	X	
	Not forested			X		X			X

For biome abbreviations see Table 4.2.

forested versus not forested. We are aware of exceptions to our classification, such as cold aridlands (although warm ones largely prevailed among our selected studies) or Mediterranean systems that are not forested but are dominated by woody species. However, these categories were purposefully broad because of our efforts to look for general patterns. Despite such broad categories, not all studies could be used to compare trajectories, species richness, or invasive alien species.

To test differences in succession trends in success, trajectories, species richness, and invasive aliens among biomes, disturbances, and latitudinal categories, we used the asymptotic generalized Pearson's χ^2 test in the case of ordered variables, with the post-hoc Cochran-Armitage test. The Cochran-Armitage test was also used in the case of ordered variables and only two categories of nonordered variables (such as Warm vs. Cold biomes); in the case of only nonordered variables, the normal χ^2 test was used (Agresti, 2007). All calculations were done in the R-package (R Development Core Team, 2015).

5 · *Volcanoes*

5.1 Disturbance Description

Volcanoes are the most destructive type of natural disturbance on earth and have been instrumental in the development of continents, mountain ranges, and the destruction of life at global and regional scales. Even today, lava produced by volcanoes is creating new land in Hawaii and other volcanic hotspots. Lava flows that obliterate all previous life are the clearest example of a natural disturbance that initiates primary succession. Initially, there is no available nitrogen or organic matter on a fresh lava flow but other elements (including phosphorus) are present, so when deficiencies are addressed, soils and plant communities can develop. Humans are often drawn to volcanoes because of the rich soils that can result. Indeed, about 12% of all humans live on or within 100 km of an active volcano ("active" in geological terms means erupting within the last 10,000 years) (Small & Neumann, 2001). We start our discussion with volcanic disturbance because it is the least influenced by humans of all disturbance regimes.

Volcanoes can be either explosive (phreatic) or effusive, and emit three basic types of eruptive material. First, molten rock within the earth (magma) that is emitted as lava can be either smooth and highly imper-meable (pahoehoe) or rough and porous (a'a). Second, tephra is magma that, when ejected, breaks into many fragments that can vary in size from large boulders or lava bombs, to intermediate-sized lapilli (cinder), to fine ash particles. Tephra is initially unstable, but fine-textured tephra can harden into tuff, especially when exposed to sea water as it cools. Where tephra deposits are shallow, secondary succession can ensue. The third product of volcanoes is gas. When superheated gases mix with tephra, searing and fast-moving pyroclastic flows race down the slopes of a volcano destroying everything in their path. Finally, volcanoes can trigger debris avalanches when a volcanic slope suddenly breaks loose (discussed in Chapter 9). When mixed with snow or ice, these avalanches become rivers of mud (lahars). Whether wet or dry, such volcanically triggered erosion is highly destructive.

5.1.1 Causes

Temperature changes in the earth and resultant flows of subsurface magma lead to shifts in position of the continental plates that are like a skin floating on a more fluid core. When the cooling plates are pushed under other plates at subduction zones, hot magma flows to the surface. The composition of the lava influences the type of volcano that forms. Basaltic lava flows readily (sometimes over distances of several kilometers) and is therefore associated with rounded, effusive shield volcanoes (e.g., Iceland, Hawaii). Andesitic and rhyolitic lavas do not flow readily and are more typical of explosive volcanoes (e.g., Indonesia).

Earthquakes sometimes trigger mud volcanoes (eruptions of mud instead of lava; USGS, 2017), but most volcanoes are associated with subduction zones of the Earth's crust and are particularly common around the Pacific Ocean, the so-called Ring of Fire. Volcanoes are also found over hotspots (e.g., Galápagos, Hawaii, Réunion) or on spreading faults (e.g., Cameroon, Galápagos, Iceland, Italy, Rwanda). Volcanic hotspots occur where a constant upwelling of magma occurs under a moving continental plate. The result is generally a chain of islands that emerge above the ocean surface, build in size, then gradually erode away after they have left the hotspot. When hotspots and plate collisions combine (Canary Islands), the result is a group of islands that do not cluster linearly by age as seen in Hawaii.

5.1.2 Spatial Patterns

Volcanoes occupy only about 1% of the earth's terrestrial surface (Fig. 5.1), but can have global consequences, such as when ash from explosive eruptions enters the upper atmosphere and circulates. Such large eruptions (e.g., Krakatau in 1883 in Indonesia or Pinatubo in 1991 in the Philippines) can color sunsets for months and even cool global climates (Parker *et al.*, 1996; del Moral & Walker, 2007). Region-ally, multiple adjacent volcanoes can create mountain ranges along active faults, with widespread effects on climate and drainage patterns, and on the movements and evolution of plants and animals. Locally, volcanoes

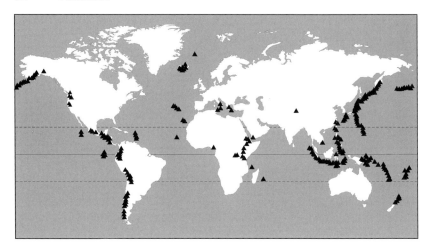

Figure 5.1 Global distribution of active volcanoes. Based on various sources.

may also be stand-alone mountains (e.g., steep-sided tuyas that erupt through a glacier) that both destroy the local biota and provide new habitats available for eventual colonization.

Volcanic eruptions vary in size from fumaroles less than a meter across to mountains such as Mauna Loa in Hawaii (5,200 km^2) or the submarine Tamu Massif in the Pacific Ocean (292,000 km^2). Volcanic eruptions are also temporally variable, with some that erupt intermittently over decades (Kilauea, Hawaii) or centuries (Mt. Etna, Sicily). For example, Anak Krakatau in Indonesia had about 10 eruptive, ash-producing episodes (each lasting 1–12 months) between its appearance above sea level in 1927 until 1980 (Whittaker *et al.*, 1992) and it is still active. Another variable influencing succession is the depth of tephra deposits, which affected understory vegetation and tree regeneration following the 1980 eruption of Mount St. Helens (Zobel & Antos, 2009, 2016) and the 1943–1952 eruption of Parícutin (Gomez-Romero *et al.*, 2006; Lindig-Cisneros *et al.*, 2006).

5.1.3 Subsequent Disturbances

Volcanic eruptions are disturbances that occur largely independent of other disturbances but they can trigger earthquakes, landslides, floods, and fires. For example, earthquakes and volcanoes share similar tectonic triggers and often occur along the same faults; landslides can occur from the erosion of unstable tephra, shifting lahars, pyroclastic flows, and post-volcanic earthquake tremors; volcanoes can trigger floods when they block rivers and cause debris avalanches when they destabilize slopes; and volcanoes can ignite fires that may spread into adjacent habitats such as forests or grasslands. Each of these subsequent disturbances increases spatial heterogeneity and can alter succession (Dale *et al.*, 2005). Timberline in Chile, for example, is depressed by persistent volcanic activity and subsequent slope instability (Veblen *et al.*, 1977). Human responses to volcanoes also influence succession by altering land use in response to devastated crops or newly fertile soils, salvage logging of killed trees, and tourism around ongoing eruptions (del Moral & Walker, 2007).

5.2 Succession

5.2.1 Abiotic Variables

The post-eruption surface of a volcano varies depending on the type of material ejected (e.g., tephra, pahoehoe, or a'a) or subsequent disruptions from debris avalanches or pyroclastic flows. Different surfaces result in a variety of abiotic conditions that can lead to distinct successional trajectories. In this section, we will focus on tephra and lava because debris avalanches are considered under landslides. Tephra particle size determines abiotic conditions. Fields of boulders resemble coarse talus slopes at the bottom of a landslide or on some spoil heaps from mining, with large crevices, rapid drainage, and slow soil development. Once water and nutrients accumulate in the crevices, succession can proceed rapidly, but the sides and tops of the boulders are likely to remain relatively bare of vegetation. Volcanic cinder results in many smaller crevices and also drains quickly, leaving an arid environment that deters plant colonization. Once cooled and spread across the land, tephra particles such as ash can harden and crack when dry, again presenting problems for plant establishment. A'a lava resembles a boulder field, with large cracks, fast drainage, and slow succession. Smooth pahoehoe lava, which resembles a hardened asphalt roadbed, is, ironically, where post-volcanic succession can occur most rapidly (Aplet *et al.*, 1998). On pahoehoe lava, plants generally establish in cracks where wind-blown organic matter and arthropods such as spiders and crickets accumulate.

The availability of nutrients limits post-volcanic succession (Dimopoulos *et al.*, 2010). Nitrogen, a key element for plant growth, is not available from fresh lava but begins to accumulate immediately (Vitousek & Walker, 1987). Several sources can add nitrogen to the surface: thermal fixation of atmospheric nitrogen at the surface of hot lava flows (Huebert *et al.*, 1999), deposition of nitrogen (e.g., in gases or particulates found in clouds or rain), and biological nitrogen fixation by colonizing cyanobacteria (Henriksson *et al.*, 1987). Cyanobacteria can be free-living, such as in leaf litter (Russell & Vitousek, 1997) and soil (Vitousek & Hobbie, 2000), or associated with plant roots (Dickson, 2000). Biological fixation on young volcanic surfaces can be limited by lack of water, colonization by cyanobacteria (Henriksson & Rodgers, 1978), or availability of phosphorus (Vitousek, 1999). In many primary seres, nitrogen limitation to plant growth declines and phosphorus limitation increases during succession (Walker & Syers, 1976; Vitousek & Farrington, 1997). However, nutrient availability for plant growth can also be influenced by other abiotic variables including substrate (phosphorus can be more limited on ash than lava; Raich *et al.*, 1996) and atmospheric inputs (phosphorus deposition from wind-blown dust; Chadwick *et al.*, 1999). Elevation appears to influence net primary productivity (it typically declines with increased elevation; Raich *et al.*, 1997) more than nutrient availability.

Successional trajectories are affected by the differential responses of plants to changes in nutrient (and water) availability. Early vascular plant colonists on volcanic surfaces often have nitrogen-fixing symbionts (Halvorson *et al.*, 1991). These nitrogen fixers may (Clarkson & Clarkson, 1995) or may not (Titus, 2009) directly facilitate the growth of other species in the vicinity (see next section on biotic variables). However, nitrogen fixers certainly have many indirect effects, including increased carbon, nitrogen, and soil microbial activity (Halvorson *et al.,* 1991). Similar but less dramatic influences can also result from plants that do not fix nitrogen (Hirose & Tateno, 1984), especially when these colonists form thickets (Walker & del Moral, 2003). Mycorrhizal fungi, which alter nutrient dynamics of many plant colonists, vary in their importance on new volcanic surfaces from abundant (Hawaii: Gemma & Koske, 1990; Japan: Obase *et al.*, 2008), to patchy (Mount St. Helens: Titus *et al.*, 1998), but are likely to facilitate establishment of both the initial and subsequent waves of pioneers (Titus & del Moral, 1998; Nara & Hogetsu, 2004). Finally, plants with high nutrient use efficiency can have an advantage in low-nutrient, early successional volcanic soils (Chiba & Hirose, 1993).

5.2.2 Biotic Variables

Biological legacies, dispersal, adaptations, species composition, and non-native species all influence post-volcanic succession. Biological legacies, or organisms that survive a disturbance, are unlikely following volcanoes because of the severity of most eruptions. However, substantial legacies remain and influence succession under shallow tephra deposits. A lava flow generally resets succession to "time zero" because it removes all life. However, lava flows sometimes leave undamaged habitat islands or kipukas. In addition, tephra depth varies with duration of and distance from an eruption (Zobel & Antos, 2016) as well as topography (Talbot et al., 2010). Where tephra is shallow enough that it erodes quickly, mycorrhizal fungi (Yamanaka & Okabe, 2006), plants (Tsuyuzaki 1989), and insects (Walker et al., 2013b) can survive. Indeed, plant colonists often sort out by favored microhabitat (e.g., erosion gullies vs. flat areas; Titus & Tsuyuzaki, 2003a). Kasatochi (Aleutian Islands) erupted in 2008 and destroyed most vegetation and nonmobile wildlife on this remote island (Talbot et al., 2010). However, some seeds and insects survived in soils that were exposed in the months following the explosive tephra eruption. Exposure of seed banks from rapid erosion of tephra in gullies can create spatial patterns in colonists (Plate 10). Similarly, following the eruption of Mount Usu in Japan in 1977, erosion in gullies exposed seeds of annuals and of stoloniferous perennials. Both life forms dominated early succession in the gullies but only the perennials persisted (Tsuyuzaki, 1994). Vegetation outside the gullies was dominated by seed immigration following the eruption. Biological legacies can also alter succession on volcanoes by providing habitat for post-eruption colonization. For example, on Mount St. Helens, leeward slopes (protected from the directional blast of the eruption) sometimes retained wet meadow and shrub species. Although these plants did not readily colonize adjacent barrens, when they resprouted they provided a habitat that facilitated the invasion of wind-dispersed pioneer and dry meadow species that could colonize the adjacent barrens (Fuller & del Moral, 2003). In addition, the timing of the eruption in the early morning in early spring meant the survival of some nocturnal animals in their burrows and some plants under snow; pre-eruption harvests of nearby forests also meant that there were lots of early successional propagules in the area (Dale et al., 2005).

Dispersal to barren volcanic surfaces by wind, water, or animals is a prerequisite to successful colonization and establishment. On continental volcanoes, such as Mount St. Helens, wind-dispersed seeds are typically the first plants to arrive (Dale, 1989; Grishin et al., 1996), although they may be preceded by wind-blown arthropods (Sugg & Edwards, 1998). The small-seeded pioneer plants may be less likely to establish and spread than later arrivals that have larger seeds or the ability to spread clonally

(Fuller & del Moral, 2003). The isolation of volcanic islands such as Krakatau (Whittaker & Bush, 1993) and Surtsey (Fridriksson, 1987) often results in the first plants arriving by sea. On Surtsey, for example, the water-dispersed forb *Honkenya* was the first plant colonist and now dominates the shoreline (Fridriksson, 1992; L. Walker, personal observation 2003). Similarly, on Krakatau, sea dispersal dominated for the first 14 years following the 1883 eruption (Whittaker & Jones, 1994). Bird dispersal (largely endozoochory) then became the most common dispersal method (34%; Thornton, 1996). Birds dispersed an estimated 36% of plants to Mount Koma, Japan (Nishi & Tsuyuzaki, 2004), 64% of plants to Surtsey, Iceland (Fridriksson, 1987), and 75% of plants to Hawaii (Carlquist, 1974). Birds are not always important, however. None of the wetland plants on Mount St. Helens were bird dispersed (Tu *et al.*, 1998). Dispersal mode clearly affects successional trajectories. Wind-dispersed seeds of the tree *Salix* lead to the formation of fertile, moist, and shaded patches on Mt. Koma in Japan that favored subsequent colonization by grasses such as *Calamagrostis* (Uesaka & Tsuyuzaki, 2004). Often, the disperser benefits from distributing seeds of plants that it eats. For example, a crow (*Corvus*) spread the shrub *Rhus* to Mt. Koma (Nishi & Tsuyuzaki, 2004); pigeons and bulbuls dispersed trees in the mahogany family (*Dysoxylum*) to Krakatau (Whittaker & Turner, 1994); and pigeons and fruit bats spread figs (*Ficus*) to Motmot near Papua New Guinea (Shanahan *et al.*, 2001). Wind and water dispersal can have the same sorting effect and influence on subsequent successional processes (Walker & del Moral, 2003).

Plants that adapt to colonizing new volcanic surfaces must cope with a shortage of nutrients, soil, shade, and water; an abundance of sunlight; and sometimes also face unstable surfaces. A rapid growth rate can help a plant establish when surfaces are unstable (Chiba & Hirose, 1993) or when nutrients and water are most available in crevices in pahoehoe lava or beneath a tephra or a'a lava flow. Microsite selectivity by colonists affects succession by determining which species colonize, and which thrive (Kamijo & Okutomi, 1995). Tree seedling growth rates can both determine distribution by microsite and have long-term consequences on stand dynamics and succession (Zobel & Antos, 1991). To date, there is little examination of the physiological or genetic links to such variation in plant traits and colonization strategies in a successional context (Kitayama *et al.*, 1997).

All plant life forms may be found on young volcanic surfaces and, combined with duration of life stages and biotic amelioration of harsh

Figure 5.2 Succession on a 250-year-old lava flow in British Columbia, Canada. Photo by Lawrence R. Walker

abiotic conditions, are key drivers of succession (Wright & Mueller-Dombois, 1988). For example, any plant that establishes can potentially ameliorate many of the physical constraints mentioned in the preceding text and also serve to entrap propagules of other plants. Wind-dispersed, perennial forbs are often dominant on isolated, low-nutrient surfaces in early succession (Suárez *et al.*, 2015), perhaps because they can effectively compete with graminoids when both life forms are widely dispersed and have clonal growth (Tsuyuzaki & del Moral, 1995). Once habitat ameli-oration has occurred, a wider range of life forms can exist (Fig. 5.2). The species composition on new volcanic surfaces generally reflects the local flora, which is adapted to the climate. Lichens (Bjarnason, 1991), liverworts (Griggs, 1933), mosses (Delgadillo & Cárdenas, 1995; Cutler *et al.*, 2008), and ferns (Howard *et al.*, 1980; Russell *et al.*, 1998) can all be important for succession, especially when they grow in dense clusters. However, trees and shrubs can be early colonizers because their roots allow extraction of water and nutrients from crevices. Grasses sometimes are the first or dominant colonists of volcanic substrates, such as *Imperata cylindrica* in the New Hebrides islands (Uhe, 1988) and the Philippines

(Gates, 1914). Grasses are most likely to dominate early volcanic succession in aridlands or tropical dry forests, where they may share the lava flows with succulents such as euphorbs (González-Mancebo *et al.*, 1996), cacti, and yuccas (Shields & Crispin, 1956).

Invasive alien species on recently formed volcanic surfaces can influence successional dynamics by usurping native species and altering resource availability. For example, nitrogen-fixing trees dramatically increased soil nitrogen in Hawaii, outcompeted native species, and favored the establishment of other invasive species in upland (*Morella faya*: Vitousek & Walker, 1989) and lowland (*Falcataria moluccana*: Hughes & Denslow, 2005) forests. The nitrogen-fixing tree, *Parasponia rugosa*, had a similarly dominant effect on succession on Mt. Pinatubo in the Philippines (Marler & del Moral, 2013). Indirect increases in soil nitrogen were also likely from the dense growth of the herb *Hypochaeris radicata* on exposed volcanic surfaces of Mount St. Helens (Schoenfelder *et al.*, 2010). The success of invasive alien plants on volcanic surfaces can be due to increased nutrient use efficiency (Funk & Vitousek, 2007), to rapid uptake and utilization of limiting nutrients such as nitrogen (Schoenfelder *et al.*, 2010), or possibly to competitor-free space. Alternatively, rapid dispersal and drought tolerance may explain the invasion of alien conifers into volcanic seres in Japan (Titus & Tsuyuzaki, 2003b) and New Zealand (Clarkson & Clarkson, 1983).

Species interactions can be critical drivers of all stages of primary succession following volcanic eruptions, but in early successional stages, where abiotic factors predominate, species interactions may be less critical. Colonization and establishment on post-volcanic surfaces have strong stochastic aspects (del Moral, 1999), which is logical considering the removal of nearly all biological components. The species composition of later stages may or may not become more predictable (Walker & del Moral, 2003), depending on such variables as the strength of priority effects (e.g., persistence of colonizers; Samuels & Drake, 1997), species saturation (proportion of total possible species pool; Clarkson, 1990), or disharmony (distinctiveness from surrounding vegetation; Whittaker *et al.*, 1997). Later stages may thus have more species interactions and more predictable species composition than early stages. Here, we briefly consider facilitative (positive), competitive (negative), and multi-trophic interactions.

The strength and successional importance of facilitative interactions likely increase with increasing physical stress, while the opposite is probably true for competitive interactions (Callaway & Walker, 1997).

Therefore, one would expect facilitation to be common on fresh volcanic surfaces. Facilitation can promote any life stage, including dispersal, germination, establishment, growth, and reproduction (Walker & del Moral, 2003); while most common in early succession, facilitation can occur throughout a sere. Dispersal can be facilitated when an early colonist provides a perch that brings in seed-defecating birds, such as on Japanese lava flows (Hiroki & Ichino, 1993) and Hawaiian tephra (Vitousek & Walker, 1989), or when a colonist entraps seeds (Uesaka & Tsuyuzaki, 2004). Germination, establishment, and growth can be inhibited or facilitated by early colonists (nurse plants), depending on the light, moisture, and root competition levels under that colonist and the requirements of the secondary colonists. For instance, in Japan, deciduous *Salix* shrubs patches promoted *Calamagrostis* grasses but not *Campanula* herbs, while under evergreen *Gaultheria* shrubs with denser shade than *Salix*, fewer species colonized (Uesaka & Tsuyuzaki, 2004). In Hawaii, fog drip from nurse plants facilitated secondary colonists (Wright & Mueller-Dombois, 1988). A nurse plant can ameliorate soil nutrients through fixation of nitrogen, as on tephra in Washington (*Lupinus*; del Moral & Wood, 1986) or Hawaii (*Morella*; Vitousek *et al.*, 1987). Sometimes the nurse plant facilitates best when it dies back, as on tephra in Japan (*Fallopia*; Adachi *et al.*, 1996). Finally, facilitation is not limited to vascular plants. Colonizing fungi provided a critical substrate for subsequent colonization of algae and bryophytes in Washington (Carpenter *et al.*, 1987).

Competitive interactions can increase with succession as available niches are gradually filled by colonizing plants (del Moral & Wood, 1988), but may also occur in early succession if resources are limiting (e.g., nitrogen; Walker & Vitousek, 1991). One can distinguish between competitive inhibition, when a plant's presence excludes other species from establishing (typically early in succession; e.g., thicket-forming shrubs in Indonesia: Whittaker *et al.*, 1989) and competitive displacement when a plant's presence leads to its own success but the removal of its competitors (typically later in succession; e.g., *Abies* outcompetes *Alnus* in stable conditions on Mt. Fuji in Japan: Ohsawa, 1984). Competitive inhibition tends to slow down or arrest succession while competitive displacement tends to accelerate succession (as does facilitation). Competition, similar to facilitation, can occur during multiple life stages of a plant. Dispersal and germination can be inhibited when dense vegetation reduces the likelihood of seeds reaching soil (ferns in Hawaii: Russell *et al.*, 1998 or shrubs in Indonesia: Tagawa *et al.*, 1985). Dense thickets of vegetation also inhibit establishment and growth through competition for light (Drake & Mueller-Dombois, 1993; Titus & Bishop, 2014), nutrients (Vitousek & Walker, 1987), and water. Rapid clonal growth of early colonists can also limit subsequent establishment (Titus *et al.*, 1999). Indirect competition occurs in a variety of ways, as when a competitor outcompetes a species only to be faced with a stronger competitor. Alternatively, competitive interactions can result in changes in disturbance regime or other abiotic variables that lead to either increased or decreased levels of competition. For example, *Morella* shrub thickets that inhibit *Metrosideros* tree establishment in Hawaii promote soil development that favors a suite of invasive species (pigs, earthworms, *Psidium* shrubs), none of which benefits the native *Metrosideros* (Aplet 1990; Aplet *et al.*, 1991).

Trophic interactions such as the *Morella* shrub affecting vertebrate and invertebrate animals influence successional rates and trajectories. Animals also influence plants, as when the rodent *Thomomys* brought critical soil nutrients to the surface of recent tephra falls after the Mount St. Helens eruption (Andersen & MacMahon, 1985). Herbivory can accelerate, arrest, or deflect successional trajectories (Walker & del Moral, 2003). Herbivores tend to retard succession when they preferentially eat later successional plants or maintain a succession–arresting thicket and accelerate succession when early colonists are preferentially eaten. For example, *Lupinus*, an early colonist on Mount St. Helens, has nitrogen-fixing symbionts and promotes herb growth. Where *Lupinus* growth is diminished due to herbivory by leaf borers and leaf miners, growth of other species is also diminished (Fagan & Bishop, 2000). Noctuid moths also feed on *Lupinus*, depending on its levels of leaf nitrogen and phosphorus (Apple *et al.*, 2009). Moth herbivory is most likely to deter *Lupinus* growth in stands of intermediate age and density. Further, succession was delayed in New Zealand when the late-successional tree *Weinmannia,* was eaten by deer, rabbits, and possums (Clarkson & Clarkson, 1995). Finally, herbivory can influence successional trajectories by preferentially affecting one species. Colonizing *Salix* shrubs were preferentially eaten by vertebrate herbivores, while rapid vegetative growth of *Populus* trees allowed them to escape intense herbivory on Mount Usu in Japan (Tsuyuzaki & Haruki, 1996).

5.2.3 Patterns within and among Biomes

Succession on a single volcano can be quite complex, reflecting the many habitats created by the interaction of lava, tephra, and gases with local

Figure 5.3 Succession on the 24-year-old blast zone of Mount St. Helens, Washington, USA. Note parallel, fallen logs.
Photo by Elizabeth Powell, with permission

topography and existing ecosystems. For example, when Mount St. Helens erupted in 1980, what remained was a mosaic of habitats from surviving wet meadows and wind-toppled forest remnants (Fig. 5.3), to newly formed lakes, tephra of varying depths including a pumice plain, and surfaces formed by lahars, a pyroclastic flow, and an enormous debris avalanche. Such complexity led to multiple successional responses (del Moral & Lacher, 2005) and a poor link between vegetation and the environment (del Moral *et al.*, 2012). When comparisons are made within a given landscape, such as among lava flows (Cutler *et al.*, 2008), lahars (Sklenář *et al.*, 2010), or lava domes (Elias & Dias, 2004), similar substrate, climate, and biota help reduce the variability and thus improve the understanding of mechanisms producing succession. For example, Korablev and Neshataeva (2016) compared similar substrates and found that plant succession in Kamchatka took twice as long on lava as it did on tephra.

Regional comparisons of volcanic succession across landscapes are rare (del Moral & Grishin, 1999). Walker (1993) compared the abundance of different types of nitrogen-fixing plants among volcanoes and other

Table 5.1 *Success of succession for volcano studies arranged by biomes (no. of studies). For the evaluation of success see Chapter 4.*

Succession successful?	TR	TD	ME	TB	CF	AA	Total
Yes	4	1	0	4	3	0	12
Partly	8	0	3	5	4	3	23
No	0	0	0	1	0	0	1
Total	12	1	3	10	7	3	36

Biome abbreviations: TR: tropical rain forests; TD: tropical dry forests; ME: Mediterranean; TB: tropical broadleaf forests; TG: temperate grasslands; CF: coniferous forests; AA: Arctic-alpine.

disturbances and soil parameters (e.g., pH, organic matter, nitrogen, phosphorus) have been compared within the Hawaiian Islands (Crews *et al.*, 1995) and globally (Walker & del Moral, 2003). We found 36 studies (Table 5.1) that examined volcanic succession at multiple sites over decades to centuries from which we distilled information about changes in recovery of pre-disturbance vegetation, successional trajectories, species richness, and nonnative species. Most of the studies we could use were from tropical rain forests, temperate broadleaf forests, or coniferous forests (N = 12, 10, and 7, respectively). No appropriate studies were found from aridlands. The estimated time to full recovery of pre-disturbance vegetation till 100 years. However, the proportion of successful or partly successful studies was high (97% overall). There were no significant differences in success among biomes and across latitude (Fig. 5.4). Divergent trajectories dominated over convergent or variable ones, sometimes appearing early in succession (García-Romero *et al.*, 2015). Species richness increased in 73% of the studies. Invasive species were only important in late successional stages in 4% of our chosen studies. There were no significant differences among groups of biomes regarding these successional characteristics (Table 5.2).

5.3 Theoretical Implications

1. Volcanic succession was least likely to approach potential natural vegetation compared to seres following other disturbances (see Fig. 16.2). Only once was volcanic succession recorded as unsuccessful; partly successful was the category that prevailed. We suggest that

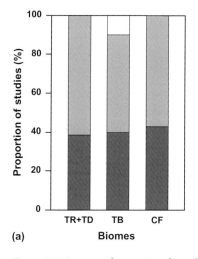
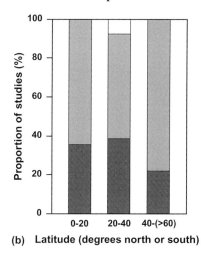

Figure 5.4 Success of succession for volcanoes by a) terrestrial biomes and b) latitude (percent of studies). Black: successful, light gray: partly successful, striped gray: not successful. TR+TD: tropical rain forests plus tropical dry forests, TB: temperate broadleaf forests, CF: coniferous forests. For sample sizes, see Table 5.1. The asymptotic generalized Pearson's χ^2 test with post-hoc test was a) $\chi^2 = 1.641$, df = 2, p = 0.440 (NS) and b) $\chi^2 = 0.128$, df = 2, p = 0.938 (NS).

factors promoting success include the relative permanence of lava on the landscape that has allowed a subset of species and a specific vegetation to evolve adaptations to such conditions. However, the burial of most vegetation and slow succession can lead to divergent pathways rather than a return to potential natural vegetation.

2. Disharmony (i.e., different plant species on volcanoes vs. the surrounding landscape) is likely to be higher than on less severe and less isolating disturbances.

3. The study of succession on volcanoes is facilitated by at least five variables that contribute greatly to our understanding of successional processes:

   1) The relatively long time frame for successional development compared to other seres in a landscape (compared to the more ephemeral disturbances such as floods, fires, or abandoned fields) means that researchers can study some very long chronosequences (e.g., 60,000 years in Chile: Gallardo *et al.*, 2012; 5,000,000 years in Hawaii: Vitousek, 2004) and also have the opportunity to study the retrogressive stages of succession (Peltzer *et al.*, 2010).

   2) Elevational gradients along surfaces of the same age and texture (Aplet *et al.*, 1998) (with varying precipitation, temperature, and

Table 5.2 Number of volcano studies (N = 36) sorted by various criteria: Warm (TR, TD, ME), Cold (TB, CF, AA), Dry (TD, ME), Wet (TR, TB, CF, AA), Forested (TR, TD, ME, TB, CF), Not forested (AA)

Successional trait		Warm	Cold	Dry	Wet	Forested	Not forested	All biomes (no.)	All biomes (%)
Succession successful? (36)	Yes	5	7	1	11	12	0	12	33
	Partly	11	12	3	20	20	3	23	64
	No	0	1	0	1	1	0	1	3
	Differences	NS		NS		NS			
Trajectory (18)	Converge	0	3	0	3	3	0	3	17
	Diverge	7	5	0	12	10	2	12	66
	Variable	2	1	1	2	3	0	3	17
	Differences	NS		NS		NS			
Species richness (22)	Increase	8	8	2	14	15	1	16	73
	Decrease	0	0	0	0	0	0	0	0
	Variable	3	3	0	6	5	1	6	27
	Differences	NS		NS		NS			
Invasive species important? (27)	Yes	1	0	0	1	1	0	1	4
	Partly	6	2	0	8	8	0	8	30
	No	3	15	2	16	15	3	18	66
	Differences	NS		NS		NS			

Sample sizes used for each successional trait are in parentheses.
For biome abbreviations see Table 5.1. χ^2 test was used for non-ordered variables, Cochran–Armitage test was used for ordered variables:
NS not significant.

surrounding vegetation) allow unusually good environments for comparative succession. Such studies suggest that succession is slower at higher elevations (Kamijo *et al.*, 2002).

3) Extremely little biological legacy (on lava, not on shallow tephra) means that succession starts from a blank slate. This situation allows the study of *de novo* community assembly (Walker, 2012).

4) The ability to measure succession at increasing distance from the disturbance source (usually a crater) (Teramoto *et al.*, 2017) provides the basis for chronosequences and disturbance gradients.

5) The deposition of tephra at varying depths is a well-studied feature of volcanoes that helps clarify the interactive roles of substrate depth and biological legacies such as seed banks (Tsuyuzaki, 2009; Zobel & Antos, 2016).

5.4 Practical Implications

1. Low predictability. Humans have almost no control over the occurrence of volcanoes or the damage they cause but more control over where we live. While avoidance is the best policy, people have long been attracted to the fertile soils on the slopes of volcanoes. Prediction of a given eruption is still in its infancy, but seismologists have had some successes and general activity levels of some volcanoes are closely monitored (see Section 5.1.2), especially for volcanoes near human populations.

2. Human responses. Because the detailed nature and consequences of an eruption are unknown, land managers are left in a purely reactionary mode when a volcano triggers fires, floods, or landslides. Historically, humans have adapted rather well to active volcanoes, retreating during an eruptive episode, then returning and incorporating the cinder into roadways, the ash into agriculture, and the lava into blocks for building roads and houses. Even tourism can thrive near a volcano, particularly when the eruption is effusive rather than explosive and viewing stations are provided.

3. Restoration. Many volcanic disturbances are left to recovery naturally. Active restoration of post-volcanic ecosystems can be hindered by the wide array of habitats that result from an explosion, and by ongoing eruptive activity (Teramoto *et al.*, 2017). However, restoration activities can also capitalize on this variation by having broad targets, supporting alternative stable states, and recognizing the

importance of priority effects (del Moral *et al.*, 2007) following volcanic disturbances.

5.5 Conclusions

Volcanoes provide a dramatic change in the landscape, creating a wide variety of habitats for succession. They also trigger a variety of secondary disturbances, from fires and floods, to landslides and earthquakes. In most cases, all previous life is destroyed, setting the stage for *de novo* assembly of plant communities and soil development. The influence of early plant colonists (particularly on nitrogen levels) is one avenue of active research. Volcanoes also provide scientists with convenient gradients in elevation and depth of tephra that have been exploited to study the successional roles of climate and biological legacies. Despite, or perhaps because of, our lack of control over volcanoes, humans remain fascinated by them. Fortuitously, volcanoes also offer diverse opportunities to study succession.

6 · Glaciers

6.1 Disturbance Description

Glaciers can be considered slow-moving rivers of ice. They cover about 10% of the earth's terrestrial surface and are concentrated in polar (e.g., Antarctica and Greenland) and alpine (e.g., Himalayas) regions (Fig. 6.1; Matthews, 1999; Boone, 2017). As glaciers flow they scour the landscape, altering the topography and drainage patterns. When they melt they leave behind typical features such as U-shaped valleys and various types of moraines. In, on, and under glacial ice there are many microorganisms and sometimes nonvascular and vascular plants, so recently deglaciated surfaces are far from sterile (Wynn-Williams, 1993). In fact, early successional heterotrophic microbial communities partially utilize carbon that predates the glacier (Bardgett *et al.*, 2007). Nevertheless, after centuries of burial beneath ice and the violent churning that occurs during melting, deglaciated surfaces have little biological legacy, so they undergo primary succession. Although glaciers also affect many riparian habitats far downstream from a melting glacier (e.g., through scouring and deposition of sediments), we focus on terrain that was formerly under the ice. Natural forces largely drive glacial retreats but recent anthropogenic global warming has accelerated this process. The most thorough, global study of succession on deglaciated terrain was by Matthews (1992); physiological adaptations to the harsh environment are described by Körner (2003).

6.1.1 Causes

Glacial advances and retreats have occurred periodically during the history of the earth. A typical pattern during periods of glacial activity has been ice advances that last about 100,000 years, interspersed with interglacial periods of ice retreat. Even within our current interglacial there have been temperature fluctuations that have affected the extent of

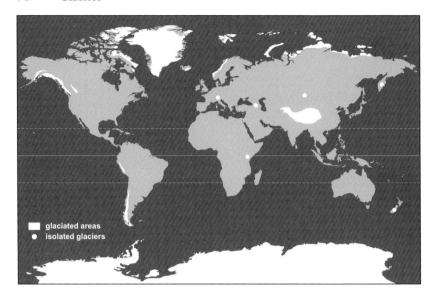

Figure 6.1 Global distribution of major glaciated areas.

glaciers, with cooler periods predominant between 1300 and 1850 AD (Matthews, 1992). We are probably due for another advance of glaciers, albeit one postponed by historical and current human activities (Vavrus *et al.*, 2008; Gray, 2015). Today, nearly all of the world's glaciers that are monitored are in retreat (Dyurgerov, 2002), although regional differences and even occasional glacial advances do occur (Whelan & Bach, 2017).

6.1.2 Spatial Patterns

The global retreat of glaciers provides a dramatic opportunity to study succession on newly deglaciated surfaces. At extreme high latitudes or elevations, peri-glacial vegetation is typically sparse and dominated by nonvascular species. For example, glaciers dominate the Himalayas, but vascular plants only persist in any abundance to approximately 6,200 m a.s.l. (Angel *et al.*, 2016). Studies of post-glacial succession typically involve Arctic-alpine or coniferous (Plate 11) vegetation (Jones & del Moral, 2005a), but also occasionally temperate broadleaf forests (Garibotti *et al.*, 2011a). Although alpine glaciers are not unknown at tropical latitudes (e.g., Mt. Kilimanjaro in Tanzania), these glaciers are the most likely to disappear in the near future (Mote & Kaser, 2007). We found only one study of post-glacial succession below 40° latitude that fit our criteria for our comparative analysis (see Chapter 4). Probably the best documented glacial retreat is located in Glacier Bay, Alaska, where various tools have been used to study succession, including permanent plots (Cooper, 1939), field experiments (Chapin *et al.*, 1994), soil analyses (Hobbie *et al.*, 1999; Bardgett & Walker, 2004), and historical reconstructions (Fastie, 1995).

6.1.3 Subsequent Disturbances

Retreating glaciers leave behind a highly variable habitat, which is affected by regional climate, rate of retreat, and type of substrate. Where the surface is unstable, it is prone to subsequent disturbances, particularly landslides and flooding. Also, snow avalanches can occur in montane landscapes and wind-blown loess can be present in dry regions.

6.2 Succession

6.2.1 Abiotic Variables

Substrate stability and texture are key variables affecting post-glacial succession and they are closely linked to topography. Succession is usually slower on unstable than stable substrates. For example, on Ellesmere Island in northern Canada, succession was slower on unstable fluvioglacial deposits than on more stable, deglaciated palaeosoils (Jones & Henry, 2003). Rock size appeared to be a factor because large (stable) rocks provided protection from wind desiccation for plants (Mori *et al.*, 2013). Similarly, species richness was greater on coarse- than fine-grained moraines in Kamchatka (Doležal *et al.*, 2008). Topographic position (upper slopes and crests of moraines vs. moraine bases), along with time, substrate texture, and distance from the edge of the deglaciated terrain influenced succession in the southern Andes (Garibotti *et al.*, 2011b). Duration of snow cover (Favero-Longo *et al.*, 2012) and seasonal persistence of ice in the soil (Doležal *et al.*, 2008) can also affect soil stability and fertility.

Substrate weathering during and after deglaciation is a key determinant of substrate fertility and is highly site specific. For example, studies have variously found either decreases (Helm & Allen, 1995; D'Amico *et al.*, 2014; Whelan & Bach, 2017) or no change (Tisdale *et al.*, 1966; Jones & Henry, 2003) in substrate pH and soluble cations such as potassium during succession. Carbon and nitrogen usually increase during succession due to the accumulation of biotic material, as is typical for primary seres (Wardle, 1979; Helm & Allen, 1995; Doležal *et al.*, 2008), but both nitrogen and phosphorus limit early primary productivity (Darcy & Schmidt, 2016). Erosion of unstable surfaces may allow pioneers to persist (Burga *et al.*, 2010), or it may slow down or even reverse succession, in what is called retrogression (Peltzer *et al.*, 2010), as described in alpine regions of Norway (Matthews & Whittaker, 1987). A typical feature of retrogression is a reduction in fertility. One way this occurs is when impermeable iron pans form in the process of podzolization in later successional stages, leading to nutrient (typically phosphorus) deficiency, and occlusion of phosphorus, which makes it unavailable for plant uptake (Walker & Syers, 1976). Another feature of retrogression is a reduction in standing biomass, usually as a consequence of the decrease of available nutrients. For example, on a moraine in New Zealand, mid successional forests changed to heathland vegetation after about 12,000 years (Wardle, 1979; Coomes *et al.*, 2013).

Air temperature and precipitation on deglaciated sites closely depend on geographical location, and particularly latitude and longitude, continentality, and elevation. Recent increases in air temperature caused by climate change are expected to modify directly successional pathways compared to earlier successional development at deglaciated sites as recently reported from Mt. Kenya (Mizuno & Fujita, 2014).

6.2.2 Biotic Variables

Nitrogen-fixing organisms often play an important role in primary seres lacking a biological legacy (Walker, 2012; Osono *et al.*, 2016). Glacial moraines are particularly suited to these organisms because they are often moist and, compared to secondary seres, competition free. Free-living nitrogen fixers can be important on glacial moraines (Worley, 1973), but where they are present vascular species with nitrogen-fixing symbionts contribute the bulk of nitrogen to the sere (Walker & del Moral, 2003). Vascular plants in the Fabaceae host *Rhizobium* bacteria (e.g., Viereck, 1966), but on moraines woody plants infected with *Frankia* bacteria were more common (Walker, 1993). Examples of moraine colonists with *Frankia* include *Dryas* spp. in Arctic North America (Chapin *et al.*, 1994; Fig. 6.2), and *Alnus* spp. in North America (Fastie, 1995) and Asia (Doležal *et al.*, 2008).

Because there is essentially no seed bank at the onset of succession, the development of vegetation depends on the transport of propagules from the surrounding vegetation (Jones & del Moral, 2009) and on the

Figure 6.2 Succession following retreat of Alaskan glacier. About 40-year-old substrate with *Dryas* plants in foreground.
Photo by Lawrence R. Walker

availability of suitable microsites (Jones & del Moral, 2005b). Anemochorous species producing a high amount of easily dispersed seeds have an advantage because they can reach often distant deglaciated areas, such as *Epilobium latifolium* in the Canadian Arctic (Mori *et al.*, 2013; Coverfront) or *Senecio* species on Mt. Kenya (Mizuno & Fujita, 2014). Therefore, isolation from species pools influences species composition on deglaciated sites (Fastie, 1995; Doležal *et al.*, 2013).

Typical vegetation on deglaciated surfaces consists of cryptogams, perennial herbs, and dwarf shrubs. Annual species are uncommon because they need more favorable temperatures to support their rapid growth. Trees are common where the glacial front is below tree line (Burga *et al.*, 2010; D´Amico *et al.*, 2014). Cryptogams are abundant at many Arctic-alpine sites (Jones & Henry, 2003), often dominating the entire sere (e.g., in sub-Antarctic sites; Favero-Longo *et al.*, 2012). During succession at these sub-Antarctic sites, widespread cryptogam species sometimes decline in abundance while Southern Hemisphere and Antarctic endemic cryptogams increase.

There are few studies that address the demography of populations of particular species participating in succession. Marcante *et al.* (2009) studied demography of early and late successional seed plants in the Alps and concluded that in demographic aspects the early successional species behaved in the same way as late successional species. This study supports the suggestion that the population dynamics of species do not substantially change during succession under harsh environmental conditions. A typical feature of post-glacial succession is little or no species turnover, although a gradual accumulation of species is commonly detected as site conditions ameliorate enough to allow species to establish. Early colonizers do not disappear because there is little or no competition and the environment does not get less favorable for them. This pattern can follow a clear progression of species composition without species exchange, which is an example of direct succession (Svoboda & Henry, 1987; Prach & Rachlewicz, 2012; Mori *et al.*, 2013).

A special case of succession connected to glaciers, but not directly to a deglaciated terrain, was described by Veblen *et al.* (1989) from the southern Andes. Landslide debris (see Chapter 9) covered the glacier and a forest developed that was dominated by *Nothofagus dombey*. The *Nothofagus* trees were about 70 years old and the forest gradually moved downslope with the glacier. The average annual rate of this forest movement was 22.5 m.

Facilitative interactions are more likely to affect succession than are competitive ones in the unproductive environments of glacial moraines where vegetation is often sparse, even in later successional stages. Under such conditions, facilitation and tolerance prevail over inhibition, and priority effects are usually unimportant (Connell & Slatyer, 1977). Stronger competition may occur under more favorable environments where woody species form a dense canopy and suppress other species (Doležal *et al.*, 2013).

Trophic interactions among plants and soil microorganisms including bacteria (Knelman *et al.*, 2018) and mycorrhizae (Welc *et al.*, 2014) are critical to post-glacial succession. Castle *et al.* (2016) conducted experiments to test the influence of soil biota on plant performance in alpine deglaciated sites and found that under low nutrient conditions, positive (facilitating) plant-soil biota interactions predominated during succession, while under high-nutrient conditions, variable relationships occurred in early stages of succession; neutral relationships prevailed in late stages. Occasionally, other relationships between plants and biota are studied on glacial moraines. For example, Albrecht *et al.* (2010) found increasing specialization of pollinators during succession.

Figure 6.3 Birch forest development on a 60-year-old moraine in Iceland. Photo by Lawrence R. Walker

6.2.3 Patterns within and among Biomes

In arctic regions many post-glacial seres share a similar set of species with circumpolar distributions (Fig. 6.3). At boreal and temperate latitudes, the differences among seres increase as regional and elevational variations in vegetation emerge. For example, on isolated mountain peaks at low latitudes, succession can be dominated by plants endemic to that mountain, e.g., giant rosette plants on Mt. Kenya (Mizuno & Fujita, 2014). At lower elevations, deglaciated sites surrounded by forests tend to develop vegetation resembling that of their surroundings. For example, in the Alps a *Larix* forest often develops (D'Amico *et al.*, 2014), and in the southern Andes both deciduous and evergreen *Nothofagus* species may dominate late successional stages (Garibotti *et al.*, 2011a,b).

The rate at which succession on moraines approaches the composition of vegetation on the surrounding unglaciated sites is highly variable. Much may depend upon whether the glaciers are at high latitude or high elevation. In the former, there may be limited sources of revegetation, while on many mountains, surviving vegetation is often adjacent to the receding glacier. In the southern Andes, initial establishment of

Figure 6.4 Succession following glacial retreat in Svalbard; the stage is ca. 20 years old.
Photo by Karel Prach

Nothofagus forest occurred within 80 years of deglaciation (Garibotti *et al.*, 2011b), while in the Alps, *Larix* forest dominated the moraine within 100 years (D'Amico *et al.*, 2014). In contrast, in the Arctic, rates of succession can be much slower. For example, Mori *et al.* (2008) reported persistence of early successional stages for several centuries on Ellesmere Island in the Canadian Arctic, despite an increasing similarity to the surrounding vegetation, which might take 1,000 years to establish. Yet in Svalbard (Fig. 6.4), Prach and Rachlewicz (2012) found all except one of the species typical of the surrounding, unglaciated tundra on moraines within 100 years of succession. Both localities are at about 80° N but Svalbard has a more favorable climate than Ellesmere Island due to the warming effects of the Gulf Stream. Landscape factors also interact. At Glacier Bay in Alaska, Milner *et al.* (2007) compared succession under terrestrial conditions with those in lake, stream, and maritime environments, and concluded that change in one ecosystem influenced the rate and direction of change in the other ecosystems through landscape-scale processes such as erosion and the accumulation of nitrogen and biomass.

Table 6.1 *Success of succession for glacier studies arranged by biomes (no. of studies). For evaluation of success see Chapter 4.*

Succession successful?	TB	CF	AL	TU	Total
Yes	1	4	8	3	16
Partly	0	2	5	2	9
No	0	0	0	0	0
Total	1	6	13	5	25

Biome abbreviations: TB: temperate broadleaf forests
CF: coniferous forests; AL: alpine, TU: tundra.

Particularly long chronosequences have been reconstructed for some glacial moraines based on various geophysical methods, including a 14,000-year chronosequence in New Zealand (Wardle, 1979); one that extends 35,000 years on Ellesmere Island (Mori *et al.*, 2008); and two of about 50,000 years: in the South Orkney Islands (Favero-Longo *et al.*, 2012) and on alpine refugia near Glacier Bay, Alaska (Boggs *et al.*, 2010). Direct comparison between succession on surfaces deglaciated at different times is limited over long time spans because the sites have inevitably experienced somewhat different histories, often under different landscape and climatic contexts (Boggs *et al.*, 2010). In conclusion, the time needed to reach target vegetation ranged from ca. 50 to several hundred years. However, slow but continuous vegetation changes are sometimes expected to continue for thousands of years (Wardle, 1979).

Based on the studies we included in our comparative analyses (N = 25; Table 6.1; for methods see Chapter 4), we found that despite the harsh environments typical of this type of succession, succession was successful in 64% of cases; we did not find any unsuccessful case. Partly successful generally indicated slow successional progress toward a target not yet reached. The target in each case was the vegetation on nearby sites that had remained ice free for at least several hundred years and that contained the potential natural vegetation for the deglaciated sites. Most (52%) of the studies were from the alpine biome, with the remainder from coniferous forest (24%) or tundra (20%) (Table 6.1). Note that because we had a number of both alpine and tundra studies for this type of disturbance, we kept them separate for analysis by biome (but pooled them as an Artic-alpine category in Chapters 5 and 7–14).

We found no significant differences among biomes with respect to success (Fig. 6.5), trajectories, species richness, or invasive alien species, probably because there were so few studies. Therefore, we combined the

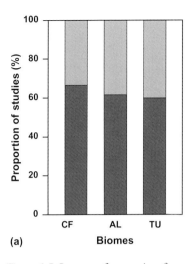 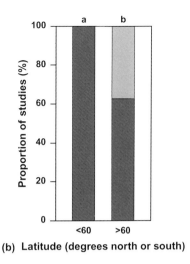

Figure 6.5 Success of succession for post-glacial succession by a) terrestrial biomes and b) latitude (percent of studies). Black: successful, light gray: partly successful; (no unsuccessful seres reported). CF: coniferous forests; AL: alpine; TU: tundra. For sample sizes, see Table 6.1. The asymptotic generalized Pearson's χ^2 test with post-hoc test a) was $\chi^2 = 0.128$, df = 2, p = 0.940 (NS) and the Cochran-Armitage test b) was Z = 4.375, p = 0.011. Different small case letters indicate statistically significant differences.

groups of biomes into high ($>60°$) and low ($<60°$) latitude (Table 6.2) and found significantly lower success at the higher latitudes, that is mostly in rather extreme Arctic environments (Fig. 6.5). Convergence (63% of studies) was more common than divergence (37%). Divergence most likely occurs if contrasting site conditions, such as substrate texture and topography, occur in the deglaciated terrain (Doležal *et al.*, 2008). Divergence tended nonsignificantly to be more common at lower than at higher latitudes. Species richness increased during succession in 71% of cases. No decreasing trend in richness was recorded, as expected in primary succession under harsh environments (Walker & del Moral, 2003). No invasive alien species were reported to influence succession. Nevertheless, invasive aliens have recently spread into higher elevations (Alexander *et al.*, 2016).

6.3 Theoretical Implications

1. The rate of succession, both in the sense of species turnover and time needed for potential natural vegetation to recover, is slow. When no species turnover occurs and only new species typical of potential natural vegetation arrive we can have direct succession.

Table 6.2 *Number of glacier studies (N = 25) sorted by latitude <60° and >60°. Sample sizes used for each successional trait are in parentheses.*

		Latitude <60°	Latitude >60°	All biomes (no.)	All biomes (%)
Succession successful? (25)	Yes	11	5	16	64
	Partly	4	5	9	36
	No	0	0	0	0
	Differences	NS			
Trajectory (19)	Converge	6	6	12	63
	Diverge	5	2	7	37
	Variable	0	0	0	0
	Differences	NS			
Species richness (17)	Increase	5	7	12	71
	Decrease	0	0	0	0
	Variable	3	2	5	29
	Differences	NS			
Invasive species important? (25)	Yes	0	0	0	0
	Partly	0	0	0	0
	No	15	10	25	100
	Differences	–			

Cochran-Armitage test was used: NS not significant; – not analyzed due to too many zero values.

2. Succession proceeded toward potential natural vegetation in all reviewed cases, although sometimes very slowly.
3. Priority effects are usually unimportant in this extreme environment.
4. Facilitation or neutral relationships among species dominate; competition (inhibition) may occur but is usually limited to late successional stages under more favorable environmental conditions.

6.4 Practical Implications

1. The increasing extent of deglaciated sites over the globe has many practical consequences, including sea level rise, changing water supply to lowlands, and perhaps emission of greenhouse gases from the

newly exposed terrain (e.g., carbon dioxide and methane releases from any newly exposed organic material).

2. However, succession results in carbon sequestration, thus decelerating additions of carbon to the atmosphere.

3. Water erosion and flooding may increase downstream due to ice melt (Boone, 2017).

4. No management or restoration activities are needed. Deglaciated sites can be left to spontaneously develop, unless local erosion control is needed using either physical barriers or native plantings (e.g., grasses).

6.5 Conclusions

Under the ongoing global warming we can expect more deglaciated sites; some glaciers, especially at lower latitudes, are expected to disappear within the next few decades (e.g., Kilimanjaro). In addition to the negative consequences for human societies mentioned in the previous section, more opportunities will arise to study colonization, species interactions, and trophic interactions under often extreme environment conditions. These opportunities may result in new theoretical insights about succession, and provide opportunities to study the influence on succession of an expected influx of new species to Arctic-alpine environments (Thuiller *et al.*, 2008).

7 · Cyclones

7.1 Disturbance Description

Cyclones (also called hurricanes or typhoons) are the first of two types of wind-caused disturbance that we discuss. The second category is dunes, covered in Chapter 8. Cyclones damage forests and infrastructure such as buildings, utility poles, and marinas. Cyclones can also be deadly, particularly in low-lying countries such as Bangladesh, which has lost hundreds of thousands of people to cyclones (Berz, 1988). They are also frequently accompanied by heavy rains, which can trigger flooding and landslides. Cyclones are primarily a disturbance of tropical climates but can also be found in temperate regions; they are most common in the Pacific Ocean, followed by the Indian and Atlantic Oceans (Plate 13).

Cyclones are categorized by the Saffir-Simpson Hurricane Scale as having sustained wind speeds >118 km hr^{-1} for a period of at least one minute. The strongest cyclones are classified as Category 5 with sustained wind speeds of >252 km hr^{-1}. In the North Atlantic Ocean between 5° and 30° North latitude, a Category 5 cyclone occurs about once every three years. Storm surges and low atmospheric pressure are other characteristics of a cyclone.

Cyclone damage to vegetation depends on many parameters, including wind speed, duration of the storm, local and regional topography, degree of soil saturation, and anatomical and stand traits of the vegetation (Lugo, 2008; Walker, 2012). Mortality of trees, generally the most vulnerable plant life form during a cyclone, is typically $<15\%$, but some cyclones kill nearly all the trees (Brokaw & Walker, 1991). Cyclones also cause defoliation, loss of branches, and snapping or uprooting of trunks. The degree and type of damage to trees is as variable as mortality, and is influenced by various plant traits including: root structure (Fraser, 1962), buttress roots (Putz et al., 1983), plant height (Dittus, 1985; Jimenez-Rodríguez et al., 2018), wood density (Walker et al., 1992; Curran et al., 2008), stand density (Foster, 1988a), forest diversity (Tanner &

Bellingham, 2006), stem diameter (Walker, 1991), specific leaf area (Bellingham *et al.*, 1995), and the presence of resprouted crowns (Putz *et al.*, 1983). Useful predictions about which species will be damaged by future cyclones are largely site-specific. Even within sites, different forest types can experience variable levels of damage, depending on exposure to wind, species composition, native vs. non-native species, and other factors (Van Bloem *et al.*, 2005; Yap *et al.*, 2016). Perhaps the most robust prediction is that later successional stands and larger trees are most likely to be damaged (Baker *et al.*, 2002; Lugo, 2008).

7.1.1 Causes

Tropical cyclones develop when warm, tropical ocean water evaporates and creates a circular wind of rising air with a calm, wind-free center or eye. These conditions occur between 5° and 30° latitude (predominantly 10–20°) in the summer season when the intertropical convergence zone is at its highest latitude. Temperate cyclones are generated between 40° and 60° latitude due to the convergence of tropical and polar air masses. The rising air cools, losing its capacity to hold moisture, so rain usually accompanies cyclones. Trade winds and the spin of the earth contribute to the rotation of cyclones. Evidence is accumulating that atmospheric changes caused by human-influenced climate change (e.g., warmer oceans and higher evaporation rates) are associated with increased frequency of intense cyclones (Goldenberg *et al.*, 2001; Webster *et al.*, 2005; Mei & Xie, 2016). These changes can mean more rain and erosion (Tzeng *et al.*, 2018) and possibly eventual shifts in species composition and abundance. Predictability of the characteristics of a given storm is poor, but taking measurements from airplanes that fly within the eye of an active storm and monitoring ozone levels that cyclones alter are tools that help predict the path, if not the intensity of a given storm (del Moral & Walker, 2007).

7.1.2 Spatial Patterns

Cyclones affect about 15% of the earth's terrestrial surface (Walker, 2012) and are abundant throughout much of the subtropics (Plate 12). Many of the storms have little impact on human population centers, but those that do can cause tremendous damage. Warm waters generate the cyclones and then trade winds push them from east to west. The strongest storms often veer north or south into higher latitudes (to about 45° latitude) before losing the thermal energy that drives them. Some even veer eastward, pushed by the westerlies. Cyclones diminish in strength when they pass over a large land mass, but can regain their strength if they return to warm ocean water. Islands are often vulnerable because of the oceanic origins of cyclones (Walker & Bellingham, 2011). The most intense and largest cyclones are in the western Pacific Ocean, frequently affecting Taiwan, the Philippines, Korea, and Japan.

Disruptions of forest vegetation by cyclones is patchy. High levels of damage might be sustained on a mountain ridge; in a plantation of uniform, fast-growing trees (Fu et al., 1996); or on steep slopes destabilized by heavy rains (Walker & Shiels, 2013). Shallow-rooted trees tend to be particularly vulnerable to damage (Foster, 1988b; Boucher et al., 1990). Less damage might occur in the lee of a ridge, among native species that might deflect the wind, or with plants adapted to strong winds (e.g., palms; but see Lugo et al., 1983). Forest gaps caused by independent tree falls (due to wind, disease, logging, senescence, etc.) have been widely described (see Chapter 15) but here we focus on more widespread damage from cyclones. We do address understory damage and succession following cyclones in the text but are primarily focused on woody overstory vegetation.

7.1.3 Subsequent Disturbances

Cyclones trigger many secondary disturbances. Floods are the first concern following wind damage by a cyclone. Hurricane Katrina (2005) and Hurricane Harvey (2017) in the United States both led to disastrous floods in New Orleans, Louisiana and Houston, Texas, respectively. Along the Louisiana shoreline, maritime forests were lost and there was significant disruption to remaining vegetation (Lucas & Carter, 2013). High rainfall in mountainous areas can also trigger landslides (Cyclone Tokage triggered >280 landslides in Japan in 2004; see Chapter 9) and Hurricane Charley in Florida (2004) appeared to trigger an earthquake, possibly creating a sub-oceanic landslide (del Moral & Walker, 2007). Crop damage can be severe, as during Cyclone Larry (2006) in Queensland, Australia. Fires are sometimes triggered by direct disruptions to gas and electric lines or occur days to months after the cyclone because of the high fuel loads that cyclones create. For example, fires that occurred after Hurricane Gilbert (1988) in Mexico killed more trees than the wind (Whigham et al., 1991). The same response occurred after Hurricane Hugo (1989) in South Carolina (Smith et al., 1997) where there was an

eight-fold increase in fuel loads (Hook *et al.*, 1991) following the cyclone. Woody debris can lead to rapid growth of insects that consume
wood, and salvage logging can disrupt soils of wind-blown and burned
forests (Everham & Brokaw, 1996). Finally, cyclones can be followed by
drought when deforested landscapes reduce evapotranspiration and alter
precipitation patterns (Lugo, 2008). Drought interacts with fires, insect
damage, and other subsequent disturbances to regulate succession.
Where mangroves or dunes are damaged, flooding and coastal erosion
can occur, sometimes leading to salt water intrusion into coastal aquifers
(Kirwan & Megonigal, 2013) and streams (Gardner *et al.*, 1991); affected
coastlines become more vulnerable to the next cyclone.

7.2 Succession

7.2.1 Abiotic Variables

Responses of abiotic variables to cyclones can fit several patterns, as noted
5 years after Hurricane Hugo in Puerto Rico (Zimmerman *et al.*, 1996).
Nitrate concentrations in streams and forest floor biomass initially
increased rapidly then declined shortly afterward to normal levels. Aboveground potassium and magnesium pools decreased sharply then rose above
pre-cyclone levels. Fine litterfall also decreased sharply then increased, but
not to pre-cyclone levels. In addition, local climatic conditions following a
cyclone influence nutrient pools, primary productivity, and processes such
as succession. A three-month drought followed Hurricane Hugo in the
Caribbean, leading to a delay in forest succession (Scatena *et al.*, 1996).

Defoliation, generally accompanied by branch and tree falls (Plate 13;
Fig. 7.1), immediately increases light penetration to the forest floor
(Fernández & Fetcher, 1991). This change can trigger germination of
pioneer species such as *Cecropia* in Central America that respond to
increases in the red/far red light ratio (Vázquez-Yanes *et al.*, 1990).
Differential responses of tree species and their seedlings and saplings to
the abrupt increase in light (Wen *et al.*, 2008) can affect successional
dynamics. The light regime changes with successional recovery of the
vegetation. In Jamaican forests, this return to original levels of shade to
pre-storm levels took <3 years (Bellingham *et al.*, 1996b). When a
cyclone damaged a tropical dry forest in Puerto Rico that was undergoing various stages of succession from previous fires, canopy shade
increased to pre-cyclone conditions more rapidly in early than in late
seral stages (Hasselquist *et al.*, 2010). When forests are damaged along

Figure 7.1 Damage from Hurricane Maria in the lowland forest of the Luquillo Mountains, Puerto Rico (2017).
Photo by Omar Gutiérrez del Arroyo, with permission

permanent streams, post-cyclone riparian succession occurs under conditions of constant rather than diminishing light resources because of the canopy opening created by the stream (Frangi & Lugo, 1998). Experimental defoliation of a Puerto Rican rainforest supported the conclusion that increased light due to canopy openness increased densities and compositional changes in woody plants and ferns and decreased leaf decomposition and litterfall; in contrast, additions of leaf litter inhibited recruitment (Shiels *et al.*, 2010; 2014; 2015). When litter was experimentally removed following Hurricane Hugo in Puerto Rico, seedlings of early successional species responded most, suggesting that litterfall during a cyclone can potentially influence successional processes (Guzmán-Grajales & Walker, 1991).

Changes in soil nutrients are minimal when a cyclone does not disrupt soil structure, and nutrients can recover quickly (McDonald & Healey, 2000). However, cyclones can deposit up to 1 year's worth of leaf litter onto the soil during a cyclone (Lodge et al., 1991), which can provide an important nutrient pulse to the forest (Silver *et al.*, 1996). Litterfall is likely to be reduced under such circumstances for several subsequent years (Vogt *et al.*, 1996). In Taiwan, annual cyclones lead to repeated loss of nutrients in litterfall and stunted forest growth (Lin *et al.*, 2008). Soils and fine roots can also be physically disrupted during cyclones (Silver & Vogt, 1993), particularly where trees are uprooted. The resulting tip up mounds and pits expose mineral soil that can serve as a site for establishment of rapidly growing pioneer trees such as *Cecropia* in tropical forests (Walker, 2000). These microhabitats result in modified soil moisture, nitrogen, carbon, and stability (Clinton & Baker, 2000).

7.2.2 Biotic Variables

Biological legacies are important following cyclones because there is no widespread disruption of soils, so the recovery is usually an example of secondary succession where surviving plants resprout (Boucher, 1990; Bellingham *et al.*, 1994; 1996a; Zimmerman et al., 1994) or germinate from existing seed banks (Hibbs, 1983). Most aboveground plants survive a cyclone, particularly subcanopy and understory plants (Dittus, 1985). Even epiphytes can survive, provided their host tree is not uprooted (Oberbauer *et al.*, 1996). Sprouting is characteristic of smaller diameter trees that tend to snap (Putz *et al.*, 1983), but can also be a mechanism for late-successional species to accelerate succession. Sprouting can be the principal form of regeneration in wind-damaged forests (Dietze & Clark, 2008). Succession varies with the type and extent of damage inflicted by the storm and the responses of the vegetation (Foster, 1988a; Merrens & Peart, 1992). Everham and Brokaw (1996) summarized successional pathways as regrowth (direct regeneration by legacy plants), recruitment (dispersal), release (of understory sapling survivors), and repression (of trees by rapid herbaceous growth).

Dispersal limitation is a concern when the dominant vegetation is too damaged to recover (e.g., a shallow-rooted pine plantation where most trees are uprooted) or where the physical environment is altered enough (e.g., sharply increased light levels) that new arrivals can establish. Dispersal is affected by the timing of the storm relative to neighboring plant phenologies (Walker & Neris, 1993). Seed dispersal into cyclone-damaged forests, typically by birds, can be an important element in succession (Vitousek & Walker, 1989; Bellingham *et al.*, 2005) and spatial distribution of recruitment (Uriarte *et al.*, 2004). Hibbs (1983) found regeneration in a New England forest to originate equally from wind-blown seeds, buried seeds, and sprouting. In Samoa, large remnant trees were key sources of seed production, attracted vertebrate seed dispersers, and provided favorable habitats for seedlings of late successional species to establish and grow (Elmqvist et al., 2002).

Pre-disturbance vegetative structure can recover within a few decades in mesic climates, but recovery of original species composition often takes about a century (Walker et al., 1996b). Succession in cooler, drier climates can take several centuries. Where 70-80% of a forested area is affected each century by cyclones, full recovery may not occur before the next storm (Lugo & Scatena, 1996). In New England (USA), where a major hurricane has impacted the forest once each century for 400 years, fast-growing, shade-intolerant species take advantage of post-cyclone conditions. However, shade-tolerant species eventually recover their initial dominance, usually from suppressed understory seedlings that take advantage of post-cyclone conditions to reach the canopy (Foster, 1988a). Seedlings of shade-intolerant species that established post-cyclone usually die out. Topography and anthropogenic disturbances also affect forest damage and succession.

Succession occurs when the existing vegetation does not fill the forest gap directly from resprouting or lateral expansion (direct regeneration). In some cases, fast-growing pioneer trees can use the higher light levels and exposed mineral soils to establish before the slower-growing species recover. Cyclones can thereby increase local forest diversity, which declines in periods without cyclones, leading to what has been con- sidered a form of cyclic succession (Lugo et al., 1983; Dittus, 1985). However, regional forest diversity is not likely to change, unless disturb- ance regimes are altered. In a Jamaican rainforest, for example, only four of 20 common tree species changed in their relative abundance following a cyclone (Bellingham et al., 1995). Three of these were so-called usurpers (low damage but highly responsive to post-cyclone conditions) and their relative abundance was projected to increase. The fourth species was called susceptible (high damage, low responsiveness) and its relative abundance was projected to decrease. Species in the other categories (resistant: low damage and responsiveness, or resilient: high damage and responsiveness) were less likely to have their relative abun- dance altered by cyclones. This classification was also used to assess cyclone damage to a temperate broadleaf forest in northern Florida (Batista & Platt, 2003). In a Puerto Rican rainforest, species diversity was maintained following a cyclone by individualistic responses of seed- lings of six common tree species to manipulations of forest debris and soil nutrients (Walker et al., 2003). The manipulations included removal of hurricane debris, a control, and an addition of fertilizer to the unaltered debris. Only some of the expected differences between pioneer and non-pioneer seedlings were apparent in seedling density, growth, and mortality. Uriarte *et al.* (2012) suggested that the maintenance of forest tree diversity following cyclones is due to trade-offs among the abilities of species to colonize, compete, and utilize newly available resources in a post-cyclone environment.

Invasive alien species can take advantage of the disruption of light regimes, alterations to stand and soil structure, addition of propagules, and loss of potential competitors. For example, *Triadica sebifera,* introduced from China, invaded temperate broadleaf forests following Hurricane Katrina in Louisiana (Henkel *et al.*, 2016). Tropical rain forests are not typically subject to invasions by alien plants (Fine, 2002), except on islands where they can cause significant disruption (Walker & Vitousek, 1991; Rothstein *et al.*, 2004). For example, the invasive tree, *Pittosporum undulatum* has invaded Jamaican forests and negatively affected native trees (Bellingham *et al.*, 2005, 2018). Climate change is expected to increase cyclone intensity, increasing the likelihood for invasive species, including woody lianas and trees in particular, to colonize tropical rain forests (Murphy & Metcalfe, 2016). These invasive species may decrease biodiversity, homogenize landscapes, and arrest forest succession, particularly in vulnerable forest fragments. Alternatively, invasive alien species can be limited to early successional stages, as in Australian rainforests following Cyclone Larry (2006) (Murphy *et al.*, 2008).

Plant-plant interactions are important following cyclones. The reestablishment of interactions is an important yet understudied aspect of forest succession (Chazdon, 2003; Uriarte *et al.*, 2012). Understory plants can play an important role in post-cyclone succession because they often show rapid changes (generally increases) in species richness and shifts in composition following a cyclone. They grow quickly in response to increased nutrients and light and can affect tree regeneration, especially when they form thickets (Walker *et al.*, 2010). For example, in northern Poland, the dominant grass, *Deschampsia flexuosa*, reduced pine tree regeneration (Skłodowski *et al.*, 2014). Cyclone Annie destroyed most of a forest in the Solomon Islands in 1967 and the dense growth of colonizing woody vines slowed but did not inhibit eventual forest recovery (Whitmore, 1974), although vines were inhibitory in Samoa (Wood, 1970). Successional shifts occur in understory as well as overstory plants (Palmer *et al.*, 2000). In Puerto Rico, there was differential mortality of species of understory ferns (Sharpe & Shiels, 2014) and in some locations, ferns and vines replaced forbs and shrubs (Royo et al., 2011). In Japan, *Rubus idaeus* and *Sasa senanensis* sequentially dominated following a cyclone; during the transition between these two species trees were able to reestablish (Ishizuka et al., 1997). Similar shifts in understory dominance during succession are common following any disturbance (e.g., landslides; Walker et al., 2010). Less extensive storms are unlikely to disrupt understory plants (Webb & Scanga, 2001), although tip up mounds and pits are areas of likely loss (Roberts, 2004), but also of later establishment (Yoshida & Noguchi, 2008) of understory plants. Understory species can also undergo successional changes (Palmer et al., 2000).

Trophic interactions are influential following cyclones. For example, increases in the level of herbivory can occur because foliage is more available, plant nutrient levels change, or plant types change in relative abundance. Foliage availability apparently supported leaf-eating monkeys in Sri Lanka and contributed to the demise of favored tree species following a 1978 cyclone (Dittus, 1985). In a simulated cyclone in Puerto Rico, herbivory on pioneer plants was most related to plant abundance while herbivory on non-pioneer plants was linked to enhanced nutrient availability and foliar quality (Prather, 2014). Herbivores are not always easily deterred. Even though cyclone-damaged trees increased anti-herbivore tannin concentrations following a cyclone in North Carolina, insect herbivory did not decrease (Hunter & Forkner, 1999).

Fungal pathogens can infect post-cyclone trees by entering wounds and leading to delayed mortality (Putz & Brokaw, 1989). Fast-growing, dense stands of pioneer trees are particularly vulnerable to pathogens once they begin to be shaded (Lodge & Cantrell, 1995). Fungi are also key components of the decomposition of the pulse of litter immediately following a cyclone (Shiels et al., 2015) and help determine understory species survival and subsequent succession (Sharpe & Shiels, 2014).

Following Hurricane Jova (2011) in a Mexican tropical dry forest, the size and complexity of plant-herbivore networks decreased while robustness of connections increased (Luviano et al., 2018). The resilience of the herbivore communities might have been related to the presence of a nearby nature reserve and the relatively mild (Category 2) cyclone. Also following Hurricane Jova, snakes, lizards, and frogs responded individualistically, with some winners (e.g., insectivorous lizards were able to colonize new habitats) and some losers (e.g., common frogs were unable to adapt to rapid changes in food availability) (Suazo-Ortuño et al., 2018).

7.2.3 Patterns within and among Biomes

Cyclones provide a useful vehicle to compare disturbance effects on succession within and among biomes because the cyclones have potentially long pathways that cross various topographical features, ecosystems, and latitudes. Various compilations of cyclone effects in the Caribbean (e.g., Bénito-Espinal & Bénito-Espinal, 1991) garnered interest because they were comprehensive examinations of damage to maritime (Woodley *et al.*, 1981), coastal (Finkl & Pilkey, 1991), and terrestrial (Walker *et al.*, 1991; Walker *et al.*, 1996a) habitats. Zimmerman *et al.* (1996) provide a useful model of potential responses of many abiotic and biotic variables to cyclones, but these compilations were largely of site-specific damage and short-term response rather than a comparison, for example, of post-cyclone succession across latitude.

Topographical differences set the stage for differences in cyclone damage (leeward and windward sides of a mountain) and therefore different successional trajectories in a Puerto Rican rainforest over several decades (Heartsill Scalley, 2017). Elevational differences in response to cyclones in the same forest were also pronounced, with fast-growing graminoids in the uplands and fast-growing *Cecropia* trees in the lowlands of Puerto Rico (Walker *et al.*, 1996b). In such a well-studied forest, landscape-level studies have been possible, including an evaluation of the interactions of land use and cyclones (Foster *et al.*, 1999; Uriarte *et al.*, 2009).

Two useful syntheses of cyclone ecology have been provided by Everham and Brokaw (1996) and Lugo (2008). Both address post-cyclone succession, or trajectory of response (i.e., any of several possible pathways to maturity (Ewel, 1980). The predicted recovery times of pre-disturbance vegetation and abiotic parameters vary from years to centuries, depending in part on what parameters are measured (in ascending order of time to recovery: light levels, vegetation structure, standing biomass, species composition) and tend to be shorter in the tropics than in temperate zones (Everham & Brokaw, 1996). Sprouting can lead to faster recovery than seedling establishment of all plants, from pioneers to late successional species (Bellingham *et al.*, 1994) and occurred more often in tropical (85% of studies) than temperate (40%) forests (Everham & Brokaw, 1996). Complete recovery may be impossible when the return time of cyclones is shorter than the life span of the dominant trees (Webb, 1958; Putz & Chan, 1986; Boucher, 1990).

For our comparative analysis, we found fewer studies that fit our criteria (for methods see Chapter 4) than we had hoped (N = 21), in

Table 7.1 *Success of succession for cyclone studies arranged by biomes (no. of studies). For the evaluation of success see Chapter 4.*

Succession successful?	TR	TD	TB	CF	Total
Yes	5	0	5	0	10
Partly	5	1	2	2	10
No	0	0	1	0	1
Total	10	1	8	2	21

Biome abbreviations: TR: tropical rain forests; TD: tropical dry forests; TB: temperate broadleaf forests; CF: coniferous forests.

part because many studies of cyclones focused more on immediate damage than on decadal changes in vegetation (Lugo, 2008). The chosen studies were almost entirely from tropical rainforests and temperate broadleaf forests (Table 7.1) with only one study from the tropical dry biome and two from the coniferous forest biome. Succession tended non-significantly to be more successful in tropical (rain and dry) forests than in temperate broadleaf forests (Fig. 7.2). Divergent trajectories were most frequent in cold habitats, while in warm habitats variable trajectories prevailed (Table 7.2). Species richness increased in three of the ten studies where we could evaluate it; most commonly richness was variable (largely curvilinear, with a typical pattern of an inverted U shape, i.e., low - high - low during the course of succession). Invasive species were never considered important and only occasionally partly important to succession, which could reflect the saturation of niches and perhaps high levels of plant-plant competition in wet forests at any latitude.

7.3 Theoretical Implications

1. Cyclone damage generally resets successional processes in a forest, with large-scale damage to trees. Fast-growing vegetation quickly covers the terrain with sprouting local trees, released understory saplings, or grasses, forbs, and vines; Vandermeer *et al.* (1998) called this the building phase. A period of thinning then ensues when species richness, after an initial increase, typically declines as the forest gradually matures.
2. Cyclone damage can accelerate succession when shade-intolerant plants with low wood density are more damaged than seedling banks

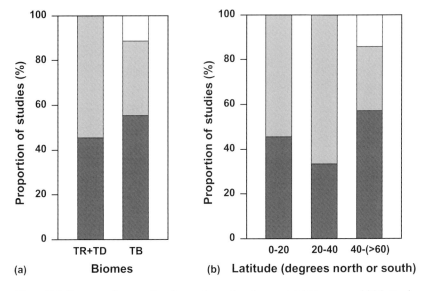

Figure 7.2 Success of succession for cyclones by a) terrestrial biomes and b) latitude (% of studies). Black: successful, light gray: partly successful, striped gray: not successful. TR+ TD: tropical rain forests plus tropical dry forests, TB: temperate broadleaf forests. For sample sizes, see Table 7.1. The Cochran-Armitage test a) was Z = –2.536; p = 0.111 (NS) and the asymptotic generalized Pearson´s χ^2 test with post-hoc test b) was χ^2 = 0.102, df = 2, p = 0.950 (NS).

    or resprouting trees of shade-tolerant, later succession species with high wood density (Curran *et al.*, 2008; Allen *et al.*, 2012). This acceleration is a common consequence of wind damage in temperate broadleaf forests but also occurs in the tropics (Zhao *et al.*, 2006).

3. Cyclones, like most disturbances, alter the distribution and availability of nutrients, increase habitat heterogeneity, influence species composition and diversity, and induce evolutionary change through the selective mortality of tree species (Lugo, 2008).

7.4 Practical Implications

1. Forests do recover from cyclones when intervals between storms are longer than tree life spans and there are no other severe disturbances (anthropogenic or natural).

2. Forest damage and recovery are closely tied to pre- and post-cyclone land use (Chazdon, 2003). Areas of high basal area (e.g., undisturbed forests) tend to lose more biomass (by the damage done to large trees)

Table 7.2 Number of cyclone studies ($N = 21$) sorted by various criteria: Warm (TR, TD), Cold (CF, TB), Dry (TD), Wet (TR, CF, TB), Forested (TR, CF, TD, TB), Not forested (not represented). Sample sizes used for each successional trait are in parentheses. For biome abbreviations see Table 7.1. All studies were evaluated for success but not for trajectory, richness, and invasive species when there was insufficient information provided.

Successional trait		Warm	Cold	Dry	Wet	Forested	Not forested	All biomes (no.)	All biomes (%)
Succession successful? (21)	Yes	5	5	0	10	10	0	10	48
	Partly	6	4	1	9	10	0	10	48
	No	0	1	0	1	1	0	1	4
	Differences	NS		NS		–			
Trajectory (11)	Converge	1	4	0	5	5	0	5	46
	Diverge	0	3	0	3	3	0	3	27
	Variable	3	0	1	2	3	0	3	27
	Differences	★		NS		–			
Species richness (10)	Increase	3	0	0	3	3	0	3	30
	Decrease	0	0	0	0	0	0	0	0
	Variable	4	3	1	6	7	0	7	70
	Differences	–		–		–			
Invasive species important? (14)	Yes	0	0	0	0	0	0	0	0
	Partly	1	3	0	4	4	0	4	28
	No	3	7	0	10	10	0	10	72
	Differences	NS		–		–			

χ^2 test was used for non-ordered variables, Cochran-Armitage test was used for ordered variables: ★ $p < 0.05$; NS not significant; – not analyzed due to too many zero values.

and experience shorter-term increases in species richness (from expansion by shade-intolerant species) than areas with less biomass (e.g., some plantations or early successional forests; Uriarte *et al.,* 2004). Signatures of historical land use up to a century old altered responses of vegetation to cyclone disturbances in New England (Motzkin *et al.,* 1999) and Puerto Rico (Zimmerman *et al.,* 1995; Foster *et al.,* 1999). Human-caused fragmentation of tropical forests affects damage and recovery from cyclones (Laurance & Curran, 2008). Salvage logging is a typical post–cyclone activity that clearly alters successional processes through species manipulations, further disruption of soils, slash debris piles, and logging roads (Lindenmayer *et al.,* 2008). When rapid production of timber is not a priority, spontaneous succession is usually preferable to manipulations of succession.

3. Climate change will likely lead to more intense cyclones but also to potential shifts in where cyclones occur as well as shifts in distributions. Future cyclones might thereby affect forests with different species composition than those of today (Shiels *et al.,* 2015). In turn, successional trajectories are likely to be altered in yet unpredictable ways based on new patterns of species composition and dominance.

4. Lugo (2008) suggested that cyclone research needs to emphasize long-term studies and networks of observations along expected cyclone paths, using remote sensing and field studies. Such an integration across multiple latitudes, longitudes, disturbance regimes, and biomes will help society interpret inevitable changes and improve management of future disturbances.

7.5 Conclusions

Cyclone damage intimately affects many people and appears to be increasing with climate change. The immediacy of cyclone damage to humans in low latitude, coastal environments has resulted in many studies of short-term forest dynamics. Key insights about these dynamics have elucidated the roles of surviving plants, plant interactions, and surrounding land use. However, more long-term studies of cyclone damage to forests and other ecosystems (e.g., coral reefs) are critical. Such studies will help clarify how humans can best mitigate the damage to ecosystems and the services that they provide.

8 · Dunes

8.1 Disturbance Description

Dunes, like cyclones, are disturbances caused by wind and only partially affected by humans. Unlike cyclones, which leave soil intact, dunes bury the soil in sand, thereby initiating primary succession. Dune formation can be triggered by such human activities as diversion of lakes or rivers, removal of vegetation by logging or overgrazing, and climate warming that increases aridity and leads to dry surface soil.

Dunes are formed when winds blowing at least 25 km per hour transport sand and build hills in places where the wind slackens and drops the sand. Dunes bury ecosystems as they advance across the land at rates ranging from meters to kilometers per year (Hesp, 2002). They range in height but are usually <100 m tall. Dunes cover about 7% of the terrestrial surface of the earth (Fig. 8.1) but are expanding in areas of desertification (such as the Sahel south of the Sahara Desert; Tucker *et al.*, 1991; Behnke & Mortimore, 2015). When dunes become relatively stable, succession can proceed, but some dunes remain unstable for thousands of years. Dunes are ultimately a consequence of long-term erosion of uplifted mountains and the deposition of sand in lake beds or floodplains and along ocean coastlines. Many past dunes have become buried and compressed into sandstone.

8.1.1 Causes

Inland dunes occur where there is a reliable source of sediment, such as from dried lakes, eroding slopes, or glacial moraines, and anywhere that humans or their livestock have removed the protective vegetative layer from underlying silts and sands. The effective overexploitation of ground water to support livestock has led to rapid expansion of grazing lands in previously less fertile aridlands. Livestock disrupt protective soil crusts and vegetation, leading to increased wind erosion and dune formation. Other

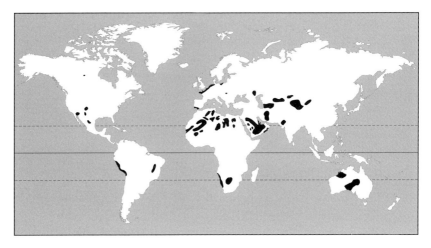

Figure 8.1 Global distribution of major areas with sand dunes.

human activities, including off-road recreational vehicles, drilling activities, highway expansion, firewood cutting, and all types of urban and suburban development also increase erosion and the potential for dune formation (del Moral & Walker, 2007). Increased aridity from climate change further exacerbates this trend of desertification.

Coastal dunes occur when upland sediments wash down to the ocean and, combined with eroded reefs and other sediments of aquatic origin, get redeposited on land as sandy beaches. The beach sand blows inland and forms dunes. Sometimes coastal dunes (Kain *et al.*, 2014) and dune succession (Hayasaka *et al.*, 2012) can be dramatically altered by tsunamis. Coastal dunes are also subject to disruption from many human activities (Kelly, 2014).

8.1.2 Spatial Patterns

Inland dunes are common in arid regions such as central Asia where receding lakes expose sediments to provide a sediment source (Fullen & Mitchell, 1994). Inland dunes are generally thought to be undesirable (Li *et al.*, 2014) (see Section 8.1.3). However, possible benefits of inland dunes include their potential role as windbreaks and the increased fertility when silty loess predominates over sand, such as the wind-blown dust from China that enriches depleted Hawaiian soils (Vitousek, 2004) or the so-call blood rain in Sicily that comes from North Africa (del Moral & Walker, 2007). In southwestern New Zealand, disturbance from a

6,500-year-old dune ridge contributed phosphorus that likely is delaying retrogression in a nearby chronosequence by promoting early successional plants such as tree ferns (Eger *et al.*, 2013). Some inland dune ecosystems (e.g., in Europe) are also actively restored for their specialized flora and fauna (Grootjans *et al.*, 2013; Rhind *et al.*, 2013).

Many coastlines support dunes that rarely advance very far inland. Instead they can form a shifting but largely effective storm barrier that protects coastal ecosystems and offers recreational opportunities for millions of beach visitors. No artificial flood barrier is as effective as a coastal dune composed of a fore dune, rows of successively more inland dunes, each parallel to the coast, and dune slacks that form between them. (Note that although dune slacks, or hollows, are mentioned here they involve a modified hydrosere, depending on elevation of the water table; our focus is on the more arid conditions of the dune slopes and ridges.) Coastal dunes vary in extent from small, localized pockets of sand to large sets of dunes such as the Cooloola Dunes in southeastern Queensland along Australia's east coast that cover 240 km^2. These dunes are well studied and have carefully dated surfaces ranging from recent to 730,000 years old (Walker *et al.*, 2018). Coastal dunes are, in contrast to inland ones, largely shrinking due to human activities such as parking lots, condominiums, and construction of seaside resorts. Sea level rise from climate warming is another cause of shrinking dunes, only partially offset in some areas (e.g., Baltic Sea, Finland) by coastal uplift (Nylén & Luoto, 2015). One cause of damage to coastal dunes is their replacement by greenhouse crops, especially in Sicily where during a 70-year period (1938–2007) there was massive loss of coastal dunes (Sciandrello *et al.*, 2015).

8.1.3 Subsequent Disturbances

Inland dunes and coastal dunes moving inland can kill trees that are then susceptible to burning if their trunks are not buried in the sand. Fire can also be promoted by dune vegetation that readily burns, thereby arresting succession (Poulson, 1999). Dunes can destroy terrestrial ecosystems through burial (e.g., of farmlands and towns). For example, the city of Paracuru in Brazil was recently covered by an advancing dune (Castro, 2005). Moving dunes can also bury or partially bury lakes and streams, in the latter case altering drainage patterns across the landscape. Particularly challenging is when villages and the oases they depend on are engulfed by advancing dunes, as has occurred to more than 10 villages in the last two decades in the Amu Darya Valley in Afghanistan (del Moral & Walker, 2007). Dune advances are also prominent in places such as Mali, Nigeria, and China.

8.2 Succession

8.2.1 Abiotic Variables

Dunes have been central to the development of ideas about succession (see Chapter 2; Miyanishi & Johnson, 2007) in Europe (Warming, 1909; Grootjans *et al.,* 1998; van der Maarel, 1998), North America (Cowles, 1901; Olson, 1958; Lichter, 1998), and Asia (Walker & Syers, 1976; Walker *et al.,* 1981). Many dune studies rely on a toposequence rather than a chronosequence approach (see Chapter 2), where physical features (dune swales, dune ridges, distance from shoreline) become substitutes for time (Pegman & Rapson, 2005). Both chronosequence and toposequence approaches are poor substitutes for direct measurements but can produce insights when used with caution. An unstable substrate is the main impediment to plant colonization of dunes (Moreno-Casasola, 1986), followed by aridity, infertility, salinity, and high light levels. Dunes stabilize where topographic barriers such as hills or large bodies of water reduce wind velocity. Other causes of stabilization include plant growth or when the source of sand is exhausted or removed (Muñoz-Reinoso, 2018). Humans intent on slowing the advance of dunes use fences or other sand traps, mechanically flatten dunes to decrease their height and sand-trapping ability, or jump-start vegetative growth through various revegetation techniques (e.g., application of biodegradable mesh to promote soil crusts and seedling growth, planting of rhizomatous grasses or trees, and fertilization to encourage plant growth). In China, large shelterbelts of trees have been planted to help stabilize dunes and reduce dust storms (Li *et al.,* 2012).

Aridity and an unstable substrate limit most colonization of dunes. For example, arid conditions, combined with loose soils and heavy grazing pressure restricted succession on Iranian inland dunes (Abdi & Afsharzadeh, 2016). Yet if plants can get roots down to the water table, they may survive. Substantial soil water can be present, even in aridland dunes, because coarse sand grains provide pore spaces too large for excessive evaporative losses from the surface.

Infertility can be ameliorated by biological soil crusts or nitrogen-fixing plants (see Section 8.2.2) and soil nutrient levels generally increase with succession (Di Palo & Fornara, 2017), affecting which plants can grow (Rohani et al., 2014; Ruocco et al., 2014). Succession is typically accelerated when subject to nitrogen deposition (Sparrius et al., 2013). However, in long chronosequences where retrogression occurs (Fig. 8.2), soil fertility and microbial biomass decline (Laliberté et al., 2012; Bokhorst et al., 2017). In fact, a pattern of declining phosphorus in old New Zealand dunes (Syers & Walker, 1969) has proven to be a widely applicable pattern with relevance to many types of retrogressive seres (Peltzer et al., 2010).

Salinity limits colonization for some plants on coastal dunes where there is ample salt spray (Young et al., 1994), but becomes less of a problem inland or in regions of high rainfall (Sykes & Wilson, 1989). Finally, differential responses of dune colonists to light availability (e.g., as altered by the shade of an earlier pioneer in coastal dune forests of South Africa; Tsvuura & Lawes, 2016) directly influence successional sequences.

8.2.2 Biotic Variables

Biological legacies can be present in or around dunes that are not extensive or tall. Such conditions can occur at the leading edge of a dune (but will likely be temporary as the dune advances) or at the edges (where vegetation may recolonize the new dune surface). Dunes advancing over previously stabilized dunes may be colonized from underneath, as vegetation grows at or faster than the pace of burial by sand. However, biological legacies are much less likely to influence succession on the largely homogeneous surface of a dune than on the more heterogeneous surfaces created by landslides, floods, or fire (Walker & del Moral, 2003).

Vegetation most readily colonizes dune slacks where there is ready access to water and sufficient nutrient availability, but also invades the leeward sides of dunes (Sewerniak & Jankowski, 2017). As one goes inland on coastal dunes, vegetation increasingly stabilizes the dunes, salt spray declines, soils start to develop, and inland plants begin to invade. Succession on inland and coastal dunes leads to the loss of the most visually distinct feature (open sand), and the former dune becomes part of the vegetated landscape (Plate 14). However, the older (retrogressive) stages of succession may not resemble surrounding upland vegetation, but instead form species-rich but nutrient-poor retrogressive communities (Peltzer et al., 2010). Cussedu et al. (2016), noted a common pattern of plant-sand interactions in dune succession in Sardinia where only a few sand-binding species colonized the fore dunes because of high

(a)

(b)

(c)

(d)

Figure 8.2 Succession on Cooloola Dunes, eastern Australia: a) early colonists, <100 years; b) developing forest, ca. 2,600 years; c) peak biomass, ca. 50,000 years, d) retrogressive phase, >500,000 years.
Photos by Lawrence R. Walker

levels of erosion that limit colonization and establishment; rapid sand burial from dune-building limited colonization in mid dunes; and competitive dominance drove succession on back dunes. However, stochastic variables can also affect later successional stages, as Lichter (2000) noted in Michigan. Establishment of *Pinus* and *Quercus* saplings depended on a coincidence of seed dispersal, favorable weather, and low rodent densities. An analysis of plant traits on Italian coastal dunes (Ciccarelli, 2015) supported Grime's (1979) CSR strategy. Ruderal (R) plants that tolerated shifting sands dominated fore dunes; competitors (C) were most prevalent in mid succession; while stress tolerators (S) dominated late-successional back dunes. Other traits followed this pattern, such as mid-successional peaks in canopy height, leaf area, and leaf dry matter content, but some traits did not, such as an early-successional peak in succulence (a stress-tolerant strategy) and a late-successional peak in specific leaf area (a competitive strategy). Tobias (2015) offered another trait-based grouping of dune plants from coastal California based on their dune-building or stabilizing properties in either the shoreline habitat or more sheltered areas.

A different type of succession can occur in inland dune fields where erosion gaps occur between mobile dunes. In such places, a typical succession proceeds from a wind erosion zone to a herb zone (with maximum species richness), to a shrub zone, to a sand burial zone, where the next dune in line begins to bury the plant community on its leeward side (Wang *et al.*, 2015). The burial at later stages of succession distinguishes this type of dune succession from the more typical burial of would-be colonists early in succession. Yet another variant of dune succession is when a moving dune continues forward without trailing dunes behind it. In this case, succession depends on how long the sand resided in the affected location, how much original organic matter was lost, and how deep the sand was. In Tanzania, succession following a moving dune's passage was rapid, with original species composition returning within 30 years (Belsky & Amundson, 1986).

Typically, the first colonists of dunes are plants with vegetative forms of expansion, especially rhizomatous grasses (e.g., *Ammophila*, *Leymus*) that begin to stabilize the dune surface. Such clonal expansion dominated over non-clonal species at all stages of succession on six Chinese dunes (Zhang & Wu, 2014). In the subarctic region of Quebec, Canada, *Leymus mollis* and *Lathyrus japonicus* both colonized coastal dunes and persisted (Imbert & Houle, 2000). Nitrogen-fixing herbs (e.g., *Lupinus*) and shrubs (e.g., *Acacia*, *Hippophaë*, *Myrica*, *Rhamnus*) can thrive if they are able to tap into the underlying ground water. Shrubs on the Canary Islands have several strategies for surviving burial by advancing dunes, including rapid vertical growth (*Tamarix canariensis*), horizontal growth (*Cyperus laevigatus*), or both (*Traganum moquinii*) (Hernández-Cordero *et al.*, 2015). Burial tolerance differed among Canadian trees on coastal dunes. Tolerance ranged from intolerant (*Pinus strobus, Picea glauca*), through intermediate (*Juniperus virginiana, Thuja occidentalis, Picea mariana*), to tolerant (*Populus balsamifera, Salix cordata*) species (Dech & Maun, 2006). Biological soil crusts can also be important to early dune succession because they can contribute nitrogen and carbon, stabilize the surface, and provide safe microsites for plant establishment (Danin, 1991; Dümig *et al.*, 2014). But such crusts are also vulnerable to sand burial and trampling by humans or animals.

Dunes are considered susceptible to invasive alien plants (Chytrý *et al.*, 2008) because of their high level of disturbance. One type of invasion is by species used previously to stabilize dunes, such as *Pinus pinea* and *Retama monosperma* in southwestern Spain (Gallego-Fernández *et al.*, 2015). Other invaders are conifers used in forestry plantations and plants chosen for landscaping (Binggeli *et al.*, 1992) or conifers simply adept at spreading, such as *Pinus taeda* that invades coastal dunes in southern Brazil where it changes the composition of understory plants (Fischer *et al.*, 2014). A third type of invader is woody plants that fix nitrogen, giving them an advantage in low-nutrient sands. For example, the nitrogen-fixing shrub, *Retama monosperma*, native to the far western Mediterranean region, has seeds that are readily spread by hares; it outcompetes native species where it invades (Muñoz Vallés *et al.*, 2013). Alien *Eleagnos angustifolia* and *Robinia pseudacacia* invade inland dunes in Hungary (K. Prach, personal observation). Nitrogen-fixing *Lupinus* invades Californian dunes where it increase nitrogen levels, reduces light availability, and lowers soil water (Alpert & Mooney, 1996). The nitrogen-fixing tree, *Robinia pseudoacacia*, invades dunes in Indiana (USA) where it reduced native diversity by shading; it also facilitates invasive *Bromus* grasses (Peloquin & Hiebert, 1999). A fourth type of invasion is by sedges or grasses. The invasive *Carex kobomugi* from Asia produces 700% more root mass than the native *Ammophila breviligulata* on mid-Atlantic dunes in the United States, making it an important factor to consider in revegetation because although it lowers species diversity it stabilizes the dunes (Charbonneau *et al.*, 2016). In Oregon, *Ammophila breviligulata* is a successful recent invader, displacing an older, established invader, *Ammophila arenaria*, and a native *Elymus mollis*. Its success is due in part to facilitation by soil microbes and in part to its lack of dependency on new disturbances to invade (David *et al.*, 2016). What is considered an invader or a native is clearly context dependent. In Europe and western Asia, a long history of human management of grazing animals has affected succession on most dunes and altered perspectives of what is invasive, naturalized, and desirable.

Plants interact during dune succession in positive (facilitative) and negative (competitive) ways. Facilitation is a common (although not omnipresent; Houle, 1997) phenomenon in the harsh habitat of dunes. On Finnish beaches, for example, facilitation was not as broadly important as expected (Nylén *et al.*, 2013). Yet the gradual build-up of organic matter is generally accepted as a form of indirect facilitation through habitat amelioration (Poulson, 1999). Shade from established vegetation can help reduce mortality of seeds and seedling from desiccation, as when *Quercus rubra* trees facilitated *Pinus resinosa* establishment in Ontario (Kellman & Kading, 1992). Established vegetation can also protect seeds and seedlings from sand burial (Teixeira *et al.*, 2016). Thicket-forming plants provide the best protection from sand. On tropical, coastal dunes of Brazil, the dense form of the evergreen tree, *Guapira opposite,* facilitated establishment of other species (Dalotto *et al.*, 2018), regardless of the distance to the shore and zone of active erosion (Castanho & Prado, 2014). At higher latitudes, *Honckenya peploides* facilitated establishment of *Leymus mollis* on coastal, subarctic dunes in Quebec (Gagné & Houle, 2001).

A stereotype of dune succession is that it proceeds from grasses to shrubs to trees, yet a close look at facilitated transitions shows many exceptions. For example, on Mexican coastal dunes, the shrub *Chamaecrista chamaecristoides* facilitated later successional grasses *Trachypogon plumosus* and *Schizachyrium scoparium* (Martínez, 2003). On Massachusetts (USA) dunes, *Myrica pensylvanica* shrubs facilitated different life history stages (growth, reproduction, recruitment) of the herbs *Ammophila beviligulata* and *Solidago sempervirens* (Shumway, 2000). Nitrogen-fixing plants, typically considered facilitators, can, in turn, be facilitated, as when *Lupinus arboreus* established under the prostrate form of *Baccharis pilularis* on coastal dunes in California (Rudgers & Maron, 2003). Finally, facilitation can involve both natives and aliens. Facilitation was species specific under two native shrubs (*Ericameria ericoides* and *Lupinus chamissonis*) on coastal dunes in California (Cushman *et al.*, 2010). Both native and alien species benefited from the ameliorated microenvironment under the shrubs but the effect was not universal.

Competitive inhibition, the opposite of facilitation, is also common during dune succession and closely intertwined with facilitative interactions. For example, a typical scenario showing the balance between competition and facilitation comes from Italian coastal dunes where the nitrogen-fixing shrub, *Medicago marina* facilitated the grass *Lophochloa pubescens* but had a negative effect on its own seedling regeneration (Bonanomi *et al.*, 2008). A facilitator can also become a competitor later in succession, as on coastal dunes in Finland where *Empetrum nigrum* facilitated *Pinus sylvestris* establishment by providing shelter in early succession but inhibited it through its allelopathic effects in mid to late succession (Grau *et al.*, 2010). Allelopathic leaf litter also helped *Artemisia halodendron* replace earlier successional species on dunes in China (Luo *et al.*, 2017). Competition, like facilitation, can also contribute to a reduction in small life forms, such as when tall grasses outcompeted tree seedlings for light in dunes slacks on Polish dunes (retrogression; Sewerniak & Jankowski, 2017). Species coexistence on New Zealand dunes has been explained by their water use patterns, an example of niche separation, thereby leading to reduced competition for water (Stubbs & Wilson, 2004).

Interactions between plant succession and soil organisms such as bacteria (Pennanen *et al.*, 2001), fungi (Roy-Bolduc *et al.*, 2016), mycorrhizae (Emery *et al.*, 2015), and nematodes (Brinkman *et al.*, 2015) can be particularly critical to plant establishment in the infertile, early successional stages on dunes (David *et al.*, 2016). Nematodes and fungi have been implicated as carriers of diseases that affect two widespread dune colonists (*Ammophila arenaria* and *Hippophaë rhamnoides*; Van der Putten *et al.*, 1993). However, this relationship can weaken during succession (Bokhorst *et al.*, 2017) and soil organisms do not necessarily alter plant growth or succession, as noted by Sikes *et al.* (2012).

Herbivory can be an important factor in dune succession. On dunes in the Netherlands, aphids preferred early-successional grasses (Van Moorleghem & de la Peña, 2016), while nematode specialists were limited to early-successional fore dunes (perhaps escaping their natural enemies, much like pioneer plants; Brinkman *et al.*, 2015). Long-term exclusion of sheep and rabbits for several decades on dune slack vegetation in England indicated that herbivory slowed dune succession but increased overall plant diversity (more herbs at the cost of woody plants) (Millett & Edmondson, 2013).

8.2.3 Patterns within and among Biomes

Coastal dunes, unlike many other disturbance types, have been compared across large geographical areas. The focus of such comparative studies tends to be on floristics and zonation patterns, but rarely on succession. Doing (1985) presented a global view of dune-colonizing plants with a focus on fore dunes. He contrasted vegetation on dunes in tropical humid, tropical dry, temperate, and boreal climates, noting such patterns as a gradual replacement of *Ammophila* by *Elymus* going from temperate to boreal habitats in the Northern Hemisphere, the prominence of halophytes or grasses in tropical dry habitats, and the wide distribution of about a dozen common dune colonists (Doing, 1985). Barbour *et al.* (1985) summarized the physiological ecology of North American dune plants. He noted decreasing frequency of shrubs and C_4 plants with increasing latitude and increasing humidity and moisture. Neither of these compilations addressed succession. Regional studies of dunes in Wales (Rhind *et al.*, 2013) and the Netherlands (Grootjans *et al.*, 2013) do mention succession in the context of restoration. They both present the perspective that active management is needed to arrest or reverse succession to keep open dune habitats, which are desired for their contribution to regional species diversity. A summary of work on Mexican dunes (Jiménez-Orocio *et al.*, 2015) noted that dune vegetation can be used to monitor climate change, but again, successional references were in relation to restoration.

Several dune studies of broad geographical scope have identified broadly repetitive patterns for dune succession. For example, in Finland Nylén and Luoto (2015) identified general trends in species richness, including the predominance of a U-shaped pattern over time (high to low to high richness). In California, Tobias (2015) identified a common replacement series of functional groups from leading edge pioneer dune builders, to mid-strand pioneer stabilizers, sheltered secondary builders, sheltered secondary stabilizers, and finally, sheltered tertiary stabilizers. Such generalized patterns transcend species identities and are encouraging for those seeking broad generalizations.

Our summary of 39 studies of dune succession suggest several patterns. In 92% of the studies, succession was projected to be partly successful or successful (Tables 8.1 and 8.2). Success did not differ among those biomes for which we have sufficient data (ME, TB, CF) and tended non-significantly to increase with latitude (Fig. 8.3). Trajectories were mostly divergent or variable. Ujházy *et al.* (2011) suggested that

Table 8.1 *Success of succession for dune studies by biomes (no. of studies). For evaluation of succession see Chapter 4.*

Succession successful?	TR	TD	AR	ME	TB	CF	AA	Total
Yes	1	0	1	4	11	3	1	21
Partly	0	1	1	5	6	2	0	15
No	1	0	0	0	2	0	0	3
Total	2	1	2	9	19	5	1	39

Biome abbreviations: TR: tropical rain forests; TD: tropical dry forests; AR: aridlands; ME: Mediterranean; TB: temperate broadleaf forests; CF: coniferous forests; AA: Arctic-alpine.

convergence in the Netherlands was more likely on inland than on coastal dunes because inland dunes were more uniformly acidic, less fertile, and had lower species richness. We found convergence in only 18% of the studies where trajectories were apparent; the remainder, either divergent or variable, were more likely to occur in forested than not forested biomes, but the sample size was small (Table 8.2). Species richness was four times more likely to increase than decrease over the course of succession. When species richness was variable, the most common trends were either U-shaped or inverted U-shaped patterns where richness either peaked or was at its lowest in mid succession. Invasive alien species were not widely considered important to succession in these 39 studies, despite the frequent occurrence of such species on dunes worldwide (Chytrý *et al.*, 2008), but were significantly more likely to be important in wet than in dry biomes (Table 8.2). We suggest that most studies that discuss invasive alien species on dunes do not consider successional implications, especially the decrease of aliens during succession. Sometimes invasive alien plant species are sown or planted to stabilize dunes, but they mostly represent early successional species.

Additional comparative studies of dune succession have examined plant dispersal and establishment across latitudes and plant-soil dynamics. Latitude may affect the role of microsites in early dune succession. In northern Canada, favorable microsites were considered critical for plant establishment (Houle, 1995), yet random factors drove establishment on tropical Brazilian dunes (Henriques & Hay, 1992). Plant-soil dynamics are key to primary succession (Walker & del Moral, 2003) and interesting patterns can be observed across time and disturbance type. For example, soil nitrogen:phosphorus ratios increased with succession on both dunes and glacial moraines in Europe, but this pattern was not reflected in plant

Table 8.2 *Number of dune studies (N = 39) sorted by various criteria: Warm (TR, TD, AR, ME), Cold (CF, TB, AA), Dry (TD, AR, ME), Wet (TR, TB, CF, AA), Forested (TR, TD, CF, AA), Not forested (AR, AA). Samples sizes used for each successional trait are in parentheses. For biome abbreviations see Table 8.1.*

Successional trait	Warm	Cold	Dry	Wet	Forested	Not forested	All biomes (no.)	All biomes (%)
Succession successful? (39)								
Yes	6	15	5	16	19	2	21	54
Partly	7	8	7	8	14	1	15	38
No	1	2	0	3	3	0	3	8
Differences	NS		NS		NS			
Trajectory (22)								
Converge	2	2	1	3	3	1	4	18
Diverge	3	7	3	7	10	0	10	46
Variable	2	6	2	6	8	0	8	36
Differences	NS		NS		–			
Species richness (34)								
Increase	7	13	6	14	19	1	20	59
Decrease	1	4	1	4	5	0	5	15
Variable	4	5	3	6	8	1	9	26
Differences	NS		NS		NS			
Invasive species important? (35)								
Yes	1	2	0	3	3	0	3	8
Partly	3	6	3	6	9	0	9	26
No	9	14	9	14	20	3	23	66
Differences	NS		***		NS			

χ^2 test was used for non-ordered variables, Cochran–Armitage test was used for ordered variables: *** $p < 0.001$; NS not significant.

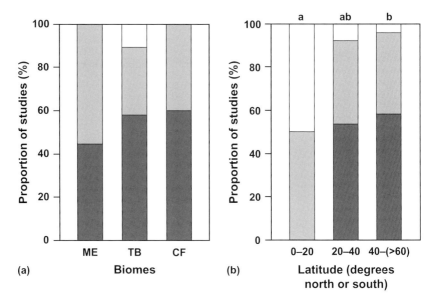

Figure 8.3 Success of succession for dunes by a) terrestrial biomes and b) latitude (% of studies). Black: successful, light gray: partly successful, white: not successful. TR + TD: tropical rain forests plus tropical dry forests, ME: Mediterranean, TB: temperate broadleaf forests, CF: coniferous forests. For sample sizes, see Table 8.1. The asymptotic generalized Pearson´s χ^2 test with post-hoc test was a) $\chi^2 = 0.225$, df = 2, p = 0.894 (NS), and b) $\chi^2 = 4.979$, df = 2, p = 0.083 (marginally significant). Different small case letters indicate statistically (marginally) significant differences.

nitrogen:phosphorus ratios, which varied more by plant functional group (grass, forb, legume) than by succession (Di Palo & Fornara, 2017). Similarly, when Bohkorst *et al.* (2017) compared soil organisms across long chronosequences following dune and glacial disturbances they found that initially strong links between soil organisms, soil fertility, and plant communities declined with age. The post-glacial sere was more fertile and with more abundant soil organisms than the dune sere.

8.3 Theoretical Implications

1. Certain generalizations are possible across dune seres regarding the inter-action of plants with tolerance of burial by sand and ability to stabilize sand (Tobias, 2015); affinities of certain plants and life forms along

topographical sequences of dunes (Doing, 1985); and general physiological traits (Barbour *et al.*, 1985), functional groupings (Nylén & Juoto, 2015), and interactions of plants (Nylén *et al.*, 2013). Despite these efforts at synthesis, most studies of dunes do not incorporate succession.

2. Success of succession increases with latitude, conforming to the majority of our disturbance examples. Success is also more likely in cold, wet habitats than in warm, dry ones.

3. Potential natural vegetation on sand dunes often clearly differs from the surroundings because of the specific dune habitat and adapted pool of species.

4. Species richness typically increases in dune succession, although richness sometimes either peaks or drops in mid succession.

5. Despite the widespread acknowledgment of the importance of invasive alien plants on dunes, few studies have evaluated the important role these species have in plant succession.

6. Human influences on coastal dunes are long-standing and must be considered in discussing succession, particularly in landscapes with a long human history such as Europe. Provoost *et al.* (2011) suggested that European coastal dune succession has, in the last century, sped up due to climate change (longer growing season, higher carbon dioxide levels), nitrogen deposition, a crash in rabbit populations, and extensive abandonment of agriculture. These trends are offset somewhat by invasive species, particularly grasses, which can arrest dune succession. In Europe, there is a push to maintain high-biodiversity open habitats that will require continued, intense human intervention in the landscape, including reducing nitrogen and organic matter levels (e.g., through reintroduction of grazing; Hršak, 2004).

8.4 Practical Implications

1. Stabilization of inland dunes where they are associated with desertification and environmental deterioration in arid regions, focuses on plantings to protect farmland and towns (Liu *et al.*, 2015). Coastal dunes have historically been stabilized as well, to augment farmland and build towns and resorts.

2. The dynamic, mobile characteristics of both inland and coastal dunes provide many ecosystem services (Lithgow *et al.*, 2013). For example,

naturally mobile dunes maintain habitats for rare flora and fauna (Grootjans *et al.*, 2017) and provide clean, fresh water lenses. In coastal regions, dunes are vulnerable to sea level rise but provide resiliency to coastlines (Feagin *et al.*, 2015) and a form of adaptive protection from floods as sea levels rise (van der Biest *et al.*, 2017).

3. Restoration must adapt to changing global conditions. For example, increased nitrogen deposition from anthropogenic sources negatively affected rates of nitrogen fixation on European dunes and accelerated acidification, with potential repercussions for the maintenance of calcareous dune grasslands (Aggenbach *et al.*, 2017). Similarly, because climate change is likely to increase storm frequency, succession on Gulf of Mexico coastal dunes might change. Gornish and Miller (2010) proposed that early- and mid-successional plant communities will become more similar, dominated by storm-resistant species, while late-successional communities will retain a more distinct flora.

4. Restoration is not always needed. For example, sand mining was once thought to be reversible only after centuries of succession or vigorous restoration efforts. Yet in South Africa, restoration efforts did not significantly increase the rate at which pre-disturbance species richness returned (Mentis & Ellery, 1998). The authors suggested that sand mining might mimic the naturally occurring instability of the substrate to which dune flora have adapted.

8.5 Conclusions

The ecology of coastal dunes is a popular topic, as witnessed by the 659 studies examined for this section. However, only 39 of those studies carefully described succession on dunes, so there is much more to learn. The popularity of dune research might reflect the obvious dynamics of sand erosion and plant regrowth often with sharply distinguished zonation, the beauty of sandy coastlines and their accessibility, the simple flora, the ecological value to dune communities, and the pressure by developers to alter dune habitats for agriculture, industry, human settlements, and tourism (Barbour *et al.*, 1985; del Moral & Walker, 2007). Dunes provide important habitat for uncommon plants and animals (Çakan *et al.*, 2011). However, in such a dynamic, frequently disturbed environment, simple toposequences cannot be assumed to faithfully represent temporal dynamics (Pegman & Rapson, 2005).

Dune vegetation might be more flexible in adapting to climate warming than other types of vegetation such as alpine habitats. Pakeman *et al.* (2015) found little change in 30 years across 89 coastal dunes in Scotland and suggested that successional dynamics and management considerations are more likely than climate change to alter dune vegetation.

9 · *Landslides*

9.1 Disturbance Description

The term landslide refers to both a sudden movement of rocks, sediments, or other debris that is gravity-driven down a slope and the newly altered surface (sometimes called a landslide scar) (Cruden, 1991). We focus on the successional processes that occur on that surface. Landslide surfaces are notoriously heterogeneous, both within and among landslides, so succession is not always easy to categorize on the gradient from primary to secondary. Landslides can occur with or without human intervention. Here, we take a broad view of landslides as a type of erosion that includes downward movement of bedrock, regolith, and sediments. We do not include seres following snow or ice avalanches but do include debris avalanches.

The movement of material in a landslide can decrease in speed from falls to flows to slides (Fig. 9.1; Coates, 1977; Walker & Shiels, 2013). Even within a given landslide, one might find different rates of movement. This variability in movement is due in part to the interior structure of many landslides. A given landslide often has three distinguishable vertical zones, a steep slip face at the top where the landslide originates (and where rapid falls are most likely), a zone of depletion in the middle called a chute (where flows of intermediate speed are likely), and a deposition zone at the bottom (where relatively slow flows are likely) (Varnes, 1958). Horizontally, landslide habitats include an undisturbed matrix (e.g., forest), an edge of intermediate disturbance, and a scoured center. Sliding movements can include rotational slumps or more linear translational slides, when sediments pass over a relatively flat and stable base. Biological consequences of landslides are related to speed and type of movement, with the most damage to preexisting vegetation occurring where speed is greatest.

9.1.1 Causes

Landslides occur when driving forces overcome resisting forces (Keller, 1996), yet such a simple statement belies the complex array of interacting

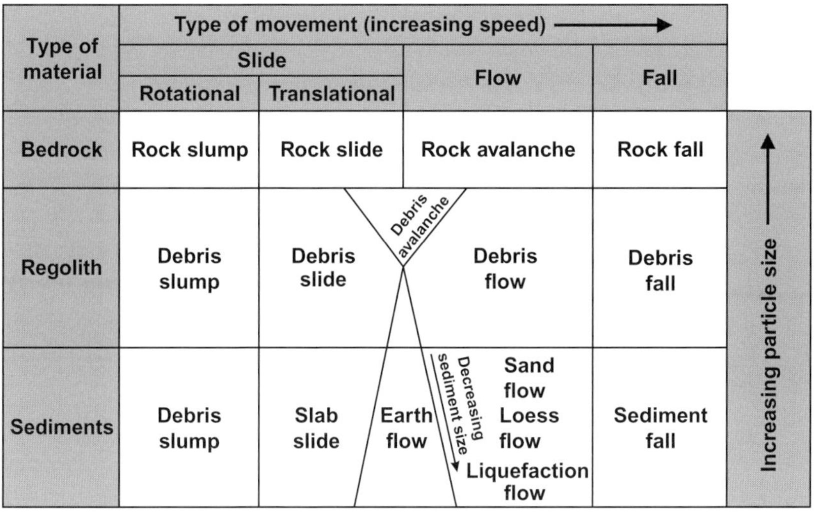

Type of material	Type of movement (increasing speed) ⟶				
	Slide		Flow	Fall	
	Rotational	Translational			
Bedrock	Rock slump	Rock slide	Rock avalanche	Rock fall	
Regolith	Debris slump	Debris slide	Debris avalanche / Debris flow	Debris fall	Increasing particle size ↑
Sediments	Debris slump	Slab slide	Earth flow / Decreasing sediment size / Sand flow Loess flow Liquefaction flow	Sediment fall	

Figure 9.1 Terrestrial landslide classification. See Coates (1977).

forces that make prediction of landslide occurrence difficult. Resisting forces come from the shear strength of the rocks and soils on a slope, from plant stems and leaves that reduce the velocity of erosive rain droplets, and from roots that grow across or funnel water away from potential slip planes (Stokes et al., 2009). Driving forces come from gravity acting on upslope rocks, soils, soil water, and vegetation. A landslide occurs when mass is added upslope (such as from growth of plants or from rain soaking the soil and reducing the shear strength of soil particles) or when resisting forces are reduced (such as removing soil to build a road across a slope). Landslides can occur on any type of rock substrate, but are most likely where weathering has created potential slip planes. Likewise, all soils on slopes can slide, provided that the adhesive properties between soil particles are sufficiently offset by factors such as a sandy texture or pore spaces filled with water (Sidle & Ochiai, 2006).

The most common triggers for landslides include rainfall, earthquakes, and human activities. Rainfall duration and intensity determine whether a landslide is triggered. For example, rain falling at a rate of 10 mm hour^{-1} needs to fall for 3.5 hr to trigger a landslide, while rain falling at a rate of 20 mm hr^{-1} need only fall for 30 minutes (global average; Larsen & Simon, 1993). In Puerto Rico, a model suggested that heavy rainfall at the end of a rain event is most likely to trigger landslides (Arnone et al., 2016). Regionally, landslide distributions are related to distances from a triggering event such as an earthquake epicenter (Keefer, 2000; Khazai & Sitar, 2003) and to the magnitude of the trigger (Schuster & Highland, 2007). Earthquakes of large magnitude trigger landslides over wider regions than earthquakes of lesser magnitude. Keefer (1984) suggests that an earthquake of magnitude 8.0 in the mountains of Ecuador could trigger landslides over an area of 35,000 km^2. Exact locations of landslides within such a vast area would be dependent on local variations in lithology (Pearce & O'Loughlin, 1985), variations in topography or aspect (Larsen & Torres-Sánchez, 1992), and presence and density of vegetation (Turner *et al.*, 2010). Erosive sandstones and water-saturated clays (especially when perched over a more water-resistant rock layer) are types of rocks prone to sliding. Aspect can influence the prevalence of landslides when a trigger event (such as driving rain or shock waves from an earthquake) differentially affects slopes facing toward the disturbance. Leeward slopes, for example, can be less prone to sliding than windward slopes that are more frequently exposed to rain (Larsen & Torres-Sánchez, 1992). Dense forest vegetation, particularly when shallow-rooted, can facilitate sliding, but extensive and deep root systems can reduce it. In addition, landslides are most likely where early successional vegetation or hydrophytic plants dominate (Perla & Martinelli, 1976; Tiwari *et al.*, 1986), although high plant biomass on slopes >45° can also create unstable conditions conducive to landslides (Myster *et al.*, 1997; Turner *et al.*, 2010).

Humans trigger landslides by increasing the driving forces on a slope (e.g., by adding mine tailings, or constructing buildings or roads), or by reducing resisting forces (e.g., by excavating a road or removing stabilizing vegetation) (Walker & Shiels, 2013). Humans can also trigger landslides by shaking the slope (e.g., from drilling activities or explosions) or by altering drainage patterns such that soil water increases. Additional causes of landslides include cryogenic processes (Khitun *et al.*, 2015) and nearly all the other disturbances covered in this book (volcanoes, melting glaciers, floods, fires, wind damage, clear cutting, and mining). Only abandonment of pastures and plowed land are not immediately associated with landslides (although deforestation and overgrazing can trigger landslides; Glade, 2003). Therefore, in a given region, it is important to consider landslides as a part of the larger set of interacting disturbances, or disturbance regime.

9.1.2 Spatial Patterns

Globally, landslides are found in about half of all terrestrial landscapes (Hong *et al.*, 2007; Plate 15), but are most commonly found where rainfall is abundant (e.g., the wet tropics) and in regions prone to earthquakes (e.g., the lands bordering the Pacific Ocean – the Ring of Fire, and other fault zones such as Tibet, northern India, and Indonesia). Areas of high human population density, especially combined with heavy rainfall or tectonic activities, are also landslide prone (e.g., southern India, eastern China, eastern Brazil) because of the many ways that humans destabilize slopes (see previous paragraph).

Where present, landslides contribute to landscape patchiness, providing often stark contrasts between the exposed soil and rock surfaces of a landslide scar with the surrounding, undisturbed vegetation. Landscape processes such as animal movements, nutrient fluxes, and microclimates are altered by landslides. Multiple landslides triggered by the same event can be considered populations of landslides and may share characteristics such as size, shape, and intensity (degree of scouring). However, because of their scattered distribution across a heterogeneous landscape, landslides within a population typically differ in successional trajectories (Restrepo & Alvarez, 2006; Walker *et al.*, 2010b). Terrestrial landslide size varies from 10 m^2 slumps to whole mountainsides. Landslides are generally longer than they are wide. Internal patchiness is also a feature of most landslides and is discussed in Section 9.2.

9.1.3 Subsequent Disturbances

Post-landslide erosion in a common feature of landslides. Slip faces, in particular, can be subject to ongoing erosion, sometimes creeping upslope until the crest is reached (Shimokawa, 1984; Walker & Shiels, 2013). Deposition zones that enter floodplains can be washed away by river erosion. Post-landslide erosion can slow successional development on a landslide by removing colonizing vegetation (Lin *et al.*, 2008), but it can also accelerate succession when intact rafts of vegetation slide into the denuded landslide from above (Walker & Shiels, 2008). Landslides have many landscape-level consequences (Swanson *et al.*, 1988) such as damming of rivers (Cruden *et al.*, 1993) and the creation of lakes (Chadwick *et al.*, 2005). These lakes alter aquatic habitats, reduce annual flood effects, attract some herbivores such as *Castor* (beaver), and destabilize steep lakeshores. The dam usually breaks after water pressure builds up behind it, and the resultant flooding down the river channel can be dramatic and destructive. In addition to altering hydrology, landslides can destroy plowed land and forest plantations, reduce downslope forest cover (Haigh *et al.*, 1995), disrupt mining activities and transportation corridors, destabilize trees at forest edges, promote the establishment of invasive alien species (Dalling, 1994), and create conditions favorable to fire (Velázquez & Gómez-Sal, 2007) and herbivore outbreaks (Walker, 1999b).

9.2 Succession

9.2.1 Abiotic Variables

A landslide creates a dramatically altered template upon which successional processes act (Figs. 9.2 and 9.3). Substrate stability, light conditions and other microclimate features, and substrate fertility are generally highly heterogeneous. Substrate stability after a landslide is a function of the size and placement of rock and soil particles and how vulnerable they are to post-landslide erosion.

Light levels are also dramatically increased by landslides (Myster & Fernández, 1995), particularly when they occur in forested regions. However, shading by adjacent forests and rapid growth of colonizers counteract the increase in light levels over time. Shade-adapted plants can experience photoinhibition from a sudden increase in light (Fetcher *et al.*, 1996). The quality of the light also changes, with an increase in red: far red ratios that can trigger germination of early successional species, such as *Cecropia* in the tropics (Vázquez-Yanes & Smith, 1982). Increased light levels typically result in hotter, drier microclimates on landslides than in the surrounding area and, in temperate regions, in greater diurnal temperature fluctuations. These changes often result in the establishment of plant colonists distinct from the undisturbed vegetation matrix around the landslide.

Initial substrate fertility is a function of which rocks and soils (or even vegetated patches) remain. Nutrient levels are highest in the deposition zone where remnant soils and organic matter collect and they are lowest in the slip face. Nitrogen levels, dependent on biological fixation, are typically low in landslides compared to adjacent forests across all latitudes, including forests in tropical (Guariguata, 1990), temperate (Pandey & Singh, 1985), and boreal (Adams & Sidle, 1987) zones. Potassium and phosphorus are rock-derived nutrients. Exposure of deep soils and rocks may increase absolute amounts from pre-landslide conditions (Zarin & Johnson, 1995), but plant-available forms are not necessarily elevated by a landslide (Guariguata, 1990; Dalling & Tanner, 1995). Soil pH generally is higher in landslides than in adjacent areas because of the loss of

Figure 9.2 Succession on a landslide in the Luquillo Mountains, Puerto Rico.
a) fresh landslide scar, b) rapid colonization after three years, and c) original scar
obscured by vegetation after five years.
Photos by Lawrence R. Walker

Figure 9.3 Initial succession (second season) on landslide in Cascades,
Washington (USA).
Photo by Karel Prach

acidic organic matter and roots in surface soils (Dalling & Tanner, 1995).
Cation exchange capacity also declines when a landslide occurs, due to
the general decline in substrate fertility. The removal of most organic
matter from landslide surfaces is critical to the cycling of all nutrients and
to subsequent succession. Typically, <1% of original organic matter
remains (Lundgren, 1978), although levels tend to be highest in the
deposition zone. Post-landslide erosion, particularly before a protective
cover of vegetation develops, can result in large losses of carbon (Walker &
Shiels, 2008) and other mobile elements, but these losses diminish as
succession proceeds (Pandey & Singh, 1985). Precipitation and sloughing
of organic matter from the sides become important sources that gradually
replenish lost nutrients in landslides (Pandey & Singh, 1985; McDowell
et al., 1990). In tropical Africa, organic carbon in landslide soils returned
to levels in undisturbed adjacent soils within 60 years; levels in older
landslides increased above adjacent soils, suggesting that landslides can
sometimes serve as carbon sinks in a landscape (Van Eynde *et al.*, 2017).

Abiotic conditions on landslides therefore present a complex stage for
the initiation of succession. Abiotic factors inhibiting succession include

post-landslide erosion, high light conditions, and non-existent or poorly developed acidic or alkaline soils with low cation exchange capacity and little organic matter or nitrogen. Depending on the substrate, levels of potassium and phosphorus can be higher or lower than surrounding soils. Factors promoting succession (through the colonization of pioneer plants) include shifts in light quality that trigger germination and high light levels.

9.2.2 Biotic Variables

In this section, we cover biological legacies, dispersal, adaptations, species composition, and non-native species in the early stages of landslide succession. The initial biotic conditions depend on what plants and soil organisms survived the landslide disturbance *in situ*. The presence, density, and spatial arrangement of these biological legacies can have a central role in determining the direction and rate of landslide succession (Shiels *et al.*, 2008), or little effect if the residual plants fail to colonize the more eroded parts of the landslide (Walker *et al.*, 1996). However, even if there is no direct regeneration from the surviving patches (or patches that raft down from post-landslide erosion), the patches can provide structure that traps seeds and litter, attracts animals, and provides shade. Legacy effects are most likely to occur in the deposition zone (Velázquez & Gómez-Sal, 2008) and their effects on succession become less pronounced as soil and vegetation develop over time.

In addition to plants that survived on rafted soil, landslide surfaces present opportunities for the dispersal of a number of colonists, particularly gap specialists adapted to unstable, low-nutrient substrates and hot and dry conditions (Neto *et al.*, 2017). Other colonists can include plants that are in the undisturbed areas adjacent to a landslide, such as understory plants (Cannone *et al.*, 2010) or even canopy trees (Kroh *et al.*, 2008). Seed rain and establishment of plants are most likely to occur around the edges of a landslide where conditions are more moderate than in the center (Walker & Neris, 1993; Shiels & Walker, 2013). Wind-dispersed plants are frequent early colonists of landslides (Nakashizuka *et al.*, 1993), but wind dispersal can be affected by the proximity and height of the spore and seed sources, the density and height of the surrounding vegetation, and weather conditions such as sinking cold air or wind patterns (Myster & Fernández, 1995; Fenner & Thompson, 2005). Frugivorous birds (Shiels & Walker, 2003), bats (Matt *et al.*, 2008), rats (Shiels, 2002), and probably monkeys (Kaplan & Moermond,

2000) are among some of the animal dispersers of plants to landslides. Other plants are dispersed using epizoochory (Mark *et al.*, 1964).

Plant adaptations to landslides include various traits characteristic of gap specialists, although there do not seem to be any plants that are strict landslide specialists (Walker & Shiels, 2013). Landslide plants must not only disperse but also successfully colonize, often under hot, dry, and infertile conditions. Plants with leaves that are small, dissected, thickened, waxy, or deciduous help prevent water loss. C_4 and CAM strategies for photosynthesis also reduce water loss, while the ability to host nitrogen-fixing bacteria can also be an advantage in low nutrient soils (Walker & Shiels, 2013).

All types of plants can colonize landslides, including bryophytes, ferns, gymnosperms, grasses, forbs, and woody angiosperms. There appears to be some tendency for bryophytes and forbs to dominate the steeper parts of landslides, while tree ferns and trees are most common on flatter parts (Walker & Shiels, 2013). Bryophytes are widely dispersed and many tolerate dry environments such as landslides. They also typically harbor cyanobacteria and fungi that aid in the acquisition of nutrients. Cover of ground-dwelling bryophtyes tends to decrease over succession but epiphytic bryophytes increase (Mark *et al.*, 1964). Ferns are common on tropical and temperate landslides, and club mosses (Dalling, 1994; Walker *et al.*, 2010a) and horsetails (Miles & Swanson, 1986; Arunachalam & Upadhyaya, 2005) can be important in early and middle stages of landslide succession. Tropical landslides often feature dense thickets of scrambling ferns (e.g., Gleicheniaceae; Russell *et al.*, 1998; Walker *et al.*, 2010a), and temperate landslides can be covered with *Pteridium aquilinum* (bracken; Kessler, 1999). Tree ferns are also frequent colonizers of tropical landslides and can persist for several decades (Restrepo & Vitousek, 2001; Brock *et al.*, 2018).

Grasses, sedges, and forbs are common colonists on temperate and tropical landslides, both as colonists and later arrivals. *Chusquea* (bamboo) can dominate at any stage of tropical succession (Kessler, 1999) but may not contribute to slope stability because of frequent uprooting (Stokes *et al.*, 2007). Invasive grasses are common following fire on tropical landslides (Velázquez & Gómez-Sal, 2007) and can be quite persistent despite removal efforts (Restrepo & Vitousek, 2001). Forbs, especially vines, can form dense stands on young landslides, but generally give way to later successional species that overtop them. However, *Smilax*, a woody vine, dominated a 130-year-old landslide in Hawaii (Restrepo & Vitousek, 2001).

Gymnosperms are frequent on temperate landslides and can be early colonists (wind-dispersed, drought tolerant; Miles & Swanson, 1986; Van der Burght et al., 2012), establish later in succession (Veblen & Ashton, 1978; Geertsema & Pojar, 2007), or both colonize and persist on landslides (Claessens et al., 2006). Woody angiosperms dominate many temperate and most tropical landslides (Walker & Shiels, 2013). Shrubs typically colonize within the first decade and provide important roles as deterrents to post-landslide erosion and as a food source for wildlife. Trees can be early or later colonists, providing links to birds and bats (Garwood et al., 1979; Brokaw, 1998) and sometimes supporting nitrogen-fixing bacteria and ectomycorrhizae that ameliorate the soil. Trees colonizing landslides can be found mostly on landslides (Nakamura, 1984) or on landslides and in the surrounding forest (Restrepo & Vitousek, 2001).

Invasive species can alter landslide succession at any stage but are particularly influential in early succession, as noted in New Zealand (Smale et al., 1997). Invasive species are also most likely where landslides are part of human-altered landscapes such as farms, towns, and roads, but less likely to be influential in remote or more pristine areas (Lepš et al., 2002; Velázquez and Gómez-Sal, 2007; Elias & Dias, 2009). Roads increased the spread of invasive plant species on landslides in Oregon (Parendes & Jones, 2000). Hawaii is particularly susceptible to invasive alien species, and some landslides there have twice as many invasive aliens as native plants (Restrepo & Vitousek, 2001). Invasive plants alter species composition, which in turn may affect ecosystem properties, slope stability, and successional trajectories on landslides (Walker & Shiels, 2013).

The absence of obvious species interactions can lead to gradual shifts in dominance without any clearly defined successional stages, such as from annuals to perennials over a 40-year period on Himalayan landslides (Pandey & Singh, 1985), or to direct replacement of long-lived species on landslides in Japan (Sakio, 1997) or New Zealand (Claessens et al., 2006). Life forms can be a factor in determining successional replacements. On Japanese landslides, herbaceous life forms were followed by shrubs and then trees (Nakamura, 1984). In Hawaii, short and creeping forms of ferns dominated early succession, followed by denser scrambling ferns and tree ferns, with some tree ferns remaining as part of the final mature forest (Restrepo & Vitousek, 2001). In Bolivia, scrambling ferns were initial colonists of landslides, followed by tree ferns and then trees (Kessler, 1999). While each of these transitions was probably driven by competition, the reemergence of scrambling ferns in gaps and new arrival of epiphytic ferns on aging tree ferns and tree trunks illustrate the role of life forms during changing successional conditions.

Facilitation is a common driver of landslide succession where early colonists that are able to establish in the exposed conditions ameliorate the environment for later colonists (Shiels & Walker, 2013). Support for the stress-gradient hypothesis comes from a large landslide in Nicaragua where facilitation was most common in the stressful zones of the landslide (Velázquez *et al.*, 2014). Trees or tall shrubs can facilitate seed dispersal by birds to young landslides (Shiels & Walker, 2003) and provide shade, leaf litter, and nutrients that enhance colonization success of later colonists (Mark *et al.*, 1989; Chaudhry *et al.*, 1996). Examples include fern thickets to trees in Puerto Rico (Walker, 1994), Ecuador (Ohl & Bussmann, 2004), and New Zealand (Brock *et al.*, 2018); shrubs to trees in New Zealand (Mark *et al.*, 1989); and pioneer to mature forest trees in Puerto Rico (Brokaw, 1998) and Nicaragua (Velázquez & Gómez-Sal, 2009a). Legumes and shrubs that host nitrogen–fixing bacteria in their roots are also typical facilitators of landslide succession (e.g., in Oregon; Miles *et al.*, 1984). However, these plants can also delay succession by their dominance in consuming scarce resources (Halvorson *et al.*, 2005) or have differential effects on subsequent species (Bellingham *et al.*, 2001).

Competition is as common as facilitation on landslides, as plants compete for scarce water and nutrients (Shiels & Walker, 2013). Thicket-forming, early successional species are typical inhibitors of landslide succession and can be forbs, graminoids, ferns, shrubs, or trees (Walker & Shiels, 2013). Grasses, sometimes introduced by humans to stabilize landslides, can inhibit succession (Velázquez & Gómez-Sal, 2009b), or give way to later successional species after the initial stabilization (Lin *et al.*, 2006). South-facing landslides in boreal Alaska are dominated by steppe vegetation that resists colonization by coniferous trees (Lewis, 1998). Scrambling ferns (Russell *et al.*, 1998; Slocum *et al.*, 2004; Walker & Sharpe, 2010) and tree ferns (Walker *et al.*, 2010a) dominate on some tropical landslides by monopolizing both light and nutrients. Shrubs (Pabst & Spies, 2001) and trees can inhibit succession through similar strategies or by their dense, acidic litter (Reddy & Singh, 1993). Sometimes, inhibiting an inhibitor leads to facilitation, as on some Puerto Rican landslides (Walker *et al.*, 2010a). Woody pioneers in Puerto Rico indirectly facilitated later successional trees by inhibiting the growth of thickets of forbs, grasses, vines, and scrambling ferns, all of which inhibited forest development.

Trophic interactions that influence succession on landslides include herbivores and pathogens. Seed loss from fungi (Myster, 1997) and seed predation by insects (Myster, 1997) and rats (Shiels, 2002) may slow colonization of landslides, as did the effect of stem borers and leaf miners on a nitrogen-fixing facilitator of erosive slopes on Mount St. Helens, Washington (USA) (Fagan & Bishop, 2000). Succession can be accelerated when early successional species are preferred by vertebrate herbivores (Bryant & Chapin, 1986; Bellingham et al., 2016). Herbivory may have little effect on succession when insect herbivores only attack but do not kill mature trees (Veblen et al., 1994), but the role of herbivory as a driver of successional change is confounded by such complicating factors as inhibition of germination by litter of other species, increased landslide frequency, or climatic shifts that may influence succession (Bellingham & Lee, 2006). Finally, herbivory and pathogens are thought to be less important on tropical islands than on continents because there has been less time for island plant-animal interactions to co-evolve (Augspurger, 1984). Yet Myster (1994, 2002) did not find differences in levels of insect herbivory or foliar pathogens between Costa Rican and Puerto Rican landslides.

9.2.3 Patterns within and among Biomes

Landslide succession is the product of plant responses to regional geology and climate; local topography, soils, species pools, and disturbance regimes; and microsite nutrients and biological legacies. Given the high variability that is commonly encountered among all these factors, it is not surprising that landslide succession within biomes varies even among neighboring landslides or landslides created by the same earthquake or rainstorm (Myster & Sarmiento, 1998). Typical trajectories of multiple landslides can be divergent, convergent, parallel, deflected, network-like, or retrogressive (Walker & del Moral, 2003). Myster and Walker (1997) found divergence of successional pathways among 16 landslides over a five-year period in a tropical rain forest in Puerto Rico (Plate 16). That variation was likely due to differences in soil type and nutrient availability, local seed availability, elevation, and aspect (Walker & Neris, 1993; Shiels et al., 2008; Shiels & Walker, 2013). There was some convergence of species that were shade tolerant during succession and total species pools were similar, although not the proportions of each common species (Walker et al., 1996). Typically, parameters such as species richness, cover, vegetation structure, and soil organic matter are more likely to converge than are species abundance and composition (Walker & Shiels, 2013), although the complex, layered structure of tropical forests may take longer to recover than biomass (Dislich & Huth, 2012). Soil parameters can also converge. For example, within 55 years on several Puerto Rican landslides, there was substantial convergence in soil nitrogen, phosphorus, potassium, and magnesium to levels found in undisturbed forest soils (Zarin & Johnson, 1995). Dalling (1994) found convergence to pre-disturbance levels of aboveground biomass on landslides in tropical rain forests in Jamaica, but over a period of 500 years. Subsequent disturbances (see Section 9.1) can result in trajectories of succession that are deflected from their original pattern of development. Complex networks of trajectories can result from multiple stable states coexisting simultaneously in a population of landslides (Slocum *et al.*, 2004). Retrogression occurs on landslides when there are declines from peak biomass, carbon, or nutrients, typically over many centuries.

There are very few comparisons of landslide succession across biomes. Comparisons are also hindered by the lack of any standard metrics. Typical measurements include soil nutrients and other physical characteristics or plant species composition. When succession is studied, there are again no standards. An additional complication is the spatial heterogeneity of a landslide, so studies of rates of succession, for example, can vary greatly between the infertile upper slip face and the more fertile deposition zone. Walker and Shiels (2013) suggested that global generalizations across biomes were unlikely because of the heterogeneity in local conditions but that regional generalizations might be possible. Landslides are most abundant (and most studied) in forested biomes of the world, especially where earthquakes are common, precipitation is high, slopes are steep, and soils are shallow. Landslides are less common but can still be present in shrublands, grasslands, and aridlands. Other patterns that emerge are the importance of soil temperature in landslides in Arctic tundra and of species interactions in the tropical rain and temperate broadleaf forests.

For our comparative analysis, we found 46 studies that examined landslide succession over several years and at several sites and from which we were able to glean information on four topics: potential recovery of pre-disturbance vegetation, the shape of successional trajectories, directional change in species richness, and the potential importance of invasive alien species affecting succession. Most of the landslide studies (85%) were from forested biomes and 94% were considered successful or partly

Table 9.1 *Success of succession for landslide studies arranged by biomes (no. of studies). For evaluation of success see Chapter 4.*

Succession successful?	TR	AR	ME	TB	CF	AA	Total
Yes	3	0	2	13	6	3	27
Partly	8	1	0	3	2	2	16
No	2	0	0	0	0	1	3
Total	13	1	2	16	8	6	46

Biome abbreviations: TR: tropical rain forests; AR: aridlands; ME: Mediterranean; TB: temperate broadleaf forests; CF: coniferous forests; AA: Arctic-alpine.

successful (potential natural vegetation is likely to return), with non-significant trends toward higher success rates in cold than warm climates (Tables 9.1 and 9.2). However, success was significantly higher in temperate broadleaf and coniferous forests than in tropical forests (Fig. 9.4). There was a significant increase in success with increasing latitude. The estimated time to recovery of pre-disturbance vegetation varied from several decades in several centuries, but was generally shorter in forested (e.g., 81% recovery in 12 years in Taiwan; Yang *et al.*, 2016) than in non-forested biomes (300 years in Arizona [USA]; Bowers et al., 1977). We found no studies with detailed data on landslide succession from tropical dry forests. Divergent trajectories prevailed over convergent ones (59 vs. 23%, respectively) overall, and were significantly more likely in warm than in cold climates (temperate broadleaf and coniferous forests) (Table 9.2). Species richness increased during succession on 52% of the landslides when pooled across biomes, which is logical given the largely denuded surface that is created. Increases in species richness tended non-significantly to be more common in cold than in hot biomes (Table 9.2). Despite the reported role of invasive species (see Section 9.2.2), we found that in 89% of the 35 studies we could evaluate, invasive alien species did not play a relevant role in late successional stages.

Given the paucity of comparative studies on landslide succession, several questions could guide future searches for patterns across biomes or regions: 1) Does lithology predict successional characteristics of landslides (e.g., patterns and rates of change of species richness; time to return of original state)? 2) Where human influences are strong, do dominant invasive plants increase convergence of landslide succession? 3) Do populations (arising from the same disturbance event) or communities

Table 9.2 *Number of landslide studies (N = 46) sorted by various criteria: Warm (TR, AR, ME), Cold (TG, TB, CF, AA), Dry (AR, ME, TG), Wet (TR, TB, CF, AA), Forested (TR, ME, TB, CF), Not forested (TR, ME, TB, CF), Not forested (AR, TB, AA). Sample sizes used for each successional trait are in parentheses. For biome abbreviations see Table 9.1.*

Successional trait		Warm	Cold	Dry	Wet	Forested	Not forested	All biomes (no.)	All biomes (%)
Succession successful? (46)	Yes	5	22	2	25	24	3	27	59
	Partly	9	7	1	15	13	3	16	35
	No	2	1	0	3	2	1	3	6
	Differences	NS		NS		NS			
Trajectory (17)	Converge	0	4	0	4	4	0	4	23
	Diverge	6	4	0	10	10	0	10	59
	Variable	0	3	0	3	3	0	3	18
	Differences	★		–		–			
Species richness (31)	Increase	3	13	1	15	11	5	16	52
	Decrease	1	2	0	2	3	0	3	10
	Variable	6	6	0	12	10	2	12	38
	Differences	NS		NS		NS			
Invasive species important? (35)	Yes	1	0	0	1	1	0	1	3
	Partly	0	3	0	3	3	0	3	8
	No	9	22	3	28	24	7	31	89
	Differences	NS		NS		NS			

$\chi 2$ test was used for non-ordered variables, Cochran–Armitage test was used for ordered variables: ★ p < 0.05; NS not significant; – not analyzed due to too many zero values.

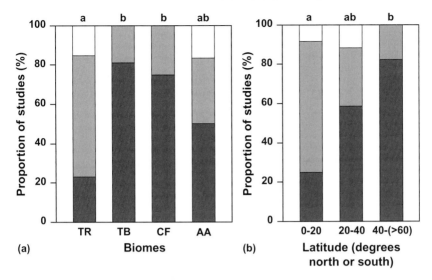

Figure 9.4 Success of succession for landslides by a) terrestrial biomes and b) latitude (% of studies). Black: successful, light gray: partly successful, white: not successful. TR: tropical rain forests, TB: temperate broadleaf forests, CF: coniferous forests, AA: Arctic-alpine. For sample sizes, see Table 9.1. The asymptotic generalized Pearson's χ^2 test with post-hoc test was a) $\chi^2 = 11.685.56$, df = 3, p = 0.009, and b) $\chi2 = 8.174$, df = 2, p = 0.017. Different small case letters indicate statistically significant differences.

(within the same region but from different triggers; see Restrepo & Alvarez, 2006) of landslides share any successional characteristics, particularly where they cross large environmental gradients?

9.3 Theoretical Implications

Landslides represent an exceptional challenge to the development of generalizations about succession because they are so spatially heterogeneous at micro to macro levels (Shiels & Walker, 2013). Erosion rills mix with pebbles that retain soil at centimeter scales; slip faces contrast with chutes and deposition zones in nearly all soil and vegetation parameters at landslide scales; and populations of landslides vary by cause, elevation, size, surrounding matrices, degree of re-sliding, and numerous other factors at landscape scales. Succession often varies more within than among landslides (Shiels *et al.*, 2006). However, that variability also offers opportunities for research to develop stronger ties between succession and restoration theory because of landslides' importance to human populations and often rapid stabilization. We offer several theoretical implications from studies of landslide succession:

1. Landslides undergo a wide range of successional trajectories. Key causes of this variation include dramatic spatial heterogeneity on a given landslide, the wide range in degree of slope stability and ongoing erosion, and the complexity of composition and developmental stages of the (mostly forested) surrounding vegetation. Comparative analyses are needed of the influence of variables such as lithology, instability, and surrounding vegetation on the rate and trajectory of landslide succession.
2. Divergence dominated, suggesting that the high spatial heterogeneity in landslide site conditions and surrounding vegetation and propagule pools direct succession in multiple directions.
3. Species richness largely increased during succession, suggesting replacement of few early colonists adapted to unstable conditions and low nutrients by more later successional species adapted to increasing substrate stability and higher nutrient levels.
4. The minimal role of invasive alien species suggests that such severe disturbances exclude them. However, many landslides are colonized by native grasses and forbs, common life forms for invasive species; landslides are often small, reducing the target for invasive aliens; and numerous studies predate the recent increase in invasive species.

9.4 Practical Implications

Humans, through our activities as road builders, urban developers, foresters, farmers, and agents of fires and climate change are increasing the frequency and severity of landslides (Sidle & Ochiai, 2006; Walker & Shiels, 2013). Therefore, it will help to better understand what causes them (prediction), how their damage can be ameliorated (mitigation), and how to speed their stabilization (restoration) (Table 9.3). Prediction relies on both local characteristics of individual slopes and on regional evaluations that incorporate rainfall thresholds, geology, topography, and vegetation. Knowledge of successional patterns on landslides can help establish past landslide history of an area based on vegetation type and cover, and provide clues for landslide prediction because these biotic variables can contribute to the likelihood of future landslides.

Table 9.3 *Three climate change implications and nine future directions for research on landslide ecology*

Climate change implication	Approach	Future directions
More variable weather and extreme events	Technology	Improve longevity of soil retention mechanisms; development of modular, replaceable units
	Ecology	Improve manipulation of succession for long-term slope stability
	Culture	Promote sustainable use of slopes and avoidance of erosion-prone areas
Spread of novel ecosystems	Technology	Improve mapping and modeling of native and novel ecosystems to forecast change and assist native ecosystem restoration
	Ecology	Determine optimal species mixes, optimal root architecture, and other biological tools to stabilize slopes
	Culture	Recognize and minimize human role in spread of non-native species through land-use patterns
More landslides; different slope failure thresholds	Technology	Improve predictive models and local applications
	Ecology	Develop robust, flexible restoration principles and applications that apply within and among ecosystems
	Culture	Develop flexible policies and infrastructures that recognize changing threats from landslides

From Walker and Shiels (2013) with permission from Cambridge University Press.

Mitigation is needed in populated areas to reduce damage from past landslides and minimize damage from re-sliding (Larsen, 2008; Boonya-nuphap, 2013). Plants with deep roots can reduce pore pressure (Stokes *et al.*, 2014). Reducing grazing pressure can lower the probability of future landslides, while fire-triggered landslides can be prevented by clearing slopes mechanically rather than by burning and by planting fire-resistant vegetation (Sidle & Ochiai, 2006). Knowledge of landslide succession helps determine the most appropriate mitigation measures.

Restoration is a broad concept with many applications to landslides. One index of successful restoration that has been tested on a landslide in the Southern Alps is an ecological index of ecosystem maturity (Giupponi *et al.*, 2015). It assesses variables such as plant cover, presence of non-native species, and successional stage. Restoration that involves an understanding of landslide succession can be easier, more affordable, and more resilient to future environmental change than a purely technical approach that uses physical amelioration (Stokes *et al.*, 2014; see Chapter 1). Sometimes the best restoration strategy is to let landslide succession proceed without assistance (Yang *et al.*, 2016). We end this section with several practical implications of the study of landslide succession:

1. Predictive models are well-developed for landslide occurrence, but little is known about subsequent successional processes. Given the destructive and often persistent nature of landslides, it is critical to explore economical, long-term, minimally invasive efforts to restore landslides.
2. Techniques that mimic early succession help with initial stabilization but deep-rooted plants that cross potential slippage zones in the soil are also needed; these plants may not readily colonize if the initial plant growth (e.g., of grasses, climbing ferns) is too dense.
3. Not all landslides can be readily stabilized, especially ones with ongoing triggers such as earthquakes, road cuts, or riverbank erosion. In such cases, the best approach might be to designate the area as a minimal-use natural area.

9.5 Conclusions

Landslides create an often abrupt contrast with their surroundings and can be slow to revegetate. The landslide scar is thus a visible and important addition to landscape heterogeneity, promoting nutrient turnover, altering slope hydrology, and providing opportunities for pioneer plants and animals, thereby promoting the maintenance of landscape-level biodiversity. Yet landslides also add sediments downslope and downstream, cause flooding that can trigger further damage, and leave nutrient-poor, often arid surfaces with diminished productivity. On this template, landslide succession does eventually proceed, unless ongoing erosion or extreme environmental conditions (e.g., drought, toxic wastes) persist. Pioneer plants adapted to conditions of high light, low nutrients, and unstable substrates colonize landslides (Seiwa *et al.*, 2013;

van der Ent *et al.*, 2015). Factors that distinguish landslide succession from other types of succession are the chronic instability of the slope, the role of gravity, and the critical role of geological forces (Walker & Shiels, 2013). Nevertheless, understanding the biological drivers of landslide succession will allow more effective management, save lives, and contribute to our understanding of succession.

10 · *Floods*

10.1 Disturbance Description

A floodplain occurs where river water leaves its normal channel and deposits or removes sediments during a flood event (Plate 17). Deposited sediments can be ephemeral because they are subject to erosion from the next high-water event. Yet where floodplains provide a stable surface, plant growth and succession can occur. Substrate texture and fertility vary, much like landslides, and this variability affects succession. The interaction of substrate quality with local topography and water quality and flow create many habitats for plant growth. Floodplains represent (like landslides) an intermediate status between primary and secondary succession. At one extreme, floods can completely remove all prior vegetation and organic matter, triggering primary succession on a layer of fresh silt, sand, or gravel. At the other extreme, intact vegetation and soils can raft down a river to a new location or new silt can simply be layered on top of an existing forest floor, leaving everything intact; both of these would trigger secondary succession. Silt deposition over an existing organic soil resembles succession following volcanic ash deposition (Zobel & Antos, 2009). The spatial scale of a flood is generally positively correlated with its intensity because large floods often provide the most intense, damaging results (Hughes, 1997). Floodplains are also intermediate in their susceptibility to human influence compared to other types of disturbance. Humans have long resided on floodplains, which are fertile and flat, and they provide many services (e.g., for drinking, fishing, washing, cooking, waste disposal, and transportation). Manipulation of floodplains began early in human history (e.g., with irrigation channels for agriculture) and has culminated in vast destruction by humans who have co-opted many floodplains for industries, hydropower, and urban growth (del Moral & Walker, 2007).

The complexity of watersheds leads to a wide variety of floodplains. At its upper reaches, a floodplain is likely to be narrow, dominated by coarse boulders, relatively infertile, and subject to many local floods of short duration. A floodplain near the terminus of a large river (delta) is typically wide, covered with fertile silts, and subject to occasional, large-scale, longer-lasting floods (Shaffer *et al.*, 1992). This generalization is not universally applicable. For example, floodplains are unpredictable or nonexistent when the river flows mostly underground (e.g., through limestone karst), is ephemeral (e.g., through desert sands), flows over cliffs (e.g., crossing a lava dike or through a sandstone slot canyon), or in very short watersheds (e.g., near an ocean). Studies of succession largely focus on wide, stable floodplains adjacent to rivers with large sediment loads (typically from upstream erosion, a large watershed, or glacial meltwater). However, even with this relative stability, details of water flow, sediment load, and plant responses are still highly stochastic (Vesipa *et al.*, 2017). Succession on fluctuating ocean, lake, and reservoir shorelines are briefly considered in Chapter 15.

10.1.1 Causes

Riverbank flooding has many causes, but essentially occurs when water inputs exceed the capacity of the channel. Proximal causes of floods fit into several categories: upstream flows, instream obstructions, and reduced riverbank absorption. 1) High water inputs from upstream are determined by each river's watershed. Conditions in the watershed determine water volume and its temporal variability. High rainfall is a typical cause of downstream flooding, and can be quite destructive, particularly in arid or semi-arid climates. Plum Creek in eastern Colorado (USA) for example, received 81% of its average annual precipitation of 445 mm in one storm in 1965 that widened the floodplain from a narrow stream to an extensive, braided channel (Friedman *et al.*, 1996). Floods are also triggered by melting ice and snow from glaciers, upstream lakes, and tributaries. Upstream urbanization agriculture or logging can also increase runoff and thereby contribute to downstream flooding. 2) Instream obstruction can occur from logjams, landslides, lava flows, or human-built dams that cause water to back up and flood the low-lying adjacent areas. Downstream flooding occurs when these obstructions suddenly break. 3) Reduced absorption from the riverbank can also cause flooding. Conditions precipitating this type of flooding include frozen soil, dry soil that has become hydrophobic, or anthropogenic structures such as levees, pavement, or urbanization (Groffman *et al.*, 2003).

Flooding will not create a floodplain by itself. The water must slow down enough to deposit sediments that then accumulate and form a floodplain. Glacial meltwaters and upstream erosion are typical sources of sediments, but volcanoes, landslides, and dunes can also contribute. Sediments accumulate behind dams (natural or anthropogenic), and those sediments form downstream floodplains when the dam is removed. Experimental releases of water from the Glen Canyon Dam into the Colorado River and the Grand Canyon (western USA) have been done to create floodplain habitats for riparian vegetation (Rood & Mahoney, 2000; Rood et al., 2005), native fishes (Gregory et al., 2002), and, incidentally, beaches for rafting tourists.

10.1.2 Spatial Patterns

Floodplains and their accompanying rivers can vary in length from >6,000 km (the Nile, Amazon, and Yangtze Rivers) to <100 m (e.g., Oregon, USA) and be several meters to many kilometers wide. An active floodplain typically occupies only a small fraction of its historical floodplain. For example, water flows most of the year through a ca. 50 m wide channel in the glacially fed Tanana River in central Alaska and active erosion moves that channel several meters a year, but the historical floodplain is tens of kilometers wide. Historical explanations for the location of floodplains include the draining of former inland lakes, often caused by melting glaciers at the end of the last ice age 12,000–15,000 years ago. Other rivers have maintained their channels for much longer, continually cutting down through uplifted rock (del Moral & Walker, 2007). Floodplains typically form on the outside of meanders (opposite an eroding shoreline) and create a variety of physical features including point bars, scroll bars, levees, back swamps, and oxbow lakes (Hickin, 1974; Malanson, 1993). Each of these features can have a characteristic zonation by sediment size, sorted by the strength of the water current. This variability in spatial pattern and sediment size is closely tied to plant establishment and subsequent succession (see Section 10.2; Grubb, 1987; Walker & del Moral, 2003).

10.1.3 Subsequent Disturbances

Floodplains are linked to many types of disturbances. They are caused by sediments from other disturbances, including dunes and, in turn, floodplains provide sand that can be blown away to create other dunes. Or, the rainstorm that brings sediment-rich floodwaters could be triggered by a cyclone. Floodplains also affect the location and intensity of riverbank undercutting, which can trigger landslides on steep slopes (see Chapter 9). Floods can trigger fires when they kill forests, leaving dry fuelwood when the waters recede (Pettit & Naiman, 2007). Fires in floodplain forests are also triggered during dry periods (Flores *et al.*, 2014); these fires may (Busch, 1995; Mann *et al.*, 1995; Timoney *et al.*, 1997) or may not (Halofsky & Hibbs, 2009) affect succession.

10.2 Succession

10.2.1 Abiotic Variables

Sediment deposition and succession on narrow floodplains formed by mountain streams can more sharply contrast with adjacent uplands (Charron *et al.*, 2011) than the parallel bands of successive plant development seen on wider floodplains where increasing distance from the river channel usually reflects increasing vegetation age (Hughes, 1997; Figs. 10.1 and 10.2). However, broad floodplains can also be heterogeneous and vegetation age may not simply correlate with distance to the main channel (Karrenberg *et al.*, 2003). Floodplains are a generally favorable place for succession. Light is not a limitation except along narrow, heavily forested streambanks (Warren *et al.*, 2016). Dissolved nutrients and organic matter deposition from upstream communities often provide sufficient soil fertility for succession. Therefore, the biggest challenges are substrate stability due to ongoing erosion from repeated flooding and substrate water-holding capacity (Kalliola *et al.*, 1991; Shaffer *et al.*, 1992). Slight shifts in river flow, direction, or sediment load can trigger erosion or deposition, flooding, or surface drought. Plants alter these physical forces through stems that slow water velocity and promote deposition or roots that stabilize floodplains, resist erosion, and promote the buildup of terraces (Hughes, 1997; Erskine *et al.*, 2009; Gran *et al.*, 2015), sometimes to the benefit of the plants (Corenblit *et al.*, 2014). Terraces can be built rapidly (as much as 0.5 m in two years; Johnson, 2000) and elevation above the river is a key variable in determining plant establishment and success because of reduced flooding and the plants' influence on flooding frequency and intensity (Menges & Waller, 1983) and nutrient availability (Smith & Lee, 1984). However, superimposed on that gradient is the irregular spatial pattern created by flooding of different patches in a floodplain, which has been analyzed as a nested hierarchical framework (van Coller *et al.*, 2000).

(a)

(b)

Figure 10.1 Succession on a Korean floodplain: a) early (ca. four-year-old), b) late (ca. 50-year-old) stages.
Photos by Karel Prach

(a)

(b)

Figure 10.2 Succession on an Alaskan floodplain: a) bare silt bar and first terrace development (ca. 30–50 years). b) 200-year-old peak biomass spruce forest. Photos by Lawrence R. Walker

Numerous modelers have analyzed the interaction of water flow, sediment load, and plant growth and succession, and these are summarized by Vesipa *et al., 2017* into five categories: 1) focus on seedling recruitment (the recruitment box model (Mahoney & Rood, 1998; see Section 10.2.2) with updates from Dixon and Turner (2006) and Benjankar *et al.* (2014); 2) stochastic models that emphasize the role of random fluctuations of water flow on vegetation dynamics (Greet *et al.*, 2011); 3) dynamic vegetation models that focus on vegetation responses to the complex of abiotic variables (Bertoldi *et al.*, 2014); 4) successional models that emphasize directional changes in vegetation, both progressive and retrogressive (Benjankar *et al.*, 2011; García-Aria & Francés, 2016); and 5) structured population models that consider the differential responses of vegetation based on its age (e.g., seedlings colonize open bars, mature trees resist flooding and produce seeds; Lytle & Merritt, 2004).

Soil development on floodplains is a complex process affected by the interaction of abiotic factors (e.g., water table, flood events, erosion, deposition) and biotic factors (e.g., root growth, organic debris, microbial processes) (Baetz *et al.*, 2015). Soil profiles on floodplains can be comprised of layers of nutrient-rich organic soils that develop during flood intervals alternating with mineral soils of variable nutrient content that are deposited by floods. Such layering can be good for roots that need a mixture of nutrients, aeration, and water-holding substrates (Werdin-Pfisterer *et al.*, 2012). Water-holding capacity varies depending on soil texture and organic matter (Gill, 1972), with drought a potential problem during periods of low water flow and high temperatures that cause high evaporation rates. In such cases, salts can accumulate on the surface of young soils that might affect successional processes (Van Cleve *et al.*, 1993), particularly if they affect keystone species such as the nitrogen-fixing *Alnus* (Chapin & Walker, 1993). In aridlands, such as northwestern China, dropping water tables (with distance from a river channel or time since flooding) were associated with increased soil and ground water salinity. These increases led to survival by those salt-tolerant plants able to keep their roots in the water table (Thevs *et al.*, 2008). In another example from northwestern China (Xi *et al.*, 2016), groundwater salinity was more important than soil salinity in determining retrogressive succession from trees to more salt-tolerant shrubs and herbs.

Later successional soils tend to be wetter than early successional soils due to the increase in organic matter (Fonda, 1974; Johnson *et al.*, 1976) and more fertile because nitrogen fixation is not inhibited by flooding

(Asaeda *et al.*, 2016). In boreal forests, the buildup of soil moisture can be associated with permafrost and a retrogressive phase of succession (Viereck *et al.*, 1993), but this stage is generally overridden by additional flooding or disturbances such as fire (Mann *et al.*, 1995). Typical of other seres, floodplain soils decline in pH during succession as organic acids build up. Leached podsols can develop where the soils are wet and acidic. Atypical of primary seres is the rapid buildup of total soil nitrogen on floodplains (Van Cleve *et al.*, 1971; Luken & Fonda, 1983). A typical asymptote of 2,000–5,000 kg of nitrogen per hectare was reached more quickly on floodplains (within 100 years) than on glacial moraines (ca. 250 years), dunes (ca. 1,000 years), or volcanoes (ca. 6,000 years) (Walker & del Moral, 2003). These comparisons suggest that floodplains are both relatively fertile initially and that they have access to continued nutrient inputs during succession. The inputs are not always from upstream. Spawning salmon contribute greatly to floodplain succession in the Kol River in Kamchatka, Russia (Morris & Stanford, 2011), altering later successional vegetation from woody to herbaceous dominants capable of abundant growth on the highly fertile soil. Ongoing inputs of nutrients and organic matter influence floodplain succession (Luken & Fonda, 1983; Walker, 1989) that can proceed more rapidly than succession in nearby uplands (Frye & Quinn, 1979). However, in arid regions where episodic drought does not favor establishment of vascular nitrogen fixers, inputs of nitrogen from upstream may be the main source (Adair *et al.*, 2004).

Most river systems are now altered by human activities that can change successional dynamics on a floodplain in complex ways (see Section 10.1.1). Logging and agriculture modify upstream flows, irrigation reduces flow, dams obstruct flow, and levees and paved surfaces reduce riverbank absorption. Many rivers (e.g., in Sweden; Hasselquist *et al.*, 2015) have been channelized to facilitate transport of logs. These disruptions by humans address the physical amount of water in the river or the channel structure. However, humans also alter water quality, which must be considered when studying floodplain succession. Pollution comes from many local and regional sources, but a short list includes agriculture (e.g., higher nitrogen, phosphorus, salts), urbanization (e.g., sewage, oils, multiple chemicals in storm runoff), heat (e.g., runoff from nuclear reactors; Landman *et al.*, 2007), and toxic wastes (e.g., from mine spills). Promoting natural flooding can help dilute toxins and promote establishment of tolerant plants and soil development needed to detoxify the floodplain substrates (Nikolic *et al.*, 2018).

10.2.2 Biotic Variables

Floods leave a highly variable biological legacy. Floods may gently cover a forest floor with a fine layer of silt or violently scour away all organic material to expose bedrock. Succession will obviously differ along such a wide gradient of disturbance severity. There can also be increasing legacy gradients from the center of the channel to the edge, where flood effects are often ameliorated by the resistance provided by surviving vegetation.

The first filter for succession is survival or dispersal. Did any plant parts survive that can resprout, root from fragments, or germinate, either *in situ* or within the now mostly barren floodplain? If so, those plants get a head start and can shape successional trajectories (priority effects; Sarneel *et al.*, 2016). If not, the river channel provides a dispersal corridor and newly exposed habitats for pioneer plants that disperse during flood events, by floating in the water, or brought in by wind or animals from the surrounding vegetation. But those links with the surrounding vegetation can be counterintuitive. For example, seed dispersal in tropical dry forests is typically highest in the dry season, yet dispersal by rivers in such areas in Mexico peaked during the wet season instead due to river overflow and bank erosion (Esper-Reyes *et al.*, 2018). Seed banks on floodplains are dynamic, reflecting largely allogenic inputs (from flooding or neighboring vegetation) rather than existing vegetation or *in situ* survival (O'Donnell *et al.*, 2016; Bourgeois *et al.*, 2017), particularly where flood damage is severe or floods are of long duration.

The surrounding vegetation shapes the nature and pattern of dispersal of new propagules to the freshly exposed floodplain. Therefore, succession will be quite different if that vegetation is a species-poor tundra (Kalliola & Puhakka, 1988) or a tropical rain forest (Kalliola *et al.*, 1991). Seasonal flooding also provides regular openings for plant colonists, such as *Salix* and *Populus* trees, whose seeds are adapted to germinate on silt banks with a receding water table (the "recruitment box model"; Rood *et al.*, 2005), as occurs following snow melt in temperate regions (Nechaev, 1967). If these early colonists survive, they can reduce local damage and slow flood water, sometimes in species–specific ways (Hortobágyi *et al.*, 2018). Expansion of *Salix* in Alaska was generally by seed, except in dry or frequently inundated sites, when vegetation expansion by root suckering was more successful (Krasny *et al.*, 1988). Both *Salix* and *Populus* acted as ecosystem engineers on gravel bars in the Italian Alps by promoting accumulation of woody debris and facilitating colonization of pioneer plants (Edwards *et al.*, 1999). Expansion of *Populus* in Alberta, Canada (Cordes *et al.*, 1997) or establishment of *Picea* populations onto the broader floodplain (Walker *et al.*, 1986) occurs primarily after infrequent and particularly high flood events. Indeed, flood frequency, represented by height of terrace above the river, is often as important a variable determining plant succession as age (Friedman *et al.*, 1996). Many studies of floodplain succession use toposequences along increasing terrace height from the river channel as a proxy for successional stage. The youngest, lowest terraces support early successional, flood tolerant species while the older, higher ones, later successional, less flood tolerant species (Prach, 1994; Nakamura *et al.*, 2007).

Floodplains can be colonized by grasses or herbs, but woody plants predominate (even in aridlands and tundra), probably because deep, fast-growing roots help stabilize woody plants in the shifting floodplain substrates and provide them with adequate water. In the Amazon basin, high and frequent flooding led to production of stilt roots, while reduced height and frequency were associated with buttress roots (Wittmann & Parolin, 2005). In backwaters, reeds and horsetails can thrive (Egger *et al.*, 2015) and late successional vegetation can be forbs (Morris & Stanford, 2011) or grasses (Bischoff *et al.*, 2009). Flooding sustains many pioneer communities adapted to the high light, high disturbance conditions and that would otherwise be outcompeted by later successional species (Basinger *et al.*, 1996). In Japan, a pioneer herb (*Aster kantoensis*) on floodplains is endangered due to habitat loss (Takenaka *et al.*, 1996). However, with one landscape-scale analysis in central Australia, frequent flooding reduced overall plant richness, while lower flooding frequency allowed more species to survive (Capon, 2005). Following a volcanic eruption (Mount St. Helens) in Washington (USA), large volumes of tephra suspended in river water scoured the drainage channels and reduced the number of floodplain colonists until the tephra has been mostly washed downstream (Kiilsgaard *et al.*, 1986). Plants tolerant of frequent flooding are represented by many common life forms, including annual monocots, perennial forbs, shrubs, and sedges. Late successional trees such as *Picea* do not tolerate the high temperatures and low soil cation concentrations of young floodplains (Angell & Kielland, 2009).

Many invasive aliens find exposed floodplains a successful place to colonize, and studying the effects of these species can elucidate floodplain succession (Pyšek & Prach, 1993). Invasive aliens can alter light, nutrient, and water conditions and compete with native species. Sometimes invaders, such as species of *Fallopia* on floodplains in France, benefit from the high light environment (Dommanget *et al.*, 2013). Yet, not all invasive species need high light conditions; *Prunus serotina* invades mature, shady floodplains in Italy (Terwei *et al.*, 2013). *Tamarix* from Asia and North Africa (Halwagy, 1961) have invaded most waterways of the western United States (Stromberg *et al.*, 2007) with severe implications for water quality and quantity and for successional processes. *Tamarix* outcompetes native plants when water flow is intermittent because it is more drought tolerant (Cleverly *et al.*, 1997). Even in its native habitat in northwestern China, *Tamarix* outcompetes *Populus* with higher growth rates (Wu *et al.*, 2016); although both species are replaced by more salt-tolerant shrubs as groundwater salinity increases (Xi *et al.*, 2016). In the southwestern United States, *Tamarix* tolerates salty soils under drought conditions better than do the natives shrubs and trees and tends to replace native vegetation following fire (Busch, 1995). *Elaeagnus angustifolia* is another invader of North American floodplains (Lesica & Miles, 2001), while *Pinus* spp. and *Acacia* spp. invade South African floodplains (Rein-ecke *et al.*, 2008) and *Robinia pseudo-acacia* invades floodplains in Japan (Maekawa & Nakagoshi, 1997). Invasive trees and shrubs (e.g., *Buddleja, Salix, Ulex*) and herbs (e.g., *Lotus, Medicago, Trifolium, Vicia*) are invasive plants on New Zealand floodplains, dramatically altering water availability, soil nutrients, and succession (Smith & Lee, 1984; Peltzer *et al.*, 2009) and *Salix* has also invaded floodplains in southern Argentina (Datri *et al.*, 2017). The invasion of *Melilotus albus* on Alaskan floodplains may, in some cases, facilitate establishment of other invasive aliens (Conn *et al.*, 2011) but appears to inhibit native species, particularly by shading (Spellman & Wurtz, 2011). Seed banks can also be influenced by invasive alien species, including in seven rivers in southeastern Australia (O'Don-nell *et al.*, 2016).

Invasive alien species are becoming a central part of most studies of floodplain succession. They contribute to divergent trajectories and novel communities. Their dispersal is largely facilitated by humans through changes in climate, hydrology, habitat pollution, management histories, or release from competitors, predators, or disease in their places of origin. For example, flow regulation by humans combined with drought favored alien plant invasions along the River Murray in Australia, probably because native species were inhibited by altered flow regimes (Catford *et al.*, 2014). Yet native and invasive alien plants often respond to different environmental drivers, as shown in a study of 19 floodplains in New Zealand (Brummer et al., 2016). Invasive alien plant cover was highest on fine substrates with high maximum flows while native cover was highest in cool, wet sites near native vegetation. Simply managing flow regimes would not necessarily promote native species. Despite the clear importance of invasive aliens on some flood-plains, few of our targeted studies considered them a big factor in altering successional pathways. This discrepancy could reflect short-term studies and floodplains with inconspicuous or recently invaded aliens. However, even inconspicuous plants can have important successional roles (Peltzer et al., 2009).

Facilitative interactions occur during floodplain succession when a species contributes a limiting resource such as shade or nitrogen, or provides surface stability and organic matter. Invasive *Acer* trees were facilitated by native *Salix* trees in France because the *Salix* provided shade in early succession (Saccone *et al.*, 2010). In contrast, succession to native forests was facilitated by the invasive shrub *Buddleja* on New Zealand floodplains (Smale, 1990). *Alnus*, with its N-fixing symbiont *Frankia*, was more likely to facilitate subsequent succession to *Picea* on an Alaskan glacier moraine that was relatively infertile than on a more fertile Alaskan floodplain (Walker, 1993). It appears that *Frankia* can be transported readily in rivers (Huss-Danell *et al.*, 1997). Similar facilitation is likely by the nitrogen-fixing *Acacia* on a floodplain in southern Texas (Van Auken & Bush, 1985). Finally, the nitrogen-fixing shrub *Carmichaelia* facilitated aboveground and below ground growth (at multiple trophic levels) on a New Zealand floodplain (St. John *et al.*, 2012). Another kind of facilitation is the accumulation of either waterborne or wind-blown silt around plants that helps concentrate organic debris and potentially reduce the damage from future floods. Such accumulation can be from mat-forming herbs (e.g., *Raoulia* in New Zealand, Gibb, 1994; or *Glinus* in Egypt, Halwagy, 1961), rhizomatous plants (e.g., *Equisetum, Carex*; Kiilsgaard *et al.*, 1986), or shrubs and trees (e.g., *Tamarix* in Egypt; Halwagy, 1961).

Competition during floodplain succession is common. For example, during a typical *Alnus* to *Populus* transition in boreal floodplains, *Populus* produces secondary chemicals that appear to reduce nitrogen cycling (Schimel *et al.*, 1998) or lead to phosphorus limitation in *Alnus* stands (Uliasii & Ruess, 2002). Competition for light occurs among fast-growing yet shade-intolerant woody pioneer species. For example, the invasive alien *Tamarix* is outcompeted by the more shade-tolerant native *Acer negundo* on western North American floodplains (Dewine & Cooper, 2008). Reduced soil fertility, acidic litter (e.g., from conifers) or copious litter (e.g., from bamboo) can restrict regeneration of some species in later stages of succession (Oliveira-Filho *et al.*, 1994; Nakamura *et al.*, 1997). Competition is often seen in conjunction with facilitation, as shown in the next three examples. 1) On the upper Amazon River (Terborgh & Petren, 1991), a stout grass (*Gynerium sagittatum*) outcompetes the first herbaceous colonist (*Tessaria integrifolia*), but then facilitates woody tree establishment (e.g., *Cecropia*) by reducing damage from annual floods and providing shade. 2) In the Andes of Colombia, a native pioneer shrub (*Tithonia diversifolia*) that was planted inhibited floodplain grasses and facilitated recruitment of desirable woody plants (Galindo *et al.*, 2017). 3) When *Alnus* and *Picea* were planted together on a central Alaskan floodplain, *Alnus* initially facilitated *Picea*, particularly at the drier of two sites. Facilitation was likely from improved soil nutrient and texture while subsequent inhibition was likely from root competition. At the wetter site, both facilitative and competitive effects were present, but competition predominated (Chapin et al., 2016). It is apparent from these three examples that facilitation and competition are both integral processes in succession.

Trophic interactions on floodplains include the key role of mycorrhizae in plant colonization (Krasny *et al.*, 1984), growth (Sarkar *et al.*, 2016), or herbivory that can alter successional trajectories (Angell & Kielland, 2009). An evaluation of invasive alien plant species on New Zealand floodplains (*Alnus* and *Salix*) found that they relied on invasive alien mycorrhizal fungi from their indigenous range rather than native fungi (Bogar *et al.*, 2015). Mycorrhizal fungi also facilitated the invasive of *Centaurea maculosa* on a floodplain in Montana (USA) (Harner *et al.*, 2010). On the Susitna River in southern Alaska, herbivory by moose, beavers, and hares all slowed, but probably did not ultimately alter the trajectory of succession by their browsing on *Salix* and *Populus* (Helm & Collins, 1997). However, an alternative view from the Tanana River in central Alaska suggests that moose accelerate succession from *Salix* to *Picea* (Feng *et al.*, 2012) but that wolves, by keeping moose populations down, can slow succession. Binkley *et al.* (1997) supported the notion that moose accelerate succession from *Populus* to *Picea* in northern Alaska. Finally, diseases are a poorly understood but important player in floodplain succession. A fungal infection of *Alnus* in Alaska (Nossov *et al.*, 2011) and decimation of *Fraxinus* on the Mississippi River (USA) by an insect (Romano, 2010) both altered species composition and successional trajectories.

Succession on floodplains is a balancing act between ongoing, abiotic disturbances (e.g., flooding, erosion, deposition, channel migration) and biotic variables (e.g., germination, growth, substrate stabilization, species interactions, and species replacements). Each successional transition is closely linked to such intertwined variables as water discharge, flooding frequency, and terrace height. Successful transition to late-successional vegetation occurs only where terraces are high enough that succession is not reset by flooding. The high variability in timing, duration, intensity, and consequences of flood events (e.g., silt load) interacts with stochastic biotic variables such as dispersal events (Salicaceae have short germination windows; *Picea* mast every several years) to produce a shifting habitat mosaic of vegetation patches in different stages of succession. Such multiple layers of patterns make comparisons within and among biomes a challenge.

10.2.3 Patterns within and among Biomes

Floodplain studies frequently involve comparisons within biomes, typically within a watershed, but occasionally across larger regions. In such comparative studies, regional differences in geomorphology, flood regime, climate, and vegetative cover can lead to different successional outcomes (Albernaz *et al.*, 2012). For example, the cool, temperate Rhine River Valley in France generally had a shorter succession than the warm-temperate lower Mississippi River Valley in the United States, likely due to higher tree species diversity in Mississippi (Schnitzler *et al.*, 2005). However, when those differences are minimal at regional scales or comparisons are made of seres within a single watershed, successional processes can be largely similar. A comparison of 10 rivers in the southeastern United States, for example, found predictable patterns of tree species composition, as long as the comparison was among single, meandering river channels with point bars, intermediate levels of water flow, and a natural hydrological regime (Robertson, 2006). Yet differences can exist within the same watershed. In northern Sweden, a comparison of the main river channel to seven of its tributaries found that the main channel had higher species richness, higher proportions of ruderal plants, and lower proportions of woody plants than the tributaries (Nilsson *et al.*, 1994). The authors attributed the differences to the 50-fold higher annual discharge, 3-fold higher silt content, and 9-fold lower peat content in the main channel compared to the tributaries. Of course, successional drivers at local and landscape scales interact, such as when landscape variability increased as seedlings aged in a Wisconsin (USA) series of 30 sandbars (Dixon *et al.*, 2002).

Abiotic constraints on floodplain succession are a popular subject for modelers, who sometimes use their models to compare among biomes.

Muñoz-Mas *et al.* (2017) used process-based models to compare flood-plain succession in Austria, Portugal, and Spain. Although the models generally supported the roles of flooding and distance to riverbed as drivers of succession, the results from the three countries differed as well, with variable importance given to drought, flash floods, and remnant patches of old forests. Rejmánek *et al.* (1987) integrated many variables including flooding history, the balance of changing sediment loads and land subsidence, historic human land use and modern development (e.g., pipelines), vegetative growth, and herbivory by nutria into a Markov model of transitions in succession on the Mississippi River delta in Louisiana (USA). They concluded that cyclic landform patterns drove a cyclic succession, where only 25% of a freshwater marsh became forest dominated. The marsh, and eventually the forests (when sediment input no longer offset land subsidence), was inundated by saltwater, leading to a salt marsh. Continued subsidence and erosion then broke up the marsh and it returned to the original open water (Rejmánek *et al.*, 1987). Modelers also need to address even broader changes in background conditions. The increased melting of glaciers due to global warming is likely to alter succession among glacially fed rivers. One prediction, based on a survey of 36 alpine streams in Montana (USA), is that species richness will decline overall from reduced scouring by meltwaters that favor *Salix* shrubs, while herbaceous species in alpine environments will increase in abundance (McKernan *et al.*, 2018).

In our comparative analysis we chose 48 manuscripts that fit our criteria. A majority of the studies were from temperate broadleaf and coniferous forests and success of succession significantly increased between those two biomes and with latitude (Tables 10.1, 10.2, and Fig. 10.3). In the Arctic-alpine biome, all four studies were successful, supporting our general trend of increased success with increased latitude. Divergent trajectories prevailed, species richness generally increased, and invasive species were important or partly important in 30% of the studies. There were no significant differences among the different groups of biomes in these characteristics (Table 10.2).

10.3 Theoretical Implications

1. Scales matter. At small scales (e.g., <100 m^2), floodplain dynamics are largely stochastic because of the variability in flooding, deposition, and colonization. At larger scales (e.g., watersheds), an overall equilibrium

Table 10.1 *Success of succession for flood studies arranged by biomes (no. of studies). For evaluation of success see Chapter 4.*

Succession successful?	TR	TD	AR	ME	TG	TB	CF	AA	Total
Yes	1	0	3	1	2	9	14	4	34
Partly	1	1	1	0	0	8	2	0	13
No	1	0	0	0	0	0	0	0	1
Total	3	1	4	1	2	17	16	4	48

Biome abbreviations: TR: tropical rain forests; TD: tropical dry forests; AR: aridlands; TG: temperate grasslands; TB: temperate broadleaf forests; CF: coniferous forests; AA: Arctic-alpine.

can be maintained between the area being disturbed by erosion and deposition and the area undergoing succession (Little *et al.*, 2013).

2. Microsites matter. *Salix* and *Populus*, two common colonists of temperate and boreal floodplains, have a one- to two-week period between seed dispersal and germination and are dependent on a wet surface and receding water levels to reproduce. When conditions of this recruitment box are not met (as when glacial meltwaters are early or do not come), these key players in succession do not establish (unless by vegetation propagation) and successional trajectories can be altered.

3. Species matter. Nitrogen-fixing, keystone colonists of floodplains, such as *Alnus*, alter succession through additions of nitrogen, leaf litter, and shade. Without them, successional pathways can vary (Nossov *et al.*, 2011), for example by being slower (St. John *et al.*, 2012), or having altered species composition (Bellingham *et al.*, 2001). Invasive species also matter, especially when they significantly alter light, nutrients, salinity, water availability, or surface stability.

4. Succession is a robust process. Despite the high degree of both spatial and temporal variability in a dynamic floodplain, a generalizable successional pattern is observable across global floodplains. The first colonizers are usually woody, fast-growing, light tolerant, and flood tolerant. These plants help stabilize the substrate, leading to terrace development. Then a new suite of species colonizes that accumulates organic matter, furthers development of soils, forms a continuous canopy, and resists erosion. Later stages are more variable and longer (hence harder to study), with purported retrogression to swamps, bogs, tundra, grasslands, or shrublands occurring at some sites, depending on the biome.

Table 10.2 Number of flood studies (N = 48) sorted by various criteria: Warm (TR, TD, AR, ME), Cold (TG, TB, CF, AA), Dry (TD, AR, ME, TG), Wet (TR, TB, CF, AA), Forested (TR, TD, ME, TB, CF), Non forested (AR, TG, AA).

Successional trait		Warm	Cold	Dry	Wet	Forested	Not forested	All biomes (no.)	All biomes (%)
Succession successful? (48)	Yes	5	29	6	28	25	9	34	71
	Partly	3	10	2	11	12	1	13	27
	No	1	0	0	1	1	0	1	2
	Differences	NS		NS		NS			
Trajectory (25)	Converge	2	3	2	3	4	1	5	20
	Diverge	3	11	2	12	11	3	14	56
	Variable	1	5	0	6	5	1	6	24
	Differences	NS		NS		NS			
Species richness (27)	Increase	5	13	5	13	14	4	18	67
	Decrease	0	1	0	1	1	0	1	4
	Variable	1	7	0	8	6	2	8	29
	Differences	NS		NS		NS			
Invasive species important? (40)	Yes	0	1	0	1	1	0	1	2
	Partly	2	9	1	10	10	1	11	28
	No	5	23	5	23	20	8	28	70
	Differences	NS		NS		NS			

Sample sizes used for each successional trait are in parentheses.

For biome abbreviations see Table 10.1.

χ^2 test was used for non-ordered variables, Cochran–Armitage test was used for ordered variables: NS not significant.

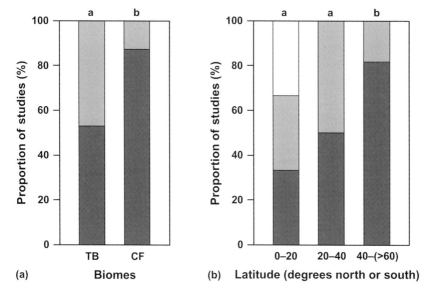

Figure 10.3 Success of succession for floods by a) terrestrial biomes and b) latitude (% of studies). Black: successful, light gray: partly successful, white: not successful. TB: temperate broadleaf forests, CF: coniferous forests. For sample sizes, see Table 10.1. The Cochran-Armitage test a) was Z = −2.1589, p = 0.031, and the asymptotic generalized Pearson's χ^2 test with post-hoc test b) was $\chi^2 = 9.370$, df = 2, p = 0.009. Different small case letters indicate statistically significant differences.

10.4 Practical Implications

Humans have dramatically altered many river channels and their flood-plains in the last several centuries with diversions for irrigation; dams for hydropower, flood control, and recreation; cooling for nuclear reactors; channeling for flood control; pollution from runoff; and many other uses. Floodplain succession therefore can occur under highly modified conditions, although there are also relatively pristine floodplains. Nevertheless, much floodplain research involves examining the effects of various restoration techniques on succession.

1. Restoration of floodplains benefits society in many ways, including to control floods, regain habitat for native plants and animals, improve water quality, and bring back ecosystem resiliency and successional processes.
2. Wildlife are either stage specialists (e.g., deer that prefer early woody vegetation for browse) or need all successional stages to meet their

nutritional and habitat needs (e.g., rhinoceros in West Bengal, India; Rawat, 2005).

3. A knowledge of plant life histories and their responses to flooding regimes is crucial to determine when and how much to intervene in natural recovery processes (Meitzen *et al.*, 2018). For example, channel widening worked best in northern Spain, followed by abandonment of agriculture or cessation of clearcutting (González *et al.*, 2017).

4. Dam removals can be successful at partially restoring previous silt loads and floodplains, with accompanying native vegetation. However, releases can also lead to damage from too much sediment, invasion by alien species, or novel successional states (Shafroth *et al.*, 2002).

10.5 Conclusions

Succession on river floodplains is a topic of clear interest to all who are affected by episodic and seasonal flooding, including the effects of the nutrients and soils deposited or the damage from flooding and erosion of soil. For example, Lawrence grew up along a small river where the size of the family property fluctuated with each flood. Extremely high spatial variability in both abiotic (e.g., timing, frequency, and intensity of floods) and biotic (e.g., legacies, dispersal, competition) factors challenge those interested in generalizations. Yet some patterns can be found at regional and global scales, especially in the sequence of plant life forms. With most rivers now altered by human activities (e.g., wildlife management, farming, dam, invasive aliens), successional studies will have to continue to adjust to the changing realities, but can continue to collect information with direct relevance to watershed management.

11 · *Fire*

11.1 Disturbance Description

Fire represents one of the most heterogeneous disturbances that we consider. Fires differ greatly in their intensity, frequency, and spatial extent. We consider here only intense fires where most aboveground biomass is consumed by fire. We focus on succession after a single fire and consider repeated fires as initiating separate seres. However, the frequency of fire in the past and the fire return interval (McKenzie *et al.*, 2011) are important factors that influence the course of succession by altering local and regional species pools (Settele *et al.*, 1996) and local site conditions (Johnstone & Chapin, 2006). Succession in ecosystems that are fire adapted differs from those that are not (Johnson, 1995) because in the former, there are species adapted to either survive the fire *in situ* or easily colonize the site immediately after the fire. Ecosystem adaptations to fires can occur over millions of years (Korasidis *et al.*, 2016). Post-fire succession is usually considered as a type of secondary succession (Walker & del Moral, 2003), but in the case of highly intense fires where all biological components, including litter and humus layer, are burned, the recovery approaches primary succession.

We found more studies of post-fire succession (ca. 1,900 in our initial search) than any other type of disturbance (Table 4.1). Indeed, fire ecology is an important subset of ecology that considers many aspects of fire's impact on ecosystems with numerous theoretical and practical implications (Whelan 1994; Johnson 1995; DeBano *et al.*, 1998; McKenzie *et al.*, 2011; Keeley *et al.*, 2012).

11.1.1 Causes

Fires have both natural (e.g., lightning, volcanoes) and anthropogenic origins. Ecosystems with a long history of predominantly natural fires include boreal coniferous forests and volcanic hotspots. Ecosystems where humans have long influenced fire regimes, especially its frequency, include African savannas and the Mediterranean region. Consequently, these ecosystems and their constituent species have developed adaptations to fires (Johnson, 1995). Recent anthropogenic changes have both increased and decreased fire frequency in different parts of the world, with usually negative effects on community and ecosystem development. Fire exclusion, in many countries ensured by legislation during the last century, appears to have an overall negative impact on biodiversity in fire-adapted systems (DeBano *et al.*, 1998). Succession after fire exclusion is not considered in our quantitative analyses. However, we did consider some well-documented studies following succession after prescribed burning. The intensity and frequency of fires are, therefore, influenced by both natural and anthropogenic factors, as well as by the accumulation of flammable biomass.

11.1.2 Spatial Patterns

Virtually all terrestrial ecosystems can burn, from tropical forests to tundra, and from lowlands to alpine zones, including even wetlands such as peatlands or floating mats of *Cyperus giganteus* (Rocha *et al.*, 2015). Fire is, therefore, one of the most widespread disturbance agents on the planet (Plate 18). Fires also exhibit large spatial heterogeneity both in their extent and intensity, often forming patches over landscapes of different size and time since the last fire. For subsequent plant regeneration and succession, minimally disturbed or undisturbed patches regardless of size can provide foci for regeneration in more severely burned sites in the vicinity (Reich *et al.*, 2001). Alternatively, severe fires that expose mineral soil can create microsites that provide favorable conditions for regeneration of some species (see Section 11.2.2). The landscape-scale mosaic patches burned at different intensities have been most frequently studied in vast areas of the North American boreal forests (Reich *et al.*, 2001). For such studies, aerial photos and GIS methodology can be effectively exploited (Franks *et al.*, 2013).

11.1.3 Subsequent Disturbances

Salvage logging is a common disturbance after fire that is practiced by traditional forestry (Lindenmayer *et al.*, 2008). It creates many changes to the environment that can affect successional trajectories. For example, salvage logging removes perches, thus reducing establishment by plants whose seeds are typically dispersal by birds (Castro *et al.*, 2012). It also removes nutrients, increases insolation (thus changing temperature and water conditions), and the soil surface is often disturbed by salvage logging. Sites logged in this way are usually reforested by planting, not left to spontaneous succession. Run off and soil erosion (e.g., landslides), may increase after fire, especially on slopes (Walker & Shiels, 2013). Burned sites may be exposed to different grazing or browsing intensity compared to unburned sites (Silva *et al.*, 2014); grazing can reduce the severity of subsequent fires for a few years (Faver *et al.*, 2011).

11.2 Succession

11.2.1 Abiotic Variables

Intensity (temperature, duration) of fire is controlled primarily by the amount of accumulated flammable material, but also by weather conditions and topography (Clarke *et al.*, 2014; Fig. 11.1). The amount of flammable material depends on the fire-return interval, that is the time

Figure 11.1 Fire effects in Nevada (USA). Note recovery of some grasses and how the fire stopped at the ridge top.
Photo by Lawrence R. Walker

since the previous fire (Johnstone & Chapin, 2006), as well as the environmentally determined rate of decomposition, and the morphology of constituent species. Summer and autumn fires are usually most intense, so seasonality plays a role (Harrod *et al.*, 2000). Aspect can also affect fire intensity because slopes facing the Equator tend to be drier than those facing away from the Equator (Buhk *et al.*, 2006). Fire severity (damage caused) determines the post-fire litter depth, which is important for subsequent successional development. For example, remaining litter depth can determine if the trajectory is toward deciduous forests (following high intensity fires) or toward coniferous forests (following low intensity fires) in the boreal zone (Shenoy *et al.*, 2013). Fires that linger have different ecological consequences than fast-moving fires (Watts & Kobziar, 2013).

Soil nutrients are variably affected by fire. They can increase immediately after fire due to their deposition in ash. However, some soil nutrients can be lost by volatilization during the fire or by increased run off and leaching after the fire (Walker & Boneta, 1995). For example, nitrogen volatilization occurs when the fire temperature reaches 200°C (Brooks, 2002). By contrast, following fire there can be a slow release of nitrogen from decaying, partially burned biomass and additional inputs from aerial deposition. Consequently, soil nitrogen levels can increase, decrease, or show no change following fires (Driscoll *et al.*, 1999; Kučerová *et al.*, 2008; Dzwonko *et al.*, 2015). Fire also has variable effects on soil phosphorus. Increases can occur when fires convert previously unavailable phosphorus (and other nutrients) bound in organic material to available forms (Dzwonko *et al.*, 2015). Cations can increase (Buhk *et al.*, 2006; Kučerová *et al.*, 2008; Dzwonko *et al.*, 2015), decrease (Driscoll *et al.*, 1999), or show no change (Ivanova *et al.*, 2017) following fire. Finally, soil pH changes closely follow changes in cations (Driscoll *et al.*, 1999).

Germination can be stimulated by smoke or high temperatures that crack impermeable seed coats (Bargmann *et al.*, 2014). Seedling growth can be stimulated by the absorption of secondary metabolites by charcoal, such as the phenolics found in humus (Calvo *et al.*, 2005). Germination and growth are also generally improved by the reduction of litter that ensures more reliable access to soil moisture and nutrients than is typically found in litter layers (Harrod *et al.*, 2000). Germination and seedling survivorship after fire were positively correlated with precipitation, especially in the first year following a fire in an *Artemisia* stand (Nelson *et al.*, 2014). As in other types of succession, the size of the disturbed area influences the subsequent colonization from the surroundings and thus the course of succession. For example, successful forest regeneration was observed only within the first 20 m from unburned patches during the first two decades of succession in New Zealand (Wiser *et al.*, 1997). Such fine-scale neighborhood effects supported divergence, multiple successional trajectories, and patch diversity in Canadian boreal forests with easier regeneration of shade-tolerant tree dominants close to undisturbed patches (Taylor & Chen, 2011). Obviously, the highly variable abiotic conditions among recently burned sites influence the variability of succession.

11.2.2 Biotic Variables

One essential variable affecting succession after fire is the proportion of plants that recolonize by seed ("seeders," Plate 19) versus those that resprout ("resprouters") (Di Castri *et al.*, 1981). In some ecosystems well adapted to fire (e.g., Mediterranean biome), resprouters, which regenerate immediately after fire, can dominate the flora. Seeders can either persist at a site in the form of a seed bank (in the soil or as an aerial seed bank such as in serotinous cones (Harvey & Holzman, 2014) or reach a site through dispersal from outside the burned area (Haire & McGarigal, 2008)). Seeds of many species can survive even severe fire and fire can stimulate germination (see Section 11.2.1). Serotinous cones represent a direct adaptation to fire because they remain closed, sometimes for many years, and then open when resins holding them closed are melted by high temperatures during a fire (Coop *et al.*, 2010). The released seeds then fall to the ground where they can germinate in open space under conditions of low competition, high light, and potentially high nutrients.

Fires leave a variable biological legacy, depending on fire intensity, management history, and species characteristics. Because we consider here only intensive fires and disregard those only lightly affecting the site, we would expect comparably little biological legacy. However, even after severe fires the biological legacy can be high, with up to 60% of species surviving the fire (Abella & Fornwalt, 2015). Even following a severe fire, some patches or micro-sites can remain intact and subsequently become nuclei for regeneration (Albornoz *et al.*, 2013). Fires can also increase the spatial heterogeneity of seed banks when fewer seeds survive in more intensely burned patches (Brooks, 2002). Surviving adult plants, ones that do not die immediately (Major *et al.*, 2013; Ivanova *et al.*, 2017), or dead standing woody plants (snags) can serve as perches and support establishment of endozoochorous species. The endozoo-chorous species usually represent late-successional species and thus succession can be accelerated (Richardson *et al.*, 2014). Burned patches and damaged individuals may attract some insect species, and lush ground layer vegetation may attract vertebrate herbivores, but the impact of these influences on succession is hard to generalize.

Growth forms that are often negatively affected by fire include cryptogams (Knuckey *et al.*, 2016), but some mosses are considered fire specialists because they readily colonize burned sites. In addition, many grasses and shrubs are well adapted to regrow rapidly after a fire. Among trees, those with thick bark are most likely to survive fire.

Invasive alien species can modify or completely change fire frequency, intensity, and subsequent successional pathways. Grass invasion arrested succession for at least four decades in tropical dry forests in Hawaii (D'Antonio *et al.*, 2011) and for at least two decades in temperate broadleaf forests in New Zealand (Wiser *et al.*, 1997). Invasive annual grasses (*Bromus*) increased fire frequency and consequently replacement of shrubland (*Artemisia*) in the Great Basin (USA) (Morris & Leger, 2016).

11.2.3 Patterns within and among Biomes

Post-fire succession has the highest probability of success of all the types of succession we consider. Success is especially high in ecosystems well adapted to regular fires, such as the Mediterranean biome, some grasslands, and boreal coniferous forests. However, there are ecosystems that are sensitive to fire where a higher fire frequency has a detrimental impact on the ecosystem structure and diversity, such as in some *Eucalyptus* forests in southwestern Australia (Gosper *et al.*, 2013) and tropical rainforests. Some biome boundaries are determined largely or in part by fire, such as the transitions between open savannas and closed tropical dry forests (Silva *et al.*, 2013; de Deus & Oliviera, 2016). Despite the generally high levels of success, fire can sometimes result in the persistence of treeless areas in otherwise forested landscapes (Coppoletta *et al.*, 2016).

The increased space, light, and nutrients after a fire provide opportunities for less competitive species (e.g., annuals) to establish. Annuals often survive in the soil seed bank and exploit the post-fire environment in the short period of favorable conditions. Ghermandi *et al.* (2004) even referred to a "phantom" community that establishes and then disappears quickly in burned Patagonian grasslands.

Variation in the frequency and severity of fires can cause differences in successional trajectories within the same biome or ecosystem. Generally, lower fire frequency and severity favor late-successional species, and higher frequency and severity favor early-successional species (Caplat & Anand, 2009). In the Mediterranean, increasing fire severity has altered the successional trajectory toward shrublands instead of forests (González-DeVega *et al.*, 2016). In North American boreal forests, the current trend toward more frequent fires, probably influenced by climate change, was considered responsible for the shift in dominance from *Picea mariana* to *Pinus banksiana* (Boiffin & Munson, 2013). Higher fire severity supported deciduous over coniferous trees because the latter more easily establish on deeply burned litter and humus (Gibson *et al.*, 2016), or in the case of *Populus*, resprout profusely from large networks of underground suckers. In tundra, more frequent fires diverted succession to graminoid-dominated instead of dwarf shrub–dominated ecosystems (Barret *et al.*, 2012). The increasing fire frequency as a consequence of global warming may also contribute to the northward movement of tall shrubs into Arctic tundra because they establish more easily in burned, sun-exposed patches (Lantz *et al.*, 2010). By contrast, on an infertile grassland in Minnesota (USA), Li *et al.* (2013) experimentally tested the influence of different fire frequencies and did not find any substantial influence, even after 27 years. In the southwestern deserts of North America, characteristics of dominant shrub species can determine post-fire successional rates and trajectories (Engel & Abella, 2011); the dominant *Larrea tridentata* recovered by sprouting after fire, while *Coleogyne ramosissima* did not, allowing other species (e.g., invasive *Bromus* grasses) to establish. Even in ecosystems adapted to a certain fire regime over millennia, changes in fire frequency or severity can disrupt the feedbacks between species traits, soil characteristics, and fire. Johnstone *et al.* (2010) documented stable cycles of forest succession for the past 6,000 years in the Alaskan boreal forests, yet unusual fire events disrupted the cycles and contributed to a shift from a coniferous to a deciduous forest.

Post-fire succession has rarely been studied using similar methods over large geographical ranges, with the exception of some studies from the North American boreal forests (Reich *et al.*, 2001) and subarctic regions (Lantz *et al.*, 2010). Velle and Vandvick (2014) experimentally tested the regeneration rate of burned *Calluna* heathlands on a 340 km latitudinal gradient along the western coast of Norway. They found that regeneration rate and the number of pioneer species decreased from south to north during the three-year study. Post-fire succession has been

Table 11.1 *Success of succession for fire studies arranged by biome (no. of studies). For the evaluation of succession see Chapter 4.*

Succession successful?	TR	TD	AR	ME	TG	TB	CF	AA	Total
Yes	1	5	4	20	6	6	26	1	69
Partly	0	2	3	3	0	2	1	1	12
No	0	1	0	0	0	1	0	0	2
Total	1	8	7	23	6	9	27	2	83

Biome abbreviations: TR: tropical rain forests; TD: tropical dry forests; AR: aridlands; ME: Mediterranean; TG: temperate grasslands; TB: temperate broadleaf forests; CF: coniferous forests; AA: Arctic-alpine.

occasionally compared with succession in clearcuts, particularly in boreal North America. Haeussler and Bergeron (2004) reported lower species richness of post-fire sites compared to clearings at multiple spatial scales. In one study, there was a lower proportion of late successional dominants in early stages following fire than after clearcutting (Rees & Juday, 2002), but succession following both disturbance types was usually convergent within the same ecosystem (Elson *et al.*, 2007).

In our comparative analyses (83 studies, for methods see Chapter 4), post-fire succession was considered successful (approaching potential natural vegetation) in 83% of the studies (Tables 11.1 and 11.2). In the two cases in which succession was unsuccessful, invasive aliens dominated, arresting succession. Success of succession differed significantly among biomes (Fig. 11.2), with the lowest success in tropical and temperate broadleaf forests and aridlands and the highest success in temperate grasslands (where all six studies reported successful regeneration after fire). Success was also high in Mediterranean ecosystems and coniferous forests. Therefore, there was a significant latitudinal trend. There were no significant differences among types of biomes for success, succession, trajectory, or the importance of alien species (Table 11.2). However, we are heartened that invasive alien species were not important in 83% of the studies and only arrested succession in two of them. Divergent and convergent successional trajectories were more or less equally present. Frelich and Reich (1995) emphasized that divergent versus convergent trajectories depend on spatial scales. They reported divergence in boreal forests at a small scale (<1 ha) where the divergence was conditioned by individual trees belonging to different species; at a larger scale (>1 ha) the tree species more or less regularly repeated in a

Table 11.2 *Number of fire studies (total N = 83) sorted by various criteria: Warm (TR, TD, AR, ME), Cold (TG, TB, CF, AA), Dry (TD, AR, ME, TG), Wet (TR, TB, CF, AA), Forested (TR, TD, ME, TB, CF), Not forested (AR, TG, AA)*

Successional trait (no. of studies)		Warm	Cold	Dry	Wet	Forested	Not forested	All biomes (no.)	All biomes (%)
Succession successful? (83)	Yes	30	39	35	34	58	11	69	83
	Partly	8	4	8	4	8	4	12	14
	No	1	1	0	2	2	0	2	3
	Differences	NS		NS		NS			
Trajectory (24)	Converge	4	4	4	4	7	1	8	33
	Diverge	1	6	1	6	7	0	7	29
	Variable	4	5	4	5	6	3	9	38
	Differences	NS		NS		NS			
Species richness (51)	Increase	6	8	6	8	13	1	14	27
	Decrease	20	8	22	6	25	3	28	55
	Variable	3	6	4	5	7	2	9	18
	Differences	NS		★		NS			
Invasive species important? (47)	Yes	1	1	1	1	2	0	2	4
	Partly	2	4	4	2	3	3	6	13
	No	15	24	17	22	33	6	39	83
	Differences	NS		NS		NS			

Sample sizes used for each successional trait are in parentheses.

For biome abbreviations see Table 11.1.

χ^2 test was used for non-ordered variables, Cochran–Armitage test was used for ordered variables: ★ $p < 0.05$; NS not significant.

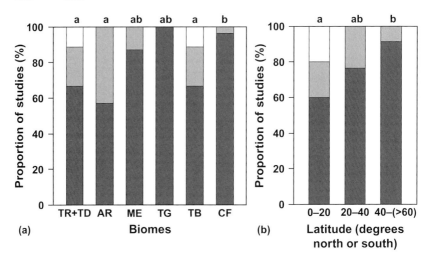

Figure 11.2 Success of succession for fire by a) terrestrial biomes and b) latitude (% of studies). Black: successful, light gray: partly successful, white: not successful. TR + TD: tropical rain forests plus tropical dry forests, AR: aridlands, ME: Mediterranean, TG: temperate grasslands, TB: temperate broadleaf forests, CF: coniferous forests. For samples sizes, see Table 11.1. The asymptotic generalized Pearson's χ^2 test with post-hoc test a) was $\chi^2 = 12.29$, df = 5, p = 0.031, and b) $\chi^2 = 8.334$, df = 2, p = 0.015. Different small case letters indicate statistically significant differences.

mosaic to which all burned sites converged. From our analyses, the only significant difference was between dry and wet biomes, with a decrease in richness with succession more likely in dry that wet climates. This pattern can be explained by dry biomes burning more frequently than wet ones. These frequent burns result in a large cohort of early successional species that appears just after fire and then disappears, causing a decrease in the total number of species. Fig. 11.3 illustrates this pattern: the highest number of species in initial stages of succession occurs in ecosystems adapted to frequent fire, and the lowest number occurs in initial stages in ecosystems not adapted to frequent fire (Delarze *et al.*, 1992).

Time to recovery varied widely. In some cases, including the Mediterranean biome or temperate grasslands, no change in species composition was recorded after fire (Tárrega *et al.*, 1995; Knops, 2006) and full recovery was completed during the first season after fire. Also, some heathlands were reported to quickly and fully recover, reaching the pre-disturbance species composition in just two years (Bullock & Webb, 1995). Forest recovery typically takes between 20 and ca. 100 years. Optimal fire return interval for maintenance of existing vegetation is also

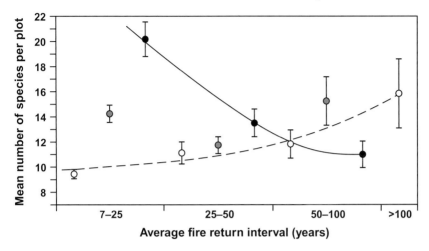

Figure 11.3 Mean number of species (±S.E.) per relevé as a function of fire frequency and time since last fire. Filled circles: last fire dating from 0 to 3 years ago; shaded circles: last fire dating from 4 to 15 years ago; open circles: last fire dating from >15 years ago. Solid curve: pattern just after a fire; dashed curve: pattern a long time after a fire.
From Delarze *et al.* (1992) with permission from Opulus Press

variable, even within the same biome. For example, *Eucalyptus* forests in southwestern Australia thrived with fire return intervals that varied between 30 and >200 years (Gosper *et al.*, 2012, 2013). Some grasslands can be burned annually without any apparent changes (Knops, 2006).

11.3 Theoretical Implications

1. Post-fire succession appeared to be the most successful among all the types of succession considered in this book. Thus, the vegetation of most biomes seems to be best adapted to this disturbance.
2. Dry biomes, which are easily burned, exhibit the highest level of resilience.
3. In biomes adapted to regular fires, species richness usually peaks shortly after the fire and then decreases. In biomes not adapted to regular fires, species richness is comparably low after fire, and then gradually increases.
4. With increasing time since fire, fire-sensitive species increase, while with decreasing time since fire, fire-tolerant species increase.
5. The Intermediate Disturbance Hypothesis does not seem to be valid here because the highest diversity in fire-adapted ecosystems is usually after intensive or frequent fires (Schwilk *et al.*, 1997).

6. Fires heterogeneous in space and time support biodiversity at the landscape scale (Burton *et al.*, 2009).
7. Invasive species only very exceptionally dominate in late successional stages.

11.4 Practical Implications

Fire has many practical consequences in forestry, a topic beyond the scope of this book. We consider instead consequences for nature conservancy and ecological restoration.

1. Fire suppression, as often practiced, leads to reduction of biodiversity in fire-adapted ecosystems (Keane *et al.*, 2002).
2. Similarly, an increase in fire frequency above the level to which ecosystems are adapted reduces biodiversity (Syphard *et al.*, 2009)
3. Prescribed fires, if carefully executed, can effectively substitute for natural fire regimes (Bates & Svejcar, 2009; Maren *et al.*, 2010).
4. A non-intervention strategy is usually better than salvage logging and replanting after a fire, unless timber production is the sole aim.
5. Satellite imagery and GIS are useful tools at broad scales to observe vegetation changes, but only to the level of some dominant species. Their use is effective in ecosystems with distinct dominants (e.g., boreal forests).

11.5 Conclusions

Biomes differ after fires in how successful the course of succession is in reaching a target. Fire plays a key role in maintaining species diversity, especially in dry ecosystems around the world. More frequent and severe fires due to global warming may change biome distributions, such as promoting the encroachment of woody species into tundra, or conversion of forests into grasslands. Wildfires shape many ecosystems. When humans disrupt natural fire frequencies (either increasing or decreasing them) there are usually detrimental consequences for ecosystem structure and functioning. The importance of fire for maintaining biodiversity was nicely illustrated by the famous 1988 Yellowstone fire (Wyoming, USA), which at first was seen as a national tragedy when about two-thirds of the world's oldest national park burned. However, it appeared soon after that the fire had a positive or neutral impact on the park's ecosystems (Romme *et al.*, 2016).

12 · *Clearcuts*

12.1 Disturbance Description

Clearcuts are a completely anthropogenic disturbance, as are the two subsequent chapters on plowed fields and mines. We consider here only disturbances that remove all tree cover or that leave only a few stems to provide seed sources for natural regeneration. Selective cutting is mentioned only if it is compared with clearcuts. Here we cover primarily clearcuts that are not subsequently managed by human intervention because our interest is in spontaneous succession. We also consider cases in which interventions are limited to immediate post-clearcut treatments including burning and chipping of residual materials (logging slash), or, rarely, tilling of the soil, or herbicide use. We excluded studies that used planting or seeding. Slash-and-burn activities in preparation for agricultural activities are mentioned in Chapter 13. Because a substantial biological legacy remains, clearcuts clearly lead to secondary succession.

Succession after clearcuts is one of the most frequently studied types of succession (we obtained ca. 1,500 studies from Web of Science). Only fire studies were more common (ca. 1,900 studies). Several recent books on forest ecology address succession following clearcuts (e.g., Peh *et al.*, 2015; Nyland, 2016).

12.1.1 Causes

The primary cause of clearcuts is for timber, but it can also be done as salvage logging, mostly after windstorms, fire, or insect outbreaks to save at least some logs or to prevent further spread of harmful insects (Lindenmayer *et al.*, 2008). Clearcuts increased in intensity in the past few centuries, though humans have cut forests selectively and sporadically at small scales for millennia. In some heavily populated parts of the world with a long history of human habitation (e.g., the Middle East, the Mediterranean basin, India, or China) impacts on forests have been substantial for a long time (Bellwood, 2005). Typical historical impacts include burning, coppicing, and conversion of forests to pastoral or cultivated land uses.

12.1.2 Spatial Patterns

Clearcuts naturally concern only those biomes dominated by forest vegetation (see Chapter 3). The current tree cover loss worldwide, mostly due to clearcuts, is estimated to be up to 30 million ha year^{-1} (World Resource Institute, www.wri.org). Most of this area is reforested either by artificial planting or spontaneous succession. The fastest and most extensive cutting is occurring now in tropical forests (Chazdon, 2014).

Clearcuts usually range in size from 10^3 to 10^6 m^2. Probably the largest continuous clearcut in the world (50,000 ha) was reported from British Columbia, Canada, as a result of salvage logging after bark beetle outbreak in the 1980s (Hawkins *et al.*, 2013). Clearcuts are mostly created in strips or square patches. In recent years, many clearcuts have been laid out with rounded or sinuous boundaries to have a more natural appearance (Perera *et al.*, 2007). Only rarely is an entire watershed cut, including the famous Hubbard Brook experimental study initiated in the 1960s in New Hampshire (USA) (Likens, 2013).

12.1.3 Subsequent Disturbances

Some intentional disturbances immediately follow clearcuts as a part of forest management operations. These include burning, soil disturbance, and herbicide use; other disturbances, such as planting or sowing, followed by artificial thinning, may follow. Clearcuts, especially large ones, can have various impacts on the site and its surroundings. Clearcut logging constitutes a sudden and severe alteration of the environment for all organisms remaining on the site. Formerly shaded environments at ground level are newly exposed to sunlight and trees are removed that formerly intercepted snow and rain and transpired water. Such changes therefore typically increase soil erosion and run off, leading potentially to landslides and avalanches. In addition, surrounding forests become more vulnerable to wind damage. Alterations of microclimates and mesoclimates can result in increased or more variable soil and water temperatures and soil moisture with potential effects on soil fauna (Tulande-M. *et al.*,

2018). Clearcuts may also attract (or deter) herbivores whose browsing activities might modify the course of succession.

12.2 Succession

12.2.1 Abiotic Variables

After clearcuts there is typically a rapid increase in available nutrients followed by a decrease (e.g., Holmes & Likens, 2016; Mylliemngap *et al.*, 2016). Absolute nutrient values are highly variable among sites due to differences in initial soil fertility, intensity of weathering, and nutrient uptake by plants. When trees are cut, the nutrient uptake suddenly drops, making nutrients more available to the understory vegetation. Gradual decay of biomass remaining after clearcutting further contributes to the nutrient increase (Bråkenhielm & Liu, 1998). Decay is usually accelerated by the warmer conditions and often moister soils that favor greater microbial activity and more rapid mineralization of the organic material. Increased availability of nitrogen can support nitrophilous, early successional species. Similar to the decrease of nutrient uptake, transpiration suddenly decreases and soil moisture may consequently increase. But soil can also become drier after clearcutting (Shiels *et al.*, 2015) due to higher insolation and wind exposure. Changes in soil properties are often ephemeral (Trefilova & Efimov, 2015), but in the wet tropics, rapid leaching of nutrients and subsequent decreases in soil fertility may cause long-lasting or even irreversible soil degradation (Chazdon, 2014). A detailed description of changes in soil chemistry in a temperate clearcut is provided by the Hubbard Brook experiment (Holmes & Likens, 2016).

Clearcutting typically results in disruption of the forest floor and exposure of mineral soil. The extent of the disruption depends on the methods used by the loggers. Where mineral soils are exposed, early successional species can invade and persist, delaying regeneration of tree species (Bainbridge & Strong, 2005). Site topography influences succession in various ways, especially through adding variability in site moisture conditions. Succession is usually faster on poleward-facing slopes in comparably drier parts of the world (Schroeder *et al.*, 2007; Halpern & Lutz, 2013). By contrast, in northern boreal forests, regeneration is slower on the cold, wet, north-facing slopes than on slopes that face south (Van Cleve & Viereck, 1981).

Light conditions after clearcutting are important. Shading from the surrounding undisturbed forest varies with the area of clearcuts, latitude, slope, aspect, and height of the surrounding canopy. For example, for a forest with trees 30 m tall at 55°N latitude, gaps would have to be >0.5 ha in area to be dominated by >75% full sunlight at level ground (Coates & Burton, 1997).

The size and shape of clearcuts can substantially influence the subsequent succession, particularly by modifying microclimate and seed inputs. Increasing the area of a clearcut is generally expected to decrease the rate of recovery by reducing seed inputs of forest species (Moktan *et al.*, 2009). In large clearings, the higher the ratio between the length of the clearcut boundary and its area, the greater the colonization from outside (Barbour *et al.*, 1998); that is, an indented boundary was better than a straight one in this respect. Obviously, edge effects are important (Harper *et al.*, 2005). The highest species richness is usually reported near the edges (ecotones) where shade tolerant and shade intolerant species typically grow together (Marozas *et al.*, 2005). For example, edge effects were detectable up to 60 m into the surrounding forest in the case of understory species, and up to 10–20 m in the case of trees, and persisted for several decades in a northern European, pine-dominated forest (Marozas *et al.*, 2005).

12.2.2 Biotic Variables

Succession in clearcuts is highly dependent on the biological legacy that remains after the trees are removed. Yet that legacy is highly variable. Understory plants can be at various stages of development at the time of the cutting and the degree of damage is influenced by the technique used for tree removal (e.g., heavy machinery, horses, or helicopters). The degree of cover of the herb layer at the time of cutting appeared in one study to be the most important predictor of establishing tree density (a negative correlation) in clearcuts (Kramer *et al.*, 2014). Clearcuts occur in pristine forests, old-growth secondary forests, young secondary forests, and plantations, further adding to the variability of the biological legacy, particularly regarding participation of late-successional species representing the respective potential natural vegetation of the area. The seed bank usually determines species composition of only the initial successional stages; therefore, seed rain from outside the site remains critical to succession (Sakai *et al.*, 2010). In some cases, seedling banks can be more important than seed banks (Leck *et al.*, 1989). If the seedling bank is composed of late-successional trees, regeneration of the pre-disturbance forest can be rapid and follow immediately in clearcuts (Allard-Duchêne *et al.*, 2014; Plate 20). However, logging operations often substantially damage the seedling bank (Archambault *et al.*, 1998). We documented up to 80% reduction of the seedling bank by salvage logging after a bark beetle outbreak in central European mountain spruce forests (Jonášová & Prach, 2004). Salvage logging after a wind disturbance led to homogenization of the stand and delayed tree recovery compared to sites left unmanaged after the disturbance (Michalová *et al.*, 2017).

Sources of propagules in the surrounding area often play a crucial role in succession. Differences in the surrounding vegetation of the Brazilian Atlantic forest caused divergence in succession among clearings (Rolim *et al.*, 2017). For the establishment of tree species typical of the potential natural vegetation, the occurrence of the respective seed trees within a distance of 50 m was the most significant factor in attempts to restore more natural forests from plantations in the Netherlands (Jonášová *et al.*, 2006).

Another decisive factor for forest regeneration in clearcuts is the ability of cut trees to regenerate vegetatively, such as by resprouting (Lévesque *et al.*, 2011). In such cases, direct succession (or regeneration) can be observed. This ability of trees is exploited in the traditional forest management of coppicing, which has pre-historic roots (Nyland, 2016). Rapid closure of the tree canopy can keep sun-demanding species from establishing. The ability to resprout is much more common among angiosperms than among gymnosperms (Del Tredici, 2001).

Early colonists of clearcuts in temperate biomes are often wind-dispersed annual species while perennial species spread by frugivorous vertebrates usually dominate among early colonists in tropical biomes (Chazdon, 2014; Carlo & Morales, 2016). Vertebrates are important vectors for spreading seeds, but vertebrates can consume seeds or seedlings. Piironen *et al.* (2017) reported that vertebrate herbivores were the main cause of seedling mortality in a logged African tropical rain forest. Later in succession, various kinds of zoochory seem to prevail in both temperate and tropical forests. Competition, facilitation, allelopathy, herbivory, and mutualistic relationships such as mycorrhizae play variable but generally important roles in succession in clearcuts. Mallik (2003) provided an interesting example of relationships in boreal coniferous forests that can substantially change successional trajectories: ericaceous species that were already present before clearcutting produced phenolic compounds that inhibited (by allelopathy) seed germination and seedling growth of conifers in clearcuts and also suppressed those ectomycorrhizae important for the conifers. Moreover, because the ericads produced protein-phenol

Figure 12.1 Forest recovery in a 10-year-old clearcut spruce-beech forest in central Europe.
Photo by Karel Prach

complexes, available nitrogen in an already nutrient-deficient habitat was consequently reduced further, which enforced inhibition of conifer establishment. The result was retrogressive succession in clearcuts where a heathland formed instead of regeneration of the original coniferous forest.

12.2.3 Patterns within and among Biomes

Succession in clearcuts is expected to proceed readily toward potential natural vegetation because typical woody species are either already present or in the surrounding forest (Fig. 12.1). Moreover, soil conditions and understory vegetation are not usually substantially changed compared to other disturbances such as volcanic activity or mining (see Chapters 5 and 14). Therefore, obstacles to forest regeneration are predominantly confined to dispersal limitation and competition. These processes often can affect succession. For example, dispersal limitations are particularly evident in clearcuts within large, monospecific plantations, such as Norway spruce (*Picea abies*) in Europe, or acacias, eucalypts,

Pinus radiata, or oil palm elsewhere (e.g., Jonášová *et al.*, 2006). Vigorously growing early successional species may limit or delay establishment of late successional species (Carleton & Maclellan, 1994). Competition can also come from post-cut invasion and then persistence of alien species such as acacias in South Africa (Galatowitch & Richardson, 2005) or Réunion (Baret *et al.*, 2007), or *Cytisus scoparius* in the Pacific Northwest (USA) (Grove *et al.*, 2017).

Woody plants, especially from the Mediterranean biome, are often good resprouters, which is primarily an adaptation to fire but useful also after clearcutting. This adaptation has probably been reinforced in Europe by 10,000 years of human activities, including grazing, frequent burning, and cutting (Blondel & Aronson, 1999). These species respond to clearcuts by rapid regeneration, and if they represent the respective potential natural vegetation, it also regenerates rapidly. Regeneration by sprouting is common, but that ability may vary even within a genus. For example, the evergreen *Quercus ilex*, one of the dominant plants in the Mediterranean, resprouts easily and immediately while the deciduous *Q. pubescens* does not. This difference may cause divergent successional trajectories in clearcuts in areas where they meet (Tatoni & Roche, 1994). Resprouting can be important in regeneration in other biomes, but is least likely in coniferous forests because many conifers do not resprout (Del Tredici, 2001).

Clearcut effects on species richness vary by spatial scale and depend on the type of vegetation considered. At the landscape level, clearcuts can be detrimental to the integrity of a forested landscape and to regional diversity, including endemic species (Huang *et al.*, 2015). However, many native species respond favorably to clearcuts, and consequently, landscape scale diversity can be maintained by clearcuts (Kellison & Young, 1997; Jenkins & Parker, 1998; Schulze *et al.*, 2014). Swanson *et al.* (2011) noted that early successional ecosystems are an understudied stage of forest succession and suggested that they play an important role in maintaining high native species diversity at the landscape scale. By contrast, clearcutting may support the establishment of alien species, thus increases in diversity may not be always desirable.

The most common comparison of succession in clearcuts is with postfire succession, particularly in boreal North America. Succession in clearcuts usually exhibited a higher proportion of late successional dominants in early stages than after fire and a faster recovery of the respective forest (Rees & Juday, 2002) but the trajectories in clearcuts or burns were usually convergent in the same ecosystem (Elson *et al.*, 2007). Hauessler and Kneeshaw (2003) concluded that clearcuts typically lacked the

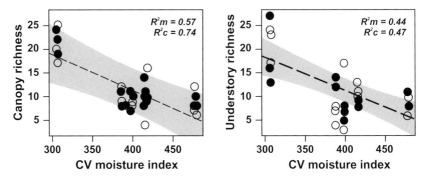

Figure 12.2 Responses of species diversity in 50- to 60-year-old secondary forests in clearcuts (open circles) and in neighboring primary forests (filled circles) studied along a broad-scale climate gradient (1,500 km along the east coast of Australia). Linear mixed-effects models (LMMs) were used. Shaded areas are 95% confidence intervals; CV: coefficient of variation of moisture index (based on precipitation and potential evapotranspiration). Coefficients of determination are given for fixed effects (R^2m) and fixed and random effects (R^2c).
From Sams *et al.* (2017) with permission from Blackwell Scientific Publications

variability in residual organic matter found after wildfires in the boreal forest. Rarely has succession in clearcuts been compared to other types of succession. Timoney *et al.* (1997) compared vegetation changes in clearcuts, after fires, and as a response to flooding in a boreal forest in Canada and found succession in clearcuts to be faster than after the two other disturbance types. This pattern could be related to more biological legacy, less environmental change, or both after clearcuts. Few studies dealt with variability of succession in clearcuts over a larger geographical area. Sams *et al.* (2017) analyzed a large set of 50- to 60-year-old forests regenerating in clearcuts along a 1,500 km transect in northeastern Australia and found that species richness decreased with increased seasonality of moisture availability (Fig. 12.2). Species richness was significantly positively correlated with landscape forest cover in the study. Kusumoto *et al.* (2015) conducted a similar study across most of Japan using functional types instead of species composition. They found higher resilience, that is a prompt return to the pre-disturbance stage, of subtropical forests compared to boreal and deciduous temperate forests, seemingly contradicting our finding of a higher likelihood of reaching potential natural vegetation at high than at low latitudes (see following text). The discrepancy might be due to higher functional redundancy among subtropical species and thus a greater chance that species substitute for each other in the subtropics, even if recovery of exact species

Table 12.1 *Success of succession for clearcut studies arrange by biome (no. of studies). For the evaluation of success see Chapter 4.*

Succession successful?	TR	TD	ME	TB	CF	Total
Yes	2	1	3	16	18	40
Partly	10	1	0	6	4	21
No	2	0	1	1	0	4
Total	14	2	4	23	22	65

Biome abbreviations: TR: Tropical rain forests; TD: tropical dry forests; ME: Mediterranean; TB: temperate broadleaf forests; CF: coniferous forests.

composition remains low compared to higher latitudes. Our evaluation was focused just on similarities in species composition.

Time to recovery of potential natural vegetation was on average faster in clearcuts than for all other disturbances except fire and cyclones, mostly due to a substantial biological legacy, less altered site environmental conditions, and often sources of propagules of late successional species in the undisturbed surroundings. The time needed for recovery in the tropics was highly variable, ranging from five years (Valdez-Hernández et al., 2014) to perhaps several hundred years (Baret et al., 2007), making succession generally less predictable than in other wooded biomes (Bishoff et al., 2005). High species richness in the tropics is likely the reason for the lower predictability and higher variability of succession in that biome. In the other biomes, recovery usually took several decades but sometimes was evident after <10 years (Floret et al., 1992). Generally, tropical forests in Africa seem to be better adapted to human impact such as clearcuts than are tropical forests in Asia or America, likely due to a longer history of anthropogenic disturbances to which species had more time to adapt (Gourlet-Fleury et al., 2013).

Our comparative analysis of 65 studies of clearcuts showed that spontaneous succession was successful in 62% of the studies, partly successful in 32%, and unsuccessful in 6% (Tables 12.1 and 12.2). There was significantly lower success in tropical forests than temperate broadleaf or coniferous forest biomes (Fig. 12.3). In the tropics, recovery was usually rapid (especially in the wet tropics) but trajectories often diverged from potential natural or pre-disturbance vegetation (d'Oliveira et al., 2011), resulting in partly successful being the most frequent category in this biome. Success was significantly higher in cold than in warm biomes (Table 12.2). Convergent trajectories prevailed over the other types of

Table 12.2 *Number of clearcut studies (N = 65) sorted by various criteria: Warm (TR, TD, ME), Cold (CF, TB), Dry (TD, ME), Wet (TR, TB, CF). Sample sizes used for each successional trait are in parentheses. For biome abbreviations see Table 12.1.*

Successional trait		Warm	Cold	Dry	Wet	All biomes (no.)	All biomes (%)
Succession successful? (65)	Yes	6	34	4	36	40	62
	Partly	11	10	1	20	21	32
	No	3	1	1	3	4	6
	Differences	***		NS			
Trajectory (10)	Converge	0	5	0	5	5	50
	Diverge	1	1	0	2	2	20
	Variable	2	1	2	1	3	30
	Differences	NS		*			
Species richness (28)	Increase	6	6	1	11	12	43
	Decrease	4	7	3	8	11	39
	Variable	1	4	1	4	5	11
	Differences	NS		NS			
Invasive species important? (39)	Yes	2	0	1	1	2	3
	Partly	1	1	1	1	2	3
	No	6	29	3	32	35	94
	Differences	**		*			

χ^2 test was used for non-ordered variables, Cochran–Armitage test was used for ordered variables: *** $p < 0.001$; ** $p < 0.01$; * $p < 0.05$; NS not significant.

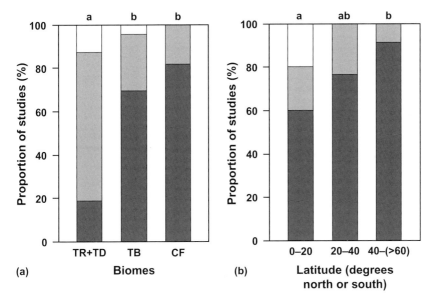

Figure 12.3 Success of succession for clearcuts by a) terrestrial biomes and b) latitude (% of studies). Black: successful, light gray: partly successful, white: not successful. TR + TD: tropical rain forests plus tropical dry forests, TB: temperate broadleaf forests, CF: coniferous forests. For sample sizes, see Table 12.1. The asymptotic generalized Pearson's χ^2 test with post-hoc test a) was χ^2 = 16.291; df = 2; p < 0.001, and b) χ^2 = 9.035, df = 2, p = 0.011. Different small case letters indicate statistically significant differences.

successional trajectories, and were significantly higher in wet than dry biomes, but sample sizes were small. The convergence pattern probably resulted from relatively high initial heterogeneity inside or among the clearcuts that then converged toward a more uniform landscape matrix (Prach *et al.*, 2014c). Other types of trajectories were less common. The two studies demonstrating parallel trajectories were determined by a different pre-disturbance vegetation type (Kramer *et al.*, 2014) and by contrasting soil fertility (Widenfalk & Weslien, 2009).

Increases and decreases of species richness during succession were approximately equally represented among the seres for which this information was available with no significant difference among the groups of biomes. Richness generally increased when the initial legacy was low and richness in the surrounding forests was high, and richness decreased under the opposite conditions. Invasion by alien species arrested succession more or less permanently in only two studies (Galatowitch & Richardson, 2005; Baret *et al.*, 2007) and alien species were significantly less likely to play an important role in cold and wet than in warm and dry biomes (Table 12.2). Though aliens are expected to arrest or deflect succession, especially in the tropics and the Mediterranean ecosystems (Pyšek *et al.*, 2017), in our data set it was not obvious.

12.3 Theoretical Implications

Many studies of succession in clearcuts have been focused on proper forest management procedures and sustainable timber production, and less on theoretical issues. We offer several theoretical implications, mostly from the studies in our meta-analysis.

1. Succession in clearcuts is usually faster than in other types of succession, especially if there is a significant legacy from vegetative recovery or a healthy seedling bank dominated by species that constitute the potential natural vegetation. Substantially unchanged soils and late successional forests in the vicinity also contribute to the rapid recovery by providing a source of propagules.
2. The recovery of potential natural vegetation (success of succession) tends to increase with latitude.
3. Invasive alien species, which may arrest or divert succession, did not appear to have strong effects, with only a few exceptions.
4. Functional diversity may follow a different pattern than species diversity during succession.
5. The impact of disturbances caused by clearcuts on biodiversity is ambiguous. Both positive and detrimental effects on biodiversity on the landscape scale have been reported. Large-scale clearcuts can be particularly detrimental to biodiversity. In the wet tropics, the original biodiversity can be hard to recover. Elsewhere, a mosaic of young and late-successional stages seems to be favorable for biodiversity unless alien species invade. Thus, structure and history of land use of a broad landscape should be considered.
6. Impacts of clearcuts on the site are also ambiguous. Effects may be ephemeral, or they may persist indefinitely (e.g., after intensive erosion following clearcutting). Persistently adverse effects should be carefully considered, especially in pristine forests where clearcutting should be avoided.

12.4 Practical Implications

Some traditional foresters may not agree with some of our points made here (e.g., 1, 2 in the following list), but based on the literature reviewed and our own experience, we suggest the following practical recommendations for most forest management scenarios.

1. Large-scale clearcuts should be avoided, even in the case of salvage logging after fire, wind, or insect outbreaks (Lindenmayer et al., 2008). A non-intervention strategy is usually the best in these cases.
2. Spontaneous succession is usually the best alternative in clearcuts, unless rapid timber production is the only interest, or alien species invade. Spontaneous succession is usually sufficiently fast and has minimal costs associated with it. Sometimes, additional management, such as artificial thinning or control of alien invasive species can be desirable (Elliott et al., 1997).
3. Well-tailored, small-scale clearings represent an effective tool for the conversion of monospecific plantations to more diverse stands favored by ecologists (Jonášová et al., 2006; Heinrichs & Schmidt, 2009; Cielo-Filho & de Souza, 2016).
4. Treeless vegetation, which can develop spontaneously due to competition or browsing, may have some benefits for maintaining species richness at small scales. Depending on the land use priorities for such areas, vegetation can be allowed to persist or may need to be displaced through native tree planting.
5. Satellite imagery and spatial modeling are often used in large-scale forestry practice. While they can be useful tools, they do not usually operate with successional changes of species composition and if they do, only dominant species are usually considered. Therefore, they must be used with caution concerning succession.

12.5 Conclusions

The rate at which forest vegetation reestablishes can impact many processes such as soil erosion, nutrient and water cycling including carbon sequestration, wildlife, trophic interactions, recreational use, and further economic use. Succession in clearcuts proceeds nearly as quickly toward potential natural vegetation (usually just a few decades) as succession following wind disturbances and fires. Spontaneous processes are usually effective and no artificial reforestation is necessary in most cases, if an ecological rather than an economical approach is preferred. Despite substantial literature on clearcuts by both foresters and plant ecologists, there is still a lack of large-scale, quantitative comparisons of responses of clearcuts within and among biomes.

13 · *Plowed Fields*

13.1 Disturbance Description

In this chapter, we consider situations in which plowed fields are left without cultivation following growth of a final crop. The crop is usually harvested but sometimes is left in place and may provide some legacy from the previous use and influence subsequent succession. Thus, succession usually starts on bare ground but with an agricultural (weedy) seed bank present, and with developed soil, though the soil is sometimes degraded by intensive use. Consequently, plowed fields represent clear examples of secondary succession (Burrows, 1990). Other terms for unused plowed fields include abandoned fields, fallows, or old fields (Cramer & Hobbs, 2007).

Most plowed fields are ploughed at least annually before their abandonment. In small-scale, slash-and-burn practice (not systematically covered in this chapter), the soil may or may not be plowed, but lasts for only a few years before the site is abandoned, and plowing can be discontinuous in space, often with solitary trees or shrubs remaining as a legacy from the pre-cultivation vegetation (Chazdon, 2014). The time scale we considered for plowed fields was up to about 100 years of succession, the time for which published data exist. Older historical cultivation, though sometimes still evident in present vegetation (Henry *et al.*, 2010), is not considered here because we cannot document subsequent seral stages and their species composition.

Succession in abandoned plowed fields is one of the most studied kinds of succession and many studies have substantially contributed to ecological theory. Rejmánek and Van Katwyk (2005) listed 1,511 references dealing with succession in plowed fields up to 1991. Since that time, Web of Science lists about 800 more studies of succession. Key book-length resources include Cramer and Hobbs (2007), with case studies from different parts of the world, and Osbornová *et al.* (1990) and Meiners *et al.* (2015b), which both summarize results of large-scale projects within specific geographical areas.

13.1.1 Causes

In the past few decades, two contrasting tendencies have become evident in agriculture: either increasing or decreasing intensity of agricultural efforts. Intensification often leads to abandonment of less productive, less accessible, or smaller fields that are difficult to cultivate with large-scale agricultural machinery. Other areas of abandonment include marginal areas, such as mountains, and sites that are too wet or too dry. The causes of abandonment include changes in ecological conditions and socio-economic conditions. Ecological changes include declining soil fertility due to nutrient depletion, increasing salinity or erosion, and decreasing water supply, all of which decrease productivity. Socio-economic changes are often linked to market factors at global scales, such as those that influence the cost of transport of agricultural products across long distances versus the cost of using local products. Depopulation of rural areas due to increasing urbanization and changing political systems also lead to abandonment (Plate 21). Ongoing global changes may have either positive or negative effects on agriculture. Either way, abandonment of plowed fields can be expected to continue.

13.1.2 Spatial Patterns

Plowed fields represent, besides fire, the most widespread disturbance among all considered in this book. They occur in a wide range of environments with various land-use histories. This variability generates a broad range of conditions, initial states, and legacy effects. By the end of the twentieth century, more than 200 million hectares of abandoned fields existed worldwide (Ramankutty & Foley, 1999). Plowed land (and its abandonment) occurs in all the major terrestrial biomes. The highest percentage of land area regularly plowed is in some parts of the tropics and subtropics (e.g., India), and in all temperate areas of the world. Steppes, including prairies and pampas, are particularly suitable for agriculture due to their fertile chernozem soils. The proportion of plowed land to total land can reach >40% in particular countries (Fig. 13.1).

Plowed land even occurs in some aridlands, when there is a short but regular wet period that is suitable for growing one crop; the rest of the year is often too dry for crops (unless they are irrigated). For example, in the desert in southern Jordan, barley or wheat grow in spring (February–May) by exploiting water from sporadic winter rains. At higher

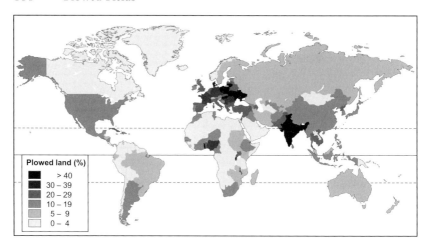

Figure 13.1 Proportion (%) of plowed land in particular countries over the world. Abandoned fields may occur in all of them. See Statistical Database of the Food and Agriculture Organization of the United Nations (http://faostat3.fao.org).

elevations in arid lands there can be sufficient water for agriculture from rainfall and melting snow. Plowing in aridlands is less limited in areas of persistent moisture (e.g., oases, floodplains), or where rainfall may be supplemented by irrigation.

Plowed land also occurs, or recently occurred, in a mild, oceanic, (sub)arctic climate, such as the coast of Iceland or the northern tip of Scandinavia. Plowed fields on the southwestern coast of Greenland are known from historical records of the twelfth and thirteenth centuries (during the Middle Age climatic optimum; Perren *et al.*, 2012). One of the highest plowed fields is in the Andes, where *Chenopodium quinoa* and potatoes are cultivated at more than 4,000 m a.s.l. In the north-western Himalayas, barley fields were even observed up to 4,300 m a.s.l. (K. Prach, personal observation). In virtually all biomes, succession occurs in abandoned plowed fields, but it has not been rigorously investigated everywhere.

In countries with rapidly increasing human populations, plowed land is increasing in extent (e.g., Brazil; FAO, 2019). In contrast, abandonment of plowed land is typical in some developed countries (e.g., in South Korea about 60% of rice paddy fields have been abandoned; Kim *et al.*, 2016). Abrupt economical changes can trigger abandonment, such as in countries of the former Soviet Union where about 45 million hectares of plowed land were abandoned in the 1990s (Kämpf *et al.*, 2016).

Most studies of abandoned plowed land originate from North America, especially the United States, followed by Europe. Rejmánek and Van Katwyk (2005) reported 42% of studies of plowed land abandonment from North America, 26% from Europe, 14% from Asia, 9% from Central and South America, 8% from Africa, and 1% from Australia and New Zealand. Many of these studies dealt with particular phenomena or with small temporal and spatial scales and thus were not utilized in this chapter.

13.1.3 Subsequent Disturbances

The majority of studies in plowed fields disregarded subsequent disturbances or considered them only marginally without directly studying their effects on the course of succession. However, some subsequent disturbances always occur and may substantially divert succession from its expected trajectory toward late successional stages. In general, subsequent disturbances maintain early successional communities or at least promote the presence of early successional species (Collins et al., 2001). In our comparative analyses, we considered only seres not obviously affected by intensive subsequent disturbances (see Chapter 4) but cannot completely ignore them.

Among abiotic disturbances, fire is one of the most important in plowed fields, especially in drier areas. Donfack et al. (1995) reported that fire arrested plowed field succession at a wooded grassland stage in dry tropical forests. Similarly, fire arrested or directed succession toward a shrub-dominated stage instead of oak forest in the Mediterranean biome in Europe (Santana et al., 2010). Fires can increase diversity when they are not too frequent (Lloret & Vila, 2003) by allowing the persistence of early successional species. Other abiotic disturbances, such as landslides, run off, and wind are only locally important in this kind of succession and less likely to be disruptive than if they occurred prior to abandonment of the plowed land.

Among biotic disturbances, grazing or browsing are the most important. For example, deer browsing maintained open forest in Minnesota (USA) (Lawson et al., 1999). Succession in Mediterranean Greece varied with intensity of grazing (Tzanopoulos et al., 2007): dwarf shrub frygana developed under intensive grazing but the more common maquis developed under low grazing pressure. Livestock grazing or hay cutting are frequently practiced in abandoned plowed fields. The former usually leads to wooded grassland in areas where forest is the potential vegetation; the latter always maintains grassland, a more valued habitat than forest from a conservation perspective in many parts of Europe (Ruprecht, 2005). Those studies dealing with intensive grazing or hay cutting were not considered here.

Asynchronous, small-scale disturbances, which create small gaps in closed vegetation, are generally expected to maintain high diversity because they open windows for establishment of additional species (Lavorel *et al.*, 1997). However, such small-scale disturbances can have the opposite effect as when mound-building activity by Mediterranean voles decreased species richness (Rebollo *et al.*, 2003). Additional disturbances may also allow invasion by alien species.

13.2 Succession

13.2.1 Abiotic Variables

One of the most important factors determining subsequent succession is the size of a plowed field, but its effect is variable. If the surrounding matrix is composed of (semi)natural vegetation, smaller fields are easily colonized by target species (Battaglia *et al.*, 2002) but are more vulnerable to invasions of alien species in the vicinity (Kupfer *et al.*, 2004). The size of a field also influences microclimatic conditions; smaller fields inside a forest exhibit fewer fluctuations in site moisture and temperature than larger ones and less shading from the surrounding vegetation. Shade-tolerant species, mostly requiring higher soil moisture, generally establish faster and in higher dominance in small than in large fields (but see Cook *et al.*, 2005).

The role of previous cultivation practices just before field abandonment has been reported by some studies. For example, there can be differences in the course of succession based on whether the field was plowed just before its abandonment or whether the last crop was left in the field. The legacy of these idiosyncratic events can be evident in species composition even after several decades (Doelle & Schmidt, 2009). The longer the previous cultivation, the longer the time was to recovery of pre-disturbance vegetation after abandonment in a study from the tropics (Lucas *et al.*, 2002).

Soil moisture is probably the most important abiotic factor shaping this kind of succession (Cramer & Hobbs, 2007). However, there are not many studies, either descriptive or experimental, that quantitatively compare the role of this essential factor among seres. Osbornová *et al.*

(1990) distinguished three subseres (wet, mesic, dry) when comparing more than a hundred abandoned fields in one landscape in the deciduous temperate forest zone of central Europe. Wet and dry seres were arrested as grass wetlands or steppe-like grasslands, respectively, while in the most common mesic sites, forests established. Similarly, soil moisture co-determined succession either toward deciduous forests on wetter sites or steppe on drier sites in the Loess Plateau of China (Jiao et al., 2007). Papanastisis (2007) reported a different trend in Greece, where woody species appeared sooner in dry than mesic sites, the latter being initially dominated by competitive herbaceous vegetation that retarded woody species establishment. Generally, however, forests seem more likely to establish in mesic than in wet or dry sites. In both dry and excessively wet sites (e.g., after the collapse of a drainage system), establishment of woody species is usually limited physiologically (Bazzaz, 2006). Soil moisture, and the presence of forests, is often related to aspect, as demonstrated by La Mantia et al. (2008) for the Mediterranean area. Succession to forest usually shifts site moisture from drier to more mesic conditions (Osbor-nová et al., 1990; Meiners et al., 2015a), but increasing transpiration by established woody species may decrease water availability to ground layer vegetation (Matlack, 1993).

Soil chemistry is another key abiotic factor affecting succession on abandoned plowed lands, but with variable effects. Increased nutrients can lead to dominance by herbaceous species that may arrest establish-ment of woody species (Smith & Olff 1998; Ruskule et al., 2016). Intriguingly, nutrient-poor soils can also lead to the slow colonization of trees and an extended period of dominance by herbaceous plants (e.g., in temperate broadleaf forests of Minnesota; Inouye et al., 1994). In plowed fields in short grass prairies in the United States, nitrogen addition supported annual, mostly alien species while nitrogen reduction supported perennial, mostly native species (Paschke et al., 2000). Yet, other studies show the opposite trend. Increasing air-borne nitrogen deposition in the last two decades of the twentieth century likely changed successional trajectories toward participation of more competi-tive, perennial, nitrophilous species, considered as generalists, in aban-doned fields in Denmark (Ejrnaes et al., 2003). An earlier emphasis on the role of nitrogen in determining the course of succession (Tilman, 1988) has recently shifted to a focus on phosphorus, particularly how phos-phorus fertilization can leave a legacy that favors certain vegetation types (Morris et al., 2011; Pätzold et al., 2013). Species diversity can be either reduced by high availability of phosphorus (plowed fields on Hungarian steppes; Boecker *et al.*, 2015) or increased (aridlands in Mongolia; Yanagawa *et al.*, 2016). Among other soil abiotic factors, pH (Jírová *et al.*, 2012) and soil texture (Kosmas *et al.*, 2000) may co-determine the course of succession.

Total soil nitrogen usually increases during succession when organic matter accumulates, but available nitrogen may decrease. Nitrogen can be trapped in organic material while phosphorus is more often sequestered in inorganic compounds during succession (Vitousek *et al.*, 2010). During succession, soil fertility generally increases on degraded land, potentially resulting in a return to agricultural use. The use of short-term fallow was a traditional agricultural practice in Europe before industrial fertilizers were introduced in the nineteenth century (Poschlod, 2017) and is still practiced in some tropical areas. Raharimalala *et al.* (2010) reported 20 years of fallow was needed for recovery of soil fertility in the tropics, while Kupfer *et al.* (2004) reported five years was needed as a minimum for recovery after slash-and-burn in the tropics. Locals often consider these processes that affect soil fertility in determining their agricultural activities (Chazdon, 2014).

13.2.2 Biotic Variables

The soil seed bank represents the most important legacy of previous cultivation. Up to a few tens of thousands of viable seeds per 1 m^2 can accumulate in plowed land (Thompson *et al.*, 1996) and the seeds determine the species composition of initial and sometimes even later seral stages (Gibson *et al.*, 2005). Slow-growing species that emerge from the initial seed bank may attain their importance later in succession following Egler's idea of Initial Species Composition (Egler, 1954). The role of the seed bank is most important in those parts of the world with a seasonal climate where species survive adverse period as seeds (Jimenéz & Armesto, 1992).

Seed dispersal can be more important than the seed bank in determining initial composition of successional communities, especially in the wet tropics. Seeds from close sources have the most influence on succession (Dovciak *et al.*, 2005), particularly if the sources are within 100 m (Ganade, 2007; Prach *et al.*, 2015) or 150 m (Kupfer *et al.*, 2004). Endozoochory is a key mode of dispersal for species of all successional stages in the tropics (Karlowski, 2006). In other regions, wind-dispersed (anemochorous) species more often dominate in early successional stages and later in succession zoochorous species (both endozoochorous and epizoochorous) usually dominate (Latzel *et al.*, 2011). For all types of dispersal and all biomes, the structure of the surrounding landscape is key to succession, especially the proximity to (semi)natural vegetation. Some studies reported seed availability in the surroundings to be more important than local environmental factors (Dovčiak *et al.*, 2005; Scott & Morgan, 2012).

Invasive alien species are another variable that affects plowed field succession. The role of invasive alien species is linked to the history of human influence in the area (Pyšek *et al.*, 2003). Reviewing the abandoned field literature, invasive alien species (mostly grasses), often participate in succession in tropical forests, temperate grasslands, Mediterranean vegetation, some aridlands (e.g., southwestern United States), and temperate broadleaf forests, especially in the Western Hemisphere. Although the proportion of species that are invasive is lower in tropical forests than in other ecosystems (Pyšek *et al.*, 2017), some invasive alien species arrest tropical forest succession or divert it to an alternative stable state (Hooper *et al.*, 2005; Erskine *et al.*, 2007). Tropical invasive plants are often vines or grasses, but occasionally woody plants (Rejmánek, 2000).

The generally accepted idea that species life strategies (*sensu* Grime, 1979) change during succession from R- to C- or S-strategists has also been documented for plowed fields (Lepš *et al.*, 1982). The strategies refer to ruderals, competitors, and stress tolerators. Osbornová *et al.* (1990) reported the shift from R- to C-strategists under mesic site conditions and to S-strategists under dry site conditions. This scheme can be tentatively accepted across all biomes. However, the details of how the strength of competition changes with site conditions is still under debate. In sites with low productivity, competition is usually below ground for water and nutrients, while in productive sites, aboveground competition for light is generally more important for succession (Wilson & Tilman, 2002). Bartha *et al.* (2014) noted that expansive, competitive herbaceous plants, which can arrest succession in abandoned fields in prairies, were wind pollinated, capable of lateral vegetative spread, and exhibited low recruitments for nitrogen and high requirements for light. This pattern may not be general, but species with intensive vegetative lateral spread often dominate old field succession, especially in productive sites. Under stressful conditions in all biomes, facilitation is generally considered important, especially in early succession. Even in sites without evident stress, facilitation may play an important role. For example, in tropical rain forests, surviving trees can facilitate establishment of other tree species by providing perches for seed dispersal through birds (Carriere *et al.*, 2002). Gómez-Aparicio (2009) concluded that semi-arid and dry tropical systems generally had more positive neighbor effects, that is facilitation, than mesic temperate systems where competition and inhibition predominate.

The physiology of germination, seedling establishment, and early growth is clearly important for species establishment in plowed fields (Burton & Bazzaz 1995; Bazzaz, 2006), but it is difficult to find generalizations for succession in agricultural land. Similarly, trophic interactions are crucial in shaping the course of succession, yet generalizations are difficult. The lack of late successional species is traditionally explained by dispersal limitation but plant-soil feedbacks might be more important. In one study, the spread of late successional species was suppressed under high soil phosphorus levels, a legacy from previous cultivation that increased their palatability to insect herbivores and root-feeding nematodes (de la Peña *et al.*, 2016). Such subtle relationships between abiotic and biotic components and how they change during succession have been rarely studied in plowed fields and no comparative study exists regarding variability within and across biomes.

13.2.3 Successional Patterns within and among Biomes

The classical successional sequence of changing dominant life forms was derived from studies of plowed fields, starting with annuals (mostly agricultural weeds), followed by perennial forbs, grasses, shrubs, and trees (Keever, 1950). This pattern applies to most plowed fields in temperate forests (Fig. 13.2) with some exceptions. For example, Jongepierová *et al.* (2004) reported an absence of annual weeds in a small, isolated field that had been cultivated for only a short period. In drier biomes, grasses usually dominate late successional stages (Plate 22), especially in steppes and savannas (Roux & Warren, 1963), and annuals can arrest succession toward perennials in aridlands (Stromberg & Griffin, 1996; Standish *et al.*, 2007). In tropical rain forests, early successional trees are often the first colonizers of plowed fields (Chazdon, 2014). Wind-dispersed trees in temperate broadleaf forests (e.g., *Betula, Populus, Salix*) sometimes colonize immediately upon abandonment of plowed fields (Baeten *et al.*, 2010), but that "colonization window" typically closes quickly due to the expansion of herbaceous vegetation (Bartha *et al.*, 2003). The next opportunity for tree establishment is then delayed until later successional stages.

Figure 13.2 Abandoned field near Prague, central Europe, ca 40 years old.
Photo by Karel Prach

There are only a few studies dealing with the variability of succession within biomes. Prach (1985) described variability of this kind of succession across Finland (largely in the coniferous forest biome), and found decreasing species diversity with latitude (Fig. 13.3) and convergent trajectories. Wright and Fridley (2010) found that the colonization rate of woody species decreased with increasing latitude for abandoned fields across the eastern United States (temperate broadleaf forest) (Fig. 13.4). They suggested that this pattern was driven by increasing competition between herbaceous and woody species with latitude. Their finding is not in full accordance with our global analysis. We expect easier establishment of late successional tree species with increasing latitude (see following, and Fig. 13.5). Perhaps different patterns can be found at different spatial scales. The same authors (Fridley & Wright 2012) reciprocally seeded woody species across the area and found that seedlings of southern pioneer species were better able to establish than northern species at all latitudes included in their experiment. Otto *et al.* (2006) found that species richness increased significantly during succession in drier areas on Tenerife Island in the Canary Islands (Mediterranean

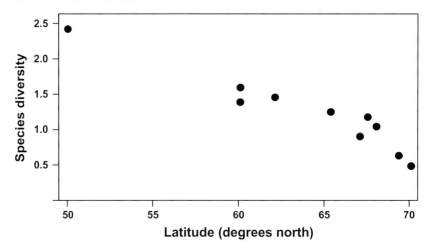

Figure 13.3 Species diversity (Shannon-Wiener index, ln) in initial stages in abandoned plowed fields across northern Europe. Sources of data for Finland (Prach, 1985); for the Czech Republic (Prach *et al.*, 2014a).

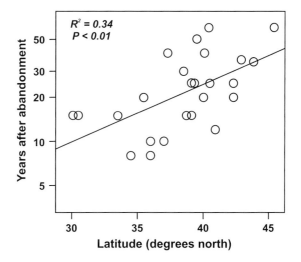

Figure 13.4 Rate of woody species colonization into abandoned plowed fields across latitudes of the eastern United States, measured as years until 50% woody cover was reached.
From Wright and Fridley (2010) with permission from Blackwell Scientific Publications

biome), whereas in the wetter areas it peaked early and then declined toward the mature stages due to stronger interspecific competition. Similar trends were found by Osbornová *et al.* (1990) in the central European temperate broadleaf forest zone. Tullus *et al.* (2013) found

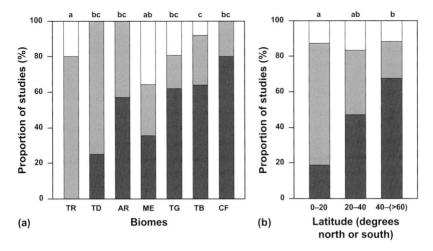

Figure 13.5 Success of succession for plowed fields by a) terrestrial biomes and b) latitude (% of studies). Black: successful, light gray: partly successful, white: not successful. Biome abbreviations: TR: tropical rain forests; TD: tropical dry forests; AR: aridlands; ME: Mediterranean; TG: temperate grasslands; TB: temperate broadleaf forests; CF: coniferous forests. For sample sizes, see Table 13.1. The asymptotic generalized Pearson's χ^2 test with post-hoc test was a) $\chi^2 = 14.387$; df = 6; p-value = 0.026), and b) $\chi^2 = 6.241$, df = 2, p = 0.044. Different small case letters indicate statistically significant differences.
Adapted from Prach and Walker (2019) with permission from Blackwell

rather uniform trajectories across Estonia that converged toward *Picea*-dominated stages in the transitional temperate broadleaf-boreal coniferous zone. Finally, Prach *et al.* (2014a) described variability of succession across the Czech Republic in central Europe (temperate broadleaf forests) with the following conclusions: 1) all measured environmental factors (age, elevation, phytogeographic region, site moisture, and bedrock type) exhibited statistically significant effects on the course of succession; 2) age and site moisture appeared to be the most important variables; 3) the number of species typical of deciduous forests, dry grasslands, and fringe communities increased during succession, while the number of alien and native synanthropic species decreased; and 4) succession was clearly divergent at the country scale.

Some generalizations presented by Cramer and Hobbs (2007) are inferred from indirect, mostly intuitive comparisons. They expected less ecosystem development in harsh than favorable environmental conditions in contrast to our findings that in aridlands spontaneous succession can be as successful as in many more favorable environments (Fig. 13.5).

Table 13.1 *Success of succession for plowed field studies by biomes (no. of studies). For the evaluation of success see Chapter 4.*

Succession successful?	TR	TD	AR	ME	TG	TB	CF	AA	Total
Yes	0	2	4	5	13	16	4	3	47
Partly	8	6	3	4	4	7	1	0	33
No	2	0	0	5	4	2	0	0	13
Total	10	8	7	14	21	25	5	3	93

Biome abbreviations: TR: tropical rain forests; TD: tropical dry forests; AR: aridlands; ME: Mediterranean; TG: temperate grasslands; TB: temperate broadleaf forests; CF: coniferous forests; AA: Arctic-alpine.

Cramer and Hobbs (2007) emphasized that succession after abandonment was often unlikely to follow trajectories toward a pre-disturbance state, especially in the Mediterranean type of ecosystems outside Europe (e.g., southwestern Australia and South Africa). These areas are also prone to invasions due to differences between life strategies of native and introduced species caused by long periods of isolation. However, in "young" postglacial landscapes of the Northern Hemisphere, native and introduced species have more similar strategies and introduced species are not as likely to change successional trajectories (Cramer & Hobbs, 2007). These conclusions are in accordance with our findings.

In our comparative analysis of succession in plowed fields among all terrestrial biomes (see Chapter 4 for methods), spontaneous succession was successful in 51% of the 93 studies, partly successful in 35%, and unsuccessful in 14% (Tables 13.1 and 13.2). Success of succession tended to increase in biomes located at higher latitudes, but declined somewhat in the Mediterranean biome where we found the highest proportion of failure of succession (Fig. 13.5; Prach & Walker, 2019). The abundance of alien species in this biome may divert or arrest succession (Groves & DiCastri, 1991; Pyšek *et al.*, 2017). Success was significantly higher in temperate broadleaf forests than in tropical rain forests and Mediterranean biomes. No full recovery was found in tropical rain forests; however, partial recovery was rather frequent. Unfortunately, few data are available from the Arctic-alpine biome, but three studies reported full success.

The time necessary to achieve recovery of potential natural vegetation differed from one decade to several centuries, with an average of several

Table 13.2 Number of plowed field studies (N = 93) sorted by various criteria: Warm (TR, TD, AR, ME), Cold (TG, TB, CF, AA), Dry (TD, AR, ME, TG), Wet (TR, TB, CF, AA), Forested (TR, TD, ME, TB, CF), Not forested (AR, TG, AA)

Biome	Warm	Cold	Dry	Wet	Forested	Not Forested	All biomes (no.)	All biomes (%)
Succession successful? (93)								
Yes	12	35	23	24	29	18	47	51
Partly	21	12	16	17	26	7	33	35
No	7	6	9	4	9	4	13	14
Differences	★★		NS	NS	NS			
Trajectory (24)								
Converge	4	5	6	3	4	5	9	38
Diverge	3	7	3	7	8	2	10	42
Variable	3	2	2	3	4	1	5	20
Differences	NS		NS	NS	NS			
Species richness (24)								
Increase	3	10	8	5	6	7	13	55
Decrease	1	4	3	2	3	2	5	20
Variable	4	2	4	2	3	3	6	25
Differences	NS		NS	NS	NS			
Invasive species important? (43)								
Yes	5	5	6	4	8	2	10	23
Partly	3	5	5	3	5	3	8	19
No	9	16	16	9	15	10	25	58
Differences	NS		NS	NS	NS			

Sample sizes used for each successional trait are in parentheses.

For biome abbreviations see Table 13.1.

χ^2 test was used for non-ordered variables, Cochran–Armitage test was used for ordered variables: ★★ p < 0.01; NS not significant.

decades. Relatively fast recovery was reported for some temperate grasslands (Albert *et al.*, 2014) and from aridlands (Castellanos *et al.*, 2005). By contrast, no signs of recovery of the original community were evident after many decades in some pampas of Argentina, due to the permanent dominance of widespread invasive aliens (Boccanelli *et al.*, 2010). The authors wrote that their results demonstrated a "requiem for the pampas grassland".

Trends in main community characteristics among the groups of biomes are summarized in Table 13.2. Succession in cold biomes was significantly more successful than in warm biomes, while arid versus humid biomes, and forested versus not forested biomes did not differ. Divergent and convergent trajectories were nearly equally represented. The resulting pattern is probably determined by initial heterogeneity within and among the fields included in the particular studies (Prach *et al.*, 2014c). Species richness mostly increased during succession but other trends were also present including decreasing or variable (e.g., U-shaped, inverted U-shaped, constant) richness. Richness is prone to increase in early stages with successful dispersal and establishment of additional species from the surrounding landscape, but can decrease when species that germinate from an abundant remnant seed bank decline from competition or a changing environment (Cramer & Hobbs, 2007). A fluctuating pattern in species richness during succession was also recorded, reflecting dominant species turnover. The lowest values occurred in the time of dominance of a species, and maximal values at the time of the dominant species exchange (Osbornová *et al.*, 1990). Participation of alien species in later successional stages was unimportant in 58% of studies and highly important in 23%. The highest abundance of alien species was typical for Mediterranean biomes outside Europe where alien species are generally frequent (Pyšek *et al.*, 2017).

13.3 Theoretical Implications

Though studies on succession in abandoned fields have contributed substantially to successional and ecological theory, broader generalizations are still difficult. Our main conclusions follow:

1. Recovery of potential natural vegetation is more likely in temperate than tropical and Mediterranean biomes. The probability of recovery generally increases with latitude (Prach & Walker, 2019). Species richness in seral vegetation decreases with latitude, in accordance with

general trends in plant species richness decreasing with latitude (Kreft & Jetz, 2007).

2. Succession in small or briefly cultivated plowed fields usually proceeds faster to potential, late-successional vegetation than does succession in large fields with a longer history of cultivation.

3. Large fields are more often colonized by generalists than are smaller fields (see also Kupfer *et al.*, 2004).

4. Under harsh environmental conditions (dry, cold, nutrient-poor) there is little species turnover. In productive sites, there is faster turnover, more subsequent dominants or stages, but a higher probability that succession will be arrested or diverted by competitive species, including invasive aliens.

5. Invasive alien species are important in decreasing the likelihood of success in reaching the potential natural vegetation among all the studied types of succession. They are most influential in altering succession in those regions where modern agriculture was recently introduced than in areas that have become adapted to this type of disturbance (see also Cramer & Hobbs, 2007). Invasive alien species were most influential at low and middle latitudes, especially in tropical forests and the Mediterranean biome, with the exception of the European Mediterranean.

7. Successional trajectories tend to converge in uniform landscapes, whether they are natural or formed by humans, and in the coniferous forest biome where the potential natural vegetation is formed by a few species. Divergence of successional trajectories is most likely in diverse (patchy) and species rich landscapes.

13.4 Practical Implications

1. Spontaneous succession (i.e., passive restoration) can often be used as a cheap and effective way to restore target vegetation in plowed fields.

2. However, potential natural vegetation, even when it recovers spontaneously, may not always be a target of ecological restoration. For example, species-rich secondary grasslands may be preferred over forests, especially if the grasslands are a traditional component of the landscapes under long-lasting agricultural impact. Grasslands can harbor more endangered and protected species than a typical forest (Ruprecht, 2006). Regular hay cutting, livestock grazing, or fire are often necessary to create and maintain grasslands, especially in

temperate forests and the Mediterranean biome. Management can be either motivated economically, and the conservation profit is only a subsidiary effect, or it can be practiced as conservation management under various conservation or restoration projects.

3. Even some novel ecosystems, usually composed of alien and native grasses and forbs and spontaneously developed, can be valued for conservation purposes or the preservation of ecosystem functions (Csecserits *et al.*, 2011). Usually, however, land managers have to either eradicate or control invasive alien species to reach a given restoration target (Tognetti *et al.*, 2010).

4. If spontaneous succession fails, intentional planting or seeding of desired species may represent restoration measures. Early planting of native trees that are poorly dispersed is very effective to accelerate succession toward targets, especially in tropical forests (Chazdon, 2014). Early seeding (sometimes as hydroseeding) can be used in arid environments to increase species establishment and thus reduce soil erosion by run off or wind (Lesschen *et al.*, 2008). In some environmentally extreme sites, early seeding of a nursery crop may facilitate subsequent spontaneous establishment of target species (Li *et al.*, 2007).

5. The ideal approach to restoration of plowed lands is with an integration of many aspects, including landscapes, biodiversity, erosion, water balance, aesthetics, and socio-economic concerns (Cramer & Hobbs, 2007; Robledano-Aymerich *et al.*, 2014).

13.5 Conclusions

Macroclimate, soil moisture, soil nutrient availability, and human impacts determine variability in successional trajectories within particular biomes. Human impacts are especially important in plowed field succession through prior influence on the site (the legacy of the previous cultivation) and through the modification of the surrounding landscape that serves as a source of species. Not only ecological but socio-economic and even political background factors are also highly relevant. This type of succession occupies a large fraction of the earth's terrestrial surface, highlighting its importance to management of abandoned fields.

Although succession on plowed lands has been frequently studied, there is still a lack of studies directly comparing successional patterns among biomes using quantitative data sampled in a comparable way.

Most generalizations are intuitive only. Careful comparisons are urgently needed to learn how ecosystems respond to ongoing global changes and future socio-economic changes. Generalizations will enable the development of scenarios on the future development of agriculture around the globe by clarifying consequences of future abandonment of plowed fields, subsequent management after abandonment, restoration of natural vegetation, or potential conversion back to cultivation if needed.

14 · *Mines*

14.1 Disturbance Description

Mining is an entirely anthropogenic activity that typically removes all biological legacy and therefore initiates a clear example of primary succession. Mines leave as severe a disturbance as do volcanoes, which are at the other end of our natural to anthropogenic disturbance gradient. We consider here succession both in sites where material is extracted (e.g., coal mines, rock quarries, sand and gravel pits) and in sites where material related to mining is deposited (e.g., spoil heaps, dumps, and slurry basins from coal or ore mining). We primarily focus on mine sites (henceforth including extraction and deposition sites) where spontaneous succession has occurred and not on mine sites that have had some anthropogenic amelioration (reclamation, i.e., the return of land to a 'useful' purpose; SER, 2004). Typical methods of mine reclamation include leveling the surface, spreading of organic material (including topsoil), the addition of lime (if needed to raise soil pH), and planting or sowing of plant species.

Studies of post-mining succession did not begin until the second half of the twentieth century and reached a peak at the end of that century (Walker, 1999a; Prach & Tolvanen, 2016). Most studies address succession on terrestrial surfaces, although aquatic habitats are often an important part of mine sites (but see Pietsch, 1996).

14.1.1 Causes

Mining disturbance started thousands of years ago when humans first quarried rocks for building materials. Mining of ores to obtain copper and tin largely started in the Bronze Age, about four thousand years ago, followed by the extraction of iron ore, lead, gold, and silver. By the Middle Ages, peat was dug for fuel, peaking in the nineteenth and early twentieth centuries. Peat was mined especially in countries where wood was sparse (e.g., Ireland; Joosten *et al.*, 2017). Coal mining increased from the eighteenth to the twentieth century. Most recently, uranium ores and oil shale have been mined.

14.1.2 Spatial Patterns

Mines are widely distributed and directly influence about 1% of the terrestrial surface of the earth (Walker, 1999a). Most studies of mine succession originate from temperate broadleaf and coniferous forest biomes, but this situation also reflects where most research on succession is conducted. Most mine sites are several hectares in size, but very extensive ones, such as those of open-cast coal mining, sand pits or quarries, can reach many square kilometers in extent. Mining can be continuous or discontinuous in space and time, and spoil material can be dumped either in disused parts of a mine or outside the mined area. Some mine sites are topographically very diverse (e.g., stone quarries, extensive spoil heaps from open-cast coal mining), while others are more homogeneous (e.g., industrially extracted peatlands).

14.1.3 Subsequent Disturbances

In topographically diverse mine sites, substrate erosion can occur on steep slopes, thereby maintaining the open character of otherwise closed vegetation. Intensively eroded slopes (landslides) are addressed in Chapter 9. Wind erosion can be expected on large, exposed mine sites formed by fine-grained substrates. Such erosion can locally slow down succession. Additional human disturbances, such as reshaping the surface, deposition of new layers of overburden, or starting a new mining can reset successional development.

14.2 Succession

14.2.1 Abiotic Variables

The chemical and physical parameters of the substrate are particularly decisive for post-mining succession and can be quite variable. For example, pH can range from 1 in pyrite residues in coal mines (Rufaut & Craw, 2010) to more than 12 in bauxite residues (Xue *et al.*, 2016), and can increase or decrease during succession due to leaching, chemical changes in the substrate, such as pyrite oxidation, aerial deposition of neutralizing substances, and development of organic layers (Takeuchi & Shimano, 2009; Young et al., 2013; Parraga-Aguado et al., 2014). Total carbon and nitrogen levels are naturally low in the case of newly exposed raw substrates, with the exception of harvested peatlands, but they generally increase during succession. Vindušková and Frouz (2013) reviewed 17 mine studies from the Northern Hemisphere and reported that a large proportion of them reached the pre-mining soil organic carbon level within 20 years or less. Changes in phosphorus content, either total or available to plants, are generally more complicated in mine sites as they largely depend on the initial chemistry of substrates.

High levels of heavy metals in some mines can delay succession (Bagatto & Shorthouse, 1999; Anawar et al., 2013), but can also provide suitable new habitats for specialized, often endangered flora (Kapusta et al., 2015). Similarly, mining can support gypsum specialists if new bedrock is exposed (Ballesteros et al., 2014).

Substrate thickness and topography are other abiotic variables that affect the course of succession (Alday et al., 2010). For example, the thickness of any peat that remains following surface harvesting determines if succession will proceed toward reestablishing original peatland vegetation or substituting fen vegetation if rewetted (Triisberg et al., 2014). The more heterogeneous the topography, the more diverse is the vegetation that develops. In heterogeneous areas, more species, including rare and endangered species, have a higher chance to find suitable microsites than on homogeneous surfaces, thus possibly making such mine sites important for nature conservation (Tropek et al., 2013). An interesting example of the influence of topography on the course of succession was described by Mudrák et al. (2016) and Frouz et al. (2018): on the flat, artificially leveled surface of spoil heaps, an expansive, competitive grass formed a continuous stand, but on more undulating surfaces a diverse mosaic of wooded and open sites developed.

Local aspect also affects succession through its influence on insolation and moisture retention. In the Northern Hemisphere, succession on spoil heaps can be faster on the wetter northern slopes than on the drier, southern ones (Alday et al., 2010). Similarly, convex microsites can be critical to successional development on post-mining surfaces in arid regions (Monokrousos et al., 2014). In harvested peatlands, the height of the ground water table has substantial influence on the course of succession and restoration (Nishimura et al., 2009). Similarly, in other mining sites, the position of ground water table determines successional trajectories (e.g., Řehounková & Prach, 2006 for sand pits). Finally, emergent parts of the topography can be subjected to persistent water or wind erosion. This erosion can sometimes negatively influence the surroundings of the mine site when the eroded material is toxic (Moreno de los Heras *et al.*, 2008), but eroded sites can also positively influence some disturbance-dependent organisms (Heneberg *et al.*, 2016).

14.2.2 Biotic Variables

Typically, there is no biological legacy remaining when mined substrates are exposed, although some spots can be locally enriched by diaspores during mining operations and substrate transport. Restoration guidelines usually require that topsoil be scraped and stored before mining and then reused for reclamation. Nevertheless, the law is not always fully respected and some organic topsoil containing diaspores can be preserved in a mine and have local effects on succession. However, succession is generally dependent on arrival of diaspores from the surroundings; thus, the surrounding vegetation composition and structure play an important role in revegetation of mine sites. In central Europe, the vast majority of colonization events on mined sites were from seeds that originated within 100 m of the mine (Řehounková & Prach, 2008; Prach *et al.*, 2015). Long-distance dispersal can also contribute to succession. For example, 7% of species occurring in large spoil heaps from coal mining in Germany dispersed a minimum of 17 km (Kirmer *et al.*, 2008) and included small, light, anemochorous seeds (often orchids) or species spread by zoochory. On spoil heaps from coal mines in central Europe, endozoochory was the most important mode of dispersal, with an average input of viable diaspores equal to 0.1 per 1 m^2 during the first year after dumping (K. Prach, unpublished data). Such inocula determined the successional trajectory for several years before anemochorous species prevailed (see also Latzel *et al.*, 2011). The role of zoochory in the early stages of succession on new substrates is often underestimated in favor of anemochory (Martín-Sanz *et al.*, 2015), except in the tropics where the importance of zoochory is widely observed (Chazdon, 2014). Particularly large mine sites may serve as huge traps for seeds moving across a landscape (Kirmer *et al.*, 2008).

The role of surrounding vegetation in determining the course of succession on a set of mines in central Europe is evident from Table 14.1 (Prach *et al.*, 2015). The vegetation types occurring in the surroundings of the studied mine sites had significant effects on the spontaneous vegetation of seral stages. The only exception was wetlands, which only

Table 14.1 *Marginal and partial canonical correspondence analysis effects[+] of main vegetation types, occurring in the surroundings up to 100 m and 1 km, on the species composition of seral stages inside various central European mine sites*

Mine sites	Surroundings	Effects	Synanthropic	Grasslands	Woodlands	Wetlands
Gravel sand pits [36]	100 m	Marg. F	1.39★	2.03★★★	2.26★★★	1.63★★★
		Part. F	1.19★	1.30★★	1.67★★★	1.25★
	1 km	Marg. F	1.40★	2.03★★★	2.58★★★	2.14★★★
		Part. F	1.19★	1.30★★	1.59★★★	1.31★★
Spoil heaps [20]	100 m	Marg. F	1.42★	3.09★	3.15★	N/A[++]
		Part. F	1.46	1.33	1.45	N/A[++]
	1 km	Marg. F	1.30★	1.07	1.36★	1.19
		Part. F	1.12	1.03	1.29	1.12
Extracted peatlands [11]	100 m	Marg. F	2.19★★★	2.01★★★	1.92★★★	2.66★★★
		Part. F	1.73★★	1.97★★	1.62★★★	1.80★★
	1 km	Marg. F	1.94★★★	2.01★★★	1.92★★★	2.59★★
		Part. F	1.80★★★	1.97★★	1.62★★★	1.79★★
Acidic stone quarries [41]	100 m	Marg. F	1.78★	1.31★	2.28★	1.56
		Part. F	1.42	1.08	1.17	1.37
	1 km	Marg. F	1.31★	1.79★	2.03★	1.62
		Part. F	1.19	1.53	1.95	1.48

Number of mines is in brackets. The statistical F values and levels of significance are provided. ★ p<0.05; ★★ p<0.01; ★★★ p<0.001. N/A – not analyzed.

Adapted from Prach *et al.* (2015) with permission.

[+] The marginal effects of environmental variables (the proportion of vegetation types in this case) denote the variability explained by any given environmental variable without considering other environmental variables, whereas partial effects denote the variability explained by a given environmental variable considering the effects of other environmental variables used as covariables (Šmilauer & Lepš, 2014).

[++] No wetlands were present in the close vicinity of the spoil heaps.

affected the course of succession in mined peatlands. Most wetland species can be transported long distances by waterfowl (Krahulec & Lepš, 1994). In addition, some common wetland species, such as cattails (*Typha*) and common reed (*Phragmites australis*) produce light seeds, which are easily wind-dispersed (Grime *et al.*, 1988). Consequently, effects of surrounding vegetation were least pronounced on wetland succession. In addition to the species composition of the surrounding vegetation, the size of a disturbed site and the intensity of propagule pressure also affect succession (Öster *et al.*, 2009; Matsamura & Takeda, 2010; Alday *et al.*, 2011a).

Some people worry that mine sites are reservoirs of alien invasive species or weeds that can potentially invade the surroundings. In fact, the opposite seems to be true: alien species were more frequent in the surroundings than on mine sites in one study (Kabrna *et al.*, 2014). In addition, alien importance dropped during succession, with aliens being unimportant in 70% of late successional stages in our comparative analyses (see Section 14.2.3).

Harsh environments of mine sites often limit successful establishment of species, even if their diaspores reach the site. For example, there are mine sites where no vegetation establishes despite rich diaspore sources nearby (Silva *et al.*, 2013; Le Stradic *et al.*, 2014). On the other hand, when all six late successional species from local steppes were experimentally sown, they established in freshly exposed substrate in a set of central European basalt quarries (Novák & Prach, 2010), indicating that dispersal, not habitat limited succession. Late successional species are generally expected to need some soil development for successful establishment (van der Valk, 1992; Walker & del Moral, 2003). Frouz *et al.* (2008) reported the decisive role of earthworms in changing soil chemistry and structure enabling establishment of late successional species after about 25 years of succession in central European coal mining spoil heaps. To decide what is habitat limitation and what is dispersal limitation is generally difficult without controlled experiments.

Individual species performances are particularly important to successional processes under the harsh site conditions of mine sites. Germination is often precluded in arid regions by low substrate moisture (Alday *et al.*, 2011b), high concentrations of heavy metals, or low pH (Anawar *et al.*, 2013). Even if seedlings survive, older plants can be exposed to many other adverse abiotic or biotic conditions. Despite these limitations, succession approached natural late successional vegetation in 54% of mine studies (see Section 14.2.3).

The most typical sequence of life forms in succession following mining goes from annuals through perennial forbs and grasses toward woody species (in forested biomes). In extreme sites, the stage with annuals can be missing and succession is often initiated directly by perennials (Randelovic *et al.*, 2014) or by cryptogams, which often occupy a broader range of environmental conditions than vascular plants and are generally less sensitive to heavy metal concentrations (Rola *et al.*, 2015). *Sphagnum* mosses dominate late successional stages in restored (formerly) harvested peatlands around the world.

Species functional groups were only rarely studied in post-mining seres, despite their current popularity as a research topic. Gilardelli *et al.* (2016) considered 25 traits of species colonizing limestone quarries and determined that their importance to succession (in decreasing order) were: life form, plant height, presence of thorns, leaf type, start of flowering period, seed dispersal, and seed dispersal distance. Wozniak *et al.* (2011) found in spoil heaps from coal mining that plant height, leaf shape and area, type of root system, seed weight, and photosynthetic pathway, were most important for succession. It is evident that traits connected to competitive ability and dispersal dominate. Some broader analyses across mining sites would be desirable.

Mycorrhizae and various groups of invertebrates affect the course of plant succession in mine sites. Often, initial plant colonists are not obligately mycorrhizal, perhaps because of the unlikelihood of finding a partner on newly exposed substrates (Rydlová & Vosátka, 2001). Close links between vegetation and soil microbial activity have also been reported (Harantová *et al.*, 2017), and activity of soil macrofauna can be pivotal to succession on mine sites (Frouz *et al.*, 2011). Belowground herbivory by wireworms (Coleoptera, Elateridae) negatively affected an early successional, highly competitive grass *Calamagrostis epigejos*, and thus accelerated succession toward a more diverse community on spoil heaps in temperate broadleaf forests in central Europe (Roubíčková *et al.*, 2012). Finally, browsing by large herbivores can modify successional pathways toward grassland or thorny shrubland rather than toward forest.

14.2.3 Patterns within and among Biomes

Woody species usually represent the late successional species in forested biomes, with gymnosperms prevailing in the boreal zone (*Picea*, *Pinus*) and on nutrient poor or drier sites at lower latitude (*Juniperus*, *Pinus*; Fig.14.1). On more mesic sites, broadleaf trees dominate: deciduous trees

(a)

(b)

Figure 14.1 Spoil heaps from coal mining in eastern Germany. a) 10 years old, b) >100 years old. Photos by Karel Prach

in temperate zones (e.g., *Alnus, Acer, Betula, Fagus, Nothofagus, Populus,* and *Quercus*) and the dry tropics (many genera), and evergreen trees (many genera) in warm-temperate and wet tropics. If mine sites are distinctly drier than their surroundings, grasses often form the late successional stages in forested areas (Bagatto & Shorthouse, 1999; Novák & Prach, 2003); grasses are typical late successional dominants in steppes and savannas. In arid biomes, various life forms can dominate late stages. These include annual forbs (e.g., from the Chenopodiaceae family); annual grasses (often introduced); or perennial, vegetatively spreading shrubs (different genera from such families as Asteraceae, Fabaceae, Tamaricaceae, and Zygophyllaceae). Sedges (Cyperaceae, Juncaceae, Restionaceae) are typical dominants on wet mine sites in various biomes. Mine sites can sometimes support a large number of species. For example, Brändle *et al.* (2000) reported 1,069 plant species from 16 unreclaimed large spoil heaps near Leipzig (Germany), which represent about one third of the county flora.

Because mine sites differ so widely, from limestone quarries to harvested peatlands, quantitative comparisons are rare within or among biomes. Prach *et al.* (2013) compared vegetation data from chronosequences in seven types of central European mine sites. The sites included various spoil heaps from coal or uranium (Fig. 14.2) mining, acidic (Plate 23) and basic stone quarries, sand and gravel pits, and harvested peatlands ranging from 1 to 100 years old. The authors concluded that: 1) the seres studied formed a vegetation continuum along a gradient determined by both substrate pH and moisture; successional age was the second important gradient; 2) the seres were more similar in their species composition in the initial stages in which synanthropic generalist species prevailed, than in later successional stages when more non-synanthropic specialists appeared; 3) in most cases, succession led to a forest, which usually established after approximately 20 years. In very dry or wet places, where woody species were limited, open habitats developed; these habitats are often valued for their maintenance of rare plant populations; 4) except in the peatlands, the total number of species and the number of target species increased during succession; 5) participation of invasive alien species was mostly unimportant; and 6) the spontaneous vegetation succession generally appears to be an ecologically suitable and cheap way of ecosystem restoration of the heavily disturbed sites.

More studies exist where one kind of succession was analyzed over a larger geographical gradient. Graf *et al.* (2008) compared 28 harvested peatlands across parts of Canada and the United States and found many similarities. They concluded that water table and residual peat layer were

Figure 14.2 Site of former uranium mine after 30 years of succession.
Photo by L. Šebelíková, with permission

the most important factors driving succession. Similarly, Triisberg *et al.* (2014) compared 64 harvested peatlands over Estonia and also found that the residual peat layer was the most important predictor of succession. In a country-wide analysis of harvested peatlands in the Czech Republic (temperate deciduous forest), Konvalinková and Prach (2014) showed that climate, geographical location, and land cover up to 1 km distant from the mine were the factors explaining the highest proportion of variability in the seral vegetation. In a similar country-wide analysis of 36 sand and gravel pits in the Czech Republic (Řehounková & Prach, 2006), climatic factors, surrounding land cover, local water table, and local substrate pH explained the highest proportion of the vegetation variability. Šebelíková *et al.* (2019) compared succession in spoil heaps from coal mining in three central European countries (Germany, Czech Republic, Hungary) and found that the vegetation developed from synanthropic vegetation through open grasslands to forests, and that macroclimatic factors were most important in determining the exact species composition. In addition to the proximity to reference target vegetation, climatic factors also appeared decisive in a regional study comparing 56 basalt quarries spread over a climatically contrasting area in central Europe (Novák & Prach, 2003). Climatic factors were responsible for divergent succession either to dry shrubby grassland, shrubby forest, or a closed mesic forest (Fig. 14.3).

In our comparative analysis of mine sites (Tables 14.2 and 14.3; for methods see Chapter 4) among all terrestrial biomes, spontaneous succession was successful in 54% of cases, partly successful in 34%, and unsuccessful in 12%. There were statistically significant differences in success of succession among some biomes (Fig. 14.4), especially between biomes at higher versus lower latitudes (Prach & Walker, 2019), though the differences were less evident than for abandoned plowed fields (see Chapter 13). In the Mediterranean biome there were no successful seres recorded. Perhaps the frequent participation of aliens in this biome diverts or arrests succession (Groves & DiCastri, 1991; Pyšek et al., 2017) although dry summers could also have contributed to arresting succession. Unfortunately, we did not have enough records to analyze aridlands and temperate grasslands. The relationship between success and latitude was very distinct (Fig. 14.4). Success was significantly higher in cold and wet biomes, while forested versus not forested biomes did not differ (Table 14.3).

Divergent trajectories were the most abundant pattern in mine sites (Table 14.3). One reason for this pattern may be that mine sites often exhibit high topographic heterogeneity, which can be reinforced with time, thereby inducing divergence. Species richness during succession was more likely to increase than to decrease or display other patterns. Increases in richness are reasonable because of the lack of a biological legacy at the onset of this type of succession (Walker & del Moral, 2003). Invasive alien species were significantly less important in cold than in warm biomes (Table 14.3).

14.3 Theoretical Implications

1. Despite the great variability among mine sites and the severity of the disturbance, spontaneous succession generally proceeds rather effectively toward reestablishment of potential natural or other target vegetation.
2. The probability of recovery of potential natural vegetation or other target vegetation (see Chapter 4) increases with increasing latitude. Recovery is more likely in cold than in warm biomes and in wet than in arid biomes. The former can be explained by the fact that in colder biomes at higher latitudes, the potential natural vegetation consists of

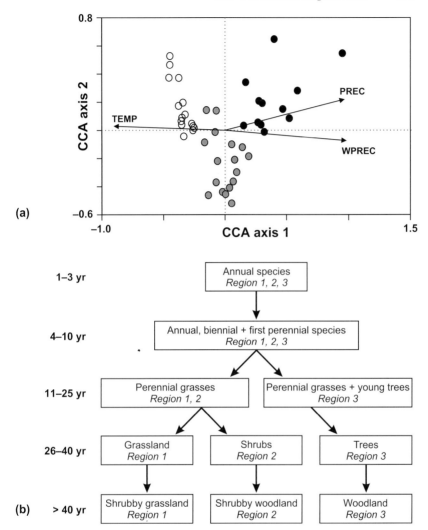

Figure 14.3 (a) CCA ordination biplot of vegetation records from basalt quarries (56) spread over a central European landscape differing largely in climatic conditions. Region 1 – comparably dry (mean annual precipitation 460-500 mm) and warm (mean annual temperature 8.1-9.0 °C), empty symbols; Region 2 – wetter (501-600 mm) and warm (7.6-9.0 °C), gray symbols; Region 3 – wet (601-820 mm) and cold (6.1-7.5 °C), black symbols. TEMP = Mean annual temperature; PREC = Mean annual precipitation; WPREC = Mean winter precipitation. (b) Generalized scheme of divergent succession among the three regions based on the dominance of life forms and physiognomy of vegetation. The arrows refer to expected vegetation based on current (< 40 years) and expected (> 40 years) trends. Adapted from Novák and Prach (2003) with permission from Wiley and Sons

Table 14.2 *Success of succession for mine studies by biomes (no. of seres). For the evaluation of success see Chapter 4.*

Succession successful?	TR	TD	AR	ME	TG	TB	CF	AA	Total
Yes	2	1	0	0	3	26	7	1	40
Partly	3	3	0	5	1	8	4	1	25
No	2	2	1	2	0	1	1	0	9
Total	7	6	1	7	4	35	12	2	74

Biome abbreviations: TR: tropical rain forests; TD: tropical dry forests; AR: aridlands; ME: Mediterranean; TG: temperate grasslands; TB: temperate broadleaf forests; CF: coniferous forests; AA: Arctic-alpine.

lower numbers of species than at lower latitudes, thus the chance that potential natural vegetation establishes is higher than in diverse, low-latitude biomes such as tropical rain forests (neutral model; Hubbell, 2001; see Chapter 16). In drier biomes, establishment of late successional species is probably limited physiologically because mine sites are usually more extreme than the surrounding undisturbed habitats.

3. Species richness usually increases during succession because it starts from "zero" and typically harsh environments often limit competitive exclusion in later stages of succession.

4. Succession is mostly divergent because a few generalists, which occur in initial stages of succession, are gradually substituted by a higher number of specialists, which share various niches available on the diverse topography.

5. Importance of alien species is mostly low in late successional stages, although they can temporarily prevail in initial and early stages of succession. Perennial aliens, which potentially prevail in later stages of succession, can occasionally be competitively superior over native perennials, especially in productive sites (perennial aliens usually require highly productive sites to be successful; Dostál *et al.*, 2013). Because mine sites are naturally unproductive, the chance of aliens to succeed is also low compared to more fertile sites such as abandoned plowed fields (see Chapter 13).

14.4 Practical Implications

For successful implementation of the modern approaches to restoration of mine sites, we offer the following suggestions. For more details, see Řehounková *et al.* (2012) and Prach (2015).

Table 14.3 *Number of mine sites studies (N = 73; seres described = 74) sorted by various criteria: Warm (TR, TD, AR, ME), Cold (TG, TB, CF, AA), Dry (TD, AR, ME, TG), Wet (TR, TB, CF, AA), Forested (TR, TD, ME, TB, CF), Not forested (AR, TG, AA)*

		Warm	Cold	Dry	Wet	Forested	Not forested	All biomes (no.)	All biomes (%)
Succession successful? (74)	Yes	3	37	4	36	36	4	40	54
	Partly	11	14	9	16	23	2	25	34
	No	7	2	5	4	8	1	9	12
	Differences	★★★		★★★		NS			
Trajectory (28)	Converge	0	3	0	3	3	0	3	11
	Diverge	4	12	5	11	14	2	16	57
	Variable	1	8	2	7	8	1	9	32
	Differences	NS		NS		NS			
Species richness (36)	Increase	10	17	9	18	22	5	27	75
	Decrease	0	1	0	1	1	0	1	3
	Variable	1	7	2	6	7	1	8	22
	Differences	NS		NS		NS			
Invasive species important? (50)	Yes	1	0	0	1	1	0	1	2
	Partly	3	11	3	11	12	2	14	28
	No	2	33	4	31	31	4	35	70
	Differences	★★		NS		NS			

Sample sizes for each successional trait are in parentheses.

For biome abbreviations see Table 14.2.

Differences among the groups of biomes were tested using χ^2 test for non-ordered variables, and Cochran–Armitage test for ordered variables: ★★★ p < 0.001; ★★ p < 0.01; NS not significant.

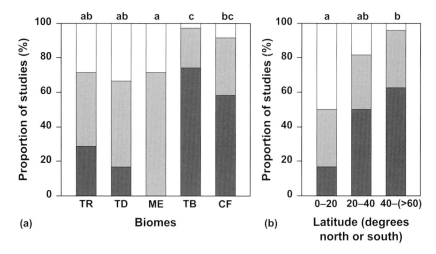

Figure 14.4 Success of succession in mine sites by a) terrestrial biomes and b) latitude (% of seres). Black: successful, light gray: partly successful, white: not successful. TR: tropical rain forests, TD: tropical dry forests, ME: Mediterranean, TB: temperate broadleaf forests, CF: coniferous forests. For sample sizes, see Table 14.2. The asymptotic generalized Pearson's χ^2 test with post-hoc test was a) $\chi^2 = 20.524$; df = 4; p-value < 0.001, and b) $\chi^2 = 10.152$, df = 2, p = 0.006. Different small case letters indicate statistically significant differences.
Adapted from Prach and Walker (2019) with permission from Blackwell

1. Reduce the extent of technical reclamation and include more spontaneous or slightly assisted succession (e.g., by eradication of invasive alien species) in restoration schemes because sites disturbed by mining often have the potential to be restored spontaneously.
2. It is important to form and preserve a heterogeneous surface during mining (high substrate diversity implies high biodiversity). Depressions enable the formation of potentially high-value wetlands, including shallow aquatic habitats, while elevated terrain and south- or north-facing slopes (in the Northern or Southern Hemisphere, respectively) provide suitable habitats for species of dry habitats.
3. In the case of technical afforestation, it is important to maintain the heterogeneous surface and not to drain the wetlands.
4. Nutrient-rich topsoil should generally be removed from the mine sites and not returned. When nutrient-rich topsoil is returned back to a mine site, or other nutrient rich substances are used, only a few competitively strong, often invasive species are typically supported,

and biodiversity generally decreases. Only extreme sites (highly acidic, dry, and toxic or particularly infertile) represent exceptions.

5. Prior to mining, it is important to conduct a biological inventory of the locality, both in the mine area and its surroundings. It is desirable to direct mining in a way that maintains as much natural habitat as possible in the immediate vicinity, which is the source of most colonizing species.

6. Restoration plans and an environmental impact assessment should be prepared by specialists who are aware of recent findings in the field of restoration ecology, and with the possibilities and limitations of mining technologies.

7. A mine should be monitored even during the mining process, which can reveal the presence of endangered species and communities as well as valuable geological and geomorphological phenomena. Mining should be modified accordingly if it is technically and economically feasible.

8. If endangered species and communities occur on the post-mining site, proper management should be applied to maintain them. Costs for such management could be paid from the funds of mining companies dedicated to reclamation or public funds dedicated to nature conservation. The most valuable mine sites should be designated as nature reserves.

9. Invasive species should be monitored before, during, and after the mining process. If these species represent a serious potential threat to successful restoration, they should be eradicated using the same financial sources as mentioned in the previous point.

10. It is possible to dedicate some spontaneously overgrown mine sites to surface-disturbing human activities, such as motocross or paintball. The irregularly and locally disturbed surface usually supports biodiversity. These conclusions should be promoted among technically oriented people, decision makers, public and politicians, because technical approaches (i.e., reclamation) are still the option typically preferred by law makers. Technical approaches are expensive, but often unnecessary and can even be detrimental to wildlife.

11. Finally, in one public survey concerning mine sites (Sklenička & Molnárová, 2010), people who saw photographs of late successional spontaneous sites, and artificially afforested and agriculturally reclaimed spoil heaps from coal mining in the Czech Republic clearly preferred spontaneous sites.

14.5 Conclusions

Mining occurs in all biomes, making it a suitable disturbance for comparative studies. However, in some biomes (aridlands, temperate grasslands) we still lack sufficient information on the course of succession. Nevertheless, as with many other types of seres, climate, available moisture, substrate pH, nutrient availability, and land use in the surrounding landscape are the factors that most influence succession. Probability of success (achieving potential natural or other target vegetation) clearly increases with latitude. Participation of aliens is surprisingly low in later stages of succession, an observation that supports using spontaneous succession as a way to restore mine sites. These generalizations reflect average trends and many exceptions occur, depending on local conditions. Unless mining destroys valuable sites with high natural, historical, or aesthetic value, it may even increase (under certain conditions) biodiversity and spatial heterogeneity of a landscape, but only if technical reclamation is avoided and spontaneous processes are allowed. The conclusions above can be applied to a certain degree to other human-disturbed sites.

15 · *Other Disturbances*

15.1 Introduction

In Chapters 5–14, we discussed 10 widely distributed disturbances and compared successional processes among biomes following each disturbance. We chose disturbances that had been sufficiently studied to permit an analysis of the scientific literature at a global scale. We kept our categories of disturbance as broad as possible to incorporate many related studies. For example, under volcanoes, we included lava, tephra, pyroclastic flows, debris avalanches, and lahars. Under landslides we included slides, flows, and falls of rock, regolith, and sediments. Under mines we included extraction of coal, rock, peat, sand, and the waste piles from these extractions. Yet the complexity of disturbances and their myriad interactions make any categorization somewhat arbitrary and incomplete: arbitrary because one could argue for different categories (e.g., we divided wind damage into dunes and cyclones but pooled all volcanic disturbances and pooled all fire-damaged ecosystems); incomplete because certain disturbances are inevitably left out. For example, under cyclones we did not address individual tree falls; under floods we focused on rivers but did not address flood zones of ocean beaches, lakeshores, or reservoirs; under fire we largely ignored low-intensity fires; while under clearcuts we did not address selective cutting or treatments followed by planting or seeding. Thus, our focus has been on disturbances that were illustrative of general successional principles without attempting a comprehensive review of all terrestrial disturbances.

For our global analyses, we did not include disturbances that were too rare or localized (e.g., the site of the former "iron curtain" separating European countries until 1989), too habitat specific (e.g., railway banks and roadsides), or too intertwined with other disturbances to have a clean identity and allow interpretation of spontaneous succession (e.g., we avoided succession in clearcuts that were extensively manipulated). Such disturbances might also not provide a clear starting point for succession, perhaps because of the complexities of changing land uses. Prach *et al.* (2014d) compared succession following such rare and habitat-specific disturbances with succession following more common disturbances and concluded that sere identity was less important in determining successional patterns than were broader categories of abiotic factors and time.

In this chapter, we briefly discuss succession following a sampling of disturbances not considered in previous chapters. These disturbances are widespread, should not be ignored, and yet often do not provide a clear successional pathway. Following the structure of previous chapters, we order these disturbances approximately by increasing human influence: tree fall gaps, shorelines, animals, silviculture, and agriculture (other than plowed fields). We do not, however, attempt any comparative analysis of successional traits (success of succession, trajectories, species richness patterns, role of invasive alien species) from individual studies as done in previous chapters. We end by mentioning additional miscellaneous disturbances that can affect succession.

15.2 Tree Fall Gaps

In Chapter 7, we focused on large-scale wind damage caused by cyclones. However, localized windstorms often cause one or more trees to fall. The gaps thereby created in a forest can undergo succession, provided that there is not simply an expansion of neighboring tree crowns or resprouting from broken limbs to fill the gap. Although small, these gaps are of cumulative importance for understory and pioneer plants, particularly when there are increases in light, moisture, and nutrients previously utilized by the downed trees (Webb, 1999). Frequent benefactors of tree fall gaps are shade-tolerant understory plants, previously suppressed by the canopy (Chazdon, 2014). The ascension into the canopy of this cohort is sometimes called advance regeneration (Martínez-Ramos & Soto-Castro, 1993) and can accelerate successional replacement of canopy species, particularly if shade-intolerant pioneer trees are selectively removed by the wind (Lorimer, 1980). Where wind-tolerant understory plants form dense, thickets, they can inhibit tree regeneration and succession (e.g., bamboo; Yamamoto, 1995). Another scenario occurs when shade-intolerant plants benefit from a tree fall gap. These plants can exist as suppressed seedlings in the understory, emerge from seed banks in the newly warmed soils that have been exposed to altered wavelengths that can trigger germination, or arrive by seed dispersal from nearby habitats where pioneer species dominate. Bare soil or root surfaces, such as that found in tip up pits and mounds formed where trees have fallen over provide opportunities for colonization on the forest floor (Plotkin *et al.*, 2017). Succession in tree fall gaps is therefore primarily affected by plant responses to shade (Lienard *et al.*, 2015), but also by other plant traits (e.g., regeneration strategies) and physical variables (e.g., soil conditions). Repeated gap formation helps maintain species diversity in forested biomes (Coates & Burton, 1997; Terborgh *et al.*, 2017).

15.3 Shorelines

In Chapter 10 on floods, we focused on riverbanks, but succession also can occur when there is a directional shift in water line on shorelines of oceans, lakes, reservoirs (Plate 24), and on newly exposed land following reservoir drainage, such as when dams are removed (Plate 25). Glacial rebound is one causal factor. The melting of glaciers from land masses in the Northern Hemisphere at the end of the last ice age (ca. 15,000–10,000 years ago) led to extensive land uplift. This geological process has strongly influenced succession, from the revegetation of forests on old bogs to the creation of new land from submerged water. The latter is prominent in the Bay of Bothnia where succession has been observed (Laine *et al.*, 2018). Regulation of water levels in reservoirs creates another opportunity for succession to occur. The so-called drawdown area provides a moist but drying surface, ideal for colonization by riparian plants. Succession often proceeds until the reservoir is filled again. Succession following dam removals is influenced by site moisture and substrate texture (Prach *et al.*, 2019), and the dynamics of dispersal and flow dynamics until regular riparian floodplain processes return (Shafroth *et al.*, 2002).

15.4 Animals

Animals, both wild and domestic, modify their habitats in ways that often trigger a loss of biomass, directly through activities such as herbivory, and indirectly through habitat modification (e.g., by trampling or the addition of manure). Intensive habitat modification has been called ecosystem engineering and a dramatic example is the effect of beavers. Beavers create ponds that change entire drainages and selectively fell and remove *Populus, Salix*, and other favored trees from adjacent forests for dam construction and for food. This selective culling can alter forest succession (Naiman & Roger, 1997). Other vertebrate herbivores such as deer and elk also influence succession. Exclusion of deer over decadal time frames in New Zealand led to changes in soil characteristics that then affected plant species replacements (Kardol *et al.*, 2014) and riparian communities in Yellowstone National Park (Wyoming, USA) are recovering since the reintroduction of wolves to control elk populations (Beschta & Ripple, 2016). Bardgett and Wardle (2003) suggested that herbivores (of leaves and roots) delay succession in fertile conditions and accelerate it in infertile conditions. Mammals are not the only influential herbivores. Insect herbivory is omnipresent and most dramatically affects succession during insect outbreaks, particularly when it alters the competitive balance between pioneers and later successional species (Walker, 2012). We briefly address the role of insect herbivory in succession in Chapter 7 (debris and tannin effects), Chapter 9 (continentality effects on plant-insect coevolution), and Chapter 12 (salvage logging). Finally, burrowing, root herbivory, and other activities by animals can directly affect plant species composition and indirectly affect succession by altering soil structure, aeration, and nutrients (Hastings *et al.*, 2007). Very little is known about the undoubtedly important influence of soil invertebrates on the course of succession (Frouz *et al.*, 2008).

15.5 Silviculture

In traditional forestry, following clearcutting, desired tree species are planted or occasionally seeded to provide future timber (Nyland, 2016). However, spontaneous succession always interferes with and often dominates silvicultural activities. Then the successional development may be close to that described in Chapter 12 on clearcuts. If species are planted that represent dominants of a potential natural vegetation, planting accelerates succession, although the forest that develops is usually more homogenous than one that would develop spontaneously. However, dense, homogeneous canopies can also develop spontaneously when dominant species establish following extensive seed rain or resprouting. Silvicultural thinning can resemble natural thinning due to competition if clearings are left to spontaneous succession. Šebelíková *et al.* (2016) compared spontaneously developed and planted pine forests in disused sand pits and concluded that in early and mid-successional stages, plantations were very species poor compared to spontaneously developed vegetation, but they gradually converged in forest structure in late succession. There is an extensive literature on vegetation development under silvicultural management but it is only loosely linked to succession and therefore beyond the scope of this book.

15.6 Agriculture

Succession following the abandonment of hay meadows, pastures, orchards, or vineyards may partially resemble succession on abandoned plowed fields (see Chapter 12). Woody plant encroachment is generally rapid in sufficiently mesic geographical areas where wooded biomes represent the main vegetation, provided that a preexisting herb layer or dense leaf litter does not inhibit it (Gibson, 2009). Succession on meadows or pastures may also differ substantially from succession on recently plowed fields because of the greater legacy of plants and intact soils in the meadows. For example, in the Amazonian rainforest, resprouting of fast-growing *Vismia* trees in abandoned pastures arrested natural forest succession for several decades compared to succession in otherwise undisturbed clearcuts (Wieland *et al.*, 2011). In contrast, succession was rapid (8–15 years) following abandonment of a vineyard in Mediterranean vegetation in Israel, with species composition stabilizing within three decades and determined by bird dispersal (Ne'eman & Izhaki, 1996). Degraded, abandoned hay meadows or pastures can be returned back to their former use, either for economic or restoration reasons. Then, succession also occurs but can be seen as only a regeneration of a previous stage. The complexity of post-agricultural seres is closely tied to the local site conditions, including soil structure and nutrients, plant seed and seedling banks, and potential dispersers from the surrounding vegetation. Human activities usually interfere.

15.7 Miscellaneous Disturbances

There are a number of miscellaneous disturbances, generally associated with human activities, which are not included in earlier sections. Industrial accidents and wastes are important triggers for succession, occasionally creating ghost towns. Nuclear power plants accidents are very disruptive. Following the failure of the Chernobyl plant in Ukraine in 1986, a formerly maintained urban forest has overgrown the streets and changed in structure and composition. Shade tolerance is now the most important factor in determining species tolerance to that environment, not radiation (Laćan *et al.*, 2015). In addition, reduced recruitment of fruit trees reliant on insect pollination and birds for fruit dispersal have been linked to radiation damage to animal populations at Chernobyl

Figure 15.1 Abandoned village after ca. 70 years. The border area between Czech
Republic and Germany.
Photo by Karel Prach

(Møller *et al.*, 2012). Other causes of ghost towns include overexploitation of resources (e.g., water or soil fertility; Diamond, 2005), collapse of
an industry (e.g., mines; see Chapter 14), or establishment or abandonment of a military base (Fig. 15.1). Landfills also offer opportunities for
colonizing species, although they are sometimes repurposed through
technical reclamation (Rebele & Lehmann, 2002). Indeed, any demol-
ished building or abandoned structure can undergo succession.

Transportation corridors, including roads, railways, power line right-
of-ways, and pipelines often undergo succession. Abandoned roads
(Fig. 15.2 and Plate 26) provide an opportunity to study succession and
are found around the world (Formann *et al.*, 2003). In the sub-tropical
rain forest of Puerto Rico, sediment erosion onto abandoned paved roads
accelerated succession and tree roots broke through the pavement at
about 25 years, with subsequent rapid recovery of the forest (Lugo &
Heartsill Scalley, 2014). In Costa Rican rainforests, colonists of unpaved
logging roads abandoned for 17 years were more diverse on the edges
than in the compacted centers of the roads, which were dominated by a

Figure 15.2 Spontaneously re-vegetated road banks after ca. 8 years, central Europe. Photo by Karel Prach

few good competitors (Guariguata & Dupuy, 1997) with projected long-term consequences to forest flora and fauna. In the Mojave Desert, abandoned dirt tracks differed in their successional recovery from bulldozed dirt roads (Bolling & Walker, 2000). Abandoned railway tracks and even entire railway stations can undergo succession. For example, one of the most important Berlin railway stations was closed due to its location close to the former Berlin Wall. Now, it is one of the most natural areas in central Berlin and is protected as a nature reserve. Additional examples include abandoned structures such as outdoor amphitheaters (Plate 27) and a military tank (Plate 28). Concern about succession on such anthropogenic disturbances increases as we continually expand our human footprint at the same time that resources are decreasing.

It is clear that disturbances inherently vary with the local site factors, so our initial 10 disturbances (Chapters 5–14) and the additional ones covered in this chapter are broad categories of that variation. In addition, succession is a highly variable process and is not triggered by every disturbance. Conditions have to be appropriate for sequential invasions of colonists and development and replacement of plant communities. These preconditions suppose a certain degree of environmental stability, which is not always guaranteed, particularly with increases in the frequency and severity of disturbances. Furthermore, successional dynamics have to be detectable and measurable with our current tools, which are still not particularly helpful with soil microbial populations, for example. In Chapter 16, we synthesize the data we have collected about succession following multiple disturbances and provide a global perspective on key topics in disturbance ecology and succession.

Part III
Synthesis

16 · *Synthesis*

16.1 Themes

In this chapter we have three themes. First, we synthesize the disturbance-specific Chapters 5–15 from Part II, examining general trends in succession among biomes, disturbances, and latitude. We summarize results from the success of succession, successional trajectories, changes in species richness, and participation of invasive alien species (Section 16.2). Second, we highlight recent advances in ecological topics that we suggest will provide a framework for future studies of succession: disturbance, temporal and spatial scales, functional traits, and predictability (Sections 16.3–16.7), we introduced these topics in Chapter 2 and now revisit them in the context of the detailed analyses of succession presented in Part II. Finally, we clarify the immediate practical relevance of successional studies through their close links to conservation and restoration (Sections 16.8 and 16.9). Section 16.9 includes subsections on stress-productivity gradients, the importance of early successional stages, and landscape and global contexts. We emphasize the reciprocal information flow between succession and conservation and restoration that will be needed to address the rapid changes occurring in our world.

16.2 Global Trends in Succession

Summarized data from our comparative analyses of 530 seres across 8 biomes and 10 types of disturbances are presented in Tables 16.1–16.3. We obtained the highest number of studies from temperate broadleaf forests (31%), followed by studies from coniferous forests (17%), tropical rain forests (14%), and Mediterranean ecosystems (12%). The lowest number of studies originated from tropical dry forests (5%) and aridlands (4%). These proportions reflect the relative intensity of study so it would be desirable in the future to focus more studies on tropical dry forests and aridlands.

Table 16.1 *Trends in succession among biomes (all disturbances combined)*

Biome	Total (No. of seres)	Succession successful (No. of seres)	Succession partly successful (No. of seres)	Succession unsuccessful (No. of seres)	Most frequent trajectory	Most frequent trend in species richness	Invasive aliens unimportant (%)
Tropical rain forests	72	19	43	10	Divergence	Increase	36
Tropical dry forests	28	10	15	3	Variable	Increase	63
Aridlands	22	12	9	1	Convergence	Increase	75
Mediterranean	63	35	20	8	Divergence	Decrease	79
Temperate grasslands	33	24	5	4	Divergence	Increase	64
Temperate broadleaf forests	163	107	47	9	Divergence	Increase	74
Coniferous forests	110	85	24	1	Divergence Convergence	Increase	89
Arctic-alpine	39	24	14	1	Divergence	Increase	97
Total	**530**	**316**	**177**	**37**	**Divergence**	**Increase**	**76**

Table 16.2 *Trends in succession among disturbance types (all biomes combined; percent of selected studies or mode of categorical data)*

Disturbance	Total (No. of seres)	Succession successful (No. of seres)	Succession partly successful (No. of seres)	Succession unsuccessful (No. of seres)	Most frequent trajectory	Most frequent trend in species richness	Invasive aliens not important (percent of seres)
Volcanoes	36	12	23	1	Divergence	Increase	66
Glaciers	25	16	9	0	Convergence	Increase	100
Cyclones	21	10	10	1	Convergence	Variable	72
Dunes	39	21	15	3	Divergence	Increase	66
Landslides	46	27	16	3	Divergence	Increase	89
Floods	48	34	13	1	Divergence	Increase	70
Fire	83	69	12	2	Variable	Decrease	83
Clearcuts	65	40	21	4	Convergence	Increase	94
Plowed fields	93	47	33	13	Divergence	Increase	58
Mines	74	40	25	9	Divergence	Increase	70
Total	**530**	**316**	**177**	**37**	**Divergence**	**Increase**	**76**

Natural disturbances are in bold font, partly natural ones in normal font, and anthropogenic ones in italics.

Table 16.3 *Number of studies among biomes (out of total 530) sorted by various criteria: Warm (TR, TD, AR, ME), Cold (TG, TB, CF, AA), Dry (TD, AR, ME, TG), Wet (TR, TB, CF, AA), Forested (TR, TD, ME, TB, CF), Not forested (AR, TG, AA)*

Successional trait		Warm	Cold	Dry	Wet	Forested	Not forested	All biomes (No.)	All biomes (%)
Succession successful? (530)	Yes	76	240	80	236	258	58	316	60
	Partly	87	90	48	129	149	28	177	33
	No	22	15	15	22	31	6	37	7
	Differences	★★★		NS		NS			
Trajectory (198)	Converge	13	45	13	45	39	19	58	29
	Diverge	28	63	14	77	75	16	91	46
	Variable	18	31	14	35	43	6	49	25
	Differences	NS		NS		★			
Species richness (280)	Increase	51	100	38	113	115	36	151	54
	Decrease	27	27	30	24	49	5	54	19
	Variable	27	48	15	60	59	16	75	27
	Differences	NS		★★★		NS			
Invasive species important? (355)	Yes	12	9	8	13	19	2	21	6
	Partly	21	44	17	48	56	9	65	18
	No	61	208	59	210	204	65	269	76
	Differences	★★★		NS		★			

Sample sizes used for each successional trait are in parentheses.

Biome abbreviations – TR: tropical rain forests, TD: tropical dry forests, AR: aridlands, ME: Mediterranean, TG: temperate grasslands, TB: temperate broadleaf forests, CF: coniferous forests, AA: Arctic-alpine.

X^2 test was used for non-ordered variables, Cochran-Armitage test was used for ordered variables: ★★★ $p < 0.001$; ★ $p < 0.05$; NS: not significant.

16.2.1 Success of Succession

In this section, we consider the success of succession (i.e., reaching potential natural vegetation or other targets by spontaneous succession) across particular biomes, groups of biomes, types of disturbances, and latitude. Success differed significantly among biomes (Fig. 16.1a and Table 16.1). Generally, success increased from biomes at lower latitude toward biomes at higher latitudes with a slight decrease at the most extreme tundra and alpine biomes. We did not have many data from the tundra biome (except retreating glaciers; see Chapter 6) so tundra was merged with the comparable alpine biome. Despite the extreme environmental conditions in these two biomes, succession was always successful or partly successful (but slow to develop potential natural vegetation). When we grouped biomes by various criteria, we found succession more successful in cold than in warm biomes (suggesting the importance of temperature and latitude), but no differences between wet and dry or forested and not forested biomes (Table 16.3).

Biome differences in success of succession were found in 6 of the 10 disturbance types (landslides, floods, fire, clearcuts, plowed fields, and mines) but not in the other 4 (volcanoes, glaciers, cyclones, dunes; see the relevant figures in Chapters 5–14). The differences correlated with latitude for floods, clearcuts, plowed fields, and mines, while success on landslides was highest at mid latitudes and success after fire was highest in fire-adapted biomes (Mediterranean ecosystems, temperate grasslands, and coniferous forests). Nonsignificant latitudinal tendencies were apparent for volcanoes and dunes. Overall, success increased with latitude when all biomes were compared (Fig. 16.1a). We must stress here that all the conclusions are based on the studies we used and represent average trends.

The 10 types of disturbances also differed significantly in success of succession (Fig. 16.1b). The most successful was succession after fire, followed by floods and glaciers. The highest proportion of unsuccessful cases was recorded in plowed fields and mines, both representing anthropogenic disturbances. No unsuccessful case was recorded among glaciers. Our results suggest that succession is most successful following disturbances to which ecosystems are well adapted, that is, plants have developed compatible strategies during their evolution. Fire, glaciers, and floods have existed for a long time, while plowed fields and mining represent recent, human initiated disturbances. When we compared the success between natural (volcanoes, glaciers, cyclones), partly natural

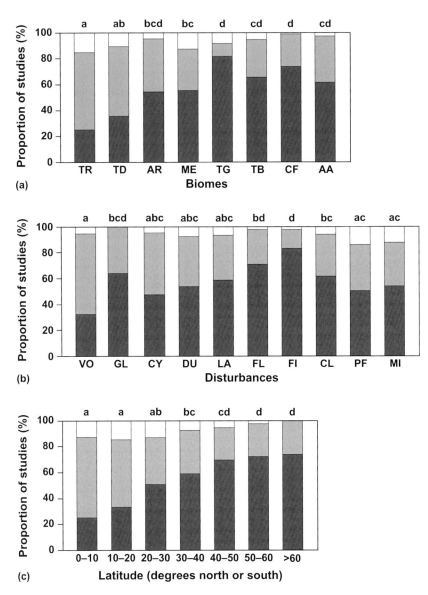

Figure 16.1 Success of succession (% of studies) among (a) terrestrial biomes, (b) types of disturbances, and (c) latitude. Black: successful, light gray: partly successful, white: not successful. Biome abbreviations: TR: tropical rain forests; TD: tropical dry forests; AR: aridlands; ME: Mediterranean; TG: temperate grasslands; TB: temperate broadleaf forests; CF: coniferous forests; AA: Arctic and alpine. Disturbance abbreviations: VO: volcanoes; GL: glaciers; CY: cyclones; DU: dunes; LA: landslides; FL: floods; FI: fire; CL: clearcuts; PF: plowed fields; MI: mines. For sample sizes see Table 16.1 (biomes) and Table 16.2 (disturbances). The asymptotic generalized Pearson's χ^2 test with post-hoc test was for (a) $\chi^2 = 58.6$, df = 7, p < 0.001; for (b) $\chi^2 = 36.20$, df = 9, p < 0.001; and for (c) $\chi^2 = 48.66$, df = 6, p < 0.001. Different letters indicate significant differences among categories.

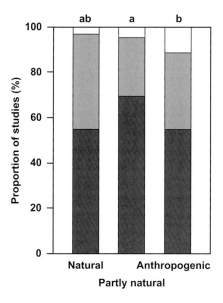

Figure 16.2 Success of succession among three groups of disturbances (% of studies), Natural, Partly natural, and Anthropogenic. Black: successful, gray: partly successful, white: not successful. The asymptotic generalized Pearson's χ^2 test with post-hoc test was $\chi^2 = 11.32$, df = 2, p < 0.01. Different letters indicate significant difference among disturbance groups.

(dunes, landslides, floods, fire), and anthropogenic (clearcuts, plowed fields, mines) disturbances, succession following anthropogenic disturbances was significantly less successful than following partly natural ones, but there was no significant difference between anthropogenic and natural disturbances (Fig. 16.2).

The data summarized across all biomes and disturbances provide a clear, highly significant pattern of increasing success of succession with increasing latitude in 10 degree increments north and south (Fig. 16.1c). This latitudinal trend was evident when we calculated an average success of succession (using the ordinal values: unsuccessful = 0, partly successful = 0.5, and successful = 1) across all disturbances (Fig. 16.3). This figure can be used to indicate the probability of reaching the target vegetation (usually the same as potential natural vegetation) at different latitudes. We suggest that at low latitudes (e.g., tropical rain forests), although favorable climatic conditions favor the rapid growth of plants and an early formation of woody vegetation (Whitmore, 1998), potential natural vegetation represents a higher number of species than it does at

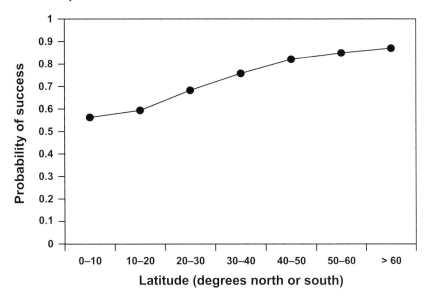

Figure 16.3 Average probability that succession reaches a target (usually potential natural vegetation) versus latitude. The probability was calculated across all disturbances as an average success of succession based on the ordinal values: unsuccessful = 0, partly successful = 0.5, and successful = 1. This graph was used for construction of Fig. 17.1.

higher latitudes (e.g., boreal coniferous forests). Therefore, early colonists at low latitudes are not as likely to represent a trajectory toward potential natural vegetation as are colonists in higher latitude ecosystems with less rapid recolonization but fewer species overall (Shugart *et al.*, 1992; Archibold, 1995). Species richness is generally known to decrease with latitude (see Fig. 3.7; Willig, 2003). Hubbell's (2001) neutral theory fits well as a general explanation of the pattern of increasing probability of success of succession with latitude resulting from the corresponding decrease in number of species. Moreover, invasive alien species are more likely to arrest or divert succession at low than at high latitudes (see Section 16.2.4). We also found a significant negative (GLM, $p < 0.01$) relationship between success and mean annual temperature, which is not surprising because temperature is correlated with latitude. By contrast, mean annual precipitation, and the interaction of temperature and precipitation were not significant (the possible role of evapotranspiration was not tested). Generally, climatic factors seemed to be less important than species pools in determining the success of succession.

We are aware of some necessary subjectivity in our evaluation of the success of succession (see Chapter 4). Other analyses might produce variable proportions of our categories of success, but we suggest that the trends would remain the same because of the high number of studies (N = 530). Therefore, we argue that our conclusion is robust that there is an increasing probability with increasing latitude that succession is likely to approach its target within ca. 100 years.

16.2.2 Trajectories

The type of trajectory implies predictability of succession: convergent trajectories are more predictable than divergent ones (Lepš & Rejmánek, 1991; Walker et al., 2010b). In our analysis of 198 seres, there were significant differences among some biomes in the type of trajectory (Fig. 16.4a) despite the fact that the overall test was not significant. Divergent trajectories prevailed (46%), while there were fewer convergent (29%) and variable (25%) trajectories. Variable trajectories included parallel and network types or occasionally cyclic or arrested types. Divergence was the most common trajectory in tropical rain forests while convergence prevailed only in aridlands. These patterns can be related to the number of species potentially composing late successional stages (or the respective potential natural vegetation), which is much higher in tropical rain forests than in aridlands (Archibold, 1995) with few potential dominants. The strength of our conclusions is limited by the low number of studies that noted trajectory patterns, especially from aridlands (N = 8). Considering groups of biomes, there were no significant differences between warm and cold or between dry and wet biomes. Trajectories in biomes that are not forested were significantly more likely to converge than in forested biomes (Table 16.3), probably because the not forested biomes (e.g., tundra, grasslands) were more homogeneous in species composition. Among disturbances, convergence prevailed for glaciers, cyclones, and clearcuts; variable trajectories prevailed for fire; and divergence prevailed in the remaining six disturbances (Fig. 16.4b). Deglaciated areas usually occur in rather uniform surrounding tundra (or alpine ecosystems) and the initial environmental heterogeneity just after deglaciation is gradually ameliorated by substrate stabilization and weathering (Matthews, 1992), thus supporting convergence. Cyclones, clearcuts, and fire (to some degree) usually impose environmental and vegetation heterogeneity onto rather homogenous forests (especially boreal coniferous forests), which gradually disappears when a disturbed

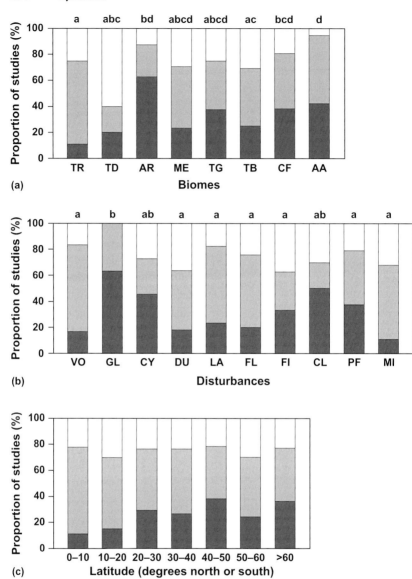

Figure 16.4 Type of successional trajectory (% of studies) among (a) terrestrial biomes, (b) disturbances, and (c) latitude. Black: convergence, light gray: divergence, white: variable (e.g., parallel, network, cyclic, or arrested). For biome and disturbance abbreviations see Fig. 16.1. For sample sizes see Table 16.1 (biomes) and Table 16.2 (disturbances). The asymptotic generalized Pearson's χ^2 test with post-hoc test was for (a) $\chi^2 = 85.253$, df = 18, p = 0.099 (NS); for (b) $\chi^2 = 19.976$, df = 9, p < 0.05; and (c) was $\chi^2 = 7.657$, df = 12, p = 0.811 (NS). Different letters indicate significant differences among categories.

site blends with its surroundings, supporting convergence. The relationship between types of trajectory and latitude were not statistically significant, although convergence tended to increase and divergence decrease with increasing latitude (Fig. 16.4c). These trends match our expectations. At lower latitudes with high number of species composing the potential natural vegetation, we would expect divergence to dominate, while at high latitudes, low numbers of potential natural vegetation species would suggest a predominance of convergent trajectories.

Detailed interpretation of the divergent or convergent status of succession is more complicated. One expectation is that the composition of vegetation in the initial stages of succession is largely determined by stochastic forces, while in later stages more determinism could be involved (Walker & del Moral, 2003); this scenario supports convergence (del Moral, 2009). However, species in the early stages of succession are usually generalists with broad ecological amplitudes and in the late stages species are usually more specialized (Grime, 2002), supporting divergence. Obviously, the extent to which succession is divergent or convergent depends on the participating species, spatial and temporal scales considered, differences in local site conditions, and landscape heterogeneity. In a 30-year study of plowed fields in Minnesota, for example, Clark *et al.* (2019) found that divergence was reliably due to contingent factors such as species traits and soil fertility rather than stochastic factors. In general, if contrasting habitats are located in the same or a similar landscape, convergence is expected. If similar habitats are located in contrasting landscapes, divergence is expected (Prach *et al.*, 2014c). This generalization is in accordance with conclusions of several previous studies on divergence versus convergence during succession (Lepš & Rejmánek, 1991; del Moral, 2009; Walker *et al.*, 2010b; Chang *et al.*, 2019). Consequently, it is easier to predict succession in a uniform than a heterogeneous landscape, unless unusual (e.g., toxic) substrates are exposed.

16.2.3 Species Richness

Species richness is a commonly measured characteristic of vegetation and the presence of many species generally indicates an established vegetation. However, a simple total number of species may not always indicate that a natural vegetation is establishing in a disturbed site. Instead, it is generally better to quantify the number of target species (van Andel & Aronson, 2012), but such data were not typically available to us so we used the total number of species. Despite this limitation, trends in the total species number indicate how succession proceeds. Species numbers increased in a majority (54%) of the 280 studies in our analyses that documented change in species richness, followed by 27% with variable richness patterns (mostly unimodal, an inverted U-shaped pattern), and 19% where richness decreased during succession. We did not consider interannual fluctuations in richness but evaluated overall trends (see Chapter 4). Increases in species richness prevailed in all biomes except the Mediterranean, where richness was most likely to decrease during succession (Fig. 16.5a). This biome is well adapted to fire and a large pool of species adapted to burned environments establishes immediately following a fire (or disturbances with similar consequences). Gradually, the species disappear under a closing canopy of resident woody species (Di Castri *et al.*, 1981). Similar situations may occur in other biomes such as coniferous forests (Johnson, 1995) and grassland ecosystems (Collins & Wallace, 1990), both of which had substantial numbers of seres with decreases in richness. No cases of decreases were recorded for the Arctic-alpine biome. Under these rather extreme environments, succession often proceeds as a slow increase of new species without competitive exclusion of earlier colonists (Svoboda & Henry, 1987; see Chapter 6) so species richness increases. When competitive exclusion appears in later stages, and site conditions become less extreme, unimodal patterns often occur (Doležal *et al.*, 2008). When we compare the groups of biomes (Table 16.3), the only significant difference was an increase in richness in wet versus dry biomes. We explain this by the influence of the frequently studied Mediterranean biome (dry with decreasing richness) described in the preceding text. Decreases in richness can also occur in wet environments when there is competitive exclusion.

Among the types of disturbances, species richness mostly increased during succession (Fig. 16.5b). Decreases in richness prevailed in succession only in the case of fire. This result can be explained by the large pool of species adapted to fire that establish immediately following a fire, as previously noted for the Mediterranean biome. Variable patterns prevailed among seres following cyclones but there were only a few studies of cyclones that mentioned richness (N = 10; see Chapter 7), making it difficult to interpret the results. Increase of species richness during succession was more frequent in primary seres, which start from bare ground and lack an initial seed bank (VO, GL, MI), than in secondary seres.

There were significant differences between trends in species richness and latitude (Fig. 16.5c). At the lowest latitudes no decrease in

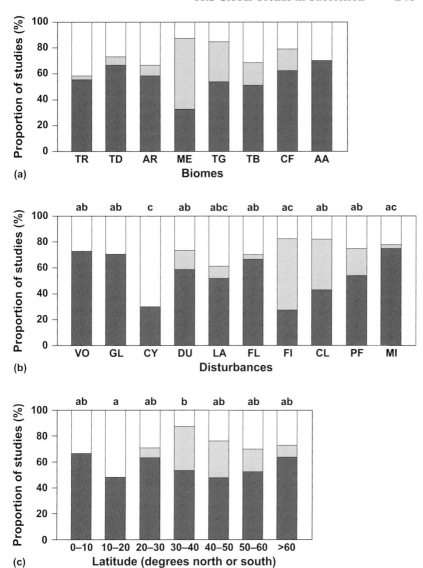

Figure 16.5 Trends in species richness changing during succession (% of studies) among (a) terrestrial biomes, (b) disturbances, and (c) latitude. Black: increase, light gray: decrease, white: variable. For biome and disturbance abbreviations see Fig. 16.1. For sample sizes see Table 16.1 (biomes) and Table 16.2 (disturbances). The asymptotic generalized Pearson's χ^2 test with post-hoc test was for (a) $\chi^2 = 55.06$, df = 14, p < 0.001 (but no significant differences in post-hoc test); for (b) $\chi^2 = 85.25$, df = 18, p < 0.001; and for (c) $\chi^2 = 34.99$, df = 12, p < 0.001. Different letters indicate significant differences among categories.

species richness was recorded. Decreasing richness was most frequent in middle latitudes, which probably reflects the decreases prevalent in the Mediterranean biome.

In general, species richness at a site is generally highest at moderate levels of stress or productivity, because the number of species able to grow is limited physiologically under conditions of high stress and low productivity, or by competition under conditions of high productivity and low stress (Grime, 2002). Species pools also tend to be highest under conditions of intermediate stress and productivity because fewer species are adapted to extremes (Safford *et al.*, 2001). At the extremes, the probability that a single species will dominate increases, either because it is a strong competitor under highly productive sites, or it is the one best adapted to the highly stressed environmental conditions; thus, dominance is high where richness is low. Also, the probability that a strongly competitive alien species will invade and dominate increases with site productivity (Ewel & Putz, 2004; Huston, 2004), a situation that may be undesirable and require intervention (see Section 16.9.1). These generalizations were easier to apply to particular seres in Chapters 5–14 than to the general trends presented in this chapter. The summary data blur the important site-specific variables such as productivity or local stressors.

16.2.4 Invasive Alien Species

Invasive alien species are clearly here to stay. Humans are homogenizing the world's flora (and fauna) and society must come to terms with new mixtures of species, including many less desirable species. Inevitably, invasive alien species participate in succession, but it has been consistently demonstrated that their participation decreases during succession (Rejmánek, 1989; Pyšek *et al.*, 2004; Prach *et al.*, 2007). Most recently, in an analysis of alien species from nearly 3,000 samples from various seral stages in the Czech Republic, the number of alien species clearly decreased during succession (Fig. 16.6). We did not have sufficient data for a detailed global analysis of changes in participation of invasive alien species in the course of succession. Instead, we concentrated on their participation in late successional stages, which is most relevant to the spontaneous recovery of potential natural vegetation.

In our comparative analyses of alien invasives in the late successional stages of 355 studies, alien species were important in 6% of cases, partly important in 18%, and unimportant in 76%. These results suggest that

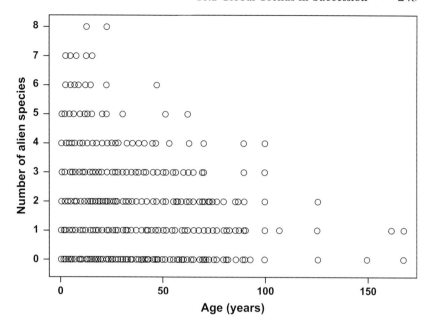

Figure 16.6 Decrease of the number of alien species per sample with successional age among seral stages belonging to 19 different seres in the Czech Republic (Prach *et al.*, unpublished).

invasive aliens do not typically overwhelm natural successional processes. There were significant differences in the participation of invasive alien species among biomes (Fig. 16.7a). Invasive aliens in late successional stages were most important in tropical rain forests (important or partly important in >50% of studies) and much less important in aridlands, coniferous forests, and the Arctic-alpine biome. Their importance was also lower in cold than warm environments (Table 16.3), suggesting a decreased role in extreme environments (Hobbs & Huenneke, 1992). Invasive alien species were also significantly less important in not forested than forested biomes. Among trees there are some competitive alien species that can dominate in late successional stages (Catford *et al.*, 2012; Řehounková *et al.*, 2018).

There were also significant differences in the participation of invasive alien species among the types of disturbances (Fig. 16.7b). Alien invasive species were most important in succession following plowed fields, dunes, and volcanoes and least important after glaciers, clearcuts, landslides, and cyclones. The regional pool of alien species is expected to be

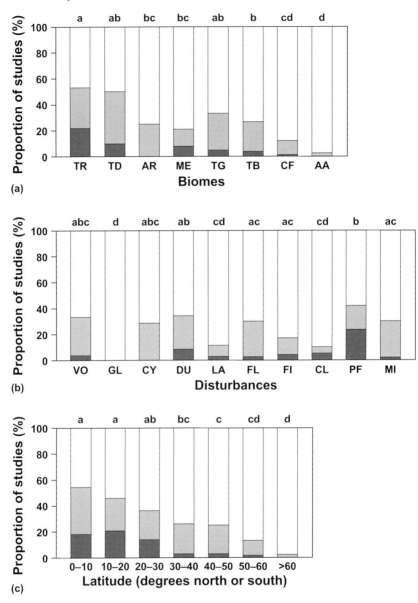

Figure 16.7 Importance of invasive alien species in late successional stages (% of studies) among (a) terrestrial biomes, (b) disturbances, and (c) latitude. Black: important, light gray: partly important, white: unimportant. For biome and disturbance abbreviations see Fig. 16.1. For sample sizes see Table 16.1 (biomes) and Table 16.2 (disturbances). The asymptotic generalized Pearson's χ^2 test with post-hoc test was for (a) $\chi^2 = 47.25$, df = 7, p < 0.001; for (b) $\chi^2 = 31.52$, df = 9, p < 0.001; and for (c) $\chi^2 = 38.37$, df = 6, p < 0.001. Different letters indicate significant differences among categories.

Plate 1 Tropical rain forest, Ecuador. Photo by Lawrence R. Walker

Plate 2 Tropical dry forest, Brazilian cerrado. Photo by Karel Prach

Plate 3 Aridland, Sonoran Desert, Arizona, USA. Photo by Lawrence R. Walker

Plate 4 Mediterranean vegetation, Crete, Greece. Photo by Lawrence R. Walker

Plate 5 Temperate grassland, central Ukraine, Photo by Karel Prach

Plate 6 Temperate broadleaf forest, central France. Photo by Karel Prach

Plate 7 Coniferous forest, Sweden. Photo by Lawrence R. Walker

Plate 8 Tundra, Svalbard. Photo by Karel Prach

Plate 9 Alpine, Sweden. Photo by Lawrence R. Walker

Plate 10 Volcanic succession two years after an eruption (Kasatochi Volcano, Alaska), with growth from buried seeds and vegetative parts that were exposed by severe erosion of the thick layer of ash deposited by the eruption. Photo by Lawrence R. Walker

Plate 11 Post-glacial succession on the Berendon Glacier near Hyder, Alaska. Surface age estimates are <5 years (most distant), 20 years (middle), and 100 years (foreground). Photo by Lawrence R. Walker

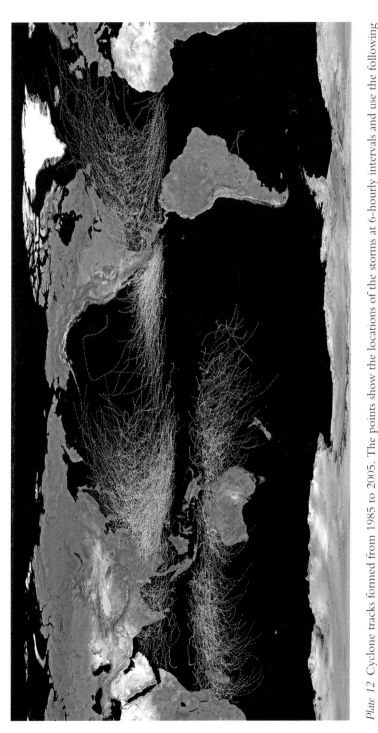

Plate 12 Cyclone tracks formed from 1985 to 2005. The points show the locations of the storms at 6-hourly intervals and use the following color scheme from the Saffir–Simpson Hurricane Scale: dark blue = tropical depression, light blue = tropical storm, light yellow = 1, dark yellow = 2, light orange = 3, dark orange = 4, red = 5. Accessed September 1, 2018 from https://commons.wikimedia.org/wiki/File:Global_tropical_cyclone_tracks-edit2.jpg

Plate 13 Damage from Hurricane Maria in the cloud forest of the Luquillo Mountains, Puerto Rico. Photo by Grizelle Gonzalez, USDA, Forest Service, with permission

Plate 14 Dune succession after ca. 120 years, The Netherlands. Photo by Karel Prach

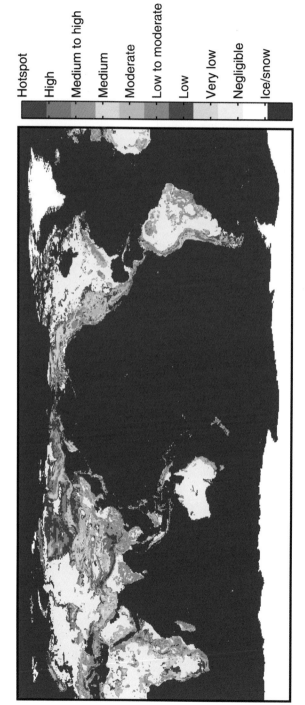

Hotspot

High

Medium to high

Medium

Moderate

Low to moderate

Low

Very low

Negligible

Ice/snow

Plate 15 Global distribution of landslides. Hong *et al.*, 2007, with permission

Plate 16 Landslide succession after six months, Puerto Rico. Photo by Lawrence R. Walker

Plate 17 Floodplain, Argentina. Photo by Lawrence R. Walker

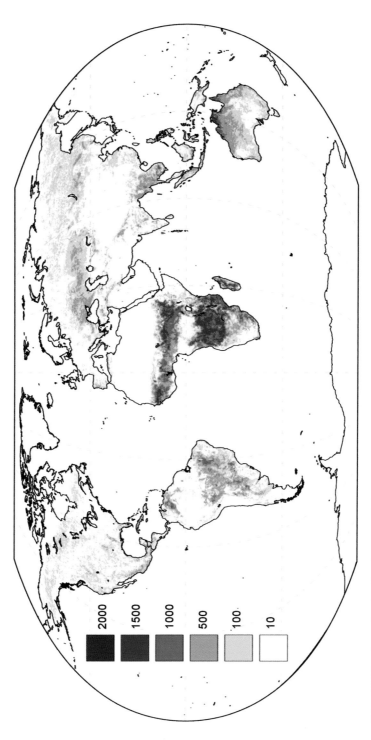

Plate 18 Number of active fire days recorded in the Global Fire Emissions Database, Version 4 (GFED4) data set during the 4,900 days covering the period August 2000 to December 2013 (Accessed February 7, 2019 from www.globalfiredata.org/data.html; from Di Giuseppe *et al.* (2016) with permission from the American Meteorological Society)

Plate 19 Fire succession after ca. five years, British Columbia. Photo by Lawrence
R. Walker

Plate 20 Clearcut succession in an experimental plot, British Columbia. Photo by Lawrence R. Walker

Plate 21 Early plowed field succession, Colombia. Photo by Karel Prach

Plate 22 Succession after abandonment of sugar cane, Oahu, Hawaii. Photo by Lawrence R. Walker

Plate 23 Mine succession in a disused stone quarry after ca. 20 years, Czech Republic. Photo by Karel Prach

Plate 24 Succession 13 years after abandonment of a boat launch due to falling water levels at Lake Mead, Nevada (USA). Photo by Lawrence R. Walker

Plate 25 Succession three years after removal of Elwha Dam, Washington (USA).
Photo by Karel Prach

Plate 26 Succession after ca. 60 years on an abandoned road, Mojave Desert, Nevada (USA). Photo by Lawrence R. Walker

Plate 27 Succession after abandonment of an outdoor amphitheater after ca. 8 years, Czech Republic. Photo by Lenka Oplatková, with permission

Plate 28 Succession on an abandoned military tank, Germany. Photo by Zuzana Veverková, with permission

larger for plowed fields (many alien weeds present) and for dunes (some aliens were used to stabilize dunes). However, further interpretation of these differences is difficult and more comparative research is needed.

The importance of invasive alien species clearly decreased with increasing latitude (Fig. 16.7c). This finding is not fully in accordance with some earlier generalizations that invasive alien species are most frequent at middle latitudes (Sax, 2001; Pyšek & Richardson, 2006). Perhaps, despite generally fewer alien species at low latitudes, those that are present are more competitive, thus playing a more important role in late successional stages in the tropics (Marler & del Moral, 2011, 2013). Fast-growing and competitive species, such as *Dicranopteris linearis*, *Andropogon gayanus*, *Lantana camara*, or *Mimosa pigra*, are very likely to serve, moreover, as biological barriers against other invasive species. Several questions are pertinent to understanding the links between invasive alien species and succession. 1) Can successional studies provide insights about which disturbed ecosystems will be prone to invasions? 2) At what stage in their successional development are ecosystems most susceptible to invasion? Studies of succession might indicate threshold conditions when nonnative organisms can start to invade. The thresholds can be determined by such factors as site abiotic conditions (moisture, nutrients), the respective traits of native and invasive alien species, the types of initial and ongoing disturbances, and the intensity of propagule pressure of the aliens from the surroundings. 3) How will invasive alien species modify succession? Invasive alien species can arrest or divert succession, thus initiating new successional pathways and increasing compositional divergence at broader scales while monopolizing space at smaller scales (Prach & Walker, 2011). New mixtures of native and alien species can have multiple and often unpredictable effects on succession, ultimately forming so-called novel ecosystems (Hobbs *et al.*, 2009). 4) What can be done to incorporate these species into successional studies (both restoration efforts and theoretical models)? Based on our comparative analyses, we can only provide partial answers to questions 1) and 3). We showed that some biomes and disturbed sites are more susceptible to alien species, and note in Chapters 5–14 where they arrest or divert succession. The role of invasive alien species in the late successional stages was more limited than we had expected. Studies of succession can demonstrate the impact of alien organisms on ecosystem structure and function. Duffin *et al.* (2019) found that whether invasive alien species differed in leaf nutrient content from native species, differences arose during succession from differential plant performance. Mechanisms of succession, such as establishment dynamics, facilitation, and competition (including inhibition) can be tested through studies of invasive organisms participating in seral stages (Meiners *et al.*, 2007). Understanding how alien species alter succession can improve management success, including perhaps control or eradication of the invasive species. There are clearly many ways to integrate studies of succession and alien species.

16.3 Disturbance

In the previous chapters we showed how succession differed following 10 different types of disturbance. We also mentioned the importance of subsequent disturbances following the focal disturbance. Examples are given in Chapters 5–15. Here, we summarize the current state of knowledge about the general links between disturbances and succession.

In ecology, a disturbance is a relatively abrupt disruption (usually loss) of biomass, structure, or function (Walker, 2012; Jentsch & White, 2019). Disturbances are involved in all aspects of succession: they provide the initial trigger and influence its course and duration. In addition, disturbances are not usually independent events, but often form parts of disturbance sequences or loops of interacting disturbances that become the disturbance regime at a given site (Lindenmayer *et al.*, 2008; Buma, 2015). The nature and composition of biological legacies are a function of the severity of a disturbance. Their presence can influence the composition of pioneer plant communities and eventual successional trajectories (Walker *et al.*, 2013; Johnstone *et al.*, 2016). The biotic response to a disturbance regime is dependent on plant-based variables (e.g., size, growth form, life history stage, and competitive status) and community-level responses that initiate succession. Disturbance effects continue to influence succession past the original trigger event through such processes as plant-soil feedbacks (Bardgett & Wardle, 2010; van der Putten *et al.*, 2013). Some reciprocal abiotic-biotic feedbacks (Geerstema & Pojar, 2007) even modify disturbances (e.g., grasses that promote fire). Disturbances can also cut short successional trajectories by removing all existing vegetation. Understanding disturbance is essential to explain successional processes.

The time lag between successive disturbances can vary from immediate (a cyclone triggers a landslide) to centuries (an aging forest becomes susceptible to bark beetles or fire if dead biomass accumulates), hence the value of understanding historical disturbances (see Section 16.4). Therefore, it is useful to distinguish between discrete or persistent disturbances that, in turn, trigger either transient or persistent responses (Wolkovich et al., 2014). For example, a single fire affects an ecosystem and successional processes differently than multiple fires in the same year. These effects can be transient to long-lasting. In addition, we can add disturbances that occur irregularly or unpredictably and alter succession in unforeseeable ways. Succession is most predictable when the ecosystem disturbances are foreseeable in both space and time. However, some species have adapted to irregular disturbances in time (e.g., with long-lasting seed banks; van der Valk & Davis, 1978) or space (e.g., with easily dispersed propagules; Debussche & Isenmann, 1994) (see Section 16.7).

The Intermediate Disturbance Hypothesis (Connell, 1978) proposed that the highest species richness would occur when disturbances are neither rare nor frequent, and neither mild nor severe. Though we generally agree with the hypothesis, there are exceptions, such as fire. We argued (Chapter 11) that severe fires lead to higher species richness in early stages of succession than do mild fires. But it is valid just for ecosystems adapted to fire. If ecosystems are adapted to a given disturbance, species richness usually peaks at the beginning because there is a pool of species adapted just to open, disturbed sites. Later, they disappear due to competition. If ecosystems are not adapted to the disturbance, species richness is usually low at the beginning, then gradually increases and peaks later in succession, a generalization that seems to be applicable across disturbance types.

The increased capabilities of scientists to measure disturbance and its ecological consequences, including succession, coincide with an increase in the types of disturbances created by humans. This combination of skills and variation in successional trajectories allows the examination of succession across a gradient of disturbance severity (Walker, 2011; Chang et al., 2019). Although anthropogenic disturbances are often more severe than natural ones (Walker, 2012), we found only slight differences in success of succession between them (Fig. 16.2). In addition, understanding the consequences of climate change on succession is aided by improved interpretation of historical disturbances and ecosystem responses (McLauchlan et al., 2014). Management and restoration measures will also benefit from understanding the variable successional consequences of disturbances (Foster et al., 2016).

16.4 Temporal Scales

In Section 16.2 we evaluated success of succession which we defined as the ability to reach the respective potential natural vegetation or other alternative states composed of native species. We used the approximate threshold of 100 years since the onset of succession for our decision if succession was successful or partly successful (or unsuccessful if arrested for a long time by invasive alien species or adverse environmental factors). However, we again stress that succession is often much longer than 100 years and may continue for millennia and reach retrogressive stages (Walker & Reddell, 2007). Here, we evaluate the time taken in our comparative studies from Chapters 5–14 to reach potential natural vegetation and summarize this information across disturbances and biomes (Table 16.4). Because most studies deal with chronosequences that encompass <100 years, we, or the authors of the individual studies, sometimes had to estimate time to potential natural vegetation; we used such extrapolations only when there were careful estimates based on the data presented.

The slowest recovery occurred in primary seres following severe natural disturbances, especially volcanoes and glaciers. Fastest recovery is typical for secondary seres, but Chang *et al.* (2019) found fastest rates of change in seres intermediate between primary and secondary succession on Mount St. Helens in Washington (USA). When a disturbance such as fire in temperate grasslands or Mediterranean ecosystems does not change species composition, recovery can occur within one year because of the fast regeneration of resident species. Overall, time to full recovery is highly variable, but potential natural vegetation typically fully recovers within several hundred years.

Prach *et al.* (2016) found a fairly consistent temporal scale for 39 seres in temperate broadleaf forests in central Europe (Fig. 16.8). The estimated average time needed to reach potential natural vegetation was ca. 180 years for primary seres and ca. 260 years for secondary seres. All 421 species found in the adjacent natural vegetation were also found in seral vegetation. Rather surprisingly, primary seres appeared to approach potential natural vegetation faster than did secondary seres, despite generalizations to the contrary (Miles & Walton, 1993). The gradual formation of soil and a soil seed bank in primary succession are expected to slow down succession compared to secondary succession (Walker & del Moral, 2003). Early stages of primary seres were indeed less similar to potential natural vegetation than were those of secondary seres (compare

Table 16.4 *Time to recovery of the potential natural vegetation or an alternative state of late successional natural vegetation among particular types of disturbances and biomes*

Disturbance	Span (years)	Comments by biomes
Volcanoes	50–2,000	Slow in AL, sometimes in TR (on unfavorable lava texture or if invaded by alien species (Hawaii); highly variable
Glaciers	80–1,000	Mostly faster in CF and AL than in TU; 80 years is for TB (the only case from this biome); highly variable
Cyclones	5–100	No clear differences among (forested only) biomes; rapid recovery
Dunes	20–several hundred	Highly variable within biomes; no pattern among biomes evident
Landslides	10–200	Fastest in wet CF, slow in AR and AL; slowest in TR
Floods	30–250	Fastest in AR (but low number of cases); variable in other biomes (most records in CF)
Fire	1–<200	Fastest records from TG, ME, TB, and TD
Clearcuts	5–>150	Fastest record in TD, slowest in TB, but generally highly variable among biomes
Plowed fields	6–150	Fastest in TG, variable in other biomes but most records between 50 and 100 years
Mines	30–several hundred	Fastest record in TG, slowest (no recovery evident) in some TR and TD; full recovery rarely <100 years
Sum	1–2,000	Highly variable within and among biomes; slow in extreme environment (AA), relatively fast in TG

For biome abbreviations, see Table 16.3; AA is composed of AL (alpine) and TU (tundra).

the respective intercepts in Fig. 16.8). In later secondary seral stages, it is likely that succession is slowed by the persistent dominance of competitors, especially in productive habitats such as plowed fields (Prach *et al.*, 2016). Although the linear relationships were predictive, the data are probably best explained as being asymptotic (Rydgren *et al.*, 2018).

Succession has traditionally been studied at local plot scales over periods of years to decades. This time span is a reasonable starting point to study succession, which has its roots in natural history observations. (It is also the average time span of an ecologist's attention and funding.) Succession is therefore in the mid-range of all temporal processes that affect ecology (seconds to millennia; Fig. 16.9a). These temporal

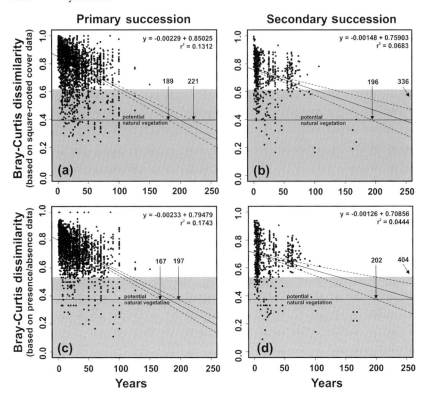

Figure 16.8 Relationships between Bray–Curtis dissimilarity and sample age calculated for primary (a, c) and secondary (b, d) seres. The dissimilarity was measured between each vegetation sample taken from seral stages and the nearest corresponding sample of natural vegetation. The horizontal line in each plot is the mean, and the gray zone is the 90th percentile of Bray–Curtis dissimilarities calculated between two of the most similar samples of potential natural vegetation. The dashed line defines the 95% confidence interval of the linear model. The dissimilarity was calculated from species cover data that were square-rooted (a, b) or converted to presence/absence (c, d).
From Prach *et al.* (2016), with permission from Wiley & Sons

processes are interactive (Fig. 16.9b) and processes at intermediate scales, such as succession, can have a pivotal role in understanding processes that occur over shorter or longer temporal scales, perhaps leading to a better integration across all ecological time (Walker & Wardle, 2014; see Chapter 2) and between temporal and spatial ecology (Wolkovich *et al.*, 2014). Such an integrative approach across temporal scales will likely improve our understanding of the global disruptions to succession and other ecological processes that are caused by climate change,

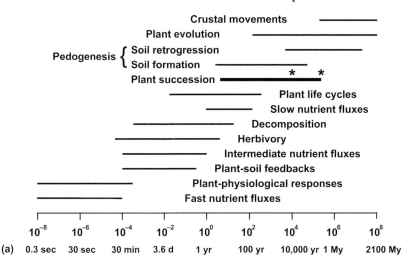

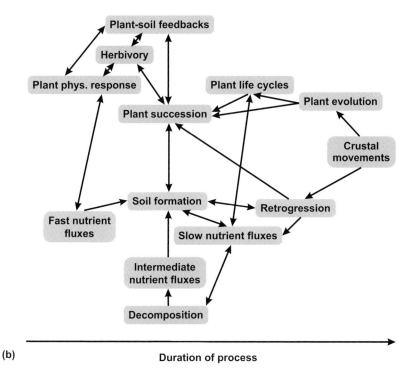

Figure 16.9 Temporal scales and linkages of ecological processes. (a) Temporal scales at which various ecological processes occur. Succession occurs at intermediate scales (heavy black bar). Asterisks denote ecosystem retrogression in very old successional stages. (b) Linkages between ecological processes. Note the many connections beween plant succession and other processes.

particularly when coupled with broad spatial comparisons such as we present in this book.

Advances are being made in the understanding of how short-term processes alter succession, particularly through plant-soil feedbacks (Wardle *et al.*, 2012; see Section 16.6). How plants respond physiologically to rapid (seconds to minutes) shifts in nutrient supply can affect plant growth during the following weeks, their competitive abilities, and consequently species replacements during years of succession (Van de Voorde *et al.*, 2012). Short-term fluctuations in resource availability may initiate invasion by aliens (Davis & Pelsor, 2001). Soil nutrient availability, locally controlled by the interaction between plants and soil organisms among other factors, also affects herbivory and decomposition, both factors that can alter succession (Kardol *et al.*, 2013). For example, species that either enrich (Callaway, 2007) or decrease (Berendse, 1998) soil nutrients have long-term influences on succession, often including the facilitation of their own replacement. Processes that take only minutes, such as grazing, can have a cumulative effect on decadal species interactions and drive succession (Walker & Wardle, 2014).

At the other end of the temporal scales we have paleoecological insights into how plant communities responded to climate fluctuations and other environmental changes in the past. More information is becoming available and can help determine how plants will respond to current changes. For example, there are increasingly sophisticated data coming from improved interpretations of sediments to supplement pollen analyses (e.g., ecosystem productivity and carbon:nitrogen ratios from compound-specific isotopes), detailed information gleaned from tree rings (e.g., historical fires, droughts, insect outbreaks), and reconstructions of past vegetation across multiple sites and centuries (Brewer *et al.*, 2012; McLauchlan *et al.*, 2014). Past events also shape the present species pool and successional processes through their influence on macro-evolution (Pickett, 1976; Cavender-Bares *et al.*, 2009). Advances are being made in testing why it appears that early-successional species represent a more tightly clustered suite of phylogenetic characteristics than the more diffuse suite of characters that are typically found among the more competitive, later-successional species (Whitfeld *et al.*, 2012; Meiners *et al.*, 2015b). Both abiotic and biotic conditions at long (historical and geological) time frames (e.g., geological events and evolution) therefore set constraints on current successional processes (Rejmánek, 1999; Walker & Wardle, 2014). Further investigation of long-term changes in these conditions will help interpret current changes in successional dynamics.

Wolkovich *et al.* (2014) argue that a fundamental challenge for ecology is to recognize that temporal processes do not occur in a stationary environment. Successional processes occur not only in a shifting spatial mosaic, but against a backdrop of shifting time scales. For example, a bog undergoes succession to a forest, typically over millennia, but only if appropriate abiotic factors such as glacial rebound and biotic factors such as propagules from upland forests are present. However, the whole process can be sped up by direct (e.g., drainage) or indirect (e.g., upland species composition changes due to human activities) land use effects. Future studies of succession do not have the liberty of assuming a relatively constant abiotic and biotic background, but instead must address the rapid community changes caused by direct or indirect human impacts on nature, including climate change. Useful approaches to understand such shifting baselines come from the analysis of both long-term and short-term ecological processes.

Ultimately, a more sophisticated approach to understanding temporal processes is required to meet our need to understand current and predict future successional dynamics. Addressing succession as not merely a process at intermediate time scales, but as integrally linked to all ecological time scales, is a good place to start. Developing a theoretical framework of temporal ecology will help predict successional dynamics and aid in manipulating them to achieve desirable goals through restoration.

16.5 Spatial Scales

Spatial and temporal processes and scales are so intertwined that physicists talk about "space-time" and ecologists talk about spatial-temporal dynamics. Scales used to measure space (micro, local, landscape, regional, global) are equally applicable to time (Walker & Wardle, 2014). Succession, though most often described as a temporal process, is just as much a spatial process as any other ecological process, and spatial aspects must always be considered in sample design and interpretation of results. We can consider particular studies dealing with one type of succession in a given locality or region, and comparative studies across more sites or seres, which naturally span larger spatial scales. In this book, we emphasize the latter approach.

Succession has been studied at scales as small as 10^{-1} m^2 (phytoplankton in microcosms; Margalef, 1958) and experimental manipulations are sometimes done at 10^0–10^1 m^2. For example, initial site conditions can be experimentally manipulated by fertilizing and biotic conditions by sowing plants (Schmidt & Brubach, 1993; Eisenhauer et al., 2016). Such small-scale experiments may provide valuable insights into detailed mechanisms of succession but should only be extrapolated to broader scales and practical applications (i.e., restoration tools) with caution. At such small scales, the influences of random events, microclimate, seed rain, or herbivory on succession may operate differently than at larger scales.

The most frequently used scale is plots that are 10^1-10^2 m^2, measured over time (permanent plots), just once (chronosequence approach), or in combination (remeasurement of plots along a chronosequence). The large number of successional studies at this scale provides data for comparative analyses, including those used in this book.

The broadest spatial scale in studying succession results from remote sensing data at 10^2-10^6 m^2. Due to limits on resolution, remote sensing usually provides repeated measures of how overall cover, biomass, or dominant species composition change during succession. Rapidly developing drone technology may soon provide more detailed data. Remote sensing data have been most frequently used in studying post-fire succession (see Chapter 11), but with increasing resolution this method is now used more frequently, including to monitor shifts in biomes and accompanying climate change (Rogers et al., 2015).

Comparative studies provide an excellent opportunity to further research on succession (Makoto & Wilson, 2019). Comparisons are also possible when detailed experimental studies are repeated at broader (regional and subcontinental) scales (van der Putten et al., 2000; Fridley & Wright, 2012; Prach et al., 2014c; Velle & Vandvik, 2014). Descriptive studies were compared within and among types of succession at regional to continental scales (see Chapter 4). Here, we present an example of a comparative study among 19 types of seres at a large spatial scale (that of the Czech Republic in the temperate broadleaf forest biome) to illustrate the power of such comparisons. We built the Database of Successional Series (DaSS) that now contains about 3,700 vegetation records (phytosociological relevés) from different seral stages aged 1–>150 years and about 1,500 species, which represent about half of the country's flora (for details see Prach et al., 2014d, 2016; Řehounková et al., 2018). The seres,

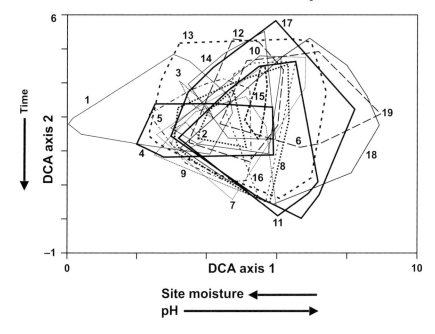

Figure 16.10 DCA ordination of vegetation samples from 19 different types of chronosequences occurring at a broad spatial scale (the entire Czech Republic). Envelopes enclose the positions of all samples of each sere. The overlaps of the particular seres indicate a successional continuum not only in time but also in space. For details see text.
Adapted from Prach *et al.* (2014d), with permission from Wiley & Sons

ranging from abandoned dry limestone quarries to extracted peatlands, formed a continuum with many overlaps along a moisture–pH gradient (Fig. 16.10). The seres were more similar in their species composition in the initial and early stages, in which ubiquitous synanthropic species prevailed, than in the later stages when the vegetation differentiated. In most cases, succession led to forest, which usually established after ca. 20 years. In very dry or wet places (with few or no woody species), open vegetation developed, often highly valuable from the restoration and conservation points of view. The total number of species and the number of target species increased in the majority of seres, while the number of alien species clearly decreased (Fig. 16.6) with successional age. When the successional pattern was related to environmental factors, the following variables appeared to have significant influence (in decreasing order): substrate acidity, macroclimate (mean annual temperature and precipitation), and land use in the surrounding area (the species pool for colonization; Vítovcová *et al.*, unpublished). At the global scale used in this book, we did not evaluate the role of substrate. Mean annual temperature appeared to significantly influence global succession patterns but precipitation did not. Species pools (number of species, number of invasive aliens) are likely key influences at the global scale (see Section 16.2). Therefore, there are some similarities in factors influencing succession between the country-wide and global scales but also some differences, suggesting that choice of spatial scale can influence research outputs.

Where data are comparable, published studies can be compared to reveal patterns during succession of disturbance regimes, community (richness) and species (life form, native or not) characteristics, and successional patterns (rate, past and perhaps future trajectories). Careful attention is needed in such comparisons, not only to potential differences in how data were collected but also to possible limitations of individual data sets (due, e.g., to differences in size and number of sampling units or technical obstacles to achieving ideal samples). With such precautions in mind, we encourage more attempts at global-level comparisons, as illustrated in this book (see also Crouzeilles *et al.*, 2016; Meli *et al.*, 2017; Prach & Walker, 2019).

16.6 Functional Traits

We did not systematically analyze changes in species functional traits or species interactions during succession among biomes or disturbances. The main reason is that sufficient comparable data do not exist. Thus, our comments here are not based on our comparative analyses but instead on a review of previous studies.

The search for general rules of community assembly has encountered difficulties (Weiher & Keddy, 1999; Götzenberger *et al.*, 2012), in much the same way that past efforts have failed to find holistic generalizations about succession (monoclimax: Clements, 1936), ecosystem assembly (cybernetics: Margalef, 1968), or both (ecosystem-level processes: Odum, 1969). Yet recent efforts to focus on functional traits of plants to explain the structure and composition (and, less often, the temporal dynamics; Prach *et al.*, 1997; Lavorel *et al.*, 2007; Latzel *et al.*, 2011; Funk *et al.*, 2016) of plant communities may prove more resilient (Raevel *et al.*, 2012). The broader the community characteristic, the easier it is to predict its outcome (see Chapter 2). For example, we are often able to predict if woody species establish and dominate over herbs in the course of succession at a particular site and region but are less able to predict exact species composition (Prach *et al.*, 1999). Typically, leaf traits (e.g., specific leaf area, leaf dry mass, leaf nitrogen concentration) are used to scale up from individual plants to community functions (Garnier *et al.*, 2004) and even global carbon budgets (De Deyn *et al.*, 2008). Some successes have been achieved in linking plant traits to environmental constraints along environmental gradients, but obstacles still remain to successfully explain biotic interactions and community assembly from the collection of plant traits (Lavorel *et al.*, 2007). And it is a big step to go from explaining the assembly of a static community to explaining community change over time (i.e., succession). Several approaches include the use of plant traits in the context of disturbance ecology (White & Jentsch, 2004) or restoration (Young *et al.*, 2001). Where interactions among species are driven by autogenic factors, plant traits may be most critical to succession. However, where species are strongly influenced by allogenic factors or stochastic events (e.g., in early primary succession), assembly rules based on plant traits are less likely to be useful predictors (Walker & del Moral, 2003; Walker *et al.*, 2006).

Additional approaches to understanding the role of plant traits in succession include experimentation and comparative analyses. Despite potential problems of scaling experimental results to larger ecosystems, for example, a grassland experiment by Fukami *et al.* (2005) provided useful insights by manipulating initial plant species composition, then allowing succession to proceed. Variation in initial compositional led to divergence of species composition but convergence of functional traits. In other words, traits may be predictable when species composition is not, due to priority effects (colonization order). Priority effects can be particularly strong in more fertile habitats where the first colonizers have an added advantage (Kardol *et al.*, 2012), but that advantage can be offset by negative feedback from soil microbes on early successional plants (Kardol *et al.*, 2007).

Comparative analyses of multiple seres have been facilitated by extensive databases that standardize the traits of species. European sources include BIOPOP (Poschlod *et al.*, 2003), LEDA (Kleyer *et al.*, 2008; www.leda-traitbase.org), and CLO-PLA (Klimešová & Klimeš 2013). Worldwide databases of species traits are also available: Database TRY (www.try-db.org/TryWeb/Home.php) and Bien (http://bien.nceas.ucsb.edu/bien/biendata/bien-2/traits/). These and other similar databases could be better exploited in studies on changing species traits in succession.

Three studies in the Czech Republic illustrate the value of comparative studies to understanding the role of functional traits in succession. In the first, Prach *et al.* (1997) compared changes in species traits during the first 10 years of succession at 13 seres after different types of disturbance. They saw an increase during succession of competitive species, woody species, VA mycorrhizae, clonal lateral spread, wind and animal dispersal, and plant height. Traits that decreased included ruderal species, annuals, propagule mass, and persistent seed banks. There was no change in stress tolerant species or pollination strategy and primary and secondary seres did not differ in any of the characteristics. The decreasing propagule mass is surprising, but early colonists can possess large seeds, less dispersed by wind than by animals, that may help the colonists to overcome the adverse environmental conditions in early seral stages (Fenner, 1985).

A second study followed post-mining chronosequences in 36 abandoned sand pits over several decades and showed contrasting trends to the first study (Řehounková & Prach, 2010). Stress-tolerant species were the most common plant strategy in early succession, although they are usually expected to follow ruderals and competitive species (Osbornová *et al.*, 1990; Grime 2002), perhaps because the initial substrate was stressful (i.e., infertile and acidic). Initial success was related to traits that determine the colonization ability of the species, such as wind-dispersal and the production of light diaspores, whereas persistence-related traits, such as vegetative reproduction and high competitive ability (height), increased in importance with time.

A final study of the Czech flora examined colonization ability (evaluated by Prach *et al.*, 2017) from a database of 21 types of succession, 39 seres, and ca. 3,700 vegetation records (DaSS; Prach *et al.*, 2014d). Functional traits that were positively correlated with colonization ability included clonal lateral spread, decreased terminal velocity of dispersing seeds, and increased canopy height (Mudrák *et al.*, unpublished). Traits that significantly predicted the successional age in which a species would occur included: plant longevity, seed longevity, clonal lateral spread, canopy height, and particularly seed mass (Fig. 16.11). Traits abundant in early successional stages included annuals, short-term seed bank viability, clonal lateral spread, low stature, and low seed mass; species in late succession had the opposite set of traits. The trait, selected as the best predictor of successional age when a species establishes, was species longevity. It is obvious that despite the same geographical area of all three studies and partly overlapping datasets, results may differ. Generalizations about the role of functional traits in succession therefore remain limited.

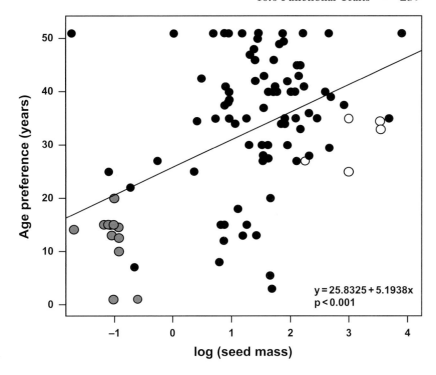

Figure 16.11 Seed mass as a significant predictor of participation of woody species in seral stages among 39 seres at a country scale (Czech Republic) from Mudrák *et al.*, unpublished, with permission. Gray points represent species of the family Salicaceae, empty circles the family Fagaceae. The former were successful colonists in early stages of succession, while the latter generally occurred in later stages of succession.

Other studies on how species traits change during succession also demonstrate variable results, but generally emphasize the importance of dispersal traits in early stages (especially in primary succession) and persistence and competitive traits in later stages of succession. However, a recent analysis by Makoto and Wilson (2019), suggested that dispersal can influence primary succession and associated long-term processes (e.g., soil carbon accumulation) for centuries. There is also increasing attention to fine-root traits (Erktan *et al.*, 2018). It seems that early successional species invest more in fine roots (and subsequent efficiency of nutrient uptake) than do late successional species (Rondina *et al.*, 2019). To the extent that generalizations about functional traits are possible across ecosystems with different species composition, they may be helpful in our search for global generalizations about succession (Cadotte *et al.*,

2011). However, several problems remain, including a lack of widespread agreement on what plant traits to measure and making the transition from a community assembly to a community dynamics perspective (Meiners *et al.*, 2015a). Despite mixed success, the search for species-based functional traits is still vital in the search for generalizations about succession.

The links between plant species traits and interactions with other organisms during succession include zoochory, palatability, and plant-soil feedbacks (Bardgett & Wardle, 2010) and represent a burgeoning area of research with implications for succession. For example, soil nutrients, along with dispersal dynamics, drove species compositional variation in secondary tropical forests in Panama (van Breugel *et al.*, 2019). Nutrient availability is largely a function of microbial processes but microbial interactions with plants are so complex that what is usually measured is the net influence on plant composition, soil nutrients, and other key drivers of succession (Meiners *et al.*, 2015b). One idea is that early colonists may benefit from largely positive interactions with soil microorganisms (e.g., symbiotic mycorrhizal fungi), but that with time plants accumulate antagonistic populations of microbes (Thrall *et al.*, 2007), potentially leading to successional change in (plant) species composition. Yet short-lived initial plant colonists may be less dependent on mycorrhizae because they have a lower chance to find a partner in undeveloped soil, especially in primary seres (Rydlová & Vosátka, 2001) than later-successional plant species (Reinhart *et al.*, 2012). Grassland succession was accelerated, for example, by mycorrhizae with a positive feedback loop with late successional species (Koziol & Bever, 2019). Clearly, the composition, function, and density of microorganisms shift during succession. For example, one potential driver of succession could be the bacterial domination of the lignin-poor environments of early succession and fungal domination of the lignin-rich environments of later succession (Bardgett & Walker, 2004). In an analysis of microbial diversity over a two-million-year chronosequence in western Australia, Turner *et al.* (2019) found highest microbial diversity in intermediate stages and highest fungal diversity in old, strongly weathered acid soils and extreme phosphorus depletion. However, changes among fungal and plant communities became increasingly decoupled as succession proceeded. Undoubtedly, there is also an important role of soil invertebrates influencing plants indirectly through changing soil structure (e.g., earthworms) or directly through root herbivory (Frouz *et al.*,

2008). As community-level consequences of soil fauna become clearer, we expect substantial insights into how they influence succession.

16.7 Predictability

The predictability of trajectories has been a constant theme of successional research (Walker & del Moral, 2009; Norden *et al.*, 2015). There is now an urgent need to go beyond predicting functional traits and species composition at each stage to predicting both individual successional trajectories and multiple trajectories across landscapes. This need comes from rapidly shifting climate conditions and widespread human alterations that reduce our confidence in a replication of past patterns of succession and the need to guide restoration of damaged ecosystems (see Section 16.9). For example, will restoration, especially if relying upon spontaneous succession, lead to predictable stages and endpoints or a random sorting of species? The easiest successional trajectories to predict (and hence the best for use of chronosequence assumptions) are convergent, parallel, or circular ones; divergent and network trajectories are more difficult (Walker *et al.*, 2010b). Also, predominantly autogenic seres (driven largely by internal processes) are easier to predict than predominantly allogenic seres, which may cause ecological surprises (e.g., the unexpected importance of acid rain in damaging the health of New Hampshire forests through its influence on nutrient availability; Paine *et al.*, 1998; Lindenmayer *et al.*, 2010). Further uncertainty comes from the arrival of new species due to altered climate regimes and also from various random or hidden factors such as those among still poorly understood plant-soil animal interactions (see Section 16.6).

Ecosystems and their constituent species are generally adapted to historic, predictable disturbances but less adapted to unpredictable ones such as disturbances recently introduced by humans. Seed banks that can germinate when conditions are favorable can be adaptations to disturbances that are more predictable in space than in exact time. Traits such as rapid seed dispersal and subsequent colonization ability can be adaptations to disturbances that are more predictable in time than in space (Grime *et al.*, 1988). Succession in a given site is more predictable in the former case and unpredictable in the latter where dispersal introduces substantial stochasticity.

One way to improve predictability is to understand past successional patterns (e.g., rates and trajectories of species change). This can be done using historical records, gathering long-term data from permanent plots, or using chronosequence assumptions to interpret temporal change (tempered by shifting temporal dynamics as previously mentioned). Where long-term data is available (see Chapter 2), some patterns emerge such as a decrease in rates of species turnover with time (Bornkamm, 1981; Prach *et al.*, 1993). As collections of such data increase, comparative analyses can interpret patterns, such as we have done in this book. However, until measurements are more standardized, the diverse nature of the data will allow exact comparisons of only a limited number of stages or the use of only broad categories, such as herbs or woody species. One of the rare attempts to predict succession among diverse disturbed sites at a broader geographical scale was presented in Section 16.4, Fig. 16.8.

Models, whether conceptual or numerical (see Chapter 2), are another useful approach to predicting successional trajectories (Lohier *et al.*, 2016), and were reviewed, for example, by Lepš (1988) and Walker and del Moral (2003). The complexity of succession means that models generally serve more of a heuristic than predictive function for a particular sere. In addition, the paucity of extensive, comparable data sets from multiple sites makes model verification difficult. Nonetheless, progress has been made in modeling succession, and advancing conceptual frameworks in which to study succession.

In general, we can predict succession by 1) using extrapolation of exact data as shown in Fig. 16.8; 2) using analogies with other successions, including broad field experience, which can be combined into expert systems (e.g., the expert system SUCCESS; Prach *et al.*, 1999); and 3) using simulation models. Simulation models use various mathematical approaches such as Lotka-Volterra equations (Lepš & Prach, 1981) or transition matrices models (Markov models; Usher, 1992). Markov models can be calibrated using data, and can take advantage of matrix algebra (estimation of succession rate and prediction of successional states using eigenvalue and eigenvector analysis; Lepš, 1987). But their predictions are conditioned by rather strict assumptions, namely stability and temporal independence of transition probabilities (Usher, 1992), which often cause poor predictability because the transitions between stages are not constant but affected by on-going environmental changes.

Some recent models link species traits to community dynamics (Soussana *et al.*, 2012). The individual-based models (Huston, 2018) are the most mechanistic in their approach. These models reflect real interactions among individuals (e.g., both intra- and inter-specific competition) and have been widely used, for example, for modeling of forest dynamics after clearcutting (e.g., the JABOWA models; Bugmann, 2001). However, these simulation models are not often realistic and need thorough validation and verification using real data. But the real data and outputs of the models do not always match. The potential to use mathematical models to predict succession was often overestimated in the past. Hopefully, in the future both the accumulation of field data on succession and further development of computer techniques will improve our ability to predict succession, including alternative successional scenarios expected from a changing climate (Lohier *et al.*, 2016).

16.8 Conservation

Conservation of ecosystems is usually the best method to protect species diversity and retain a functional ecosystem with intact processes such as nutrient cycling, productivity of biomass, species interactions, and succession following disturbances. However, even well-preserved natural ecosystems may occasionally require some human intervention to resist degradation such as that due to invasion by alien species. Intervention is essential in human-managed habitats where a certain stage of succession is desirable. For example, species-rich hay meadows or pastures need mowing (Dengler et al., 2014) or extensive pasturing of grazing animals (Rejmánek & Rosén, 1992) to arrest succession to shrubland or forest. With the increasing human impact on all ecosystems, the traditional conservation approach (e.g., when a nature reserve is designated and no intervention is allowed), is insufficient and conservation management or ecological restoration is needed to either arrest, accelerate, or even reverse succession. Such active manipulation of succession overlaps with restoration (Section 16.9). Late successional ecosystems, developed after a disturbance and composed of native species, are usually a priority for conservation. However, sometimes early successional stages are preferred, such as in some abandoned mines that may provide habitat for rare species. These species are often poor competitors and need open, unproductive sites as refugia. Such sites are typically rare in modern landscapes in intensively used and populated parts of the world and the human-made sites may serve as surrogates of natural habitats for the species (Řehounková *et al.*, 2016). Given the need to conserve a range of habitats and ecosystems characteristic of different stages of succession, it is clear that understanding successional processes is key to conservation. Conservation is increasingly concerned with landscape and regional approaches as well. Wildlife corridors, regional systems of (ideally) interconnected nature reserves, and conservation across international borders are part of this trend (Rosenberg *et al.*, 1997). In addition, conservation of meta-population dynamics (Hanski, 1999) at landscape or regional scales is important for the persistence of species.

The importance of early, middle, and late successional stages for endangered species was illustrated by Řehounková *et al.* (in press). Ten successional seres in various post-mining sites across the Czech Republic were analyzed regarding different categories of Red List species (2,597 vegetation samples and 935 vascular plant species). The authors found 235 species in this sample to be on the Red List. Nearly all (223) of the threatened species colonizing the spontaneously revegetated post-mining sites avoided late-successional stages totally overgrown by woody species. The open, early successional stages were important for critically endangered plants, especially for the heliophilous plants that were poor competitors. Different Red List categories were confined to different successional stages (Fig. 16.12), indicating the importance of each stage, but the early stages of succession had significant conservation value.

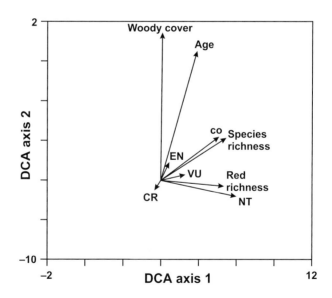

Figure 16.12 Ordination (DCA) of vegetation samples (their pattern is not displayed) from variously aged mine sites (N = 2,597) with passively projected successional age, total cover of woody species, total species richness, co – common species and different categories of Red List species: red richness – all Red List species; CR – critically endangered; EN – endangered; VU – vulnerable; NT – near threatened. Adapted from Řehounková *et al.* (in press), with permission

16.9 Restoration

Successional processes are already so modified by humans that restoration, the purposeful manipulation of succession to a desired target, is a reasonable extension of human influence. Through restoration activities, we manipulate succession for many reasons, including to maintain critical ecosystem services and to (re)establish desired plant communities (van Andel & Aronson, 2012). The target is typically, but not always, potential natural vegetation corresponding to environmental conditions of a site (SER, 2004), which can usually be found intact somewhere in the vicinity of the disturbed site. Such intact vegetation can be used as a reference for restoration efforts (Fig. 16.13a; van Andel & Aronson, 2012). The reference ecosystem can represent a target for restoration efforts, but is not always achieved due to ecological, economic, or other constraints. Alternatively, the target can be represented by younger successional stages than are those corresponding to potential natural vegetation (Fig. 16.13b). Restoration is one of several related processes that involve site improvement (e.g., rehabilitation, revitalization, reclamation; for terminology see SER, 2004; Cross *et al.*, 2018) but all the

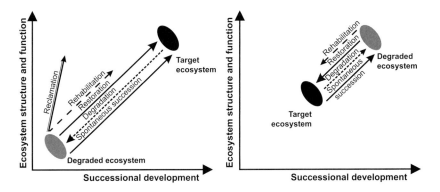

Figure 16.13 Hypothetical diagrams demonstrating the main processes that link succession and restoration. We assume that there is increasing complexity of ecosystem structure and function in each successional stage. Succession spontaneously proceeds or is manipulated by restoration measures to follow or reverse this natural process. Left: A potential natural vegetation is the target. Right: Succession is manipulated to reverse the process as we consider successionally more advanced stages to be degraded. Under restoration, we consider here a full recovery of a target, under rehabilitation at least partial improvement in the right direction toward a target, and under reclamation some measures taken in the direction of the target but not meeting it (e.g., to increase productivity of a site or decrease erosion). Adapted from Prach *et al.* (2007) and other sources with permission from Springer

related processes can be considered as restoration *sensu lato* (van Andel & Aronson, 2012) and this broader meaning is the one that we use here. From a generalized viewpoint of ecological succession, there are two principal directions by which succession can proceed or be manipulated to attain a target, either to accelerate it or to reverse it if it has proceeded beyond the target. In the former case, the starting capital of soil nutrients and biota is often low or even nonexistent. Here, there is a need to build an ecosystem that will hopefully follow a successional trajectory with increasing ecosystem complexity. The latter case is exactly the reverse (Marrs & Bradshaw, 1993; Marrs, 2002; Prach *et al.*, 2007).

As we showed in Section 16.2, spontaneous succession usually does lead, or provides indications that it is leading toward the respective potential natural vegetation. However, when undesirable vegetation develops, restoration measures are indicated. Undesirable communities are often those dominated by non–target species such as invasive aliens, and restorationists try to avoid such trajectories. Based on our comparative analyses, the role of invasive alien species in late successional stages is comparably low among biomes and moreover, it decreases with latitude (Fig. 16.7c). This is a good message for restoration ecologists, but individual situations can differ substantially from average trends. Local site conditions must be considered when applying knowledge of succession to restoration.

Knowledge about succession can help predict the nature of the target and the timing and trajectories of succession needed to reach it. This knowledge can come from detailed case studies, comparative studies, and field experience (Fig. 16.14). When a restoration program is implemented, monitoring should begin (del Moral *et al.*, 2007). Results of monitoring provide a feedback for predictions and facilitate adaptations to the restoration program if required (adaptive management; Williams, 2011). Monitoring can also serve as a convenient base for other scientific research, including testing ideas about succession. The scheme in Fig. 16.14 summarizes how knowledge of succession can be integrated into the process of ecological restoration and illustrates relationships between key elements of the process.

Efforts to restore ecosystem functions, biotic interactions, and community structure are more effective when restoration goals (i.e., targets) are not narrowly focused on static conditions but instead focus on the recovery of dynamic community processes. Restoration ecologists can both contribute to the development of successional theory (through their replicated studies) and benefit from it by utilizing any generalizations

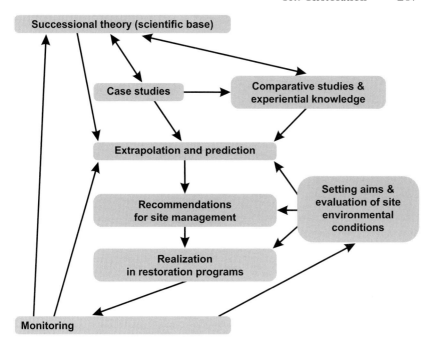

Figure 16.14 General scheme showing how knowledge of spontaneous succession can be integrated into ecological restoration.
Adapted from Prach *et al.* (2001), with permission from Wiley & Sons

about succession that supersede site-specific details. Successional concepts can guide future restoration activities by suggesting the most effective techniques and the best timing for manipulations to mimic natural successional mechanisms. Bradshaw (1987) suggested that restoration is an acid test for ecology and, by extension, for succession as well.

We distinguish three strategies for creating new ecosystems that represent increasing intensity of management (Prach & Hobbs, 2008). The first approach is called spontaneous (passive) restoration (Parker, 1997; Prach *et al.*, 2001; DellaSala *et al.*, 2003; Walker & del Moral, 2003). Based on our comparative analyses, we argue that the usefulness of this approach is generally underestimated and that it should be more often used in restoration projects around the world, especially at higher latitudes (temperate and boreal biomes; see Section 16.2). A second approach, called directed or assisted succession, is when spontaneous succession is assisted by limited physical site improvements or biotic manipulations (e.g., additions of desirable species; control of invasive aliens; Luken, 1990). A third approach is technical reclamation where

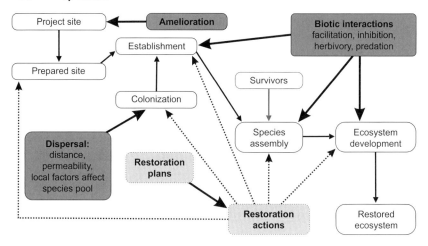

Figure 16.15 Restoration actions (dashed arrows) can affect all stages of the course of succession (illustrated by thin arrows). Dark gray boxes represent natural mechanisms that alter the success of organisms and are linked to successional processes (thick arrows). From del Moral *et al.* (2007), with permission from Springer

the entire system is controlled (Cross *et al.*, 2018). Mines often use this approach that can include sowing or planting a desirable mix of species. Choosing which restoration strategy to use requires some knowledge about the predictability of succession (see Section 16.7) and local environmental conditions. Whichever approach is used, restoration efforts can be applied to each successional stage (Fig. 16.15). Yet the focus of restoration efforts can shift depending on what ecological process or condition is most prominent at a given site and sere. We next address how restoration concerns are affected by stress–productivity gradients, early successional stages, and landscape and global contexts.

16.9.1 Stress-Productivity Gradients

At either end of a stress–productivity gradient, the probability of attaining a target stage by spontaneous succession decreases and the feasibility of technical reclamation increases (Prach & Hobbs, 2008; Fig. 16.16). Spontaneous succession can be most effectively used in the middle of environmental gradients where site environmental conditions are not extreme. At extremely nutrient-poor, toxic, dry, or intensively eroded sites with little or no vegetation (e.g., some mine sites; see Chapter 14), spontaneous succession is least reliable so technical measures are typically

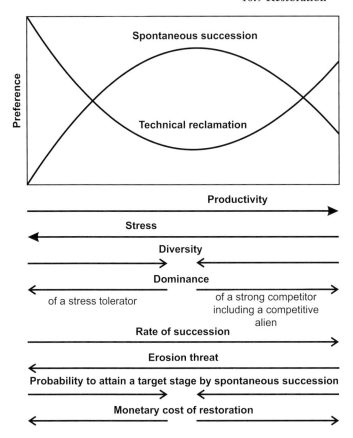

Figure 16.16 Relative preference of spontaneous succession (i.e., spontaneous or passive restoration) and technical reclamation along a productivity-stress gradient. Some core characteristics, relevant to restoration, are also related to the gradient. See Prach *et al.* (2007) and Prach and Hobbs (2008).

used to increase natural or productive values of the land (Whisenant, 1999) or to push the system over a particular threshold and initiate spontaneous succession (Whisenant *et al.*, 1995; King & Hobbs, 2006). Under conditions of high productivity, (e.g., some plowed fields; see Chapter 13), technical measures, such as topsoil removal (Grootjans & Verbeek, 2002) or carbon addition (Prober *et al.*, 2005; Kulmatiski *et al.*, 2006) may be adopted to encourage the reestablishment of diverse native plant communities and perhaps promote desirable trajectories of spontaneous succession. Invasive alien species, if important in late successional stages, may also require some restoration measures to eradicate or at least control them. Because the probability that invasive alien species modify successional trajectories decreases with latitude (Fig. 16.7c) such measures are particularly needed at lower latitudes.

In many restoration projects, the main goal is to re-vegetate a site as soon as possible, either to decrease the threat of erosion or to increase the productivity or aesthetic value of a site (Luken, 1990; Perrow & Davy, 2002). Spontaneous succession in productive sites, where environmental factors do not limit plant growth, is usually fast, in the sense of rapid formation of continuous vegetation cover. While rapid colonization can decrease the threat of erosion (Walker & del Moral, 2003), it often does not ensure desirable species composition, which might have to be manipulated. Such situations can occur when tropical rain forests are disturbed (see Section 16.2). In unproductive sites, where vegetation cover is sparse and forms slowly, the threat of erosion is usually higher than in productive sites (Ninot *et al.*, 2001), so technical reclamation is often needed (e.g., mine sites; see Chapter 14). In Arctic and alpine environments and other relatively pristine landscapes there is generally less need for intervention because of the available target species pool, and reduced invasion by alien species (see Chapter 6, Section 16.2).

16.9.2 Importance of Early Successional Stages

Early successional stages, such as meadows in a forested landscape, often support higher biodiversity, have more desirable species, and have higher conservation value than do closed forests (e.g., Wilson *et al.*, 2012; Řehounková *et al.*, 2016; see also Section 16.8). Therefore, early successional stages can enhance biodiversity within a late successional vegetation matrix. Such young stages can be maintained either through competition by an early successional dominant species, which can temporarily arrest succession, by grazing or browsing by wild animals, or through regular management (Walker *et al.*, 2007; Alday & Marrs, 2014). Even in heavily disturbed sites, such as those on mine tailings, early successional stages that develop by passive restoration can have more conservation value than does the surrounding landscape (Prach & Pyšek, 2001; Kirmer *et al.*, 2008). Řehounková *et al.* (2016) reported about five times more protected and endangered species from initial successional stages, maintained by additional disturbances, than from adjacent undisturbed late successional stages in an abandoned sand pit. Generally, we consider the value of initial and early successional stages to be underestimated by restoration ecologists. Their existence in a landscape may support and maintain regional biodiversity (see also Section 16.8) as demonstrated, for example, by studies of clearcuts and post-fire succession in boreal coniferous forests (see Chapters 11 and 12). The restoration goal of maintaining early successional stages is also typically valued in landscapes that have a long influence of traditional human impact under which valuable anthropogenic habitats developed (e.g., secondary hay meadows in Europe; see Chapter 15). However, in most landscapes the maintenance of early successional stages is not a priority. For example, in the tropics where maximal species diversity occurs in mature forests, rapid reforestation seems to be the prevailing goal of restoration (Lamb *et al.*, 2005). Additionally, forest gaps may be colonized by undesirable species such as pasture grasses (Riege & del Moral, 2004). Reforestation, whether spontaneous or from planting or sowing of a few native woody species, may not be the best approach for enhancement of species diversity, but is much better than doing nothing when large areas of agricultural land are abandoned and then dominated by invasive aliens.

16.9.3 Landscape and Global Contexts

The degree to which humans have altered the landscape affects the potential for immigration by suitable species. In less altered and traditionally managed landscapes, passive restoration usually proceeds toward valued (e.g., high biodiversity) ecosystems (Ruprecht, 2006). In strongly altered, uniform landscapes (e.g., arable lands lacking corridors or remnant, semi-natural vegetation), passive restoration cannot be expected to produce a desirable result (Boccanelli *et al.*, 2010). Such landscapes are often dominated by generalists and invasive alien species and target species are lacking (Hobbs *et al.*, 2009). In such cases, active restoration measures are needed.

Most restoration projects concentrate on a restored site while ignoring the surroundings. However, in the case of primary succession, which is characterized by an absence of biological legacy, colonization depends on 1) propagule availability in the surrounding landscape (Zobel *et al.*, 1998), 2) the presence and intensity of dispersal vectors (Settele *et al.*, 1996), and 3) the recruitment ability of species (Öster *et al.*, 2009). In secondary succession, such as on abandoned arable land (see Chapter 13), restoration of (semi)natural vegetation also depends on these same factors because late successional target species rarely occur in the propagule bank (Cramer & Hobbs, 2007). An exception would be in clearcuts or fire-adapted vegetation where seeds of late successional species may survive in the soil or the species regenerate by resprouting (Abella & Fornwalt,

2015). Generally, spontaneous restoration depends on external sources if target species are not present at a site. The surrounding vegetation can positively influence restoration through colonization by desirable target species. Negative effects of the surrounding vegetation on a restored site result from invasion of undesirable species, aliens, and other competitive synanthropic species. In some cases, if target species are not present, the development of such ecosystems is tolerable to provide at least some ecosystem services (Hobbs *et al.*, 2009).

Surrounding vegetation usually influences spontaneous succession (Prach & Řehounková, 2006; Prach *et al.*, 2015), although colonization may be through long-distance dispersal by wind or birds. In the case of vascular plants in some terrestrial habitats, proximity (up to 100 m) to populations of target plant species dictated the degree to which restoration occurred spontaneously (del Moral *et al.*, 2005; Řehounková & Prach, 2008), but some species may arrive from much longer distances (Kirmer *et al.*, 2008; Kepfer-Rojas *et al.*, 2014). In Chapter 14 (Table 14.1), we demonstrated the importance of vegetation at both 100 m and 1 km distance to succession, regarding colonization of seral stages by forest, grassland, and synanthropic species but not wetland species. Similarly, restoration activities of any kind are affected by surrounding vegetation. Therefore, increased consideration of the character of the surroundings of disturbed sites, prior to and during restoration activities will improve prediction of success or failure of the restoration. Prach *et al.* (2015) proposed several actions to improve restorations success: 1) provide an inventory of species of the surrounding habitats to distances of at least 100 m from a disturbed site prior to design of a restoration project and identify desirable and undesirable species; 2) with anthropogenic disturbances preserve, if possible, semi-natural habitats in close vicinity to a disturbed site even before restoration begins; 3) control invasive aliens or other undesirable species not only in the disturbed site, but also in its surroundings, at least up to 100 m distant; and 4) consider additional restoration measures of the surrounding areas if ownership and legislation allow.

Our global approach to the study of succession, and therefore to restoration, clearly indicates that the success of spontaneous succession (i.e., passive restoration) increases with latitude (Fig. 16.3). Among biomes, spontaneous restoration was most effective in temperate grasslands, and coniferous forests (Fig. 16.1a). These generalizations offer guidelines for when a focus on passive or active interventions might be needed for restoration. However, these are general trends and site-

Table 16.5 *Main processes and concepts concerning succession and possible restoration measures to manipulate succession*

Processes and concepts	Restoration measures
Primary succession	Manipulation of abiotic site factors
Secondary succession	Manipulation of biotic site factors
Facilitation	Use of nursery plants or crop
Inhibition	Control or eradication of undesirable competitive species
Safe sites	Fine-scale mechanical disturbances of surface; mulching
Gap dynamics	Mechanical creation of artificial gaps
Patch dynamics	Creation of differentially aged successional stages, e.g. by consecutive cutting; rotational management
Intermediate Disturbance Hypothesis	Adjustment of management
Species pool	Seeding, planting, eradication, or control of undesirable species in the surroundings and support of desirable species or communities
Metapopulation dynamics	Increasing connectivity among restored sites; e.g. establishing corridors, or supporting vectors transporting propagules (e.g., movement of domestic animals)

Adapted from Prach *et al.* (2007), with permission.

Scientific experiments vs. Practical restoration

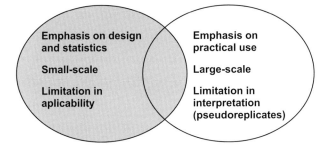

Figure 16.17 Different requirements of a scientific approach to succession and of a practical approach to ecological restoration. A larger overlap is desirable.

specific details must always be considered. In Table 16.5 we present tentative analogies between ecological processes and concepts concerning succession and possible corresponding restoration measures to manipulate succession. It is evident that the theoretical concepts and practical measures are very closely linked. However, basic research on succession and ecological restoration are often conducted as separate activities. While basic research mostly consists of experiments and a strict design of data sampling, which should follow statistical requirements with independent replicates, ecological restoration usually does not meet the criteria simply because of technical and practical reasons. This issue is summarized in Fig. 16.17. Because the need for restoration of degraded or destroyed ecosystems will continue to increase, we expect closer links between studies on succession and ecological restoration.

17 · Conclusions and Future Research Challenges

17.1 Comparative Analyses

We undertook the writing of this book because of the lack of comparative studies of (plant) succession across biomes and disturbance types and because of the potential benefit to restoration efforts if site-specific studies were generalizable. Despite reviewing about 7,000 studies, we found only 530 of those studies useful for our detailed comparisons of various trends in succession. We used broad categories for comparison because of the large variability in site conditions, sampling methods, and documented patterns. We found some patterns that we summarize in this chapter before discussing what we see as some outstanding challenges and opportunities in successional research. Both the summarized patterns and future challenges are briefly presented in Table 17.1.

Our four characteristics of succession (success of succession in achieving target vegetation, predominance of convergent or divergent trajectories, increases or decreases in species richness, and the importance of invasive aliens) revealed several interesting patterns. The most prominent pattern was one we detected earlier in mines and plowed fields (Prach & Walker, 2019): a pronounced increase in success with increasing latitude. This pattern was reflected in the biome distributions and was linked to decreasing temperature and participation of invasive alien species in late successional stages with increasing latitude. The main explanation for this pattern is likely to be the decreasing pool of species with increased latitude, which increases the probability of reaching the relatively species-poor target vegetation. Patterns of success are probably influenced more by the available species than by climate, although biomes and latitude incorporate both of these variables.

Success also varied by disturbance type, and was slightly higher after natural or partly natural than after anthropogenic disturbances. Disturbance severity was not as clear a driver of success. Success was highest in the case of fire and lowest for volcanoes. Overall, we found several

Table 17.1 *Conclusions and gaps in research on succession. For biome and disturbance abbreviations see Fig. 16.1*

Characteristic of succession	Main conclusions	Gaps and future research challenges
Success of succession to reach target	Success is positively influenced by increasing latitude, decreasing temperature, and decreasing presence of invasive alien species; the three main factors are correlated	More exact data needed to enable quantitative comparisons; common criteria of success should be developed
Trajectory	Divergence prevails, especially at low latitude (in tropical rain forests) and in heterogeneous landscapes	Many studies describe one, linear chronosequence; we need more studies investigating more stages along environmental gradients to reveal successional networks
Trends in species richness	Increases during succession prevail, but the total number of species is not particularly informative	We need more investigations on participation of desired (target) species, how they establish and persist, and how they assemble with other species
Importance of invasive alien species	Decreases in succession and with latitude; alien species in late successional stages still unimportant in three-quarters of seres but increasing influence expected in the future	Research needed on how they integrate into ecosystems in the process of succession and how they influence ecosystem structure and functions
Disturbance	Recovery is faster when a system is adapted to a given type of disturbance, such as fire in ME, TG, or CF biomes, than after a disturbance to which a system is not adapted (e.g., mining); in the former systems, the Intermediate Disturbance Hypothesis often does not fit	Lack of generalizations about how initial and repeated disturbances affect succession; disturbance gradient studies are a particular lack
Temporal scales	Time to recovery largely varies among biomes and disturbances, averaging	Time to recovery is the core information for prediction of succession, thus more

Table 17.1 (*cont.*)

Characteristic of succession	Main conclusions	Gaps and future research challenges
	several centuries but ranging from 1 to 2,000 years, then retrogression can be expected; slowest recovery in primary, natural seres (VO, GL) and at extreme low (TR) or high latitudes (TU)	investigations are needed; retrogression should be examined more often in studies of succession (but there is a lack of old chronosequences)
Spatial scales	Comparative studies across larger scales are possible now; at the global scale they are presented here with some promising results (see other boxes)	Do processes occur differently at different spatial scales? Few studies at very small (microbe role) and very large (continental, global) scales; the large-scale gap partially filled by this book
Functional traits	Dispersal traits and traits supporting competition of species seem to be most important; functional species traits are promising tool to explain mechanisms of succession, despite still ambiguous results	More integration of traits into studies on succession is desired; generalizations still lacking about traits that alter species roles in succession
Interactions among biota	Propagule dispersal by animals, and grazing or browsing are generally recognized as highly important in succession	Large gaps exist especially in interactions among plants and soil microbes and invertebrates despite their decisive impact on succession
Predictability	Prediction is one important goal of successional studies; convergent or linear successions are easier to predict, as well as patterns of functional species groups rather than exact species composition	Practical implications in ecological restoration and land management will be more and more appreciated under ongoing global change, and models and expert systems may help
Reaction to global climate change	Some shifts in distribution of vegetation types and even biomes already distinguished	More shifts expected in the future, together with homogenization of vegetation due to expansion of generalists and aliens; past data from permanents plots will serve as reference

Table 17.1 (*cont.*)

Characteristic of succession	Main conclusions	Gaps and future research challenges
Implications for conservation	Successional stages of every age may be important for the occurrence of rare and retreating species, thus whole chronosequences and not only mature stages should be protected in some cases	Threats represented by invasive alien species to native ones should be further investigated in succession; there are many gaps and challenges for future research in this area
Implications for restoration	Restoration is closely linked with succession; spontaneous succession is a more effective tool in restoration than usually expected and can be used more frequently	Identification of additional links between succession and restoration and their practical implications represent a fertile area for additional research

clearly global patterns in success and also much variation among biomes and disturbance types. A clear benefit to future analyses (of success and of all variables) will be a larger data base of collections using similar methods, thus providing directly comparable data.

Successional trajectories were not as influenced by the other factors we considered as was success. Divergence prevailed and patterns were largely due to differences among biomes. Although convergence was least at low latitudes, there was no significant latitudinal effect overall. There were minor influences by disturbances and the presence or absence of forest cover. There was a mixed response to human influence and disturbance severity. Local site variability is a likely cause of the paucity of global influences on successional trajectories.

Richness typically increased during succession, and the trends in species richness were influenced by biome, latitude, moisture, and disturbance type. Richness increased most at mid latitudes (except in the Mediterranean biome), in wetter biomes, and following severe disturbances such as mines, volcanoes, and glaciers; the smallest increases were found following cyclones.

Invasive alien species were not reported as influencing the majority of studies, but their importance in late-successional stages varied by biome, latitude, temperature, disturbance type, site age, and presence or absence of forest cover. A negative relationship occurred between the importance of invasive alien species and increasing latitude, while higher levels of human influence increased their role in succession. The relationships between the importance of invasive alien species and disturbance type and severity were less clear, in part because of large variation among and within disturbance types. No invasive species were reported to influence post-glacial succession, while plowed fields, volcanoes, and dunes were the most influenced.

Overall, success of succession was the characteristic of succession that showed the clearest patterns, despite the necessary subjectivity of its evaluation (see Chapter 4). In addition to its clear increase with latitude (Figs. 16.1c and 16.3), success generally declines with increased human alteration of the landscape, in part because of decreasing availability of target species and increasing influence of invasive alien species (Prach et al., 2019). We can also expect the degree of human alteration to be highest at mid latitudes and lowest at high latitudes (Newbold et al., 2015). Therefore, in Fig. 17.1, we combined these three patterns, increasing success with latitude, decreasing success with the degree of human transformation of the landscape, and a peak of human influence at mid latitudes. This figure illustrates how one can broadly predict the probability that spontaneous succession reaches its target, a feature critical in determining appropriate restoration activities (Prach & Walker, 2019). However, this figure should be considered as a general guideline and not as a template for a particular site. Intervention appears to be least important in pristine landscapes at high latitudes and most important in human altered landscapes at low latitudes.

There are other key influences, either direct or indirect, on the success of succession than just latitude and the degree of human transformation of the landscape (Fig. 17.2). Increasing latitude is negatively correlated with the number of invasive alien species (compare Fig. 16.7c) and the number of species in the regional species pool (Gilman et al., 2015). Both the alien and high regional species pools negatively affect the success of succession as defined here (see Chapters 4 and 16), and affect the target species pool, but not in a clearly positive or negative direction. The degree of human transformation of the landscape directly decreases success of succession and indirectly decreases success through increases in the alien species pool and decreases in the target species pool (Prach et al., 2019). Human transformation also increases the differences of site conditions between seral and reference sites, which, in turn, negatively affects success. Human transformation has further negative effects on success by reducing the adaptability of the system to disturbance, which

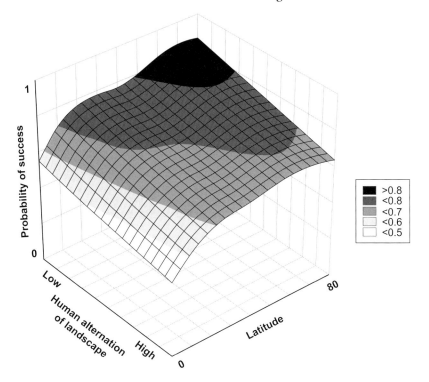

Figure 17.1 Probability of succession to reach a target increases with latitude and decreases with the degree of human transformation of landscape, while the degree of human transformation is generally highest at middle latitudes and lowest at highest latitudes. These three main relationships are combined in this graph (fitted by Spline method in Statistica).

can lead to species experiencing more environmental stress. Many other factors affect success of succession (e.g., disturbance regimes, soil fertility, climatic fluctuations, and species life history characteristics and inter-actions), but Fig. 17.2 focuses on broadly generalizable topics that were central to this book.

17.2 Future Research Challenges

The human domination of the planet has altered succession in many ways, particularly through our influence on nitrogen and carbon cycles, global temperatures, spread of invasive alien species, and alteration of disturbance regimes. It is unclear exactly how these changes will alter

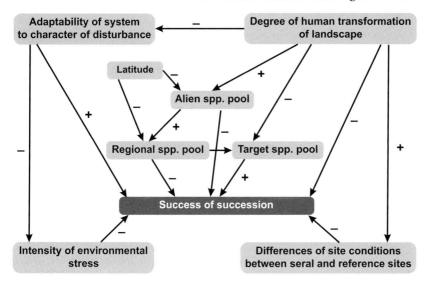

Figure 17.2 Principal factors influencing the success of succession and their positive or negative interactions. For details, see text.

succession, but there are many possibilities that provide a clear challenge to future research in succession. Nitrogen enrichment (Vitousek *et al.*, 1997) may decelerate succession by promoting fast-growing, competitive pioneers that dominate resources and lower local species richness (Southon *et al.*, 2013; Walker & Wardle, 2014). The effects of atmospheric carbon dioxide enrichment on succession are less clear. To the extent more carbon dioxide leads to increased plant growth, nitrogen limitation can ensue (Norby & Zak, 2011), which can retard succession by limiting colonization and growth. Another possible outcome of higher carbon dioxide levels is an acceleration of succession in less fertile habitats by the promotion of woody plant invasion (Wright *et al.*, 2013), or other shifts in plant life forms or longevities (Bugman & Bigler, 2011; Walker & Wardle, 2014). Clearly, many challenges are presented for future succession research by the current global shifts in nutrient cycles.

Warming temperatures alter successional trajectories, lead to shifting species distributions particularly at higher latitudes and elevations, and have variable effects on successional rates and alpha diversity (Walker & Wardle, 2014). A related and especially difficult problem, sometimes accompanying global warming, is the introduction of alien species and their influence on succession. For example, invasive species can displace early-successional species and accelerate succession (Smale, 1990) or inhibit late-successional species and arrest succession (Davis *et al.*, 2005). In addition to changes in rates of succession, trajectories might demonstrate increasing divergence due to the introduction of new species. By contrast, homogenization of biota worldwide might support convergence. Invasive species can also alter successional trajectories by changing nutrient status (Hughes & Denslow, 2005) or fire regime (D'Antonio *et al.*, 2011). Irregular precipitation regimes, another common consequence of climate change, can affect succession by decreasing species diversity, as observed in dry tropical forests in Mexico (Maza-Villalobos *et al.*, 2013), or limit establishment of woody species in drier areas, thus changing the physiognomy of seral stages.

We see future research tacking these issues in six ways. First, we hope that more detailed ecological studies are conducted about disturbance and its link to succession. Despite much interest from land use planners about risk management and several books (e.g., Walker, 1999a, 2012; Reice, 2003; Johnson & Miyanishi, 2007; Wohlgemuth *et al.*, 2019) and review papers (e.g., White & Jentsch, 2001; Platt & Connell, 2003; Jentsch & White, 2019) about the ecology of disturbance, its link to succession remains understudied. Interactions among different disturbances (e.g., Buma, 2015), have complex but poorly understood effects on succession. With human alteration of fire regimes, for example, what will be the implications for insect outbreaks, logging, the spread of disease, and other disturbances on coniferous forest succession (Lindenmayer *et al.*, 2008; Burton, 2010; Johnstone *et al.*, 2016)?

A second, fruitful approach to the study of succession is the use of comparisons of temporal and spatial scales. A spatial approach to ecology, and to some degree succession, has long been utilized and continues to offer insights, particularly as scales are contrasted (van Bruegel *et al.*, 2019). Surprisingly, fewer studies have explicitly addressed the temporal variation in succession (Walker & Wardle, 2014; Wolkovitch *et al.*, 2014), despite occasional examinations of rates (Bornkamm, 1981; Anderson, 2007; del Moral & Chang, 2015). In studies of temporal variation, it is rare that multiple seres are compared (Prach *et al.*, 1993). We see hopeful trends in the inclusion of different scales in comparative approaches to studying rates of succession (van Breugel *et al.*, 2019; Chang *et al.*, 2019), yet more work is needed on both rates of species turnover and recovery times to potential natural vegetation.

Third, we emphasize the value of better linkages between the large set of studies on functional traits of plants and their successional roles (Latzel *et al.*, 2011; Funk *et al.*, 2016). The recent expansion of studies on species traits should lead to new findings about succession, despite the frequent lack of explicit connections between traits and succession. We expect that functional species traits will substantially help to explain mechanisms of succession and functioning of seral ecosystems. However, we are convinced, species identity still remains the basis for description and explanation of successional processes.

A fourth opportunity for succession research involves an expansion of the traditional study of plant interactions to include more plant-microbe (Turner *et al.*, 2019) and plant–invertebrate interactions (Fagan *et al.*, 2005), particularly regarding soil organisms (Frouz *et al.*, 2008). This avenue of research is exploding with improved technology for identifying soil microbes. Successional implications include insights into nutrient availability and its role in driving succession (Koziol & Bever, 2019; Teste & Laliberté, 2019). In addition to increased measurements of the role of soil microbes in succession, what is now needed is a further emphasis on generalizations across seres.

A fifth topic involves the role of alien species in succession, including when and how they establish (e.g., invasion windows, Johnstone, 1986; Gill *et al.*, 2018), and how they influence ecosystem functions. Again, in this growing field of research, what is still inadequately covered is the nature of the link between alien species and succession (Pyšek *et al.*, 2004). Despite our results suggesting that invasive aliens do not often modify succession, we can expect them to have an increasing role. Indeed, some invasive aliens are already becoming central components of certain "novel" ecosystems (Hobbs *et al.*, 2009). Land managers are already learning to adapt to this reality and further insights about how invasive aliens influence succession are a task for future research.

Finally, the link between restoration and succession is well established (Luken, 1990; Walker *et al.*, 2007; Prach & Hobbs, 2008) and continues to provide vital insights for the application of successional principles to issues of land management. Of particular importance going forward is prediction of successional change at varying temporal scales and associated lessons for restoration activities.

Table 17.1 summarizes our main conclusions and what we see as future research challenges, encapsulating the ideas in this chapter and Chapter 16. We cover the four principal foci of this book, success of succession, trajectories, species richness, and invasive alien species. We also include other key themes: disturbance, temporal and spatial scales, interactions among biota, and predictability of succession. We conclude with management concerns of how succession will respond to global climate change and successional links to conservation and restoration topics. We hope that this book serves to focus more attention on large spatial scale aspects of succession. We expect more comparative studies at continental and global scales in the future. Hopefully such studies will continue to refine and quantify the effort that we have begun here.

Appendix 1

Glossary

Abiotic: pertaining to nonliving factors (e.g., wind, temperature, erosion)

Alien species: *see* invasive alien species

Allelopathy: form of inhibition based on release of chemicals that deter competitors

Allogenic: force originating from outside a community or ecosystem (e.g., wind)

Anthropogenic: created or influenced by humans

Arrested succession: succession stalled at a given stage, typically from inhibition or recurring disturbance

Assembly rules: predictions concerning mechanisms of community organization

Autogenic: force originating from inside a community or ecosystem (e.g., competition)

Biological legacy: biotic characteristics (biomass, structure, finction) that remain after a disturbance

Biome: ecosystem with similar vegetation conditioned largely by macroclimate

Boreal: biome dominated by coniferous forests with cold winters (e.g., taiga)

CAM photosynthesis: Crassulacean acid metabolism, a water-saving form of photosynthesis used by cacti and other succulent plants

Chernozem soils: black, humus-rich soils capable of high agricultural yields that are typical of steppe vegetation

Chronosequence: space-for-time substitution that allows study of long-term succession

Climax vegetation: vegetation that has reached a more or less stable state in late succession

Competition:	negative effect of one organism on another in exploitation of resources
Continentality:	distant from oceanic shorelines
Convergence:	successional trajectories where communities become more similar with time
Cryptogam:	plant with no true flowers or seeds (e.g., fern, moss, alga)
Desertification:	conversion of rangeland or semi-desert to desert
Diaspore:	*see* propagule
Disharmony:	distinctive from surrounding vegetation
Dispersal:	movement of propagules (e.g., seeds, offspring) away from parent
Disturbance:	relatively abrupt loss of biomass or structure from autogenic or allogenic forces
Divergence:	successional trajectories where communities become less similar with time
Ecosystem service:	ecosystem benefit for humans (e.g., clean water)
Ecotone:	boundary between two ecosystems; the edge of a patch
Ectomycorrhizae:	*see* mycorrhizae
Endemism:	restricted geographic range
Endozoochory:	seed dispersal via ingestion by animals. Antonym: epizoochory
Epiphyte:	plant growing on another plant
Evapotranspiration:	sum of evaporation and transpiration from vegetation to the atmosphere
Facilitation:	positive influence of one organism on another
Fallow:	period of no cultivation to restore soil fertility
Functional trait:	any characteristics of a species that influences its interactions with the environment (e.g., growth rate)
Geophyte:	a perennial plant that seasonally regenerates from underground storage organ (e.g., tuber, rhizome)
GIS:	Geographical Information Systems, used to manage and present geographical data

Glacial refugia:	areas where species survived glacial periods
Holism:	approach that emphasizes connectivity and that the whole is greater than the sum of the parts; *see* reductionism
Hydrosere:	succession in water
Inhibition:	negative effect of one organism on another
Initial floristic composition:	concept that all species are present initially and succession is a process of sequential conspicuousness
Intermediate Disturbance Hypothesis:	maximum diversity is obtained at intermediate levels of disturbance
Intertropical convergence zone:	zone near the Equator where northern and southern air masses converge and produce low atmospheric pressure
Invasive alien species:	generally undesirable species spreading into a new landscape. Synonym: nonnative invasive species
Keystone species:	species with a pivotal role in ecosystem function
Macroclimate:	average climate of a large geographic area
Mesoclimate:	climate of a geographically restricted area, such as a valley
Mesophyllous leaves:	large, soft leaves adapted to humid environment
Metapopulation:	group of populations of the same species interacting in space
Microclimate:	climate within meters of a plant
Mine tailings:	*see* spoil heap
Mycorrhizae:	mutualistic interactions between fungi and vascular plants largely within (endomycorrhizae) or largely on the surface (ectomycorrhizae) of plant roots
Naturalized species:	alien species established and reproducing in its new location
Nitrophilous:	nitrogen-loving plant
Novel ecosystem:	new ecosystem created by human influences
Nurse plant:	plant that facilitates another plant, particularly under its larger canopy
Phenology:	life stages of an organism

Physiognomy:	the physical structure of a plant
Plant community:	group of interacting plants in a specific place and time
Podzolization:	soil formation in humid climates where upper soil layers heavily leached
Potential natural vegetation:	a late successional plant community that is adapted to a site's environmental conditions; it may correspond to adjacent, undisturbed vegetation, and often represents a target of ecological restoration
Priority effects:	successional consequences of arrival order of colonists where an early colonist determines subsequent species composition
Propagule:	any reproductive unit that is adapted to dispersal. Synonym: diaspore
Reductionism:	approach that emphasizes individual processes and entities; *see* holism
Refugia:	*see* glacial refugia
Resilience:	ability of an ecosystem to return to its pre-disturbance condition
Resistance:	ability of an ecosystem to persist unchanged in the face of disturbance
Restoration:	returning a damaged or destroyed ecosystem to at least some of its former biological state
Retrogression:	successional process of decreasing biomass, diversity, or function. Antonym: progression
Richness:	*see* species diversity
Ruderal:	weedy plant that colonizes recent disturbances
Sclerophyllous leaves:	small, thick, leathery leaves adapted to arid environment
Seed bank:	pool of all seeds found on a plant, on the soil surface, or buried in the soil
Sere:	successional sequence
Serotiny:	having cones that open when heated by fire; a form of delayed seed dispersal
Slash-and-burn agriculture:	short-term agriculture following cutting and burning of a forest

Solifluction:	downhill movement of usually saturated soil, often where underlain by frozen layer
Species diversity:	combination of evenness of distribution and number of species (richness) in a given area; diversity commonly used to imply only richness
Spoil heap:	piled mine wastes. Synonym: mine tailings
Spontaneous succession:	succession that occurs without human interference. It is used in passive or natural restoration. Antonym: directed or assisted succession
Stochastic:	unpredictable
Success of succession:	establishment of target vegetation, often potential natural vegetation
Succession:	species and community replacement, or ecosystem development over time following a disturbance that leaves little or no (primary) or substantial (secondary) biological legacy and may reach a relatively equilibrial state (climax)
Succulent plant:	one with leaves or stems that are thickened and fleshy to store water
Synanthropic plant:	plant that thrives in association with human habitats
Target species:	species desired for restoration purposes
Therophyte:	annual plant that survives harsh conditions as a seed
Toposequence:	sequence of soils related to local topography; sometimes used instead of chronosequence
Trait:	see functional trait
Transpiration:	loss of water from a plant's surface due to biological activity
Topography:	the surface features of the land
Trichome:	small outgrowth on plant surface (e.g., hair, scale)
Vivipary:	germination and early seedling growth while still attached to parent plant

Appendix 2

Literature and Search Phrases Used in Comparative Analyses

N = sample size of studies that fit our criteria (see Chapter 4). Biome is in parentheses (TR: tropical rain forests, TD: tropical dry forests, AR: aridlands, ME: Mediterranean, TG: temperate grasslands, TB: temperate broadleaf forests, CF: coniferous forests, TU: tundra, AL: alpine). Web of Science was used for searching the phrases. Full citations are in the Reference section.

Volcanoes (N = 36) Search terms: succession AND (plant OR vegetation) AND (volcano OR tephra OR lava OR ash OR lahar OR pyroclastic flow)
Aplet *et al.* 1998 (TR), Atkinson 1970 (TR), Brown *et al.* 1917 (TR), Clarkson 1997 (TR), Clarkson & Clarkson 1994 (TB), Clarkson & Clarkson 1995 (TB), Cutler *et al.* 2008 (TU), del Moral *et al.* 2011 (CF), Dickson & Crocker 1953 (CF), Dimopoulos *et al.* 2010 (ME), Elias & Dias 2004 (ME), Gallardo *et al.* 2012 (TB), García-Romero *et al.* 2015 (TR), Grishin 2010 (CF), Grishin *et al.* 1996 (CF), Heath 1967 (CF), Hendrix 1981 (TD), Horrocks & Ogden 1998 (TB), Kamijo *et al.* 2002 (TB), Korablev & Neshataeva 2016 (CF), Magnússon & Magnússon 2000 (TU), Nakamura 1985 (TB), Partomihardjo *et al.* 1992 (TR), Raus 1988 (ME), Rejmánek *et al.* 1982 (CF), Sklenář *et al.* 2010 (AL), Tagawa 1964 (TB), Tagawa *et al.* 1985 (TR), Taylor 1957 (TR), Teramoto *et al.* 2017 (TB), Tezuka 1961 (TB), Thornton *et al.* 2001 (TR), Tsuyuzaki 1995 (TB), Uhe 1988 (TR), Whittaker & Bush 1993 (TR), Wilmshurst & McGlone 1996 (TB).

Glaciers (N = 25) Search terms: succession AND (plant OR vegetation) AND (glacier OR deglaciated OR deglaciation)
Albrecht *et al* 2010 (AL), Birks 1980 (CF), Burga *et al.* 2010 (AL), D´ Amico *et al.* 2014 (AL), Doležal *et al.* 2008 (AL), Fastie 1995 (CF), Favero-Longo *et al.* 2012 (TU), Garibotti *et al.* 2011a (AL), Garibotti

et al. 2011b (TB), Helm & Allen (1995 (CF), Jones & Henry 2003 (TU), Kaufmann & Raffl 2002 (AL), Marcante *et al.* 2009 (AL), Matthews & Whittaker 1987 (AL), Mizuno & Fujita 2014 (AL), Moreau *et al.* 2008 (TU), Mori *et al.* 2013 (TU), Prach & Rachlewicz 2012 (TU), Reiners *et al.* 1971 (CF), Sommerville *et al.* 1982 (AL), Tisdale *et al.* 1966 (CF), Vetaas 1994 (AL), Viereck 1966 (AL), Wardle 1979 (CF), Whelan & Bach 2017 (AL).

Cyclones (N = 21) Search terms: succession AND (plant OR vegetation) AND (cyclone OR hurricane OR typhoon OR wind damage) Allen *et al.* 2012 (TB), Burley *et al.* 2008 (CF), Crow 1980 (TR), FÖ 1988a (TB), Frangi & Lugo 1998 (TR), Franklin 2007 (TR), Harcombe *et al.* 2002 (TB), Heartsill Scalley 2017 (TR + TR), Hibbs 1983 (TB), Imbert & Portecop 2008 (TD), Mabry & Korsgren 1998 (TB), Royo *et al.* 2011 (TR), Shimizu 2005 (CF), Skłodowski *et al.* 2014 (TB), Smith *et al.* 1997 (TB), Tanner & Bellingham 2006 (TR), Vandermeer *et al.* 2000 (TR), Weaver 1989 (TR), Webb & Scanga 2001 (TB), Whitmore 1989 (TR).

Dunes (N = 39) Search terms: succession AND (plant OR vegetation) AND (dune) Aggenbach *et al.* 2017 (TB), Álvarez-Molina *et al.* 2012 (TR), Angiolini *et al.* 2013 (ME), Avis & Lubke 1996 (ME), Ayyad 1973 (ME), Belsky & Amundson 1986 (TD), Berendse *et al.* 1998 (TB), Binggeli *et al.* 1992 (TB), Bokhorst *et al.* 2017 (TB), Bossuyt *et al.* 2005 (TB), Çakan *et al.* 2011 (ME), Chadwick & Dalke 1965 (AR), Ciccarelli 2015 (ME), Cussedu *et al.* 2016 (ME), Dilustro & Day 1997 (TB), Emery *et al.* 2015 (TB), Henriques & Hay 1998 (TR), Imbert & Houle 2000 (TU), Isermann 2011 (TB), Johnson 1997 (TB), Kuiters *et al.* 2009 (TB), Kumler 1962 (CF), Lichter 1998 (CF), Londo 1974 (TB), Mantilla-Contreras *et al.* 2012 (TB), Miller *et al.* 2010 (TB), Muñoz-Reinoso 2018 (ME), Nylén & Luoto 2015 (CF), Olff *et al.* 1993 (TB), Olson 1958 (TB), Parker-Nance *et al.* 1991 (ME), Pegman & Rapson 2005 (TB), Roy-Bolduc *et al.* 2016 (CF), Sciandrello *et al.* 2015 (ME), Sparrius *et al.* 2013 (TB), Tissier *et al.* 2013 (CF), Ujházy *et al.* 2011 (TB), van der Maarel *et al.* 1985 (TB), Wang *et al.* 2015 (AR).

Landslides (N = 46) Search terms: succession AND (plant OR vegetation) AND (landslide OR debris flow OR debris avalanche OR rock slide) Arunachalam & Upadhyaya 2005 (TR), Bartleman *et al.* 2001 (TU), Basher *et al.* (unpublished) (AL), Bellingham *et al.* 2001 (TB), Bowers *et al.* 1997 (AR), Burn & Friele 1989 (CF), Cannone *et al.* 2010 (TU),

Chou *et al.* 2009 (TB), Curtin 1994 (AL), Dale & Adams 2003 (CF), Dalling 1994 (TR), Dislich & Huth 2012 (TR), Elias & Dias 2009 (ME), Flaccus 1959 (TB), Francescato *et al.* 2001 (TB), Frenzen *et al.* 1988 (CF), Guariguata 1990 (TR), Hull & Scott 1982 (TB), Kessler 1999 (TR), Khitun *et al.* 2015 (TU), Kroh *et al.* 2008 (CF), Lambert 1972 (TU), Li *et al.* 2017 (TB), Lin *et al.* 2008 (TB), Lundgren 1978 (TR), Mark *et al.* 1989 (TB), Miles & Swanson 1986 (CF), Myster & Walker 1997 (TR), Myster *et al.* 1997 (TR), Nakashizuka *et al.* 1993 (TB), Neto *et al.* 2017 (ME), Ohl & Bussman 2004 (TR), Pabst & Spies 2001 (CF), Pandey & Singh 1985 (TB), Reddy & Singh 1993 (TB), Restrepo *et al.* 2003 (TR), Rood 2006 (CF), Schumacher 1997 (TB), Seiwa *et al.* (TB), Shiels & Walker 2013a (TR), Smale *et al.* 1997 (TB), Smith *et al.* 1986 (CF), Takeuchi & Shimano 2009 (TB), Walker *et al.* 2010a (TR), Walker *et al.* 2013a (TR), Yang *et al.* 2016 (TB).

Floods (N = 48) Search terms: succession AND (plant OR vegetation) AND (floodplain OR flood plain OR riverbank OR river bank OR riparian)

Baker & Walford 1995 (AR), Bellingham *et al.* 2001 (TB), Bellingham *et al.* 2005 (TB), Biondini & Kandus 2006 (TR), Binkley *et al.* 1997 (CF), Bliss & Cantlon 1957 (TU), Boggs & Weaver 1994 (TG), Bush *et al.* 2006 (TB), Clement 1985 (CF), Cline & McAllister 2012 (TB), Cordes *et al.* 1997 (TG), Crampton 1987 (CF), Dahlskog 1982 (TU), Davis & Smith 2013 (TB), Egger *et al.* 2015 (CF), Fonda 1974 (CF), Friedman *et al.* 1996 (TB), Frye & Quinn 1979 (TB), Fyles & Bell 1986 (CF), Garófano-Gómez *et al.* 2017 (TB), Gibb 1994 (TB), Gill 1973 (CF), Halwagy 1961 (AR), Helm & Collins 1997 (CF), Hollingsworth *et al.* 2010 (CF), Ignjatović *et al.* 2013 (TB), Johnson *et al.* 1976 (TB), Kalliola & Puhakka 1988 (TU), Kalliola *et al.* 1991 (TR) Korkmaz *et al.* 2017 (ME), Lindsey *et al.* 1961 (TB), Little *et al.* 2013 (CF), Luken & Fonda 1983 (CF), Morris & Stanford 2011 (TU), Mouw *et al.* 2013 (CF), Nakamura *et al.* 1997 (TB), Nanson & Beach 1977 (CF), Oliveira-Filho *et al.* 1994 (TD), Prach 1994 (AR), Prach *et al.* 2014b (TB), Rejmánek *et al.* 1987 (TB), Smith & Lee 1984 (TB), Terborgh & Petren 1991 (TR), Timoney *et al.* 1997 (CF), Van Auken & Bush 1985 (AR), Viereck 1970 (CF), Wilson 1970 (TB), Van Pelt *et al.* 2006 (CF).

Fire (N = 83) Search terms: succession AND (plant OR vegetation) AND (fire OR wildfire OR burn*)

Álvarez *et al.* 2009 (TB), Aslan 2015 (TG), Atkinson 2004 (TB), Barret *et al.* 2012 (TU), Benscoter & Vitt 2008 (CF), Bouchon & Arseneault 2004 (CF), Brulisauer *et al.* 1996 (CF), Buhk *et al.* 2006 (ME), Bullock & Webb 1995 (TB), Calder *et al.* 1992 (TG), Calvo *et al.* 2005 (ME), Campbell & Antos 2003 (CF), Capitano & Carcaillet 2008 (ME), Carleton & Maclellan 1994 (CF), Clark *et al.* 2003 (CF), Coop *et al.* 2010 (CF), D'Antonio *et al.* 2011 (TD), de Deus & Oliviera 2016 (TD), De Villiers & O'Connor 2011 (TD), Delarze *et al.* 1992 (TB), Donato *et al.* 2009 (ME), Doyle *et al.* 1998 (CF), Driscoll *et al.* 1999 (CF), Dzwonko *et al.* 2015 (TB), Ehrensperger *et al.* 2013 (TD), Engel & Abella 2011 (AR), Franklin *et al.* 2004 (ME), Freestone *et al.* 2015 (ME), Frelich & Reich 1995 (CF), Gibson *et al.* 2016 (CF), Gloaguen 1993 (TB), González-DeVega *et al.* 2016 (ME), González-Tagle *et al.* 2008 (ME), Gosper *et al.* 2013 (ME), Guedo & Lamb 2013 (TG), Hanna & Fulgham 2015 (AR), Harrod *et al.* 2000 (TB), Harvey & Holzman 2014 (ME), Heinl *et al.* 2007 (TD), Huff 1995 (CF), Huffman *et al.* 2012 (AR), Humphrey 1984 (AR), Ivanova *et al.* 2017 (CF), Jacquet & Prodon 2009 (ME), Johnstone & Chapin III 2006 (CF), Kavgaci *et al.* 2010 (ME), Kazanis & Arianoutsou 1996 (ME), Kellman & Meave 1997 (TD), Knops 2006 (TG), Knuckey *et al.* 2016 (AR), Lantz *et al.* 2010 (TU), Lesieur *et al.* 2002 (CF), Mallik *et al.* 2010 (CF), McCoy *et al.* 1999 (TR), Meira-Neto *et al.* 2011 (ME), Morisson *et al.* 1995 (ME), Morris & Leger 2016 (AR), Nadeau & Corns 2002 (CF), Nelson *et al.* 2014 (AR), Overbeck *et al.* 2005 (TD), Powers *et al.* 2009 (TD), Privett *et al.* 2001 (ME), Purdie & Slatyer 1976 (ME), Rees & Juday 2002 (CF), Reich *et al.* 2001 (CF), Richardson *et al.* 2014 (TB), Romme *et al.* 2016 (CF), Ruokolainen & Salo 2009 (CF), Schaffhauser *et al.* 2012 (ME), Schulze *et al.* 2005 (CF), Sedláková & Chytrý 1999 (TG), Smirnova *et al.* 2008 (CF), Spellman *et al.* 2014 (CF), Strong 2009 (CF), Tárrega *et al.* 1995 (ME), Tavţanoďlu & Gürkan 2014 (ME), Taylor & Chen 2011 (CF), Tepley *et al.* 2014 (CF), Trabaud & Campant 1991 (ME), Türkmen & Düzenli 2005 (ME), Wiser *et al.* 2012 (TB), Wu *et al.* 2014 (TG), Yates *et al.* 2003 (ME).

Clearcuts (N = 65) Search terms: succession AND (plant OR vegetation) AND (clearcut* OR clearings OR opening OR glade)

Aiba *et al.* 2001 (TB), Allard-Duchene *et al.* 2014 (CF), Archambault *et al.* 1998 (CF), Bainbridge & Strong 2005 (CF), Banner & LePage 2008 (CF), Barbour *et al.* 1998 (CF), Baret *et al.* 2007 (TR), Bermúdez *et al.* 2007 (ME), Bishoff *et al.* 2005 (TR), Bradshaw *et al.* 2005 (TB), Brĺkenhielm & Liu 1998 (CF), Carleton & Maclellan 2016 (CF), Cazzolla Gatti *et al.* 2015 (TR), Cielo-Filho & de Souza 2016 (TR), Crowell & Freedman 1994 (TB), Dierschke 2014 (TB), Doležal *et al.* 2009 (TB), Dupuch & Fortin 2013 (CF), Elliott *et al.* 1997 (TB), Elson *et al.* 2007 (CF), Ferracin *et al.* 2013 (TD), Floret *et al.* 1992 (ME), Fujii *et al.* 2009 (TR), Galatowitsch & Richardson 2005 (ME), Garcia-Florez *et al.* 2017 (TR), Gilliam *et al.* 1995 (TB), Halpern & Lutz 2013 (CF), Hanley & Barnard 1998 (CF), Huang *et al.* 2015 (TB), Ishida *et al.* 2005 (TB), Jenkins & Parker 1998 (TB), Jonášová *et al.* 2006 (TB), Kellison & Young 1997 (TB), Kramer *et al.* 2014 (TB), Kubota *et al.* 2005 (TR), Kurulok & Mcdonald 2007 (CF), Levesque *et al.* 2011 (TD), McDonald & Reynolds 1999 (CF), McKee *et al.* 2012 (TB), Michalová *et al.* 2017 (CF), Moola & Vasseur 2004 (CF), Mylliemngap *et al.* 2016 (TR), Nagashima *et al.* 2009 (TB + TB), Nguyen-Xuan *et al.* 2000 (CF), d´Oliviera *et al.* 2011 (TR), Olsson & Staaf 1995 (CF), Orwig & Abrams 1994 (TB), Rees & Juday 2002 (CF), Reich *et al.* 2001 (CF), Renard *et al.* 2016 (CF), Ribeiro *et al.* 2010 (TR), Rolim *et al.* 2017 (TR), Royo *et al.* 2016 (TB), Schuler & Gillespie 2000 (TB), Serong & Lill 2008 (TB), Tang *et al.* 2010 (TB), Tatoni & Roche 1994 (ME), Timoney *et al.* 1997 (TB), Tovilla-Hernández *et al.* 2001 (TR), Trefilova & Efimov 2015 (CF), van Andel 2001 (TR), Wieland *et al.* 2011 (TR), Widenfalk & Weslien 2009 (CF), Yao *et al.* 2012 (TB).

Plowed fields (N = 93) Search terms: succession AND (plant OR vegetation) AND (old field OR abandoned field)

Albert *et al.* 2014 (TG), Baar *et al.* 2004 (TR), Baeten *et al.* 2010 (TB), Bartha *et al.* 2014 (TG), Battaglia *et al.* 2002 (TB), Becker *et al.* 2011 (TG), Boccanelli *et al.* 1999 (TG), Boecker *et al.* 2015 (TG), Bonet & Pausas 2004 (ME), Carriere *et al.* 2007 (TR), Castellanos *et al.* 2005 (AR), Clewell 2011 (TB), Cook *et al.* 2005 (TB), Copenheaver 2008 (TB), Cramer *et al.* 2007 (ME), Csetserits *et al.* 2011 (TG), Davis *et al.* 2005 (TG), de la Peńa *et al.* 2016 (TB), De Wilde *et al.* 2012 (TR), Dean & Milton 1995 (AR), Debussche *et al.* 1996 (ME), Doelle & Schmidt 2009 (TB), Donfack *et al.* 1995 (TD), Ejrnaes *et al.* 2003 (TB), Erskine *et al.* 2007 (TR), Fenesi *et al.* 2015 (TB), Fensham *et al.* 2016 (TD), Fike & Niering 1999 (TB), Ganade 2007 (TR), Gardescu & Marks 2004 (TB), Grau *et al.* 1997 (TD), Gross & Emery 2007 (TB), Harmer *et al.* 2001 (TB), Hooper *et al.* 2005 (TR), Howard &

Lee 2002 (TB), Jírová *et al.* 2012 (TB), Jongepierová *et al.* 2004 (TG), Karlowski 2006 (AL), Keever 1979 (TB), Kou *et al.* 2016 (AL), Krug & Krug 2007 (ME), Kupfer *et al.* 2004 (TD), LaMantia *et al.* 2008 (ME), Lawson *et al.* 1999 (TB), Lebrija-Trejos *et al.* 2008 (TD), Lee *et al.* 2002 (TB), Lesschen *et al.* 2008 (AR), Li *et al.* 2016 (TB), Lucas *et al.* 2002 (TR), Martínez-Duro *et al.* 2010 (AR), McLendon *et al.* 2012 (AR), Molnár & Botta-Dukát 1998 (TG), Mora *et al.* 2012 (ME), Morris *et al.* 2011 (AR), Neeman & Izhaki 1996 (ME), Nemet *et al.* 2016 (TG), Otto *et al.* 2006 (AR), Prach 1985 (CF), Prach *et al.* 2014a (TB), Pueyo & Alados 2007 (ME), Riedel & Epstein 2005 (TB), Riege & del Moral 2004 (CF), Robledano-Aymerich *et al.* 2014 (ME), Roux & Warren 1963 (TG + TG), Ruprecht 2006 (TG), Ruskule *et al.* 2016 (TB), Santana *et al.* 2010 (ME), Sarmiento *et al.* 2003 (AL), Scott & Morgan 2012 (TD), Smith & Olff 1998 (TB), Sojneková & Chytrý 2015 (TG), Stadler *et al.* 2007 (TG + TG), Standish *et al.* 2007 (ME), Stover & Marks 1998 (TB), Stromberg & Griffin 1996 (TG), Sulieman 2014 (TD), Tatoni *et al.* 1994 (ME), Tognetti *et al.* 2010 (TG), Toh *et al.* 1999 (TR), Török *et al.* 2011 (TG), Tullus *et al.* 2013 (TB), Tyler 2008 (CF), Tzanopoulos *et al.* 2007 (ME), van der Merwe & van Rooyen 2011 (ME), van Gemerden *et al.* 2003 (TR), Wang *et al.* 2010 (TG), Wong *et al.* 2010 (TD), Yanagawa *et al.* 2016 (TG), Yannelli *et al.* 2014 (TG), Zhu *et al.* 2009 (TB), Zimmerman *et al.* 2007 (TR).

Mines (N = 74) Search terms: succession AND (plant OR vegetation) AND (mining OR mine OR spoil heap)

Amaral *et al.* 2013 (TR), Anawar *et al.* 2013 (ME), Baasch *et al.* 2012 (TB), Bagatto & Shorthouse 1999 (CF), Bétard 2013 (TB), Biswas *et al.* 2014 (TR), Boyer *et al.* 2011 (TD), Brofas & Varelides 2000 (ME), Burke 2014 (AR), Celi *et al.* 2013 (CF), Copenheaver *et al.* 2006 (TB), Correa *et al.* 2007 (TD), Craw *et al.* 2007 (TB), Densmore 1994 (CF), dos Santos *et al.* 2008 (TR), Duan *et al.* 2008 (TR), Ekka & Behera 2011 (TD), Escarré *et al.* 2011 (ME), Game *et al.* 1982 (TB), Gilardelli *et al.* 2016 (TB), González *et al.* 2013 (TB), Graf *et al.* 2008 (TB), Hilgartner *et al.* 2009 (TB), Hodačová & Prach 2003 (TB), Huang *et al.* 2016 (TG), Ivakina *et al.* 2013 (TB), Jha & Singh 1991 (TD), Jorgenson & Joyce 1994 (TU), Kasowska & Koszelnik-Leszek 2014 (TB), Kirmer *et al.* 2008 (TB), Koch 2007 (ME), Kompala-Baba & Baba 2013 (TB), Konvalinková & Prach 2010 (TB), Koronatova & Milyaeva 2011 (CF), Koyama & Tsuyuzaki 2010 (CF), Le Stradic *et al.*

2014 (TD), Li *et al.* 2008 (TB), Markowicz *et al.* 2015 (TB), Martínez-Ruiz & Marrs 2007 (ME), Mentis 2006 (TD), Montoni *et al.* 2014 (TG), Mota *et al.* 2004 (ME), Mudrák *et al.* 2016 (TB), Nikolic *et al.* 2016 (TB), Ninot *et al.* 2001 (TB), Nishimura *et al.* 2009 (CF), Novák & Prach 2003 (TB), Nurtjahya *et al.* 2009 (TR), Osipov *et al.* 2008 (CF), Párraga-Aguado *et al.* 2014 (ME), Pensa *et al.* 2004 (CF), Peterson & Heemskerk 2001 (TR), Piekarska-Stachowiak *et al.* 2014 (TB), Pietsch 1996 (TB), Randelovic *et al.* 2014 (TB), Řehounková & Prach 2006 (TB), Robert *et al.* 1999 (CF), Rydgren *et al.* 2011 (AL), Shooner *et al.* 2015 (CF), Silva *et al.* 2013 (TR), Skousen *et al.* 1994 (TB), Szarek-Lukaszewska 2009 (TB), Takeuchi & Shimano 2009 (TB), Tischew *et al.* 2014 (TB), Triisberg *et al.* 2014 (CF), Tropek *et al.* 2010 (TB), Tropek *et al.* 2013 (TB), Wali 1999 (TG), Wassenaar *et al.* 2005 (TD), Wiegleb & Felinks 2001 (TB), Wilcox *et al.* 2005 (TB), Woch *et al.* 2016 (TB), Woziwoda & Kopec 2014 (TB), Young *et al.* 2013 (CF).

References

Abdi, M. & Afsharzadeh, S. (2016). An analysis of vegetation and species diversity patterns in sand dunes and gravel desert ecosystem. *Botanical Sciences*, **94**, 499–511.

Abella, S. R. & Fornwalt, P. J. (2015). Ten years of vegetation assembly after a North American mega fire. *Global Change Biology*, **21**, 789–802.

Adachi, N., Terashima, I., & Takahashi, M. (1996). Central die-back of monoclonal stands of *Reynoutria japonica* in an early stage of primary succession on Mount Fuji. *Annals of Botany*, **77**, 477–486.

Adair, E. C., Binkley, D., & Andersen, D. C. (2004). Patterns of nitrogen accumulation and cycling in riparian floodplain ecosystems along the Green and Yampa rivers. *Oecologia*, **139**, 108–116.

Adams, J. (2007). *Vegetation – Climate Interactions*. New York: Springer.

Adams, P. W. & Sidle, R. C. (1987). Soil conditions in three recent landslides in southeast Alaska. *Forest Ecology and Management*, **18**, 93–102.

Aggenbach, C. J. S., Kooijman, A. M., Fujita, Y., *et al.* (2017). Does atmospheric nitrogen deposition lead to greater nitrogen and carbon accumulation in coastal sand dunes? *Biological Conservation*, **212**, 416–422.

Agresti, A. (2007). *An Introduction to Categorical Data Analysis*. 2nd ed. New York: Wiley & Sons.

Aiba, S., Hill, D. A., & Agetsuma, N. (2001). Comparison between old-growth stands and secondary stands regenerating after clear-felling in warm-temperate forests of Yakushima, southern Japan. *Forest Ecology and Management*, **140**, 163–175.

Albernaz, A. L., Pressey, R. L., Costa, L. R. F., *et al.* (2012). Tree species compositional change and conservation implications in the white-water flooded forests of the Brazilian Amazon. *Journal of Biogeography*, **39**, 869–883.

Albert, A. J., Kelemen, A., Valko, O., *et al.* (2014). Secondary succession in sandy old-fields: A promising example of spontaneous grassland recovery. *Applied Vegetation Science*, **17**, 214–224.

Albornoz, F. E., Gaxiola, A., Seaman, B. J., Pugnaire, F. I., & Armesto, J. J. (2013). Nucleation-driven regeneration promotes post-fire recovery in a Chilean temperate forest. *Plant Ecology*, **214**, 765–776.

Albrecht, M., Riesen, M., & Schmid, B. (2010). Plant-pollinator network assembly along the chronosequence of a glacier foreland. *Oikos*, **119**, 1610–1624.

Alday, J. G. & Marrs, R. H. (2014). A simple test for alternative states in ecological restoration: The use of principal response curves. *Applied Vegetation Science*, **17**, 302–311.

Alday, J. G., Marrs, R. H., & Martinez-Ruiz, C. (2010). The importance of topography and climate on short-term revegetation of coal wastes in Spain. *Ecological Engineering*, **36**, 579–585.

Alday, J. G., Marrs, R. H., & Martinez-Ruiz, C. (2011a). Vegetation convergence during early succession on coal wastes: A 6-year permanent plot study. *Journal of Vegetation Science*, **22**, 1072–1083.

Alday, J. G., Marrs, R. H., & Martinez-Ruiz, C. (2011b). Vegetation succession on reclaimed coal wastes in Spain: The influence of soil and environmental factors. *Applied Vegetation Science*, **14**, 84–94.

Alexander, J. M., Lembrechts, J. J., Cavieres, L. A., et al. (2016). Plant invasions into mountains and alpine ecosystems: Current status and future challenges. *Alpine Botany*, **126**, 89–103.

Allard-Duchêne, A., Pothier, D., Dupuch, A., & Fortin, D. (2014). Temporal changes in habitat use by snowshoe hares and red squirrels during post-fire and post-logging forest succession. *Forest Ecology and Management*, **313**, 17–25.

Allen, M. S., Thapa, V., Arévalo, J. R., & Palmer, M. W. (2012). Windstorm damage and forest recovery: Accelerated succession, stand structure, and spatial pattern over 25 years in two Minnesota forests. *Plant Ecology*, **213**, 1833–1842.

Alpert, P. & Mooney, H. A. (1996). Resource heterogeneity generated by shrubs and topography on coastal sand dunes. *Vegetatio*, **122**, 83–93.

Álvarez, R., Munñoz, A., Pesqueira, X. M., García-Duro, J., Reyes, O., & Casal, M. (2009). Spatial and temporal patterns in structure and diversity of Mediterranean forest of *Quercus pyrenaica* in relation to fire. *Forest Ecology and Management*, **257**, 1596–1602.

Álvarez-Molina, L. L., Martínez, M. L., Pérez-Maqueo, O., Gallego-Fernández, J. B., & Flores, P. (2012). Richness, diversity, and rate of primary succession over 20 years in tropical coastal dunes. *Plant Ecology*, **213**, 1597–1608.

Amaral, W. G., Pereira, I. M., Amaral, C. S., Machado, E. L. M., & Rabelo, L. D. O. (2013). Dynamics of the shrub and tree vegetation colonizing an area degraded by gold mined in Diamantina, Minas Gerais State. *Ciência Florestal*, **23**, 713–725.

Amarasekare, P. & Possingham, H. (2001). Patch dynamics and metapopulation theory: The case of successional species. *Journal of Theoretical Biology*, **209**, 333–344.

Anawar, H. M., Canha, N., Santa-Regina, I., & Freitas, M. C. (2013). Adaptation, tolerance, and evolution of plant species in a pyrite mine in response to contamination level and properties of mine tailings: Sustainable rehabilitation. *Journal of Soils and Sediments*, **13**, 730–741.

Andersen, D. C. & MacMahon, J. A. (1985). Plant succession following the Mount St. Helens volcanic eruption: Facilitation by a burrowing rodent, *Thomomys talpoides*. *The American Midland Naturalist*, **114**, 62–69.

Anderson, K. J. (2007). Temporal patterns in rates of community change during succession. *The American Naturalist*, **169**, 780–793.

Angel, R., Conrad, R., Dvorský, M., et al. (2016). The root-associated microbial community of the world's highest growing vascular plants. *Microbial Ecology*, **72**, 394–406.

Angell, A. C. & Kielland, K. (2009). Establishment and growth of white spruce on a boreal forest floodplain: Interactions between microclimate and mammalian herbivory. *Forest Ecology and Management*, **258**, 2475–2480.

Angiolini, C., Landi, M., Pieroni, G., Frignani, F., Finoia, M. G., & Gaggi, C. (2013). Soil chemical features as key predictors of plant community occurrence in a Mediterranean coastal ecosystem. *Estuarine, Coastal and Shelf Science*, **119**, 91–100.

Aplet, G. H. (1990). Alteration of earthworm community biomass by the alien *Myrica faya* in Hawaii. *Oecologia*, **82**, 414–416.

Aplet, G. H., Anderson, S. J., & Stone, C. P. (1991). Association between feral pig disturbance and the composition of some alien plant assemblages in Hawaii Volcanoes National Park. *Vegetatio*, **95**, 55–62.

Aplet, G. H., Flint, H. R., & Vitousek, P. M. (1998). Ecosystem development on Hawaiian lava flows: Biomass and species composition. *Journal of Vegetation Science*, **9**, 17–26.

Apple, J. L., Wink, M., Wills, S. E., & Bishop, J. G. (2009). Successional change in phosphorus stoichiometry explains the inverse relationship between herbivory and lupin density on Mount St. Helens. *PLoS ONE*, **4**, e7807, 1–10.

Archambault, L., Morissette, J., & Bernier-Cardou, M. (1998). Forest succession over a 20-year period following clearcutting in balsam fir yellow birch ecosystems of eastern Quebec, Canada. *Forest Ecology and Management*, **102**, 61–74.

Archibold, O. (1995). *Ecology of World Vegetation*. New York: Springer.

Arnone, E., Dialynas, Y. G., Noto, L. V., & Bras, R. L. (2016). Accounting for soil parameter uncertainty in a physically based and distributed approach for rainfall-triggered landslides. *Hydrological Processes*, **30**, 927–944.

Arroyo, M. T. K., Zedler, P. H., & Fox, M. D., eds. (1995). *Ecology and Biogeography of Mediterranean Ecosystems in Chile, California, and Australia*. New York: Springer.

Arunachalam, A. & Upadhyaya, K. (2005). Microbial biomass during revegetation of landslides in the humid tropics. *Journal of Tropical Forest Science*, **17**, 306–311.

Asaeda, T., Rashin, Md. H., & Ohta, K. (2106). Nitrogen fixation by *Pueraria lobata* as a nitrogen source in the midstream sediment bar of a river. *Ecohydrology*, **9**, 995–1005.

Aslan, M. (2015). Succession of steppe area after fire in the Gap Region of Turkey. *Bangladesh Journal of Botany*, **44**, 489–497.

Atkinson, I. A. E. (1970). Successional trends in the coastal and lowland forest of Mauna Loa and Kilauea Volcanoes, Hawaii. *Pacific Science*, **24**, 387–400.

Atkinson, I. A. E. (2004). Successional processes induced by fires on the northern offshore islands of New Zealand. *New Zealand Journal of Ecology*, **28**, 181–193.

Augspurger, C. K. (1984). Seedling survival of tropical tree species: Interactions of dispersal distance, light-gaps and pathogens. *Ecology*, **65**, 1705–1712.

Austin, M. P. (1985). Continuum concept, ordination methods, and theory. *Annual Review of Ecology and Systematics*, **16**, 39–61.

Avis, A. M. & Lubke, R. A. (1996). Dynamics and succession of coastal dune vegetation in the Eastern Cape, South Africa. *Landscape and Urban Planning*, **34**, 237–254.

Ayyad, M. A. (1973). Vegetation and environment of the western Mediterranean coastal land of Egypt. I. The habitat of sand dunes. *Journal of Ecology*, **61**, 509–523.

Baar, R., Cordeiro, M. D., Denich, M., & Folster, H. (2004). Floristic inventory of secondary vegetation in agricultural systems of East-Amazonia. *Biodiversity and Conservation*, **13**, 501–528.

Baasch, A., Kirmer, A., & Tischew, S. (2012). Nine years of vegetation development in a postmining site: Effects of spontaneous and assisted site recovery. *Journal of Applied Ecology*, **49**, 251–260.

Baeten, L., Velghe, D., Vanhellemont, M., De Frenne, P., Hermy, M., & Verheyen, K. (2010). Early trajectories of spontaneous vegetation recovery after intensive agricultural land use. *Restoration Ecology*, **18**, 379–386.

Baetz, N., Verrecchia, E. P., & Lane, S. N. (2015). The role of soil in vegetated gravelly river braid plains: More than just a passive response? *Earth Surface Processes and Landforms*, **40**, 143–156.

Bagatto, C. & Shorthouse, J. D. (1999). Biotic and abiotic characteristics of ecosystems on acid metalliferous mine tailings near Sudbury, Ontario. *Canadian Journal of Botany*, **77**, 410–425.

Bainbridge, E. L. & Strong, W. L. (2005). *Pinus contorta* understory vegetation dynamics following clearcutting in west-central Alberta, Canada. *Forest Ecology and Management*, **213**, 133–150.

Baker, W. L. & Walford, G. M. (1995). Multiple stable states and models of riparian vegetation succession on the Animas River, Colorado. *Annals of the Association of American Geographers*, **85**, 320–338.

Baker, W. L., Flaherty, P. H., Lindemann, J. D., Veblen, T. T., Eisenhart, K. S., & Kulakowski, D. W. (2002). Effects of severe blowdown in the southern Rocky Mountains, USA. *Forest Ecology and Management*, **168**, 63–75.

Ballesteros, M., Cañadas, E. M., Foronda, A., Peñas, J., Valle, F., & Lorite, J. (2014). Central role of bedding materials for gypsum-quarry restoration: An experimental planting of gypsophile species. *Ecological Engineering*, **70**, 470–476.

Banner, A. & LePage, P. (2008). Long-term recovery of vegetation communities after harvesting in the coastal temperate rainforests of northern British Columbia. *Canadian Journal of Forest Research*, **38**, 3098–3111.

Barbour, M. G. & Billings, W. D. (2000). *North American Terrestrial Vegetation*. 2nd ed. Cambridge: Cambridge University Press.

Barbour, M. G., De Jong, T. M., & Pavlik, B. M. (1985). Marine beach and dune plant communities. In B. F. Chabot & H. A. Mooney, eds., *Physiological Ecology of North American Plant Communities*, pp. 296–322. New York: Chapman & Hall.

Barbour, M. G., Fernau, R. F., Benayas, J. M. R., Jurjavcic, N., & Royce, E. B. (1998). Tree regeneration following clearcut logging in red fir forests of California. *Forest Ecology and Management*, **104**, 101–111.

Bardgett, R. D. & Walker, L. R. (2004). Impact of coloniser plant species on the development of decomposer microbial communities following deglaciation. *Soil Biology and Biochemistry*, **36**, 555–559.

Bardgett, R. D. & Wardle, D. A. (2003). Herbivore mediated linkages between above-ground and below-ground communities. *Ecology*, **84**, 2258–2268.

Bardgett, R. D. & Wardle, D. A. (2010). *Aboveground-Belowground Linkages: Biotic Interactions, Ecosystem Processes, and Global Change.* Oxford: Oxford University Press.

Bardgett, R. D., Richter, A., Bol, R., *et al.* (2007). Heterotrophic microbial communities use ancient carbon following glacial retreat. *Biology Letters*, **3**, 487–490.

Baret, S., Le Bourgeois, T., Rivière, J.-N., Pailler, T., Sarrailh, J.-M., & Strasberg, D. (2007). Can species richness be maintained in logged endemic *Acacia heterophylla* forests (Reunion Island, Indian Ocean)? *Revue D'Écologie-La Terre Et La Vie*, **62**, 273–284.

Bargmann, T., Maren, I. E., & Vandvik, V. (2014). Life after fire: Smoke and ash as germination cues in ericads, herbs and graminoids of northern heathlands. *Applied Vegetation Science*, **17**, 670–679.

Barrett, K., Rocha, A., van de Weg, M. J., & Shaver, G. (2012). Vegetation shifts observed in arctic tundra 17 years after fire. *Remote Sensing Letters*, **3**, 729–736.

Bartha, S., Meiners, S. J., Pickett, S. T. A., & Cadenasso, M. L. (2003). Plant colonization windows in a mesic old field succession. *Applied Vegetation Science*, **6**, 205–212.

Bartha, S., Szentes, S., Horvath, A., *et al.* (2014). Impact of mid-successional dominant species on the diversity and progress of succession in regenerating temperate grasslands. *Applied Vegetation Science*, **17**, 201–213.

Barthlott, W., Lauer, W., & Placke, A. (1996). Global distribution of species diversity in vascular plants: Towards a world map of phytodiversity. *Erdkunde*, **50**, 317–327.

Bartleman, A.-P., Miyanishi, K., Burn, C. R., & Côté, M. M. (2001). Development of vegetation communities in a retrogressive thaw slump near Mayo, Yukon Territory: A 10-year assessent. *Arctic*, **54**, 149–156.

Basher, L. R., Daly, G. T., & Tonkin, P. J. Unpublished. Succession in subalpine scrub and grassland communities, Cropp River, Central Westland, New Zealand. Landcare Research, Lincoln, New Zealand.

Basinger, M. A., Franklin, S. B., & Shimp, J. P. (1996). Vegetation of a sandstone outcrop along the Ohio River in Hardin County, Illinois. *Castanea*, **61**, 327–338.

Bates, J. D. & Svejcar, T. J. (2009). Herbaceous succession after burning of cot western juniper trees. *Western North American Naturalist*, **69**, 9–25.

Batista, W. B. & Platt, W. J. (2003). Tree population responses to hurricane disturbance: Syndromes in a south-eastern USA old-growth forest. *Journal of Ecology*, **91**, 197–212.

Battaglia, L. L., Minchin, P. R., & Pritchett, D. W. (2002). Sixteen years of old-field succession and reestablishment of a bottomland hardwood forest in the Lower Mississippi Alluvial Valley. *Wetlands*, **22**, 1–17.

Bazzaz, F. A. (2006). *Plants in Changing Environments: Linking Physiological, Population, and Community Ecology.* Cambridge: Cambridge University Press.

Becker, T., Andres, C., & Dierschke, H. (2011). Young and old steppe-like grasslands in the "Badra Lehde-Grosser Eller" Reserve (Kyffhauser Mountains, central Germany). *Tuexenia*, **31**, 173–210.

Behnke, R. & Mortimore, M. (2015). *The End of Desertification? Disputing Environmental Change in the Drylands*. Berlin: Springer.

Bellingham, P. J. & Lee, W. G. (2006). Distinguishing natural processes from impacts of invasive mammalian herbivores. In R. B. Allen & W. G. Lee, eds., *Biological Invasions in New Zealand*, pp. 323–336. New York: Springer.

Bellingham, P. J., Kohyama, T., & Aiba, S.-I. (1996a). The effects of a typhoon on Japanese warm temperate forests. *Ecological Research*, **11**, 229–247.

Bellingham, P. J., Peltzer, D. A., & Walker, L. R. (2005). Contrasting impacts of a native and an invasive exotic shrub on flood-plain succession. *Journal of Vegetation Science*, **16**, 135–142.

Bellingham, P. J., Tanner, E. V. J., & Healey, J. R. (1994). Sprouting of trees in Jamaican montane forests, after a hurricane. *Journal of Ecology*, **82**, 747–758.

Bellingham, P. J., Tanner, E. V. J., & Healey, J. R. (1995). Damage and responsiveness of Jamaican montane tree species after disturbance by a hurricane. *Ecology*, **76**, 2562–2580.

Bellingham, P. J., Tanner, E. V. J., & Healey, J. R. (2005). Hurricane disturbance accelerates invasion by the alien tree *Pittosporum undulatum* in Jamaican montane rain forests. *Journal of Vegetation Science*, **16**, 675–684.

Bellingham, P. J., Walker, L. R., & Wardle, D. A. (2001). Differential facilitation by a nitrogen-fixing shrub during primary succession influences relative performance of canopy tree species. *Journal of Ecology*, **89**, 861–875.

Bellingham, P. J., Tanner, E. V. J., Rich, P. M., & Goodland, T. C. R. (1996b). Changes in light below the canopy of a Jamaican montane rainforest after a hurricane. *Journal of Tropical Ecology*, **12**, 699–722.

Bellingham, P. J., Tanner, E. V. J., Martin, P. H., Healey, J. R., & Burgea, O. R. (2018). Endemic trees in a tropical biodiversity hotspot imperilled by an invasive tree. *Biological Conservation*, **217**, 47–53.

Bellingham, P. J., Kardol, P., Bonner, K. I., *et al.* (2016). Browsing by an invasive herbivore promotes development of plant and soil communities during primary succession. *Journal of Ecology*, **104**, 1505–1517.

Bellwood, P. (2005). *First Farmers: The Origins of Agricultural Societies*. Oxford: Blackwell.

Belsky, A. J. & Amundson, R. G. (1986). Sixty years of successional history behind a moving sand dune near Olduvai Gorge, Tanzania. *Biotropica*, **18**, 231–235.

Bénito-Espinal, F. P. & Bénito-Espinal, E., eds. (1991). *L'Ouragan Hugo: Genese, Incidences Géographiques et Écologiques sur la Guadeloupe*. Parc National de la Guadeloupe, Délégation Régionale a l'Action Culturelle, and Agence Guadeloupéenne de l'Environnement du Tourism et des Loisirs. Fort-de-France, Martinique: Imprimerie Désormeaux.

Benjankar, R., Burke, M., Yager, E., *et al.* (2014). Development of a spatially-distributed hydroecological model to simulate cottonwood seedling recruitment along rivers. *Journal of Environmental Management*, **145**, 277–288.

Benjankar, R., Egger, G., Jorde, K., Goodwin, P., & Glenn, N. (2011). Dynamic floodplain vegetation model development for the Kootenai River, USA. *Journal of Environmental Management*, **92**, 3058–3070.

Benscoter, B. W. & Vitt, D. H. (2008). Spatial patterns and temporal trajectories of the bog ground layer along a post-fire chronosequence. *Ecosystems*, **11**, 1054–1064.

Berendse, F. (1998). Effects of dominant plant species on soils during succession in nutrient poor ecosystems. *Biogeochemistry*, **42**, 73–88.

Berendse, F., Lammerts, E. J., & Olff, H. (1998). Soil organic matter accumulation and its implications for nitrogen mineralization and plant species composition during succession in coastal dune slacks. *Plant Ecology*, **137**, 71–78.

Bermingham, E., Dick, Ch. W., & Moritz G. (2005). *Rainforests: Past, Present & Future*. Chicago: University of Chicago Press.

Bermúdez, A. M., Fernández-Palacios, J. M., González-Mancebo, J. M., Patiño, J., Arévalo, J. R., Otto, R., & Delgado, J. D. (2007). Floristic and structural recovery of a laurel forest community after clear-cutting: A 60 years chronosequence on La Palma (Canary Islands). *Annals of Forest Science*, **64**, 109–119.

Bertoldi, W., Siviglia, A., Tettamanti, S., Toffolon, M., Vetsch, D., & Francalanci, S. (2014). Modeling vegetation controls on fluvial morphological trajectories. *Geophysical Research Letters*, **41**, 7167–7175.

Berz, G. (1988). List of major natural disasters, 1960–1987. *Natural Hazards*, **1**, 97–99.

Beschta, R. L. & Ripple, W. J. (2016). Riparian vegetation recovery in Yellowstone: The first two decades after wolf reintroduction. *Biological Conservation*, **198**, 93–103.

Bétard, F. (2013). Patch-scale relationships between geodiversity and biodiversity in hard rock quarries: Case study from a disused quartzite quarry in NW France. *Geoheritage*, **5**, 59–71.

Bhaskar, R., Dawson, T. E., & Balvanera, P. (2014). Community assembly and functional diversity along succession post-management. *Functional Ecology*, **28**, 1256–1265.

Binggeli, P., Eakin, M., Macfadyen, A., Power, J., & McConnell, J. (1992). Impact of the alien sea buckthorn (*Hippophaë rhamnoides* L.) on sand dune ecosystems in Ireland. In R. W. G. Carter, T. G. F. Curtis, & M. J. Sheehy-Skeffington, eds., *Coastal Dunes: Geomorphology, Ecology and Management*, pp. 325–337. Rotterdam: Balkema.

Binkley, D., Suarez, F., Stottlemyer, R., & Caldwell, B. (1997). Ecosystem development on terraces along the Kugururok River, northwest Alaska. *Écoscience*, **4**, 311–318.

Biondini, M. & Kandus, P. (2006). Transition matrix analysis of land-cover change in the accretion area of the lower delta of the Paraná River (Argentina) reveals two succession pathways. *Wetlands*, **26**, 981–991.

Birks, H. J. B. (1980). The present flora and vegetation of the moraines of the Klutlan Glacier, Yukon Territory, Canada: A study in plant succession. *Quaternary Research*, **14**, 60–86.

Bischoff, A., Warthemann, G., & Klotz, S. (2009). Succession of floodplain grasslands following reduction in land use intensity: The importance of environmental conditions, management and dispersal. *Journal of Applied Ecology*, **46**, 241–249.

Bishoff, W., Newbery, D. M., Lingenfelder, M., *et al.* (2005). Secondary succession and dipterocarp recruitment in Bornean rain forest after logging. *Forest Ecology and Management*, **218**, 174–192.

Biswas, C. K., Mishra, S. P., & Mukherjee, A. (2014). Diversity and composition of vegetation on aged coalmine overburden dumps in Sonepur Bazari area, Raniganj, West Bengal. *Journal of Environmental Biology*, **35**, 173–177.

Bjarnason, Á. H. (1991). Vegetation on lava fields in the Hekla area, Iceland. *Acta Phytogeographica Suecica*, **77**, 1–110.

Bliss, L. C. & Cantlon, J. E. (1957). Succession on river alluvium in northern Alaska. *The American Midland Naturalist*, **58**, 452–469.

Blondel, J. & Aronson, J. (1999). *Biology and Wildlife of the Mediterranean Region.* Oxford: Oxford University Press.

Boccanelli, S., Pire, E., & Lewis. J. (2010). Vegetation changes after 15 years of abandonment of crop fields in the Pampas Region (Argentina). *Ciencia E Investigacion Agraria*, **37**, 45–53.

Boccanelli, S. I., Pire, E. F., Torres, P. S., & Lewis, J. P. (1999). Vegetation changes in a field abandoned after a wheat crop. *Pesquisa Agropecuaria Brasileira*, **34**, 151–157.

Boecker, D., Centeri, C., Welp, G., & Moseler, B. (2015). Parallels of secondary grassland succession and soil regeneration in a chronosequence of central-Hungarian old fields. *Folia Geobotanica*, **50**, 91–106.

Bogar, L. M., Dickie, I. A., & Kennedy, P. G. (2015). Testing the co-invasion hypothesis: Ectomycorrhizal fungal communities on *Alnus glutinosa* and *Salix fragilis* in New Zealand. *Diversity and Distributions*, **21**, 268–278.

Boggs, K. & Weaver, T. (1994). Changes in vegetation and nutrient pools during riparian succession. *Wetlands*, **14**, 98–109.

Boggs, K., Klein, S. C., Grunblatt, J., *et al.* (2010). Alpine and subalpine vegetation chronosequences following deglaciation in coastal Alaska. *Arctic, Antarctic and Alpine Research*, **42**, 385–395.

Boiffin, J. & Munson, A. D. (2013). Three large fire years threaten resilience of closed crown black spruce forests in eastern Canada. *Ecosphere*, **4**, 1–20.

Bokhorst, S., Kardol, P., Bellingham, P. J., *et al.* (2017). Responses of communities of soil organisms and plants to soil aging at two contrasting long-term chronosequences. *Soil Biology and Biochemistry*, **106**, 69–79.

Bolling, J. D. & Walker, L. R. (2000). Plant and soil recovery along a series of abandoned desert roads. *Journal of Arid Environments*, **46**, 1–24.

Bonanomi, G., Rietkerk, M., Dekker, S. C., & Mazzoleni, S. (2008). Islands of fertility induce co-occurring negative and positive plant-soil feedbacks promoting coexistence. *Plant Ecology*, **197**, 207–218.

Bonet, A. & Pausas, J. G. (2004). Species richness and cover along a 60-year chronosequence in old-fields of southeastern Spain. *Plant Ecology*, **174**, 257–270.

Boone, M., ed. (2017). *Deglaciation: Processes, Causes and Consequences.* Happauge, NY: Nova Science Publishers.

Boonyanuphap, J. (2013). Cost-benefit analysis of vetiver system-based rehabilitation measures for landslide-damaged mountainous agricultural lands in the lower Northern Thailand. *Natural Hazards*, **69**, 599–629.

Bormann, F. H. & Likens, G. E. (1979). *Patterns and Process in a Forested Ecosystem: Disturbance, Development, and the Steady State Based on the Hubbard Brook Ecosystem Study.* New York: Springer.

Bornkamm, R. (1981). Rates of change in vegetation during secondary succession. *Vegetatio*, **47**, 213–220.

Bossuyt, B., Honnay, O., & Hermy, M. (2005). Evidence for community assembly constraints during succession in dune slack plant communities. *Plant Ecology*, **178**, 201–209.

Boucher, D. H. (1990). Growing back after hurricanes. *BioScience*, **40**, 163–166.

Boucher, D. H., Vandermeer, J. H., Yih, K., & Zamora, N. (1990). Contrasting hurricane damage in tropical rain forest and pine forest. *Ecology*, **71**, 2022–2024.

Bouchon, E. & Arseneault, D. (2004). Fire disturbance during climate change: Failure of postfire forest recovery on a boreal floodplain. *Canadian Journal of Forest Research*, **34**, 2294–2305.

Bourgeois, B., Boutin, C., Vannase, A., & Poulin, M. (2017). Divergence between riparian seed banks and standing vegetation increases along successional trajectories. *Journal of Vegetation Science*, **28**, 787–797.

Bowers, J. E., Webb, R. H., & Pierson, E. A. (1997). Succession of desert plants on debris flow terraces, Grand Canyon, Arizona, U.S.A. *Journal of Arid Environments*, **36**, 67–86.

Boyer, S., Wratten, S., Pizey, M., & Weber, P. (2011). Impact of soil stockpiling and mining rehabilitation on earthworm communities. *Pedobiologia*, **54**, S99–S102.

Boyes, L. J., Gunton, R. M., Griffiths, M. E., & Lawes, M. J. (2011). Causes of arrested succession in coastal dune forest. *Plant Ecology*, **212**, 21–32.

Bradshaw, A. D. (1987). Restoration: An acid test for ecology. In W. R. Jordan, M. E. Gilpin, & J. D. Aber, eds., *Restoration Ecology: A Synthetic Approach to Ecological Research*, pp. 23–29. Cambridge: Cambridge University Press.

Bradshaw, A. D. (2000). The use of natural processes in reclamation – Advantages and difficulties. *Landscape and Urban Planning*, **51**, 89–100.

Bradshaw, R. H. W., Wolf, A., & Moller, P. F. (2005). Long-term succession in a Danish temperate deciduous forest. *Ecography*, **28**, 157–164.

Bråkenhielm, S. & Liu, Q. (1998). Long-term effects of clear-felling on vegetation dynamics and species diversity in a boreal pine forest. *Biodiversity and Conservation*, **7**, 207–220.

Brändle, M., Durka, W., & Altmoos, M. (2000). Diversity of surface dwelling beetle assemblages in open-cast lignite mines in Central Germany. *Biodiversity and Conservation*, **9**, 1297–1311.

Breckle, S.-W. (2002). *Walter's Vegetation of the Earth*. Berlin: Springer.

Brewer, S., Jackson, S. T., & Williams, J. W. (2012). Paleoecoinformatics: Applying geohistorical data to ecological questions. *Trends in Ecology and Evolution*, **27**, 104–112.

Brinkman, E. P., Duyts, H., Karssen, G., van der Stoel, C. D., & van der Putten, W. H. (2015). Plant-feeding nematodes in coastal sand dunes: Occurrence, host specificity and effects on plant growth. *Plant and Soil*, **397**, 17–30.

Brock, J. M. R., Perry, G. L. W., Lee, W. G., Schwendenmann, L., & Burns, B. R. (2018). Pioneer tree ferns influence community assembly in northern New Zealand forests. *New Zealand Journal of Ecology*, **42**, 18–30.

Brofas, G. & Varelides, C. (2000). Hydro-seeding and mulching for establishing vegetation on mining spoils in Greece. *Land Degradation & Development*, **11**, 375–382.

Brokaw, N. V. L. (1998). *Cecropia schreberiana* in the Luquillo Mountains of Puerto Rico. *Botanical Review*, **64**, 91–120.

Brokaw, N. V. L. & Walker, L. R. (1991). Summary of the effects of Caribbean hurricanes on vegetation. *Biotropica*, **23**, 442–447.

Brooks, M. L. (2002). Peak fire temperatures and effects on annual plants in the Mojave Desert. *Ecological Applications*, **12**, 1088–1102.

Brown, W. H., Merrill, E. D., & Yates, H. S. (1917). The revegetation of Volcano Island, Luzon, Philippine Islands, since the eruption of Taal Volcano in 1911. *The Philippine Journal of Science*, **12**, 177–243.

Brulisauer, A. R., Bradfield, G. E., & Maze, J. (1996). Quantifying organisational change after fire in lodgepole pine forest understorey. *Canadian Journal of Botany*, **74**, 1773–1782.

Brummer, T. J., Byrom, A. E., Sullivan, J. J., & Hulme, P. E. (2016). Alien and native plant richness and abundance respond to different environmental drivers across multiple gravel floodplain ecosystems. *Diversity and Distributions*, **22**, 823–835.

Bryant, J. P. & Chapin III, F. S. (1986). Browsing-woody plant interactions during local forest plant succession. In K. Van Cleve, F. S. Chapin III, P. W. Flanagan, L. A. Viereck, & C. T. Dyrness, eds., *Forest Ecosystems in the Alaskan Taiga: A Synthesis of Structure and Function*, pp. 213–225. New York: Springer.

Bugmann, H. (2001). A review of forest gap models. *Climatic Change*, **51**, 259–305.

Bugman, H. & Bigler, C. (2011). Will the CO_2 fertilization effect in forests be offset by reduced tree longevity? *Global Change Ecology*, **165**, 533–544.

Buhk, C., Götzenberger, L., Wesche, K., Gomez, P. S., & Hensen, I. (2006). Post-fire regeneration in a Mediterranean pine forest with historically low fire frequency. *Acta Oecologica*, **30**, 288–298.

Bullock, J. M. & Webb, N. R. (1995). Responses to severe fires in heathland mosaics in southern England. *Biological Conservation*, **73**, 207–214.

Buma, B. (2015). Disturbance interactions: Characterization, prediction, and the potential for cascading effects. *Ecosphere*, **6**, 1–15.

Burga, C. A., Krusi, B., Egli, M., *et al.* (2010). Plant succession and soil development on the foreland of the Morteratsch glacier (Pontresina, Switzerland): Straightforward or chaotic? *Flora*, **205**, 561–576.

Burke, A. (2014). Natural recovery of dwarf shrubs following topsoil and vegetation clearing on gravel, and sand plains in the southern Namib Desert. *Journal of Arid Environments*, **100**, 18–22.

Burley, S., Robinson, S. L., & Lundholm, J. T. (2008). Post-hurricane vegetation recovery in an urban forest. *Landscape and Urban Planning*, **85**, 111–122.

Burn, C. R. & Friele, P. A. (1989). Geomorphology, vegetation succession, soil characteristics and permafrost in retrogressive thaw slumps near Mayo, Yukon Territory. *Arctic*, **42**, 31–40.

Burrows, C. J. (1990). *Processes of Vegetation Change*. London: Unwin Hyman.

Burton, P. J. (2010). Striving for sustainability and resilience in the face of unprecedented change: The case of the mountain pine beetle outbreak in British Columbia. *Sustainability*, **2**, 2403–2423.

Burton, P. J. & Bazzaz, F. A. (1995). Ecophysiological responses to tree seedlings invading different patches of old-field vegetation. *Journal of Ecology*, **83**, 99–112.

Burton, P. J., Parisien, M. A., Hicke, J. A., Hall, R. J., & Freeburn, J. T. (2009). Large fires as agents of ecological diversity in the North American boreal forest. *International Journal of Wildland Fire*, **17**, 754–767.

Busch, D. E. (1995). Effects of fire on southwestern riparian plant community structure. *The Southwestern Naturalist*, **40**, 259–267.

Bush, J. K., Richter, F. A., & Van Auken, O. W. (2006). Two decades of vegetation change on terraces of a south Texas river. *The Journal of the Torrey Botanical Society*, **133**, 280–288.

Cadotte, M. W., Carscadden, K., & Mirotchnick, N. (2011). Beyond species functional diversity and the maintenance of ecological processes and services. *Journal of Applied Ecology*, **48**, 1079–1087.

Cain, S. A. (1959). Henry Allan Gleason – Eminent ecologist. *Bulletin of the Ecological Society of America*, **40**, 105–110.

Çakan, H., Yilmaz, K. T., Alphan, H., & Ünlükaplan, Y. (2011). The classification and assessment of vegetation monitoring coastal sand dune succession: The case of Tuzla in Adana, Turkey. *Turkish Journal of Botany*, **35**, 697–711.

Calder, J. A., Wilson, J. B., Mark, A. F., & Ward, G. (1992). Fire, succession and reserve management in a New Zealand snow tussock grassland. *Biological Conservation*, **62**, 35–45.

Callaway, R. M. (1995). Positive interactions among plants. *Botanical Review*, **61**, 306–349.

Callaway, R. M. (2007). *Positive Interactions and Interdependence in Plant Communities*. New York: Springer.

Callaway, R. M. & Walker, L. R. (1997). Competition and facilitation: A synthetic approach to interactions in plant communities. *Ecology*, **78**, 1958–1965.

Calvo, L., Tárrega, R., Luis, E., Valbuena, L., & Marcos, E. (2005). Recovery after experimental cutting and burning in three shrub communities with different dominant species. *Plant Ecology*, **180**, 175–185.

Campbell, E. M. & Antos, J. A. (2003). Postfire succession in *Pinus albicaulis* – *Abies lasiocarpa* forests of southern British Columbia. *Canadian Journal of Botany*, **81**, 383–397.

Cannone, N., Lewkowicz, A. G., & Guglielmin, M. (2010). Vegetation colonization of permafrost-related landslides, Ellesmere Island, Canadian High Arctic. *Journal of Geophysical Research – Biogeosciences*, **115**, article number G04020. doi: 10.1029/2010JG001384.

Capitanio, R. & Carcaillet, C. (2008). Post-fire Mediterranean vegetation dynamics and diversity: A discussion of succession models. *Forest Ecology and Management*, **255**, 431–439.

Caplat, P. & Anand, M. (2009). Effects of disturbance frequency, species traits and resprouting on directional succession in an individual-based model of forest dynamics. *Journal of Ecology*, **97**, 1028–1036.

Capon, S. J. (2005). Flood variability and spatial variation in plant community composition and structure on a large arid floodplain. *Journal of Arid Environments*, **60**, 283–302.

Carleton, T. J. & Maclellan, P. (1994). Woody vegetation responses to fire versus clear-cutting logging: A comparative survey in the central Canadian boreal forest. *Ecoscience*, **1**, 141–152.

Carlo, T. A. & Morales, J. M. (2016). Generalist birds promote tropical forest regeneration and increase plant diversity via rare-biased seed dispersal. *Ecology*, **97**, 1819–1831.

Carlquist, S. (1974). *Island Biology*. New York: Columbia University Press.

Carpenter, S. E., Trappe, J. M., & Ammirati, J., Jr. (1987). Observations of fungal succession in the Mount St. Helens devastation zone, 1980–1983. *Canadian Journal of Botany*, **65**, 716–728.

Carriere, S. M., Letourmy, P., & McKey, D. B. (2002). Effects of remnant trees in fallows on diversity and structure of forest regrowth in a slash-and-burn agricultural system in southern Cameroon. *Journal of Tropical Ecology*, **18**, 375–396.

Carson, W. P. & Schnitzer, S. A., eds. (2008). *Tropical Forest Community Ecology*. Chichester, UK: Wiley-Blackwell.

Castanho, C. de T. & Prado, P. I. (2014). Benefit of shading by nurse plant does not change along a stress gradient in a coastal dune. *PLoS ONE*, **9**, e105082.

Castellanos, A. E., Martinez, M. J., Llano, J. M., Halvorson, W. L., Espiricueta, M., & Espejel, I. (2005). Successional trends in Sonoran Desert abandoned agricultural fields in northern Mexico. *Journal of Arid Environments*, **60**, 437–455.

Castle, S. C., Lekberg, Y., Affleck, D., & Cleveland, C. C. (2016). Soil abiotic and biotic controls on plant performance during primary succession in a glacial landscape. *Journal of Ecology*, **104**, 1555–1565.

Castro, J., Puerta-Piñero, C., Leverkus, A. B., Moreno-Rueda, G., & Sánchez-Miranda, A. (2012). Post-fire salvage logging alters a key plant-animal interaction for forest regeneration. *Ecosphere*, **3**, 90.

Castro, J. W. A. (2005). Burying processes carried out by a mobile transversal dunefield, Paracuru County, State of Ceará, Brazil. *Environmental Geology*, **49**, 214.

Catford, J. A., Morris, W. K., Vesk, P. A., Gippel, C. J., & Downes, B. J. (2014). Species and environmental characteristics point to flow regulation and drought as drivers of riparian plant invasion. *Diversity and Distributions*, **20**, 1084–1096.

Catford, J. A., Daehler, C. C., Helen T., Murphy, H. T., *et al.* (2012). The intermediate disturbance hypothesis and plant invasions: Implications for species richness and management. *Perspectives in Plant Ecology, Evolution and Systematics*, **14**, 231–241.

Cavender-Bares, J., Kozak, K. H., Fine, P. V. A., & Kembel, S. W. (2009). The merging of community ecology and phylogenetic biology. *Ecology Letters*, **12**, 693–715.

Cazzolla Gatti, R., Castaldi, S., Lindsell, J. A., *et al.* (2015). The impact of selective logging and clearcutting on forest structure, tree diversity and above-ground biomass of African tropical forests. *Ecological Research*, **30**, 119–132.

Celi, L., Cerli, C., Turner, B. L., Santoni, S., & Bonifacio, E. (2013). Biogeochemical cycling of soil phosphorus during natural revegetation of *Pinus sylvestris* on disused sand quarries in northwestern Russia. *Plant and Soil*, **367**, 121–134.

Chadwick, H. W. & Dalke, P. D. (1965). Plant succession on dune sands in Fremont County, Idaho. *Ecology*, **46**, 765–780.

Chadwick, J., Dorsch, S., Glenn, N., Thackray, G., & Shilling, K. (2005). Application of multi-temporal high-resolution imagery and GPS in a study of the motion of a canyon rim landslide. *Journal of Photogrammetry & Remote Sensing*, **59**, 212–221.

Chadwick, O. A., Derry, L. A., Vitousek, P. M., Huebert, B. J., & Hedin, L. O. (1999). Changing sources of nutrients during four million years of ecosystem development. *Nature*, **397**, 491–497.

Chang, C. C. & Turner, B. L. (2019). Ecological succession in a changing world. *Journal of Ecology*, **107**, 503–509.

Chang, C. C., Halpern, C. B., Antos, J. A., *et al.* (2019). Testing conceptual models of early plant succession across a disturbance gradient. *Journal of Ecology*, **107**, 517–530.

Chapin, F. S. III & Walker, L. R. (1993). Direct and indirect effects of calcium sulfate and nitrogen on growth and succession of trees on the Tanana River floodplain, interior Alaska. *Canadian Journal of Forest Research*, **23**, 995–1000.

Chapin, F. S. III, Walker, L. R., Fastie, C. L., & Sharman, L. C. (1994). Mechanisms of primary succession following deglaciation at Glacier Bay, Alaska. *Ecological Monographs*, **64**, 149–175.

Chapin, F. S. III, Conway, A. J., Johnstone, J. F., Hollingsworth, T. N., & Hollingsworth, J. (2016). Absence of long-term successional facilitation by alder in a boreal Alaska floodplain. *Ecology*, **97**, 2986–2997.

Chapin, F. S. III & Körner, Ch., eds. (1995). *Arctic and Alpine Biodiversity*. New York: Springer.

Chapin F. S. III, Sale, O. E., & Huber-Sannwald E., eds. (2013). *Global Biodiversity in a Changing Environment*. 2nd ed. New York: Springer.

Chapin, F. S. III, Jeffries, R. L., Reynolds, J. F., Shaver, G. R., & Svoboda, J., eds. (1992). *Arctic Ecosystems in a Changing Climate*. San Diego: Academic Press.

Charbonneau, B. R., Wnek, J. P., Langley, J. A., Lee, G., & Balsamo, R. A. (2016). Above vs. belowground plant biomass along a barrier island: Implications for dune stabilization. *Journal of Environmental Management*, **182**, 126–133.

Charron, I., Johnson, E. A., & Martin, Y. E. (2011). Tree establishment on bars in low-order gravel-bed mountain streams. *Earth Surface Processes and Landforms*, **36**, 1522–1533.

Chaudhry, S., Singh, S. P., & Singh, J. S. (1996). Performance of seedlings of various life forms on landslide-damaged forest sites in Central Himalaya. *Journal of Applied Ecology*, **33**, 109–117.

Chazdon, R. L. (2003). Tropical forest recovery: Legacies of human impact and natural disturbances. *Perspectives in Plant Ecology, Evolution and Systematics*, **6**, 51–71.

Chazdon, R. L. (2014). *Second Growth: The Promise of Tropical Forest Regeneration in an Age of Deforestation*. Chicago: University of Chicago Press.

Chiba, N. & Hirose, T. (1993). Nitrogen acquisition and use in three perennials in the early stage of primary succession. *Functional Ecology*, **7**, 287–292.

Chou, W.-C., Lin, W.-T., & Lin, C.-Y. (2009). Vegetation recovery patterns assessment at landslides caused by catastrophic earthquake: A case study in central Taiwan. *Environmental Monitoring and Assessment*, **152**, 245–257.

Chytrý, M., Maskell, L. C., Pino, J., *et al.* (2008). Habitat invasions by alien plants: A quantitative comparison among Mediterranean, subcontinental and oceanic regions of Europe. *Journal of Applied Ecology*, **45**, 448–458.

Ciccarelli, D. (2015). Mediterranean coastal dune vegetation: Are disturbance and stress the key selective forces that drive the psammophilous succession? *Estuarine, Coastal and Shelf Science*, **165**, 247–253.

Cielo-Filho, R. & de Souza, J. A. D. (2016). Assessing passive restoration of an Atlantic forest site following a *Cupressus lusitanica* Mill. Plantation clearcutting. *Ciencia Florestal*, **26**, 475–488.

Claessens, L., Verburg, P. H., Schoorl, J. M., & Veldkamp, A. (2006). Contribution of topographically based landslide hazard modeling to the analysis of the spatial distribution and ecology of kauri (*Agathis australis*). *Landscape Ecology*, **21**, 63–76.

Clark, A. T., Knops, J. M. H., & Tilman, D. (2019). Contingent factors explain average divergence in functional composition over 88 years of old field succession. *Journal of Ecology*, **107**, 545–558.

Clark, D. F., Antos, J. A., & Bradfield, G. E. (2003). Succession in sub-boreal forests of west-central British Columbia. *Journal of Vegetation Science*, **14**, 721–732.

Clarke, P. J., Knox, K. J. E., Bradstock, R. A., Munoz-Robles, C., & Kumar, L. (2014). Vegetation, terrain and fire history shape the impact of extreme weather on fire severity and ecosystem response. *Journal of Vegetation Science*, **25**, 1033–1044.

Clarkson, B. D. (1990). A review of vegetation development following recent (<450 years) volcanic disturbance in North Island, New Zealand. *New Zealand Journal of Ecology*, **14**, 59–71.

Clarkson, B. D. (1997). Vegetation succession (1967–89) on five recent montane lava flows, Mauna Loa, Hawaii. *New Zealand Journal of Ecology*, **22**, 1–9.

Clarkson, B. R. & Clarkson, B. D. (1983). Mt. Tarawera 2. Rates of change in the vegetation and flora of high domes. *New Zealand Journal of Ecology*, **2**, 107–119.

Clarkson, B. D. & Clarkson, B. R. (1994). Vegetation decline following recent eruptions on White Island (Whakaari), Bay of Plenty, New Zealand. *New Zealand Journal of Botany*, **32**, 21–26.

Clarkson, B. R. & Clarkson, B. D. (1995). Recent vegetation changes on Mount Tarawera, Rotorua, New Zealand. *New Zealand Journal of Botany*, **33**, 339–354.

Clement, C. J. E. (1985). Floodplain succession on the West Coast of Vancouver Island. *Canadian Field-Naturalist*, **99**, 34–39.

Clements, F. E. (1916). *Plant Succession: An Analysis of the Development of Vegetation.* Washington, DC: Carnegie Institution of Washington Publication, p. 242.

Clements, F. E. (1928). *Plant Succession and Indicators.* New York: H. W. Wilson.

Clements, F. E. (1936). Nature and structure of the climax. *Journal of Ecology*, **24**, 252–284.

Cleverly, J. R., Smith, S. D., Sala, A., & Devitt, D. A. (1997). Invasive capacity of *Tamarix ramosissima* in the Mojave Desert floodplain: The role of drought. *Oecologia*, **111**, 12–18.

Clewell, A. (2011). Forest succession after 43 years without disturbance on ex-arable land, northern Florida. *Castanea*, **76**, 386–394.

Cline, S. P. & McAllister, L. S. (2012). Plant succession after hydrologic disturbance: Inferences from contemporary vegetation on a chronosequence of bars, Willamette River, Oregon, USA. *River Research and Applications*, **28**, 1519–1539.

Clinton, B. D. & Baker, C. R. (2000). Catastrophic windthrow in the southern Appalachians: Characteristics of pits and mounds and initial vegetation responses. *Forest Ecology and Management*, **126**, 51–60.

Coates, D. R. (1977). Landslide perspectives. In D. R. Coates, ed., *Landslides*, pp. 3–28. Washington, DC: Geological Society of America.

Coates, K. D. & Burton, P. J. (1997). A gap-based approach for development of silvicultural systems to address ecosystem management objectives. *Forest Ecology and Management*, **99**, 339–356.

Collins, B., Wein, G., & Philippi, T. (2001). Effects of disturbance intensity and frequency on early old-field succession. *Journal of Vegetation Science*, **12**, 721–728.

Collins, S. L. & Wallace, L. L., eds. (1990). *Fire in North American Tallgrass Prairies*. Norman: University of Oklahoma Press.

Conn, J. S., Werdin-Pfisterer, N. R., Beattie, K. L., & Densmore, R. V. (2011). Ecology of invasive *Melilotus albus* on Alaskan glacial river floodplains. *Arctic, Antarctic, and Alpine Research*, **43**, 343–354.

Connell, J. H. (1978). Diversity in tropical rain forests and coral reefs. *Science*, **199**, 1302–1310.

Connell, J. H. & Slatyer, R. O. (1977). Mechanisms of succession in natural communities and their role in community stability and organization. *The American Naturalist*, **111**, 1119–1144.

Connell, J. H., Noble, I. R., & Slatyer, R. O. (1987). On the mechanisms producing successional change. *Oikos*, **50**, 136–137.

Connor, E. F. & Simberloff, D. (1976). The assembly of plant communities: Chance or competition? *Ecology*, **60**, 1132–1140.

Cook, W. M., Yao, J., Foster, B. L., Holt, R. D., & Patrick, L. B. (2005). Secondary succession in an experimentally fragmented landscape: Community patterns across space and time. *Ecology*, **86**, 1267–1279.

Coomes, D. A., Bentley, W. A., Tanentzap, A. J., & Burrows, L. E. (2013). Soil drainage and phosphorus depletion contribute to retrogressive succession along a New Zealand chronosequence. *Plant and Soil*, **367**, 77–91.

Coop, J. D., Massatti, R. T., & Schoettle, A. W. (2010). Subalpine vegetation pattern three decades after stand-replacing fire: Effects of landscape context and topography on plant community composition, tree regeneration, and diversity. *Journal of Vegetation Science*, **21**, 472–487.

Cooper, W. S. (1939). A fourth expedition to Glacier Bay, Alaska. *Ecology*, **20**, 130–155.

Copenheaver, C. A. (2008). Old-field succession in western New York: The progression of forbs and woody species from abandonment to mature forest. *Rhodora*, **110**, 157–170.

Copenheaver, C. A., Matthews, J. M., Showalter, J. M., & Auch, W. E. (2006). Forest stand development patterns in the southern Appalachians. *Northeastern Naturalist*, **13**, 477–494.

Coppoletta, M., Merriam, K. E., & Collins, B. M. (2016). Post-fire vegetation and fuel development influences fire severity patterns in reburns. *Ecological Applications*, **26**, 686–699.

Cordes, L. D., Hughes, F. M. R., & Getty, M. (1997). Factors affecting the regeneration and distribution of riparian woodlands along a northern prairie river: The Red Deer River, Alberta, Canada. *Journal of Biogeography*, **24**, 675–695.

Corenblit, D., Steiger, J., González, E., *et al.* (2014). The biogeomorphological life cycle of poplars during the fluvial bioogeomorphological succession: A special focus on *Populus nigra* L. *Earth Surface Processes and Landforms*, **39**, 546–563.

Correa, R. S., de Mello Filho, B., & de Mello Baptista, G. M. (2007). Phytosociological evaluation of the autogenic succession in mined areas in the Brazilian Federal District. *Cerne*, **13**, 406–415.

Cowles, H. C. (1901). The physiographic ecology of Chicago and vicinity: A study of the origin, development, and classification of plant societies. *Botanical Gazette*, **31**, 73–108, 145–82.

Cramer, V. A., Standish, R. J., & Hobbs, R. J. (2007). Prospects for the recovery of native vegetation in Western Australian old fields. In V. A. Cramer & R. J. Hobbs, eds., *Old Field Dynamics and Restoration of Abandoned Farmland*, pp. 286–306. Washington, DC: Island Press.

Cramer, V. A. & Hobbs, R. J., eds. (2007). *Old Field Dynamics and Restoration of Abandoned Farmland*. Washington, DC: Island Press.

Crampton, C. B. (1987). Soils, vegetation and permafrost across an active meander of Indian River, Central Yukon, Canada. *Catena*, **14**, 157–163.

Craw, D., Rufaut, C. G., Hammit, S., Clearwater, S. G., & Smith, C. M. (2007). Geological controls on natural ecosystem recovery on mine waste in southern New Zealand. *Environmental Geology*, **51**, 1389–1400.

Crews, T., Kitayama, K., Fownes, J., *et al.* (1995). Changes in soil phosphorus fractions and ecosystem dynamics across a long chronosequences in Hawaii. *Ecology*, **76**, 1407–1424.

Cross, A. T., Young, R., Nevill, P., *et al.* (2018). Appropriate aspirations for effective post-mining restoration and rehabilitation: A response to Kaźmierczak et al. *Environmental Earth Sciences*, **77**, 256. doi: 10.1007/s12665-018-7437-z.

Crouzeilles, R., Curran, M., Ferreira, M. S., Lindenmayer, D. B., Grelle, C. E. V., & Rey Benayas, J. M. (2016). A global meta-analysis on the ecological drivers of forest restoration success. *Nature Communications*, **7**, 11666.

Crow, T. R. (1980). A rainforest chronicle: A 30-year record of change in structure and composition at El Verde, Puerto Rico. *Biotropica*, **12**, 42–55.

Crowell, M. & Freedman, B. (1994). Vegetation development in a hardwood-forest chronosequence in Nova-Scotia. *Canadian Journal of Forest Research*, **24**, 260–271.

Cruden, D. M. (1991). A simple definition of a landslide. *Bulletin of the International Association of Engineering Geology*, **43**, 27–29.

Cruden, D. M., Keegan, T. R., & Thomson, S. (1993). The landslide dam on the Saddle River near Rycroft, Alberta. *Canadian Geotechnical Journal*, **30**, 1003–1015.

Csecserits, A., Czucz, B., Halassy, M., *et al.* (2011). Regeneration of sandy old-fields in the forest steppe region of Hungary. *Plant Biosystems*, **145**, 715–729.

Curran, T. J., Gersbach, L. N., Edwards, W., & Krockenberger, A. K. (2008). Wood density predicts plant damage and vegetative recovery rates caused by cyclone disturbance in tropical rainforest tree species of north Queensland, Australia. *Austral Ecology*, **33**, 442–450.

Curtin, C. G. (1994). The gothic earthflow revisited: A chronosequence examination of colonization on a subalpine earthflow. *Vegetatio*, **111**, 137–147.

Cushman, J. H., Waller, J. C., & Hoak, D. R. (2010). Shrubs as ecosystem engineers in a coastal dune: Influences on plant populations, communities and ecosystems. *Journal of Vegetation Science*, **21**, 821–831.

Cussedu, V., Ceccherelli, G., & Bertness, M. (2016). Hierarchical organization of a Sardinian sand dune plant community. *PeerJ*, **4**, e2199.

Cutler, N. A., Belyea, L. R., & Dugmore, A. J. (2008). The spatiotemporal dynamics of a primary succession. *Journal of Ecology*, **96**, 231–246.

Dahlskog, S. (1982). Successions in a Lapland mountain delta. *Meddelanden fran Växtbiologiska Institutionen*, **3**, 54–62.

Dale, V. H. (1989). Wind dispersed seeds and plant recovery on the Mount St. Helens debris avalanche. *Canadian Journal of Botany*, **67**, 1434–1441.

Dale, V. H. & Adams, W. M. (2003). Plant reestablishment 15 years after the debris avalanche at Mount St. Helens, Washington. *Science of the Total Environment*, **313**, 101–113.

Dale, V. H., Crisafulli, C. M., & Swanson, F. J. (2005). 25 years of ecological change at Mount St. Helens. *Science*, **308**, 961–962.

Dalling, J. W. (1994). Vegetation colonization of landslides in the Blue Mountains, Jamaica. *Biotropica*, **26**, 392–399.

Dalling, J. W. & Tanner, E. V. J. (1995). An experimental study of regeneration on landslides in montane rain forests in Jamaica. *Journal of Ecology*, **83**, 55–64.

Dalotto, C. E. S., Sühs, R. B., Dechoum, M. S., Pugnaire, F. I., Peroni, N., & Castellani, T. (2018). Facilitation influences patterns of perennial species abundance and richness in a subtropical dune system. *AOB Plants*, **10**, ply017.

D'Amico, M. E., Freppaz, M., Filippa, G., & Zanini, E. (2014). Vegetation influence on soil formation rate in a proglacial chronosequence (Lys Glacier, NW Italian Alps). *Catena*, **113**, 122–137.

D'Antonio, C. M., Hughes, R. F., & Tunison, J. T. (2011). Long-term impacts of invasive grasses and subsequent fire in seasonally dry Hawaiian woodlands. *Ecological Applications*, **21**, 1617–1628.

Danin, A. (1991). Plant adaptations in desert dunes. *Journal of Arid Environments*, **21**, 193–212.

Darcy, J. L. & Schmidt, S. K. (2016). Nutrient limitation of microbial phototrophs on a debris-covered glacier. *Soil Biology and Biochemistry*, **95**, 156–163.

Datri, L., Faggi, A., & Gallo, L. (2017). Crack willow changing riverine landscapes in Patagonia. *Ecohydrology*, **10**, e1837.

David, A. S., May, G., Schmidt, D., & Seabloom, E. W. (2016). Beachgrass invasion in coastal dunes is mediated by soil microbes and lack of disturbance dependence. *Ecosphere*, **7**, e01527.

Davis, M. A. & Pelsor, M. (2001). Experimental support for a resource-based mechanistic model of invasibility. *Ecology Letters*, **4**, 421–428.

Davis, M. A., Bier, L., Bushelle, E., Diegel, C., Johnson, A., & Kujala, B. (2005). Non-indigenous grasses impede woody succession. *Plant Ecology*, **178**, 249–264.

Davis, M. B. 1996. *Eastern Old-growth Forests: Prospects for Rediscovery and Recovery.* Washington, DC: Island Press.

Dean, W. R. J. & Milton, S. J. (1995). Plant and invertebrate assemblages on old fields in the arid southern Karoo, South-Africa. *African Journal of Ecology*, **33**, 1–13.

DeBano, L. F., Neary, D. G., & Folliot, P. F. (1998). *Fire's Effects on Ecosystems*. New York: Wiley.

Debussche, M. & Isenmann, P. (1994). Bird-dispersed seed rain and seedling establishment in patchy Mediterranean vegetation. *Oikos*, **69**, 414–426.

Debussche, M., Escarré, J., Lepart, J., Houssard, C., & Lavorel, S. (1996). Changes in Mediterranean plant succession: Old-fields revisited. *Journal of Vegetation Science*, **7**, 519–526.

Dech, J. P. & Maun, M. A. (2006). Adventitious root production and plastic resource allocation to biomass determine burial tolerance in woody plants from central Canadian coastal dunes. *Annals of Botany*, **98**, 1095–1105.

de Deus, F. F. & Oliveira, P. E. (2016). Changes in floristic composition and pollination systems in a "Cerrado" community after 20 years of fire suppression. *Brazilian Journal of Botany*, **39**, 1051–1063.

De Deyn, G. B., Cornelissen, J. H. C., & Bardgett, R. D. (2008). Plant functional traits and soil carbon sequestration in contrasting biomes. *Ecology Letters*, **11**, 516–531.

De Frenne, P., Baeten, L., Braae, B. J., *et al.* (2011). Interregional variation in the floristic recovery of post-agricultural forests. *Journal of Ecology*, **99**, 600–609.

de la Peña, E., Baeten, L., Steel, H., *et al.* (2016). Beyond plant-soil feedbacks: Mechanisms driving plant community shifts due to land-use legacies in post-agricultural forests. *Functional Ecology*, **30**, 1073–1085.

Delarze, R., Caldelari, D., & Hainard, P. (1992). Effects of fire on forest dynamics in southern Switzerland. *Journal of Vegetation Science*, **3**, 55–60.

Delgadillo, C. M. & Cárdenas, A. S. (1995). Observations on moss succession on Paricutín Volcano, Mexico. *The Bryologist*, **98**, 606–608.

DellaSala, D. A., Martin, A., Spivak, R., *et al.* (2003). A citizens' call for ecological forest restoration: Forest restoration principles and criteria. *Ecological Restoration*, **21**, 14–23.

del Moral, R. (1999). Predictability of primary successional wetlands on pumice, Mount St. Helens. *Madroño*, **46**, 177–186.

del Moral, R. (2009). Increasing deterministic control of primary succession on Mount St. Helens, Washington. *Journal of Vegetation Science*, **20**, 1145–1154.

del Moral, R. & Chang, C. C. (2015). Multiple assessments of succession rates on Mount St. Helens. *Plant Ecology*, **216**, 165–176.

del Moral, R. & Grishin, S. Y. (1999). Volcanic disturbances and ecosystem recovery. In L. R. Walker, ed., *Ecosystems of Disturbed Ground: Ecosystems of the World 16*, pp. 137–160. Amsterdam: Elsevier.

del Moral, R. & Lacher, I. L. (2005). Vegetation patterns 25 years after the eruption of Mount St. Helens, Washington. *American Journal of Botany*, **92**, 1948–1956.

del Moral, R. & Walker, L. R. (2007). *Environmental Disasters, Natural Recovery and Human Responses*. Cambridge: Cambridge University Press.

del Moral, R. & Wood, D. M. (1986). Subalpine vegetation recovery five years after the Mount St. Helens eruptions. In S. A. C. Keller, ed., *Mount St. Helens: Five Years Later*, pp. 215–221. Cheney: Eastern Washington University Press.

del Moral, R. & Wood, D. M. (1988). Dynamics of herbaceous vegetation recovery on Mount St. Helens, Washington, USA, after a volcanic eruption. *Vegetatio*, **74**, 11–27.

del Moral, R., Walker, L. R., & Bakker, J. P. (2007). Insights gained from succession for the restoration of landscape structure and function. In L. R. Walker, J. Walker, & R. J. Hobbs, eds., *Linking Restoration and Succession in Theory and Practice*, pp. 19–44. New York: Springer.

del Moral, R., Thomason, L. A., Wenke, A. C., Lozanoff, N., & Abata, M. D. (2012). Primary succession trajectories on pumice at Mount St. Helens, Washington. *Journal of Vegetation Science*, **23**, 73–85.

Del Tredici, P. (2001). Sprouting in temperate trees: A morphological and ecological review. *Botanical Review*, **67**, 121–140.

Dengler, J., Janisová, M., Török, P., & Wellstein, C. (2014). Biodiversity of Palaearctic grasslands: A synthesis. *Agriculture, Ecosystems and Environment*, **182**, 1–14.

Densmore, R. V. (1994). Succession on regraded placer mine spoil in Alaska, USA, in relation to initial site characteristics. *Arctic and Alpine Research*, **26**, 354–363.

De Villiers, A. D. & O'Connor, T. G. (2011). Effect of a single fire on woody vegetation in catchment IX, Cathedral Peak, KwaZulu-Natal Drakensberg, following extended partial exclusion of fire. *African Journal of Range and Forage Science*, **28**, 111–120.

De Wilde, M., Buisson, E., Ratovoson, F., Randrianaivo, R., Carriere, S. M., & Ii, P. P. L. (2012). Vegetation dynamics in a corridor between protected areas after slash-and-burn cultivation in south-eastern Madagascar. *Agriculture Ecosystems & Environment*, **159**, 1–8.

Dewine, J. M. & Cooper, D. J. (2008). Canopy shade and the successional replacement of tamarisk by native box elder. *Journal of Applied Ecology*, **45**, 505–514.

Diamond, J. (2005). *Collapse: How Societies Choose to Fail or Succeed*. New York: Penguin Books.

Diamond, J. M. (1975). The assembly of species communities. In M. L. Cody & J. M. Diamond, eds., *Ecology and Evolution of Communities*, pp. 342–344. Cambridge, MA: Harvard University Press.

Díaz, S., Hodgson, J. G., Thompson, K., *et al.* (2004). The plant traits that drive ecosystems: Evidence from three continents. *Journal of Vegetation Science*, **15**, 295–304.

Di Castri, F., Goodall, D. W., & Specht, R. L., eds. (1981). *Mediterranean-Type Shrublands: Ecosystems of the World 2*. Amsterdam: Elsevier.

Dickson, B. A. & Crocker, R. L. (1953). A chronosequence of soils and vegetation near Mt. Shasta, California. 1. Definition of the ecosystem investigated and features of the plant succession. *Journal of Soil Science*, **4**, 123–141.

Dickson, L. G. (2000). Constraints to nitrogen fixation by cryptogamic crusts in a polar desert ecosystem, Devon Island, N.W.T., Canada. *Arctic, Antarctic, and Alpine Research*, **32**, 40–45.

Dierschke, H. (2014). Secondary succession in clear-cut areas of a beech forest: Permanent plot research 1971–2013. *Tuexenia*, **34**, 107–130.

Dietze, M. C. & Clark, J. S. (2008). Changing the gap dynamics paradigm: Vegetative regeneration control on forest response to disturbance. *Ecological Monographs*, **78**, 331–347.

Di Giuseppe, F., Pappenberger, F., Wetterhall, F., *et al.* (2016). The potential predictability of fire danger provided by numerical weather prediction. *Journal of Applied Meteorology and Climatology*, **55**, 2469–2491.

Dilustro, J. J. & Day, F. P. (1997). Aboveground biomass and net primary production along a Virginia barrier island dune chronosequence. *The American Midland Naturalist*, **137**, 27–38.

Dimopoulos, P., Raus, T., Mucina, L., & Tsiripidis, I. (2010). Vegetation patterns and primary succession on sea-born volcanic islands (Santorini archipelago, Aegean Sea, Greece). *Phytocoenologia*, **40**, 1–14.

Di Palo, F. & Fornara, D. A. (2017). Plant and soil nutrient stoichiometry along primary ecological successions: Is there any link? *PLoS ONE*, **12**, e0182569.

Dirzo, R., Young, H. S., Mooney, H. A., & Ceballos, G. (2011). *Seasonally Dry Tropical Forests: Ecology and Conservation*. Washington, DC: Island Press.

Dislich, C. & Huth, A. (2012). Modelling the impact of shallow landslides on forest structure in tropical montane forests. *Ecological Modelling*, **239**, 40–53.

Dittus, W. P. J. (1985). The influence of cyclones on the dry evergreen forest of Sri Lanka. *Biotropica*, **17**, 1–14.

Dixon, M. & Turner, M. (2006). Simulated recruitment of riparian trees and shrubs under natural and regulated flow regimes on the Wisconsin River, USA. *River Research Applications*, **22**, 1057–1083.

Dixon, M. D., Turner, M. G., & Jin, C. F. (2002). Riparian tree seedling distribution on Wisconsin River sandbars: Controls at different spatial scales. *Ecological Monographs*, **72**, 465–485.

Doelle, M. & Schmidt, W. (2009). The relationship between soil seed bank, aboveground vegetation and disturbance intensity on old-field successional permanent plots. *Applied Vegetation Science*, **12**, 415–428.

Doing, H. (1985). Coastal fore-dune zonation and succession in various parts of the world. *Vegetatio*, **61**, 65–75.

Doležal, J., Yakubov, V., & Hara, T. (2013). Plant diversity changes and succession along resource availability and disturbance gradients in Kamchatka. *Plant Ecology*, **214**, 477–488.

Doležal, J., Song, J. S., Altman, J., Janeček, S., Černý, T., Šrůtek, M., & Kolbek, J. (2009). Tree growth and competition in a post-logging *Quercus mongolica* forest on Mt. Sobaek, South Korea. *Ecological Research*, **24**, 281–290.

Doležal, J., Homma, K., Takahashi, K., *et al.* (2008). Primary succession following deglaciation at Koryto Glacier Valley, Kamchatka. *Arctic, Antarctic, and Alpine Research*, **40**, 309–322.

d'Oliveira, M. V. N., Alvarado, E. C., Santos, J. C., & Carvalho Jr., J. A. (2011). Forest natural regeneration and biomass production after slash and burn in a seasonally dry forest in the Southern Brazilian Amazon. *Forest Ecology and Management*, **261**, 1490–1498.

Dommanget, F., Spiegelberger, T., Cavaille, P., & Evette, A. (2013). Light availability prevails over soil fertility and structure in the performance of Asian knotweeds on riverbanks: New management perspectives. *Environmental Management*, **52**, 11453–1462.

Donato, D. C., Fontaine, J. B., Robinson, W. D., Kauffman, J. B., & Law, B. E. (2009). Vegetation response to a short interval between high-severity wildfires in a mixed-evergreen forest. *Journal of Ecology*, **97**, 142–154.

Donfack, P., Floret, C., & Pontanier, R. (1995). Secondary succession in abandoned fields of dry tropical northern Cameroon. *Journal of Vegetation Science*, **6**, 499–508.

dos Santos, R., Citadini-Zanette, V., Leal-Filho, L. S., & Hennies, W. T. (2008). Spontaneous vegetation on overburden piles in the Coal Basin of Santa Catarina, Brazil. *Restoration Ecology*, **16**, 444–452.

Dostál, P., Dawson, W., van Kleunen, M., Keser, L. H., & Fischer, M. (2013). Central European plant species from more productive habitats are more invasive at a global scale. *Global Ecology and Biogeography*, **22**, 64–72.

Dovciak, M., Frelich, L. E., & Reich, P. B. (2005). Pathways in old-field succession to white pine: Seed rain, shade, and climate effects. *Ecological Monographs*, **75**, 363–378.

Doyle, K. M., Knight, D. H., Taylor, D. L., Barmore, W. J., & Benedict, J. M. (1998). Seventeen years of forest succession following the Waterfalls Canyon Fire in Grand Teton National Park, Wyoming. *International Journal of Wildland Fire*, **8**, 45–55.

Drake, D. (1990). Communities as assembled structures: Do rules govern pattern? *Trends in Ecology and Evolution*, **5**, 159–164.

Drake, D. R. & Mueller-Dombois, D. (1993). Population development of rain forest trees on a chronosequence of Hawaiian lava flows. *Ecology*, **74**, 1012–1019.

Driscoll, K. G., Arocena, J. M., & Massicotte, H. B. (1999). Post-fire soil nitrogen content and vegetation composition in Sub-Boreal spruce forests of British Columbia's central interior, Canada. *Forest Ecology and Management*, **121**, 227–237.

Duan, W. J., Ren, H., Fu, S. L., Wang, J., Yang, L., & Zhang, J. P. (2008). Natural recovery of different areas of a deserted quarry in South China. *Journal of Environmental Sciences*, **20**, 476–481.

Duffin, K. I., Li, S., & Meiners, S. J. (2019). Species pools and differential performance generate variation in leaf nutrients between native and exotic species in succession. *Journal of Ecology*, **107**, 595–605.

Dümig, A., Veste, M., Hagedorn, F., et al. (2014). Organic matter from biological soil crusts induces the initial formation of sandy temperate soils. *Catena*, **122**, 196–208.

Dupuch, A. & Fortin, D. (2013). The extent of edge effects increases during post-harvesting forest succession. *Biological Conservation*, **162**, 9–16.

Dyurgerov, E. (2002). Glacier Mass Balance and Regime: Data of Measurements and Analysis. Occasional Paper Number 55, Institute of Arctic and Alpine Research, University of Colorado, Boulder, CO.

Dzwonko, Z., Loster, S., & Gawronski, S. (2015). Impact of fire severity on soil properties and the development of tree and shrub species in a Scots pine moist forest site in southern Poland. *Forest Ecology and Management*, **342**, 56–63.

Edwards, P. J., Kollmann, J., Gurnell, A. M., Petts, G. E., Tockner, K., & Ward, J. V. (1999). A conceptual model of vegetation dynamics on gravel bars of a large Alpine river. *Wetlands Ecology and Management*, **7**, 141–153.

Eger, A., Almond, P. C., Wells, A., & Condron, L. M. (2013). Quantifying ecosystem rejuvenation: Foliar nutrient concentrations and vegetation communities across a dust gradient and a chronosequences. *Plant and Soil*, **367**, 93–109.

Egger, G., Politti, E., Lautsch, E., Benjankar, R., Gill, K. M., & Rood, S. B. (2015). Floodplain forest succession reveals fluvial processes: A hydrogeomorphic model for temperate riparian woodlands. *Journal of Environmental Management*, **161**, 72–82.

Egler, F. E. (1954). Vegetation science concepts 1. Initial floristic composition, a factor in old-field vegetation development. *Vegetatio*, **4**, 412–417.

Ehrenfeld, J. G. (2000). Defining the limits of restoration: The need for realistic goals. *Restoration Ecology*, **8**, 2–9.

Ehrensperger, T., Urech, Z. L., Rehnus, M., & Sorg, J. P. (2013). Fire impact on the woody plant components of dry deciduous forest in Central Menabe, Madagascar. *Applied Vegetation Science*, **16**, 619–628.

Eisenhauer, N., Barnes, A. D., Cesarz, S., *et al.* (2016). Biodiversity-ecosystem function experiments reveal the mechanisms underlying the consequences of biodiversity change in real world ecosystems. *Journal of Vegetation Science*, **27**, 1061–1070.

Ejrnaes, R., Hansen, D. N., & Aude, E. (2003). Changing course of secondary succession in abandoned sandy fields. *Biological Conservation*, **109**, 343–350.

Ekka, N. J. & Behera, N. (2011). Species composition and diversity of vegetation developing on an age series of coal mine spoil in an open cast coal field in Orissa, India. *Tropical Ecology*, **52**, 337–343.

Elias, R. B. & Dias, E. (2004). Primary succession on lava domes on Terceira (Azores). *Journal of Vegetation Science*, **15**, 331–338.

Elias, R. B. & Dias, E. (2009). Effects of landslides on the mountain vegetation of Flores Island, Azores. *Journal of Vegetation Science*, **20**, 706–717.

Elliott, K. J., Boring, L. R., Swank, W. T., & Haines, B. R. (1997). Successional changes in plant species diversity and composition after clearcutting a Southern Appalachian watershed. *Forest Ecology and Management*, **92**, 67–85.

Elmqvist, T., Wall, M., Berggren, A.-L., Blix, L., Fritioff, Å., & Rinman, U. (2002). Tropical forest reorganization after cyclone and fire disturbance in Samoa: Remnant trees as biological legacies. *Conservation Ecology*, **5**, article no. 10.

Elson, L. T., Simon, N. P. P., & Kneeshaw, D. (2007). Regeneration differences between fire and clearcut logging in southeastern Labrador: A multiple spatial scale analysis. *Canadian Journal of Forest Research*, **37**, 473–480.

Emery, S. M., Master, J. A., Benanti, S., & Gottshall, C. B. (2015). Patterns of trophic-level diversity associated with herbaceous dune vegetation across a primary successional gradient. *The American Midland Naturalist*, **173**, 177–190.

Engel, E. C. & Abella, S. R. (2011). Vegetation recovery in a desert landscape after wildfires: Influences of community type, time since fire and contingency effects. *Journal of Applied Ecology*, **48**, 1401–1410.

Erktan, A., Roumet, C., Bouchet, D., *et al.* (2018). Two dimensions define the variation of fine root traits across plant communities under the joint influence of ecological succession and annual mowing. *Journal of Ecology*, **106**, 2031–2042.

Erskine, P. D., Catterall, C. P., Lamb, D., & Kanowski, J. (2007). Patterns and processes of old fields reforestation in Australian rain forest landscapes. In V. A.

Cramer & R. J. Hobbs, eds., *Old Field Dynamics and Restoration of Abandoned Farmland*, pp. 119–144. Washington, DC: Island Press.

Erskine, W., Chalmers, A., Keene, A., Cheetham, M., & Bush, R. (2009). Role of a rheophyte in bench development on a sand-bed river in southeast Australia. *Earth Surface Processes and Landforms*, **34**, 941–953.

Escarré, J., Lefèbvre, C., Raboyeau, S., *et al.* (2011). Heavy metal concentration survey in soils and plants of the Les Malines mining district (Southern France): Implications for soil restoration. *Water Air and Soil Pollution*, **216**, 485–504.

Esler, K. J., Jacobsen, A. L., & Pratt, R. B. (2018). *The Biology of Mediterranean-Type Ecosystems*. Oxford: Oxford University Press.

Esper-Reyes, K. A., Mariano, N. A., Alcalá, R. E., Bonilla-Barbosa, J. R., Flores-Franco, G., & Wehncke, E. V. (2018). Seed dispersal by rivers in tropical dry forests: An overlooked process in tropical central Mexico. *Journal of Vegetation Science*, **29**, 62–73.

Everham, E. M. & Brokaw, N. V. L. (1996). Forest damage and recovery from catastrophic wind. *The Botanical Review*, **62**, 113–185.

Ewel, J. (1980). Tropical succession: Manifold routs to maturity. *Biotropica*, **12** (Supplement), 2–7.

Ewel, J. J. & Putz, F. E. (2004). A place for alien species in ecosystem restoration. *Frontiers in Ecology and the Environment*, **2**, 354–360.

Fagan, W. F. & Bishop, J. G. (2000). Trophic interactions during primary succession: Herbivory slows a plant reinvasion at Mount St. Helens. *The American Naturalist*, **155**, 238–251.

Fagan, W. F., Lewis, M., Neubert, M. G., *et al.* (2005). When can herbivores slow or reverse the spread of an invading plant? A test case from Mount St. Helens. *American Naturalist*, **166**, 669–685.

FAO (2019). Food and Agriculture Organization of the United Nations. www.fao.org.

Fastie, C. L. (1995). Causes and ecosystem consequences of multiple pathways on primary succession at Glacier Bay, Alaska. *Ecology*, **76**, 1899–1916.

Faucon, M.-P., Houben, D., & Lambers, H. (2017). Plant functional traits: Soil and ecosystem services. *Trends in Plant Science*, **22**, 385–394.

Faver, S., Jain, T., Bradford, J. B., *et al.* (2011). The efficacy of salvage logging in reducing subsequent fire severity in conifer-dominated forests of Minnesota, USA. *Ecological Applications*, **21**, 1895–1901.

Favero-Longo, S. E., Worland, M. R., Convey, P., *et al.* (2012). Primary succession of lichen and bryophyte communities following glacial recession on Signy Island, South Orkney Islands, Maritime Antarctic. *Antarctic Science*, **24**, 323–336.

Feagin, R. A., Figlus, J., Zinner, J. C., *et al.* (2015). Going with the flow or against the grain? The promise of vegetation for protecting beaches, dunes, and barrier islands from erosion. *Frontiers in Ecology and the Environment*, **13**, 203–210.

Fenesi, A., Vagasi, C. I., Beldean, M., *et al.* (2015). *Solidago canadensis* impacts on native plant and pollinator communities in different-aged old fields. *Basic and Applied Ecology*, **16**, 335–346.

Feng, Z., Alfaro-Murillo, J. A., DeAngelis, D. L., *et al.* (2012). Plant toxins and trophic cascades alter fire regime and succession on a boreal forest landscape. *Ecological Modelling*, **244**, 79–92.

Fenner, M. (1985). *Seed Ecology*. London: Chapman & Hall.

Fenner, M. & Thompson, K. (2005). *The Ecology of Seeds*. Cambridge: Cambridge University Press.

Fensham, R. J., Fairfax, R. J., Quintin, A. R., & Dwyer, J. M. (2016). Passive restoration of subtropical grassland after abandonment of cultivation. *Journal of Applied Ecology*, **53**, 274–283.

Fernández, D. S. & Fetcher, N. (1991). Changes in light availability following Hurricane Hugo in a subtropical montane forest in Puerto Rico. *Biotropica*, **23**, 393–399.

Ferracin, T. P., Medri, P. S., Batista, A. C. R., Mota, M. C., Bianchini, E., & Torezan, J. M. D. (2013). Passive restoration of Atlantic forest following *Pinus taeda* harvesting in southern Brazil. *Restoration Ecology*, **21**, 770–776.

Fetcher, N., Haines, B. L., Cordero, R. A., *et al.* (1996). Responses of tropical plants to nutrients and light on a landslide in Puerto Rico. *Journal of Ecology*, **84**, 331–341.

Fike, J. & Niering, W. A. (1999). Four decades of old field vegetation development and the role of *Celastrus orbiculatus* in the northeastern United States. *Journal of Vegetation Science*, **10**, 483–492.

Fine, P. V. A. (2002). The invasibility of tropical forests by exotic plants. *Journal of Tropical Ecology*, **18**, 687–705.

Finkl, C. W. & Pilkey, O. H., eds. (1991). Impact of Hurricane Hugo: September 10–22, 1989. *Journal of Coastal Research*, special issue **8**, 1–356.

Fischer, F. M., Oliveira, J. M., Dresseno, A. L. P., & Pillar, V. D. (2014). The role of invasive pine on changes of plant composition and functional traits in a coastal dune ecosystem. *Natureza and Conservação*, **12**, 19–23.

Flaccus, E. (1959). Revegetation of landslides in the White Mountains of New Hampshire. *Ecology*, **40**, 692–703.

Flores, B. M., Piedade, M.-T. F., & Nelson, B. W. (2014). Fire disturbance in Amazonian blackwater floodplain forests. *Plant Ecology and Diversity*, **7**, special issue S1, 319–327.

Floret, C., Galan, M. J., Floch, E., & Romane, F. (1992). Dynamics of holm oak (*Quercus ilex* L.) coppices after clearcutting in southern France. *Plant Ecology*, **99–100**, 97–105.

Fonda, R. W. (1974). Forest succession in relation to river terrace development in Olympic National Park, Washington. *Ecology*, **55**, 927–942.

Formann, R. T. T., Sperling, D., Bissonette, J. A., *et al.* (2003). *Road Ecology: Science and Solutions*. Washington, DC: Island Press.

Foster, C. N., Sato, C. F., Lindenmayer, D. B., & Barton, P. S. (2016). Integrating theory into disturbance interaction experiments to better inform ecosystem management. *Global Change Biology*, **22**, 1325–1335.

Foster, D. R. (1988a). Disturbance history, community organization and vegetation dynamics of the old-growth Pisgah Forest, south-western New Hampshire, U.S.A. *Journal of Ecology*, **76**, 105–134.

Foster, D. R. (1988b). Species and stand response to catastrophic wind in central New England, U.S.A. *Journal of Ecology*, **76**, 135–151.

Foster, D. R., Fluet, M., & Boose, E. R. (1999). Human or natural disturbance: Landscape-scale dynamics of the tropical forests of Puerto Rico. *Ecological Applications*, **9**, 555–572.

Fox, B. J., Fox, M. D., Taylor, J. E., et al. (1996). Comparison of regeneration following burning, clearing or mineral sand mining at Tomago, NSW. 1. Structure and growth of the vegetation. *Australian Journal of Ecology*, **21**, 184–199.

Francescato, V., Scotton, M., Zarin, D. J., Innes, J. C., & Bryant, D. M. (2001). Fifty years of natural revegetation on a landslide in Franconia Notch, New Hampshire, U.S.A. *Canadian Journal of Botany*, **79**, 1477–1485.

Frangi, J. L. & Lugo, A. E. (1998). A flood plain palm forest in the Luquillo Mountains of Puerto Rico five years after Hurricane Hugo. *Biotropica*, **30**, 339–348.

Franklin, J. (2007). Recovery from clearing, cyclone and fire in rain forests of Tonga, South Pacific: Vegetation dynamics 1995–2005. *Austral Ecology*, **32**, 789–797.

Franklin, J., Coulter, C. L., & Rey, S. J. (2004). Change over 70 years in a southern California chaparral community related to fire history. *Journal of Vegetation Science*, **15**, 701–710.

Franks, S., Masek, J. G., & Turner, M. G. (2013). Monitoring forest regrowth following large scale fire using satellite data: A case study of Yellowstone National Park, USA. *European Journal of Remote Sensing*, **46**, 551–569.

Fraser, A. I. (1962). The soil and roots as factors in tree stability. *Forestry*, **35**, 117–127.

Freestone, M., Wills, T. J., & Read, J. (2015). Post-fire succession during the long-term absence of fire in coastal heathland and a test of the chronosequence survey method. *Australian Journal of Botany*, **63**, 572–580.

Frelich, L. E. (2002). *Forest Dynamics and Disturbance Regimes: Studies from Temperate Evergreen-Deciduous Forests*. Cambridge: Cambridge University Press.

Frelich, L. E. & Reich, P. B. (1995). Spatial patterns and succession in a Minnesota southern-boreal forest. *Ecological Monographs*, **65**, 325–346.

Frenzen, P. M., Krasny, M. E., & Rigney, L. P. (1988). Thirty-three years of plant succession on the Kautz Creek mudflow, Mount Rainier National Park, Washington. *Canadian Journal of Botany*, **66**, 130–137.

Fridley, J. D. & Wright, J. P. (2012). Drivers of secondary succession rates across temperate latitudes of the Eastern USA: Climate, soils, and species pools. *Oecologia*, **168**, 1069–1077.

Fridriksson, S. (1987). Plant colonization of a volcanic island, Surtsey, Iceland. *Arctic and Alpine Research*, **19**, 425–431.

Fridriksson, S. (1992). Vascular plants on Surtsey (1981–1990). *Reykiavik, Surtsey Research Progress Report*, **10**, 17–30.

Friedman, J. M., Osterkamp, W. R., & Lewis, W. M., Jr. (1996). Channel narrowing and vegetation development following a Great Plains flood. *Ecology*, **77**, 2167–2181.

Frouz, J., Kalčík, J., & Velichová, V. (2011). Factors causing spatial heterogeneity in soil properties, plant cover, and soil fauna in a non-reclaimed post-mining site. *Ecological Engineering*, **37**, 1910–1913.

Frouz, J., Mudrák, O., Reitschmiedová, E., et al. (2018). Rough wave-like heaped overburden promotes establishment of woody vegetation while leveling promotes grasses during unassisted. *Journal of Environmental Management*, **205**, 50–58.

Frouz, J., Prach, K., Pizl, V., *et al.* (2008). Interactions between soil development, vegetation and soil fauna during spontaneous succession in post mining sites. *European Journal of Soil Biology*, **44**, 109–121.

Frye, R. J. II & Quinn, J. A. (1979). Forest development in relation to topography and soils on a floodplain of the Raritan River, New Jersey. *Bulletin of the Torrey Botanical Club*, **106**, 334–345.

Fu, S., Rodríguez Pedraza, C., & Lugo, A. E. (1996). A twelve-year comparison of stand changes in a mahogany plantation and a paired natural forest of similar age. *Biotropica*, **28**, 515–524.

Fujii, S., Kubota, Y., & Enoki, T. (2010). Long-term ecological impacts of clear-fell logging on tree species diversity in a subtropical forest, southern Japan. *Journal of Forest Research*, **15**, 289–298.

Fukami, T., Bezemer, T. M., Mortimer, S. R., & van der Putten, W. H. (2005). Species divergence and trait convergence in experimental plant community assembly. *Ecology Letters*, **8**, 1283–1290.

Fullen, M. A. & Mitchell, D. J. (1994). Desertification and reclamation in North-Central China. *Ambio*, **23**, 131–135.

Fuller, R. N. & del Moral, R. (2003). The role of refugia and dispersal in primary succession on Mount St. Helens, Washington. *Journal of Vegetation Science*, **14**, 637–644.

Funk, J. & Vitousek, P. (2007). Resource-use efficiency and plant invasion in low-resource systems. *Nature*, **446**, 1079–1081.

Funk, J. L., Larson, J. E., Ames, G. M., *et al.* (2016). Revisiting the Holy Grail: Using plant functional traits to understand ecological processes. *Biological Reviews*, **92**, 1156–1173.

Fyles, J. W. & Bell, M. A. M. (1986). Vegetation colonizing river gravel bars in the Rocky Mountains of southeastern British Columbia. *Northwest Science*, **60**, 8–14.

Gagne, J.-M. & Houle, G. (2001). Facilitation of *Leymus mollis* by *Honckenya peploides* on coastal dunes in subarctic Quebec, Canada. *Canadian Journal of Botany*, **79**, 1327–1331.

Galatowitsch, S. & Richardson, D. M. (2005). Riparian scrub recovery after clearing of invasive alien trees in headwater streams of the Western Cape, South Africa. *Biological Conservation*, **122**, 509–521.

Galindo, V., Calle, Z., Chará, J., & Armbrecht, I. (2017). Facilitation by pioneer shrubs for the ecological restoration of riparian forests in the Central Andes of Colombia. *Restoration Ecology*, **25**, 731–737.

Gallardo, M.-B., Pérez, C., Núñez-Ávila, M., & Armesto, J. J. (2012). Decoupling of soil development and plant succession over a 60,000 year chronosequence in the Llaima Volcano, Chile. *Chilean Journal of Natural History*, **85**, 291–306.

Gallego-Fernández, J. B., Muñoz-Valles, S., & Dellafiore, C. M. (2015). Spatio-temporal patterns of colonization and expansion of *Retama monosperma* on developing coastal dunes. *Journal of Coastal Conservation*, **19**, 577–587.

Game, M., Carrel, J. E., & Hotrabhavandra, T. (1982). Patch dynamics of plant succession on abandoned surface coal-mines: A case-history Approach. *Journal of Ecology*, **70**, 707–720.

Ganade, G. (2007). Processes affecting succession in old fields of Brazilian Amazonia. In V. A. Cramer & R. J. Hobbs, eds., *Old Field Dynamics and Restoration of Abandoned Farmland*, pp. 75–92. Washington, DC: Island Press.

García-Aria, A. & Francés, F. (2016). The RVDM: Modelling impacts, evolution and competition processes to determine riparian vegetation dynamics. *Ecohydrology*, **3**, 438–459.

Garcia-Florez, L., Vanclay, J. K., Glencross, K., & Nichols, J. D. (2017). Understanding 48 years of changes in tree diversity, dynamics and species responses since logging disturbance in a subtropical rainforest. *Forest Ecology and Management*, **393**, 29–39.

García-Romero, A., Alanís-Anaya, R. M., & Muñoz-Jiménez, J. (2015). Environmental factors that affect primary plant succession trajectories on lahars (Popocatépetl Volcano, Mexico). *Journal of Mountain Science*, **12**, 1254–1266.

Gardescu, S. & Marks, P. L. (2004). Colonization of old fields by trees vs. shrubs: Seed dispersal and seedling establishment. *Journal of the Torrey Botanical Society*, **131**, 53–68.

Gardner, L. R., Michener, W. K., Blood, E. R., Williams, T. M., Lipscomb, D. J., & Jefferson, W. H. (1991). Ecological impact of Hurricane Hugo – Salinization of a coastal forest. *Journal of Coastal Research*, special issue **8**, 301–318.

Garibotti, I. A., Pissolito, C. I., & Villalba, R. (2011a). Spatiotemporal pattern of primary succession in relation to meso-topographic gradients on recently deglaciated terrains in the Patagonian Andes. *Arctic, Antarctic, and Alpine Research*, **43**, 555–567.

Garibotti, I. A., Pissolito, C. I., & Villalba, R. (2011b). Vegetation development on deglaciated rock outcrops from Glaciar Frias, Argentina. *Arctic, Antarctic, and Alpine Research*, **43**, 35–45.

Garnier, E., Cortez, J., Billès, G., et al. (2004). Plant functional markers capture ecosystem properties during secondary succession. *Ecology*, **85**, 2630–2637.

Garwood, N. C., Janos, D. J., & Brokaw, N. (1979). Earthquake-caused landslides: A major disturbance to tropical forests. *Science*, **205**, 997–999.

Gates, F. C. (1914). The pioneer vegetation of Taal Volcano. *Philippine Journal of Science Section C*, **9**, 391–431.

Geertsema, M. & Pojar, J. J. (2007). Influence of landslides on biophysical diversity – A perspective from British Columbia. *Geomorphology*, **89**, 55–69.

Gemma, J. N. & Koske, R. E. (1990). Mycorrhizae in recent volcanic substrates in Hawaii. *American Journal of Botany*, **77**, 1193–1200.

Ghermandi, L., Guthmann, N., & Bran, D. (2004). Early post-fire succession in northwestern Patagonia grasslands. *Journal of Vegetation Science*, **15**, 67–76.

Gibb, J. A. (1994). Plant succession on the braided bed of the Orongorongo River, Wellington, New Zealand, 1973–1990. *New Zealand Journal of Ecology*, **18**, 29–40.

Gibson, C. M., Turetsky, M. R., Cottenie, K., Kane, E. S., Houle, G., & Kasischke, E. S. (2016). Variation in plant community composition and vegetation carbon pools a decade following a severe fire season in interior Alaska. *Journal of Vegetation Science*, **27**, 1187–1197.

Gibson, D. J. (2009). *Grasses and Grassland Ecology*. Oxford: Oxford University Press.

Gibson, D. J., Middleton, B. A., Foster, K., Honu, Y. A. K., Hoyer, E. W., & Mathis, M. (2005). Species frequency dynamics in an old-field succession: Effects of disturbance, fertilization and scale. *Journal of Vegetation Science*, **16**, 415–422.

Gilardelli, F., Sgorbati, S., Armiraglio, S., Citterio, S., & Gentili, R. (2016). Assigning plant communities to a successional phase: Time trends in abandoned limestone quarries. *Plant Biosystems*, **150**, 799–808.

Gill, D. (1972). The point bar environment in the Mackenzie River Delta. *Canadian Journal of Earth Sciences*, **9**, 1382–1393.

Gill, D. (1973). Floristics of a plant succession sequence in the Mackenzie Delta, Northwest Territories. *Polarforschung*, **43**, 55–65.

Gill, R. A., O'Connor, R. C. Rhodes, A., Bishop, T. B. B., Laughlin, D. C., & St. Clair, S. B. (2018). Niche opportunities for invasive annual plants in dryland ecosystems are controlled by disturbance, trophic interactions, and rainfall. *Oecologia*, **187**, 755–765.

Gilliam, F. S., Turrell, N. L., & Adams, M. B. (1995). Herbaceous-layer and overstory species in clear-cut and mature central Appalachian hardwood forests. *Ecological Applications*, **5**, 947–955.

Gilman, L. N., Wright, S. D., Cusens, J., McBride, P. D., Malhi, Y., & Whittaker, R. J. (2015). Latitude, productivity and species richness. *Global Ecology and Biogeography*, **24**, 107–117.

Giupponi, L., Bischetti, G. B., & Giorgi, A. (2015). Ecological index of maturity to evaluate the vegetation disturbance of areas affected by restoration work: A practical example of its application in an area of the Southern Alps. *Restoration Ecology*, **23**, 635–644.

Glade, T. (2003). Landslide occurrence as a response to land use change: A review of evidence from New Zealand. *Catena*, **51**, 297–314.

Gleason, H. A. (1926). The individualistic concept of the plant association. *Bulletin of the Torrey Botanical Club*, **53**, 7–26.

Glenn-Lewin, D. C. (1980). The individualistic nature of plant community development. *Vegetatio*, **43**, 141–146.

Glenn-Lewin, D. C., Peet, R. K., & Veblen, T. T., eds. (1992). *Plant Succession: Theory and Prediction*. London: Chapman & Hall.

Gloaguen, J. C. (1993). Spatiotemporal patterns in postburn succession on Brittany heathlands. *Journal of Vegetation Science*, **4**, 561–566.

Goldenberg, S. B., Landsea, C. W., Mestas-Nuñez, A. M., & Gray, W. M. (2001). The recent increase in Atlantic hurricane activity: Causes and implications. *Science*, **293**, 474–479.

Goméz-Aparicio, L. (2009). The role of plant interactions in the restoration of degraded ecosystems: A meta-analysis across lifeforms and ecosystems. *Journal of Ecology*, **97**, 1202–1214.

Gomez-Romero, M., Lindig-Cisneros, R., & Galindo-Vallejo, S. (2006). Effect of tephra depth on vegetation development in areas affected by volcanism. *Plant Ecology*, **183**, 207–213.

González, E., Rochefort, L., & Poulin, M. (2013). Trajectories of plant recovery in block-cut peatlands 35 years after peat extraction. *Applied Ecology and Environmental Research*, **11**, 385–406.

González, E., Masip, A., Tabacchi, E., & Poulin, M. (2017). Strategies to restore floodplain vegetation after abandonment of human activities. *Restoration Ecology*, **25**, 82–91.

González-De Vega, S., De las Heras, J., & Moya, D. (2016). Resilience of Mediterranean terrestrial ecosystems and fire severity in semiarid areas: Responses of Aleppo pine forests in the short, mid and long term. *Science of the Total Environment*, **573**, 1171–1177.

González-Mancebo, J. M., Beltrán Tejera, E., Losada-Lima, A., & Sánchez-Pinto, L. (1996). *La Vida Vegetal en las Lavas Históricas de Canarias: Colonización y Recubrimiento Vegetal, con Especial Referencia al Parque Nacional de Timanfaya.* Madrid: Organismo Autónomo Parques Nacionales.

González-Ollauri, A. & Mickovski, S. B. (2017). Shallow landslides as drivers for slope ecosystem evolution and biophysical diversity. *Landslides*, **14**, 1699–1714.

González-Tagle, M. A., Schwendenmann, L., Pérez, J. J., & Schulz, R. (2008). Forest structure and woody plant species composition along a fire chronosequence in mixed pine-oak forest in the Sierra Madre Oriental, Northeast Mexico. *Forest Ecology and Management*, **256**, 161–167.

Goodall, D. W. (1986). Classification and ordination: Their nature and role in taxonomy and community studies. *Coenoses*, **1**, 3–9.

Gornish, E. S. & Miller, T. E. (2010). Effects of storm frequency on dune vegetation. *Global Change Biology*, **16**, 2668–2675.

Gosper, C. R., Yates, C. J., & Prober, S. M. (2013). Floristic diversity in fire-sensitive eucalypt woodlands shows a "U"-shaped relationship with time since fire. *Journal of Applied Ecology*, **50**, 1187–1196.

Gosper, C. R., Yates, C. J., Prober, S. M., & Parsons, B. C. (2012). Contrasting changes in vegetation structure and diversity with time since fire in two Australian Mediterranean-climate plant communities. *Austral Ecology*, **37**, 164–174.

Götzenberger, L., de Bello, F., Brathen, K. A., *et al.* (2012). Ecological assembly rules in plant communities-approaches, patterns and prospects. *Biological Reviews*, **87**, 111–127.

Gourlet-Fleury, S., Beina, D., Fayolleet, A., *et al.* (2013). Silvicultural disturbance has little impact on tree species diversity in a Central African moist forest. *Forest Ecology and Management*, **304**, 322–332.

Graf, M. D., Rochefort, L., & Poulin, M. (2008). Spontaneous revegetation of cutaway peatlands of North America. *Wetlands*, **28**, 28–39.

Gran, K. B., Tal, M., & Wartman, E. D. (2015). Co-evolution of riparian vegetation and channel dynamics in an aggrading braded river system, Mount Pinatubo, Philippines. *Earth Surface Processes and Landforms*, **40**, 1101–1115.

Grau, H. R., Arturi, M. F., Brown, A. D., & Aceñolaza, P. G. (1997). Floristic and structural patterns along a chronosequence of secondary forest succession in Argentinean subtropical montane forests. *Forest Ecology and Management*, **95**, 161–171.

Grau, O., Rautio, P., Heikkinen, J., Saravesi, K., Kozlov, M. V., & Markkola, A. (2010). An ericoid shrub plays a dual role in recruiting both pines and their fungal symbionts along primary succession gradients. *Oikos*, **119**, 1727–1734.

Gray, N. F. (2015). *Facing Up to Global Warming: What Is Going on and How You Can Make a Difference?* New York: Springer.

Greet, J., Webb, J., & Downes, B. (2011). Flow variability maintains the structure and composition of in-channel riparian vegetation. *Freshwater Biology*, **56**, 2514–2528.

Gregory, S., Li, H., & Li, J. (2002). The conceptual basis for ecological responses to dam removal. *BioScience*, **52**, 713–723.

Griggs, R. F. (1933). The colonization of the Katmai ash, a new and inorganic "soil." *American Journal of Botany*, **20**, 92–113.

Grime, J. P. (1977). Evidence for the existence of three primary strategies in plants and its relevance to ecological and evolutionary theory. *The American Naturalist*, **111**, 1169–1194.

Grime, J. P. (1979). *Plant Strategies and Vegetation Processes*. Chichester, UK: Wiley.

Grime, J. P. (2002). *Plant Strategies and Vegetation Processes*. 2nd ed. Chichester, UK: Wiley.

Grime, J. P., Hodgson, J. G., & Hunt, R. (1988). *Comparative Plant Ecology: A Functional Approach to Common British Species*. London: Unwin Hyman.

Grishin, S. Yu. (2010). Vegetation changes under the impact of volcanic ashfall (Tolbachinsky Dol, Kamchatka). *Russian Journal of Ecology*, **41**, 436–439.

Grishin, S. Yu., del Moral, R., Krestov, P. V., & Verkholat, V. P. (1996). Succession following the catastrophic eruption of Ksudach volcano (Kamchatka, 1907). *Vegetatio*, **127**, 129–153.

Groffman, P. M., Bain, D. J., Band, L. E., *et al.* (2003). Down by the riverside: Urban riparian ecology. *Frontiers in Ecology and the Environment*, **1**, 315–321.

Grootjans, A. P. & Verbeek, S. K. (2002). A conceptual model of European wet meadow restoration. *Ecological Restoration*, **20**, 6–9.

Grootjans, A. P., Ernst, W. H. O., & Stuyfzand, P. J. (1998). European dune slacks: Strong interactions of biology, pedogenesis and hydrology. *Trends in Ecology and Evolution*, **13**, 96–100.

Grootjans, A. P., Dullo, B. S., Kooijman, A. M., Bekker, R. M., & Aggenbach, C. (2013). Restoration of dune vegetation in The Netherlands. In M. L. Martínez, J. B. Gallego-Fernández, & P. A. Hesp, eds., *Restoration of Coastal Dunes*, pp. 235–254. New York: Springer.

Grootjans, A. P., Shahrudin, R., van de Craats, A., *et al.* (2017). Window of opportunity of *Liparis loeselii* populations during vegetation succession on the Waddern Sea islands. *Journal of Coastal Conservation*, **21**, 631–641.

Gross, K. I. & Emery, S. M. (2007). Succession and restoration in Michigan old field communities. In V. A. Cramer & R. J. Hobbs, eds., *Old Field Dynamics and Restoration of Abandoned Farmland*, pp. 162–179. Washington, DC: Island Press.

Grove, S., Parker, I. M., & Haubensak, K. A. (2017). Do impacts of an invasive nitrogen-fixing shrub on Douglas-fir and its ectomycorrhizal mutualism change over time following invasion? *Journal of Ecology*, **105**, 1687–1697.

Groves, R. H. & DiCastri, F., eds. (1991). *Biogeography of Mediterranean Invasions*. Cambridge: Cambridge University Press.

Grubb, P. J. (1987). Some generalizing ideas about colonization and succession in green plants and fungi. In A. J. Gray, M. J. Crawley, & P. J. Edwards, eds., *Colonization, Succession and Stability*, pp. 81–102. Oxford: Blackwell.

Guariguata, M. R. (1990). Landslide disturbance and forest regeneration in the Upper Luquillo Mountains of Puerto Rico. *Journal of Ecology*, **78**, 814–832.

Guariguata, M. R. & Dupuy, J. M. (1997). Forest regeneration in abandoned logging roads in lowland Costa Rica. *Biotropica*, **29**, 15–28.

Guedo, D. D. & Lamb, E. G. (2013). Temporal changes in abundance-occupancy relationships within and between communities after disturbance. *Journal of Vegetation Science*, **24**, 607–615.

Guzmán-Grajales, S. M. & Walker, L. R. (1991). Differential seedling responses to litter after Hurricane Hugo in the Luquillo Experimental Forest, Puerto Rico. *Biotropica*, **23**, 407–413.

Haeussler, S. & Bergeron, Y. (2004). Range of variability in boreal aspen plant communities after wildfire and clear-cutting. *Canadian Journal of Forest Research*, **34**, 274–288.

Haigh, M. J., Rawat, J. S., Rawat, M. S., Bartarya, S. K., & Rai, S. P. (1995). Interactions between forest and landslide activity along new highways in the Kumaun Himalaya. *Forest Ecology and Management*, **78**, 173–189.

Haire, S. L. & McGarigal, K. (2008). Inhabitants of landscape scars: Succession of woody plants after large, severe forest fires in Arizona and New Mexico. *Southwestern Naturalist*, **53**, 146–161.

Halofsky, J. E. & Hibbs, D. E. (2009). Controls on early post-fire plant colonization in riparian areas. *Forest Ecology and Management*, **258**, 1350–1358.

Halpern, C. B. & Lutz, J. A. (2013). Canopy closure exerts weak controls on understory dynamics: A 30-year study of overstory-understory interactions. *Ecological Monographs*, **83**, 221–237.

Halvorson, J. J., Smith, J. L., & Franz, E. H. (1991). Lupine influence on soil carbon, nitrogen and microbial activity in developing ecosystems at Mount St. Helens. *Oecologia*, **87**, 162–170.

Halvorson, J. J., Smith, J. L., & Kennedy, A. C. (2005). Lupine effects on soil development and function during early primary succession at Mount St. Helens. In V. H. Dale, F. J. Swanson, & C. M. Crisafulli, eds., *Ecological Responses to the 1980 Eruption of Mount St. Helens*, pp. 243–254. New York: Rotterdam.

Halwagy, R. (1961). Studies on the succession of vegetation on some islands and sand banks in the Nile near Khartoum, Sudan. *Vegetatio*, **11**, 217–234.

Hanley, T. A. & Barnard, J. C. (1998). Red Alder, *Alnus rubra*, as a potential mitigating factor for wildlife habitat following clearcut logging in southeastern Alaska. *Canadian Field-Naturalist*, **112**, 647–652.

Hanna, S. K. & Fulgham, K. O. (2015). Post-fire vegetation dynamics of a sagebrush steppe community change significantly over time. *California Agriculture*, **69**, 36–42.

Hanski, I. (1999). *Metapopulation Ecology*. Oxford: Oxford University Press.

Harantová, L., Mudrák, O., Kohout, P., Elhottová, D., Frouz, J., & Baldrián, P. (2017). Development of microbial community during primary succession in areas degraded by mining activities. *Land Degradation and Development*, **28**, 2574–2584.

Harcombe, P. A., Bill, C. J., Fulton, M., Glitzenstein, J. S., Marks, P. L., & Elsik, I. S. (2002). Stand dynamics over 18 years in a southern mixed hardwood forest, Texas, USA. *Journal of Ecology*, **90**, 947–957.

Harmer, R., Peterken, G., Kerr, G., & Poulton, P. (2001). Vegetation changes during 100 years of development of two secondary woodlands on abandoned arable land. *Biological Conservation*, **101**, 291–304.

Harner, M. J., Mummey, D. L., Stanford, J. A., & Rillig, M. C. (2010). Arbuscular mycorrhizal fungi enhance spotted knapweed growth across a riparian chronosequences. *Biological Invasions*, **12**, 1481–1490.

Harper, J. L. (1977). *Population Biology of Plants*. New York: Academic Press.

Harper, K. A., Macdonald, S. E., Burton, P. J., et al. (2005). Edge influence on forest structure and composition in fragmented landscapes. *Conservation Biology*, **19**, 768–782.

Harrod, J. C., Harmon, M. E., & White, P. S. (2000). Post-fire succession and 20th century reduction in fire frequency on xeric southern Appalachian sites. *Journal of Vegetation Science*, **11**, 465–472.

Harvey, B. J. & Holzman, B. A. (2014). Divergent successional pathways of stand development following fire in a California closed-cone pine forest. *Journal of Vegetation Science*, **25**, 88–99.

Hasselquist, E. M., Nilsson, C., Hjältén, J., Jørgensen, D., Lind, L., & Polvi, L. E. (2015). Time for recovery of riparian plants in restored northern Swedish streams: A chronosequences study. *Ecological Applications*, **25**, 1373–1389.

Hasselquist, N. J., Santiago, L. S., & Allen, M. F. (2010). Belowground nutrient dynamics in relation to hurricane damage along a tropical dry chronosequence. *Biogeochemistry*, **98**, 89–100.

Hastings, A., Byers, J. E., Crooks, J. A., et al. (2007). Ecosystem engineering in space and time. *Ecology Letters*, **10**, 153–164.

Haussler, S. & Kneeshaw, D. (2003). Comparing forest management to natural processes. In P. J. Burton, C. Messier, D. W. Smith, & W. L. Adamowicz, eds., *Towards Sustainable Management of the Boreal Forest*, pp. 307–368. Ottawa, ON: NRC Research Press.

Hawkins, C. D., Dhar, A., & Bittencourt, E. (2013). Improving site index estimates for pine and spruce plantations: A case study in the sub-boreal spruce zone in British Columbia. *Forest Science and Technology*, **9**, 51–58.

Hayasaka, D., Goka, K., Thawatchai, W., & Fujiwara, K. (2012). Ecological impacts of the 2004 Indian Ocean tsunami on coastal sand-dune species on Phuket Island, Thailand. *Biodiversity Conservation*, **21**, 1971.

Heartsill Scalley, T. (2017). Insights on forest structure and composition from long-term research in the Luquillo Mountains. *Forests*, **8**, 204.

Heath, J. P. (1967). Primary conifer succession, Lassen Volcanic National Park. *Ecology*, **48**, 270–275.

Heinl, M., Sliva, J., Murray-Hudson, M., & Tacheba, B. (2007). Post-fire succession on savanna habitats in the Okavango Delta wetland, Botswana. *Journal of Tropical Ecology*, **23**, 705–713.

Heinrichs, S. & Schmidt, W. (2009). Short-term effects of selection and clear cutting on the shrub and herb layer vegetation during the conversion of even-aged Norway spruce stands into mixed stands. *Forest Ecology and Management*, **258**, 667–678.

Helm, D. J. & Allen, E. B. (1995). Vegetation chronosequence near Exit Glacier, Kenai Fjords National Park, Alaska, USA. *Arctic and Alpine Research*, **27**, 246–257.

Helm, D. J. & Collins, W. B. (1997). Vegetation succession and disturbance on a boreal forest floodplain, Susitna River, Alaska. *Canadian Field-Naturalist*, **111**, 553–566.

Hendrix, L. B. (1981). Post-eruption succession on Isla Fernandina, Galápagos. *Madroño*, **28**, 242–254.

Heneberg, P., Hesoun, P., & Skuhrovec, J. (2016). Succession of arthropods on xerothermophilous habitats formed by sand quarrying: Epigeic beetles (Coleoptera) and orthopteroids (Orthoptera, Dermaptera and Blattodea). *Ecological Engineering*, **95**, 340–356.

Henkel, T. K., Chambers, J. Q., & Baker, D. A. (2016). Delayed tree mortality and Chinese tallow (*Triadica sebifera*) population explosion in a Louisiana bottomland hardwood forest following Hurricane Katrina. *Forest Ecology and Management*, **378**, 222–232.

Henriksson, E., Henriksson, L. E., Norrman, J. O., & Nyman, P. O. (1987). Biological dinitrogen fixation (acetylene reduction) exhibited by blue-green algae (cyanobacteria) in association with mosses gathered on Surtsey, Iceland. *Arctic and Alpine Research*, **19**, 432–436.

Henriksson, L. E. & Rodgers, G. A. (1978). Further studies in the nitrogen cycle of Surtsey, 1974–1976. *Surtsey Research Progress Report*, **8**, 30–40.

Henriques, R. P. B. & Hay, J. D. (1992). Nutrient content and the structure of a plant community on a tropical beach-dune system in Brazil. *Acta Ecologica*, **13**, 101–117.

Henriques, R. P. B. & Hay, J. D. (1998). The plant communities of a foredune in southeastern Brazil. *Canadian Journal of Botany*, **76**, 1323–1330.

Henry, F., Talon, B., & Dutoit, T. (2010). The age and history of the French mediterranean steppe revisited by soil wood charcoal analysis. *Holocene*, **20**, 25–34.

Hernández-Cordero, A. I., Hernández-Calvento, L., & Pérez-Chacon Espino, E. (2015). Relationship between vegetation dynamics and dune mobility in an arid transgressive coastal system, Maspalomas, Canary Islands. *Geomorphology*, **238**, 160–176.

Hesp, P. (2002). Foredunes and blowouts: Initiation, geomorphology and dynamics. *Geomorphology*, **48**, 245–268.

Hibbs, D. E. (1983). Forty years of forest succession in central New England. *Ecology*, **64**, 1394–1401.

Hickin, E. J. (1974). The development of meanders in natural river-channels. *American Journal of Science*, **274**, 414–442.

Hilgartner, W. B., Nejako, M., & Casey, R. (2009). A 200-year paleoecological record of *Pinus virginiana*, trace metals, sedimentation, and mining disturbance in a Maryland serpentine barren. *Journal of the Torrey Botanical Society*, **136**, 257–271.

Hiroki, T. & Tateno, M. (1984). Soil nitrogen patterns induced by colonization of *Polygonum cuspidatum* on Mt. Fuji. *Oecologia*, **61**, 218–223.

Hirose, S. & Ichino, K. (1993). Difference of invasion behavior between two climax species, *Castanopsis cuspidata* var. *sieboldii* and *Mechilus thunbergii*, on lava flows on Miyakejima, Japan. *Ecological Research*, **8**, 167–172.

Hobbie, E. A., Macko, S. A., & Shugart, H. H. (1999). Insights into nitrogen and carbon dynamics of ectomycorrhizal and saprotrophic fungi from isotopic evidence. *Oecologia*, **118**, 353–360.

Hobbs, R. J. & Huenneke, L. F. (1992). Disturbance, diversity and invasion: Implications for conservation. *Conservation Biology*, **6**, 324–337.

Hobbs, R. J., Higgs, E., & Harris, J. A. (2009). Novel ecosystems: Implications for conservation and restoration. *Trends in Ecology and Evolution*, **24**, 599–605.

Hobbs, R. J. & Suding, K. N., eds. (2009). *New Models for Ecosystem Dynamics and Restoration*. Washington, DC: Island Press.

Hodačová, D. & Prach, K. (2003). Spoil heaps from brown coal mining: Technical reclamation versus spontaneous revegetation. *Restoration Ecology*, **11**, 385–391.

Holling, C. S. (1973). Resilience and stability of ecological systems. *Annual Review of Ecology and Systematics*, **4**, 1–23.

Hollingsworth, T. N., Lloyd, A. H., Nossov, D. R., Ruess, R. W., Charlton, B. A., & Kielland, K. (2010). Twenty-five years of vegetation change along a putative successional chronosequence on the Tanana River, Alaska. *Canadian Journal of Forest Research*, **40**, 1273–1287.

Holmes, R. T. & Likens, G. E. (2016). *Hubbard Brook: The Story of a Forest Ecosystem*. New Haven, CT: Yale University Press.

Hong, Y., Adler, R. F., & Huffman, G. J. (2007). Satellite remote sensing for global landslide monitoring. *EOS, Transactions of the American Geophysical Union*, **88**, 357–358.

Hook, D. D., Buford, M. A., & Williams, T. M. (1991). Impact of Hurricane Hugo on the South Carolina coastal plain forest. *Journal of Coastal Research*, **8**, 291–300.

Hooper, E., Legendre, P., & Condit, R. (2005). Barriers to forest regeneration of deforested and abandoned land in Panama. *Journal of Applied Ecology*, **42**, 1165–1174.

Horrocks, M. & Ogden, J. (1998). The effects of the Taupo tephra eruption of c. 1718 BP on the vegetation of Mt. Hauhungatahi, central North Island, New Zealand. *Journal of Biogeography*, **25**, 649–660.

Hortobágyi, B., Corenblit, D., Steiger, J., & Peiry, J-L. (2018). Niche construction within riparian corridors. Part 1. Exploring biogeomorphic feedback windows of three pioneer riparian species (Allier River, France). *Geomorphology*, **305**, special issue, 94–111.

Houle, G. (1995). Environmental filters and seedling recruitment on a coastal dune in subarctic Quebec (Canada). *Canadian Journal of Botany*, **74**, 1507–1513.

Houle, G. (1997). No evidence for interspecific interactions between plants in the first stage of succession on coastal dunes in subarctic Quebec, Canada. *Canadian Journal of Botany*, **75**, 902–915.

Howard, L. F. & Lee, T. D. (2002). Upland old-field succession in southeastern New Hampshire. *Journal of the Torrey Botanical Society*, **129**, 60–76.

Howard, R. A., Portecop, J., & de Montaignac, P. (1980). The post-eruptive vegetation of La Soufrière, Guadeloupe, 1977–1979. *Journal of the Arnold Arboretum*, **61**, 749–764.

Hršak, V. (2004). Vegetation succession and soil gradients on inland sand dunes. *Ekológia (Bratislava)*, **23**, 24–39.

Huang, L., Zhang, P., Hu, Y. G., & Zhao, Y. (2016). Vegetation and soil restoration in refuse dumps from open pit coal mines. *Ecological Engineering*, **94**, 638–646.

Huang, Y. T., Ai, X. R., Yao, L., et al. (2015). Changes in the diversity of evergreen and deciduous species during natural recovery following clear-cutting in a subtropical evergreen-deciduous broadleaved mixed forest of central China. *Tropical Conservation Science*, **8**, 1033–1052.

Hubbell, S. P. (2001). *The Unified Neutral Theory of Biodiversity and Biogeography*. Princeton, NJ: Princeton University Press.

Huebert, B., Vitousek, P., Sutton, J., et al. (1999). Volcano fixes nitrogen into plant-available forms. *Biogeochemistry*, **47**, 111–118.

Huff, M. H. (1995). Forest age structure and development following wildfires in the western Olympic Mountains, Washington. *Ecological Applications*, **5**, 471–483.

Huffman, D. W., Crouse, J. E., Chancellor, W. W., & Fule, P. Z. (2012). Influence of time since fire on pinyon-juniper woodland structure. *Forest Ecology and Management*, **274**, 29–37.

Hughes, F. M. R. (1997). Floodplain biogeomorphology. *Progress in Physical Geography*, **21**, 501–529.

Hughes, R. & Denslow, J. (2005). Invasion by a N_2-fixing tree alters function and structure in wet lowland forests of Hawaii. *Ecological Applications*, **15**, 1615–1628.

Hull, J. C. & Scott, R. C. (1982). Plant succession on debris avalanches of Nelson County, Virginia. *Castanea*, **47**, 158–176.

Humboldt, A. de & Bonpland, A. (1807). *Essai Súr la Geographie des Plantes*. Lyon, France: Fr. Schoell.

Humphrey, L. D. (1984). Patterns and mechanisms of plant succession after fire on Artemisia-grass sites in southeastern Idaho. *Vegetatio*, **57**, 91–101.

Hunter, M. D. & Forkner, R. E. (1999). Hurricane damage influences foliar polyphenolics and subsequent herbivory on surviving trees. *Ecology*, **80**, 2676–2682.

Huntly, B. J. & Walker, B. H., eds. (1982). *Ecology of Tropical Savannas*. New York: Springer.

Huss-Danell, K., Uliassi, D., & Renberg, I. (1997). River and lake sediments as sources of infective *Frankia* (*Alnus*). *Plant and Soil*, **197**, 35–39.

Huston, M. (2018). Individual-based forest succession models and the theory of plant competition. In D. L. DeAngelis, ed., *Individual-Based Models and Approaches in Ecology*, pp. 408–420. London: Chapman & Hall/CRC.

Huston, M. A. (2004). Management strategies for plant invasions: Manipulating productivity, disturbance, and competition. *Diversity & Distribution*, **10**, 167–178.

Ignjatović, M., Kaligarič, M., Škornik, S., & Ivajnšič, D. (2013). Spatio-temporal patterns along a primary succession on alluvial sediments. *Central European Journal of Biology*, **8**, 888–897.

Imbert, D. & Portecop, J. (2008). Hurricane disturbance and forest resilience: Assessing structural *vs.* functional changes in a Caribbean dry forest. *Forest Ecology & Management*, **255**, 3494–3501.

Imbert, É. & Houle, G. (2000). Persistence of colonizing plant species along an inferred successional sequence on a subarctic coastal dune (Québec, Canada). *Écoscience*, **7**, 370–378.

Inouye, R. S., Allison, T. D., & Johnson, N. C. (1994). Old field succession on a Minnesota Sand Plain – Effects of deer and other factors on invasion by trees. *Bulletin of the Torrey Botanical Club*, **121**, 266–276.

Isermann, M. (2011). Patterns in species diversity during succession of coastal dunes. *Journal of Coastal Research*, **27**, 661–671.

Ishida, H., Hattori, T., & Takeda, Y. (2005). Comparison of species composition and richness between primary and secondary lucidophyllous forests in two altitudinal zones of Tsushima Island, Japan. *Forest Ecology and Management*, **213**, 273–287.

Ishizuka, M., Toyooka, H., Osawa, A., Kushima, H., Kanazawa, Y., & Sato, A. (1997). Secondary succession following catastrophic windthrow in a boreal forest in Hokkaido, Japan. *Journal of Sustainable Forestry*, **6**, 367–388.

Ivakina, E. V., Jakubov, V. V., & Osipov, S. V. (2013). Vascular plants of the Luzanovskii open-pit coal-mining station (Russian Far East). *Contemporary Problems of Ecology*, **6**, 187–198.

Ivanova, G. A., Ivanov, V. A., Kovaleva, N. M., Conard, S. G., Zhila, S. V., & Tarasov, P. A. (2017). Succession of vegetation after a high-intensity fire in a pine forest with lichens. *Contemporary Problems of Ecology*, **10**, 52–61.

Jackson, S. T. (2013). Natural, potential and actual vegetation in North America. *Journal of Vegetation Science*, **24**, 772–776.

Jacquet, K. & Prodon, R. (2009). Measuring the postfire resilience of a bird-vegetation system: A 28-year study in a Mediterranean oak woodland. *Oecologia*, **161**, 801–811.

Jenkins, M. A. & Parker, G. R. (1998). Composition and diversity of woody vegetation in silvicultural openings of southern Indiana forests. *Forest Ecology and Management*, **109**, 57–74.

Jentsch, A. & White, P. S. (2019). A theory of pulse dynamics and disturbance in ecology. *Ecology*, **100**, e02734.

Jha, A. K. & Singh, J. S. (1991). Spoil characteristics and vegetation development of an age series of mine spoils in a dry tropical environment. *Vegetatio*, **97**, 63–76.

Jiao, J. Y., Tzanopoulos, J., Xofis, P., Bai, W. J., Ma, X. H., & Mitchley, J. (2007). Can the study of natural vegetation succession assist in the control of soil erosion on abandoned croplands on the Loess Plateau, China? *Restoration Ecology*, **15**, 391–399.

Jimenéz, H. E. & Armesto, J. J. (1992). Importance of the soil seed bank of disturbed sites in Chilean mattoral in early secondary succession. *Journal of Vegetation Science*, **3**, 579–586.

Jiménez-Orocio, O., Espejel, I., & Martínez, M. L. (2015). La investigación científica sobre dunas costeras de México: Origin, evolucion y retos. *Revista Mexicana de Biodiversidad*, **86**, 486–507.

Jimenez-Rodríguez, D. L., Alvarez-Añorve, M. Y., Pineda-Cortes, M., et al. (2018). Structural and functional traits predict short term response of tropical dry forests to a high intensity hurricane. *Forest Ecology and Management*, **426**, 101–114.

Jírová, A., Klaudisová, A., & Prach, K. (2012). Spontaneous restoration of target vegetation in old-fields in a central European landscape: A repeated analysis after three decades. *Applied Vegetation Science*, **15**, 245–252.

Johnson, A. F. (1997). Rates of vegetation succession on a coastal dune system in northwest Florida. *Journal of Coastal Research*, **13**, 373–384.

Johnson, E. A. (1995). *Fire and Vegetation Dynamics: Studies from the North American Boreal Forest*. Cambridge: Cambridge University Press.

Johnson, E. A. & Miyanishi, K. (2008). Testing the assumptions of chronosequences in succession. *Ecology Letters*, **11**, 419–431.

Johnson, E. A. & Miyanishi, K., eds. (2007). *Plant Disturbance Ecology: The Process and the Response*. Amsterdam: Elsevier.

Johnson, W. (2000). Tree recruitment and survival in rivers: Influence of hydrological processes. *Hydrological Processes*, **14**, 3051–3074.

Johnson, W. C., Burgess, R. L., & Keammerer, W. R. (1976). Forest overstory vegetation and environment on the Missouri River floodplain in North Dakota. *Ecological Monographs*, **46**, 59–84.

Johnstone, I. M. (1986). Plant invasion windows: A time-based classification of invasion potential. *Biological Reviews*, **61**, 369–394.

Johnstone, J. F. & Chapin, F. S. (2006). Fire interval effects on successional trajectory in boreal forests of northwest Canada. *Ecosystems*, **9**, 268–277.

Johnstone, J. F., Chapin, F. S., Hollingsworth, T. N., Mack, M. C., Romanovsky, V., & Turetsky, M. (2010). Fire, climate change, and forest resilience in interior Alaska. *Canadian Journal of Forest Research*, **40**, 1302–1312.

Johnstone, J. F., Allen, C. D., Franklin, J. F., et al. (2016). Changing disturbance regimes, ecological memory, and forest resilience. *Frontiers in Ecology and the Environment*, **14**, 369–378.

Jonášová, M. & Prach, K. (2004). Central-European mountain spruce (*Picea abies* (L.) Karst) forest: Regeneration of tree species after a bark beetle outbreak. *Ecological Engineering*, **23**, 15–27.

Jonášová, M., van Hees, A., & Prach, K. (2006). Rehabilitation of monotonous exotic coniferous plantations: A case study of spontaneous establishment of different tree species. *Ecological Engineering*, **28**, 141–148.

Jones, C. C. & del Moral, R. (2005a). Patterns of primary succession on the foreland of Coleman Glacier, Washington, USA. *Plant Ecology*, **180**, 105–116.

Jones, C. C. & del Moral, R. (2005b). Effects of microsite conditions on seedling establishment on the foreland of Coleman Glacier, Washington. *Journal of Vegetation Science*, **16**, 293–300.

Jones, C. C. & del Moral, R. (2009). Dispersal and establishment both limit colonization during primary succession on a glacier foreland. *Plant Ecology*, **204**, 217–230.

Jones, G. & Henry, G. H. R. (2003). Primary plant succession on recently deglaciated terrain in the Canadian High Arctic. *Journal of Biogeography*, **30**, 277–296.

Jongepierová, I., Jongepier, J. W., & Klimeš, L. (2004). Restoring grassland on arable land: An example of a fast spontaneous succession without weed-dominated stages. *Preslia*, **76**, 361–369.

Joosten H., Tanneberger F., & Moen A., eds. (2017). *Mires and Peatlands of Europe: Status, Distribution and Conservation*. Stuttgart: Schweizerbart Science Publishers.

Jorgenson, M. T. & Joyce, M. R. (1994). Six strategies for rehabiliting land disturbed by oil development in arctic Alaska. *Arctic*, **47**, 374–390.

Jørgenson, S. E. (1997). *Integration of Ecosystem Theories: A Pattern*. 2nd ed. Amsterdam: Kluwer.

Kabrna, M., Hendrychová, M., & Prach, K. (2014). Establishment of target and invasive plant species on a reclaimed coal mining dump in relation to their occurrence in the surroundings. *International Journal of Mining Reclamation and Environment*, **28**, 242–249.

Kain, C., Gomez, C., Wassmer, P., Levine, F., & Hart, D. (2014). Truncated dunes as evidence of the 2004 tsunami in North Sumatra and environmental recovery post-tsunami. *New Zealand Geographer*, **70**, 165–178.

Kalliola, R. & Puhakka, M. (1988). River dynamics and vegetation mosaicism: A case study of the River Kamajohka, northernmost Finland. *Journal of Biogeography*, **15**, 703–719.

Kalliola, R., Salo, J., Puhakka, M., & Rajasilta, M. (1991). New site formation and colonizing vegetation in primary succession on the western Amazon floodplains. *Journal of Ecology*, **79**, 877–901.

Kamijo, T. & Okutomi, K. (1995). Seedling establishment of *Castanopsis cuspidata* var. *sieboldii* and *Persea thunbergii* on lava and scoria of the 1962 eruption on Miyake-jima Island, the Izu Islands. *Ecological Research*, **10**, 235–242.

Kamijo, T., Kitayama, K., Sugawara, A., Urushimichi, S., & Sasai, K. (2002). Primary succession of the warm-temperate broad-leaved forest on a volcanic island, Miyake-Jima, Japan. *Folia Geobotanica*, **37**, 71–91.

Kämpf, I., Mathar, W., Kuzmin, I., Holzel, N., & Kiehl, K. (2016). Post-Soviet recovery of grassland vegetation on abandoned fields in the forest steppe zone of Western Siberia. *Biodiversity and Conservation*, **25**, 2563–2580.

Kaplan, B. A. & Moermond, T. C. (2000). Foraging ecology of the mountain monkey (*Cercopithecus l'hoesti*): Implications for its evolutionary history and use of disturbed forest. *American Journal of Primatology*, **50**, 227–246.

Kapusta, P., Szarek-Lukaszewska, G., Jedrzejczyk-Korycinska, M., & Zagorna, M. (2015). Do heavy-metal grassland species survive under a Scots pine canopy during early stages of secondary succession? *Folia Geobotanica*, **50**, 317–329.

Kardol, P., Souza, L., & Classen, A. T. (2012). Resource availability mediates the importance of priority effects in plant community assembly and ecosystem function. *Oikos*, **122**, 84–94.

Kardol, P., Cornips, N. J., van Kempen, M. M. L., Bakx-Schotman, J. M. T., & van der Putten, W. H. (2007). Microbe-mediated plant-soil feedback causes historical contingency effects in plant community assembly. *Ecological Monographs*, **77**, 147–162.

Kardol, P., De Deyn, G. B., Laliberté, E., Mariotte, P., & Hawkes, C. V. (2013). Biotic plant-soil feedbacks across temporal scales. *Journal of Ecology*, **101**, 309–315.

Kardol, P., Dickie, I. A., St. John, M. G., et al. (2014). Soil-mediated effects of invasive ungulates on native tree seedlings. *Journal of Ecology*, **102**, 622–631.

Karlowski, U. (2006). Afromontane old-field vegetation: Secondary succession and the return of indigenous species. *African Journal of Ecology*, **44**, 264–272.

Karrenberg, S., Kollman, J., Edwards, P. J., Gurnell, A. M., & Petts, G. E. (2003). Patterns in woody vegetation along the active zone of a near-natural Alpine river. *Basic and Applied Ecology*, **4**, 157–166.

Kasowska, D. & Koszelnik-Leszek, A. (2014). Ecological features of spontaneous vascular flora of serpentine post-mining sites in Lower Silesia. *Archives of Environmental Protection*, **40**, 33–52.

Kaufmann, R. & Raffl, C. (2002). Diversity in primary succession: The chronosequence of a glacier foreland. In C. Korner & E. Spehn, eds., *Global Mountain Biodiversity: A Global Assessment*, pp. 177–190. London: Parthenon Publishing.

Kavgaci, A., Carni, A., Basaran, S., et al. (2010). Long-term post-fire succession of *Pinus brutia* forest in the east Mediterranean. *International Journal of Wildland Fire*, **19**, 599–605.

Kazanis, D. & Arianoutsou, M. (1996). Vegetation composition in a post-fire successional gradient of *Pinus halepensis* forests in Attica, Greece. *International Journal of Wildland Fire*, **6**, 83–91.

Keane, R. E., Ryan, K. C., Veblen, T. T., et al. (2002). The cascading effects of fire exclusion in Rocky Mountain ecosystems. In J. S. Baron, ed., *Rocky Mountain Futures: An Ecological Perspective*, pp. 133–152. Washington, DC: Island Press.

Keefer, D. K. (1984). Landslides caused by earthquakes. *Geological Society of America Bulletin*, **95**, 406–421.

Keefer, D. K. (2000). Statistical analysis of an earthquake-induced landslide distribution – The 1989 Loma Prieta, California event. *Engineering Geology*, **58**, 231–249.

Keeley, J. E., Bond, W. J., Bradstock, R. A., Pausas, J. G., & Rundel, P. W. (2012). *Fire in Mediterranean Ecosystems: Ecology, Evolution and Management*. Cambridge: Cambridge University Press.

Keever, C. (1950). Causes of succession on old fields of the Piedmont, North Carolina. *Ecological Monographs*, **20**, 229–250.

Keever, C. (1979). Mechanisms of plant succession on old fields of Lancaster County, Pennsylvania. *Bulletin of the Torrey Botanical Club*, **106**, 299–308.

Keller, E. A. (1996). *Environmental Geology*, 7th ed. Upper Saddle River, NJ: Prentice Hall.

Kellison, R. C. & Young, M. J. (1997). The bottomland hardwood forest of the southern United States. *Forest Ecology and Management*, **90**, 101–115.

Kellman, M. & Kading, M. (1992). Facilitation of tree seedling establishment in a sand dune succession. *Journal of Vegetation Science*, **3**, 679–688.

Kellman, M. & Meave, J. (1997). Fire in the tropical gallery forests of Belize. *Journal of Biogeography*, **24**, 23–34.

Kelly, J. F. (2014). Effects of human activities (raking, scraping, off-road vehicles) and natural resource protections on the spatial distribution of beach vegetation and related shoreline features in New Jersey. *Journal of Coastal Conservation*, **18**, 383–398.

Kepfer-Rojas, S., Schmidt, I. K., Ransijn, J., Riis-Nielsen, T., & Verheyen, K. (2014). Distance to seed sources and land-use history affect forest development over a long-term heathland to forest succession. *Journal of Vegetation Science*, **25**, 1493–1503.

Kessler, M. (1999). Plant species richness and endemism during natural landslide succession in a perhumid montane forest in the Bolivian Andes. *Ecotropica*, **4**, 123–136.

Khazai, B. & Sitar, N. (2003). Evaluation of factors controlling earthquake-induced landslides caused by Chi-Chi earthquake and comparison with the Northridge and Loma Prieta events. *Engineering Geology*, **71**, 79–95.

Khitun, O., Ermokhina, K., Czernyadjeva, I., Leibman, M., & Khomutov, A. (2015). Floristic complexes on landslides of different age in Central Yamal, West Siberian Low Arctic, Russia. *Fennia International Journal of Geography*, **193**, 31–52.

Kiilsgaard, C. W., Greene, S. E., Stafford, S. G., & McKee, W. A. (1986). Recovery of riparian vegetation in the northeastern region of Mount St. Helens. In S. A. C. Keller, ed., *Mount St. Helens Five Years Later*, pp. 222–230. Cheney: Eastern Washington University Press.

Kim, S., Lee, S., McCormick, M., Kim, J. G., & Kang, H. (2016). Microbial community and greenhouse gas fluxes from abandoned rice paddies with different vegetation. *Microbial Ecology*, **72**, 692–703.

King, E. G. & Hobbs, R. J. (2006). Identifying linkages among conceptual models of ecosystem degradation and restoration: Towards an integrative framework. *Restoration Ecology*, **14**, 369–378.

Kirmer, A., Tischew, S., Ozinga, W. A., von Lampe, M., Baasch, A., & van Groenendael, J. M. (2008). Importance of regional species pools and functional traits in colonization processes: Predicting re-colonization after large-scale destruction of ecosystems. *Journal of Applied Ecology*, **45**, 1523–1530.

Kirwan, M. L. & Megonigal, J. P. (2013). Tidal wetland stability in the face of human impacts and sea-level rise. *Nature*, **504**, 53–60.

Kitayama, K., Pattison, R., Cordell, S., Webb, D., & Mueller-Dombois, D. (1997). Ecological and genetic implications of foliar polymorphism in *Metrosideros polymorpha* Gaud. (Myrtaceae) in a habitat matrix on Mauna Loa, Hawaii. *Annals of Botany*, **80**, 491–497.

Kleyer, M., Bekker, R. M., Knevel, I. C., *et al.* (2008). The LEDA Traitbase: A database of life-history traits of the Northwest European flora. *Journal of Ecology*, **96**, 1266–1274.

Klimešová, J. & Klimeš, L. (2013). *CLO-PLA3 – Database of Clonal Growth of Plants from Central Europe*, 3rd ed. Třeboň, Czech Republic: Institute of Botany CAS (available at http:clopla.butbn.cas.cz).

Knapp, A. K., Briggs, J. M., Hartnett, D. C., & Collins, S. L. (1998). *Grassland Dynamics: Long-Term Ecological Research in Tallgrass Prairie*. Oxford: Oxford University Press.

Knelman, J. E., Graham, E. B., Prevey, J. S., *et al.* (2018). Interspecific plant interactions reflected in soil bacterial community structure and nitrogen cycling in primary succession. *Frontiers in Microbiology*, **9**, article 128.

Knops, J. M. H. (2006). Fire does not alter vegetation in infertile prairie. *Oecologia*, **150**, 477–483.

Knuckey, C. G., Van Etten, E. J. B., & Doherty, T. S. (2016). Effects of long-term fire exclusion and frequent fire on plant community composition: A case study from semi-arid shrublands. *Austral Ecology*, **41**, 964–975.

Koch, J. M. (2007). Restoring a jarrah forest understorey vegetation after bauxite mining in Western Australia. *Restoration Ecology*, **15**, S26–S39.

Kollmann, J. & Rasmussen, K. K. (2012). Succession of a degraded bog in NE Denmark over 164 years – Monitoring one of the earliest restoration experiments. *Tuexenia*, **32**, 67–85.

Kompala-Baba, A. & Baba, W. (2013). The spontaneous succession in a sand-pit: The role of life history traits and species habitat preferences. *Polish Journal of Ecology*, **61**, 13–22.

Konvalinková, P. & Prach, K. (2010). Spontaneous succession of vegetation in mined peatlands: A multi-site study. *Preslia*, **82**, 423–435.

Konvalinková, P. & Prach, K. (2014). Environmental factors determining spontaneous recovery of industrially mined peat bogs: A multi-site analysis. *Ecological Engineering*, **69**, 38–45.

Korablev, A. P. & Neshataeva, V. Yu. (2016). Primary plant successions of forest belt vegetation on the Tolbachinskii Dol Volcanic Plateau, (Kamchatka). *Biology Bulletin*, **43**, 307–317.

Korasidis, V. A., Wallace, M. W., Wagstaff, B. E., Holdgate, G. R., Tosolini, A. M. P., & Jansen, B. (2016). Cyclic floral succession and fire in a Cenozoic wetland/peatland system. *Palaeogeography, Palaeoclimatology, Palaeoecology*, **461**, 237–252.

Korkmaz, H., Yildirim, C., & Yalçin, E. (2017). Relationships between soil and plant communities distribution throughout primary succession in deltaic plains of Gölyazi Natural Reserved Area (Terme/Samsun, Turkey). *Rendiconti Lincei-Scienze Fisiche e Naturali*, **28**, 503–517.

Körner, Ch. (2003). *Alpine Plant Life: A Functional Plant Ecology of High Mountain Ecosystems*. Berlin: Springer.

Koronatova, N. G. & Milyaeva, E. V. (2011). Plant community succession in post-mined quarries in the northern-taiga zone of West Siberia. *Contemporary Problems of Ecology*, **4**, 513–518.

Kosmas, C., Gerontidis, S., & Marathianou, M. (2000). The effect of land use change on soils and vegetation over various lithological formations on Lesvos (Greece). *Catena*, **40**, 51–68.

Kou, M., Jiao, J. Y., Yin, Q. L., *et al.* (2016). Successional trajectory over 10 years of vegetation restoration of abandoned slope croplands in the Hill-Gully Region of the Loess Plateau. *Land Degradation & Development*, **27**, 919–932.

Koyama, A. & Tsuyuzaki, S. (2010). Effects of sedge and cottongrass tussocks on plant establishment patterns in a post-mined peatland, northern Japan. *Wetlands Ecology and Management*, **18**, 135–148.

Koziol, L. & Bever, J. D. (2019). Mycorrhizal feedbacks generate positive frequency dependence accelerating grassland succession. *Journal of Ecology*, **107**, 622–632.

Kraft, N. J. B., Godoy, O., & Levine, J. M. (2015). Plant functional traits and the multidimensional nature of species coexistence. *Proceedings of the National Academy of Sciences of the United States of America*, **112**, 797–802.

Krahulec, F. & Lepš, J. (1994). Establishment success of plant immigrants in a new water reservoir. *Folia Geobotanica & Phytotaxonomica*, **29**, 3–14.

Kramer, K., Brang, P., Bachofenet H., Bugmann, H., & Wohlgemuth, T. (2014). Site factors are more important than salvage logging for tree regeneration after wind disturbance in Central European forests. *Forest Ecology and Management*, **331**, 116–128.

Krasny, M. E., Vogt, K. A., & Zasada, J. C. (1984). Root and shoot biomass and mycorrhizal development of white spruce seedlings naturally regenerating in interior Alaskan floodplain communities. *Canadian Journal of Forest Research*, **14**, 554–558.

Krasny, M. E., Vogt, K. A., & Zasada, J. C. (1988). Establishment of four Salicaceae species on river bars in interior Alaska. *Holarctic Ecology*, **11**, 210–219.

Kreft, H. & Jetz, W. (2007). Global patterns and determinants of vascular plant diversity. *Proceedings of the National Academy of Science*, **104**, 5925–5930.

Kroh, G. C., McNew, K., & Pinder III, J. E. (2008). Conifer colonization of a 350-year old rock fall at Lassen Volcanic National Park in northern California. *Plant Ecology*, **199**, 281–294.

Krug, C. B. & Krug, R. M. (2007). Restoration of olf fields in Renosterveld: A case study in a Mediterranean-type shrubland of South Africa. In V. A. Cramer & R. J. Hobbs, eds., *Old Field Dynamics and Restoration of Abandoned Farmland*, pp. 265–285. Washington, DC: Island Press.

Kubota, Y., Katsuda, K., & Kikuzawa, K. (2005). Secondary succession and effects of clear-logging on diversity in the subtropical forests on Okinawa Island, southern Japan. *Biodiversity and Conservation*, **14**, 879–901.

Kučerová, A., Rektoris, L., Štechová, T., & Bastl, M. (2008). Disturbances on a wooded raised bog: How windthrow, bark beetle and fire affect vegetation and soil water quality? *Folia Geobotanica*, **43**, 49–67.

Kuiters, A. T., Kramer, K., Van der Hagen, H. G. J. M., & Schaminée, J. H. J. (2009). Plant diversity, species turnover and shifts in functional traits in coastal dune vegetation: Results from permanent plots over a 52-year period. *Journal of Vegetation Science*, **20**, 1053–1063.

Kulmatiski, A., Beard, K. H., & Stark, J. M. (2006). Soil history as a primary control on plant invasion in abandoned agricultural fields. *Journal of Applied Ecology*, **43**, 868–876.

Kumler, M. L. (1962). Plant succession on the sand dunes of the Oregon coast. *Ecology*, **50**, 695–704.

Kunstler, G., Falster, D., Coomes, D. A., *et al.* (2016). Plant functional traits have globally consistent effects on competition. *Nature*, **529**, 204–207.

Kupfer, J. A., Webbeking, A. L., & Franklin, S. B. (2004). Forest fragmentation affects early successional patterns on shifting cultivation fields near Indian Church, Belize. *Agriculture Ecosystems & Environment*, **103**, 509–518.

Kurulok, S. E. & Macdonald, S. E. (2007). Impacts of postfire salvage logging on understory plant communities of the boreal mixedwood forest 2 and 34 years after disturbance. *Canadian Journal of Forest Research*, **37**, 2637–2651.

Kusumoto, B., Shiono, T., Miyoshi, M., *et al.* (2015). Functional response of plant communities to clearcutting: Management impacts differ between forest vegetation zones. *Journal of Applied Ecology*, **52**, 171–180.

Laćan, I., McBride, J. R., & De Witt, D. (2015). Urban forest condition and succession in the abandoned city of Pripyat, near Chernobyl, Ukraine. *Urban Forestry and Urban Greening*, **14**, 1068–1078.

Laine, A. M., Selänpää, T., Oksanen, J., Sevakivi, M., & Tuittila, E.-S. (2018). Plant diversity and functional trait composition during mire development. *Mires and Peat*, **21**, Article 02, 1–19.

Laliberté, E., Turner, B., Costes, T., *et al.* (2012). Experimental assessment of nutrient limitation along a 2-million-year dune chronosequences in the south-western Australia biodiversity hotspot. *Journal of Ecology*, **100**, 631–642.

La Mantia, T., Ruhl, J., Pasta, S., Campisi, D. G., & Terrazzino, G. (2008). Structural analysis of woody species in Mediterranean old fields. *Plant Biosystems*, **142**, 462–471.

Lamb, D., Eskrine, P. D., & Parrotta, J. A. (2005). Restoration of degraded tropical forest landscape. *Science*, **310**, 1628–1632.

Lambert, J. D. H. (1972). Plant succession on tundra mudflows: Preliminary observations. *Arctic*, **25**, 99–106.

Landman, G. B., Kolka, R. K., & Sharitz, R. R. (2007). Soil seed bank analysis of planted and naturally revegetating thermally-disturbed riparian wetland forests. *Wetlands*, **27**, 211–223.

Lantz, T. C., Gergel, S. E., & Henry, G. H. R. (2010). Response of green alder (*Alnus viridis* subsp. *fruticosa*) patch dynamics and plant community composition to fire and regional temperature in north-western Canada. *Journal of Biogeography*, **37**, 1597–1610.

LaPage, P. & Banner, A. (2014). Long-term recovery of forest structure and composition after harvesting in the coastal temperate rainforests of northern British Columbia. *Forest Ecology and Management*, **318**, 250–260.

Larsen, M. C. (2008). Rainfall-triggered landslides, anthropogenic hazards, and mitigation strategies. *Advances in Geoscience*, **14**, 147–153.

Larsen, M. C. & Simon, A. (1993). A rainfall intensity-duration threshold for landsides in a humid-tropical environment, Puerto Rico. *Geografiska Annaler*, **75A**, 13–23.

Larsen, M. C. & Torres-Sánchez, A. J. (1992). Landslides triggered by Hurricane Hugo in eastern Puerto Rico, September 1989. *Caribbean Journal of Science*, **28**, 113–125.

Latzel, V., Klimešová, J., Doležal, J., Pyšek, P., Tackenberg, O., & Prach, K. (2011). The association of dispersal and persistence traits of plants with different stages of succession in Central European man-made habitats. *Folia Geobotanica*, **46**, 289–302.

Lauenroth, W. K. & Burke, I. C. (2008). *Ecology of the Shortgrass Steppe: A Long-Term Perspective*. Oxford: Oxford University Press.

Lavorel, S., McIntyre, S., Landsberg, J., & Forbes, T. D. A. (1997). Plant functional classification: From general groups to specific groups based on response to disturbance. *Trends in Ecology and Evolution*, **12**, 474–478.

Lavorel, S., Díaz, S., Cornelissen, H. C., *et al.* (2007). Plant functional types: Are we getting any closer to the Holy Grail? In J. G. Canadell, D. E. Pataki, & L. F. Pitelka, eds., *Terrestrial Ecosystems in a Changing World*, pp. 149–164. New York: Springer.

Lawson, D., Inouye, R. S., Huntly, N., & Carson, W. P. (1999). Patterns of woody plant abundance, recruitment, mortality, and growth in a 65 year chronosequence of old-fields. *Plant Ecology*, **145**, 267–279.

Lebrija-Trejos, E., Bongers, F., Pérez-García, E. A., & Meave, J. A. (2008). Successional change and resilience of a very dry tropical deciduous forest following shifting agriculture. *Biotropica*, **40**, 422–431.

Leck, M. A., Parker, V. T., & Simpson, R. L., eds. (1989). *Ecology of Soil Seed Banks*. San Diego: Academic Press.

Lee, C. S., You, Y. H., & Robinson, G. R. (2002). Secondary succession and natural habitat restoration in abandoned rice fields of central Korea. *Restoration Ecology*, **10**, 306–314.

Leibold, M. A. & Chase, J. M. (2018). *Metacommunity Ecology*. Princeton, NJ: Princeton University Press.

Lepš, J. (1987). Vegetation dynamics in early old field succession: A quantitative approach. *Vegetatio*, **72**, 95–102.

Lepš, J. (1988). Mathematical modelling of ecological succession: A review. *Folia Geobotanica et Phytotaxonomica*, **23**, 79–94.

Lepš, J. & Prach, K. (1981). A simple mathematical model of the secondary succession of shrubs. *Folia Geobotanica et Phytotaxonomica*, **16**, 61–72.

Lepš, J. & Rejmánek, M. (1991). Convergence or divergence: What should we expect from vegetation succession? *Oikos*, **62**, 261–264.

Lepš, J., Osbornová-Kosinová, J., & Rejmánek, M. (1982). Community stability, complexity and species life history strategies. *Vegetatio*, **50**, 53–63.

Lepš, J., Novotný, V., Čížek, L., et al. (2002). Successful invasion of a neotropical species *Piper aduncum* in rain forests in Papua New Guinea. *Applied Vegetation Science*, **5**, 255–262.

Lesica, P. & Miles, S. (2001). Natural history and invasion of Russian olive along eastern Montana rivers. *Western North American Naturalist*, **61**, 1–10.

Lesieur, D., Gauthier, S., & Bergeron, Y. (2002). Fire frequency and vegetation dynamics for the south-central boreal forest of Quebec, Canada. *Canadian Journal of Forest Research*, **32**, 1996–2009.

Lesschen, J. P., Cammeraat, L. H., Kooijman, A. M., & van Wesemael, B. (2008). Development of spatial heterogeneity in vegetation and soil properties after land abandonment in a semi-arid ecosystem. *Journal of Arid Environments*, **72**, 2082–2092.

Le Stradic, S., Buisson, E., & Fernandes, G. W. (2014). Restoration of Neotropical grasslands degraded by quarrying using hay transfer. *Applied Vegetation Science*, **17**, 482–492.

Lévesque, M., McLaren, K. P., & McDonald, M. A. (2011). Recovery and dynamics of a primary tropical dry forest in Jamaica, 10 years after human disturbance. *Forest Ecology and Management*, **262**, 817–826.

Levins, R. (1969). Some demographic and genetic consequences of environmental heterogeneity for biological control. *Bulletin of the Entomological Society of America*, **15**, 237–240.

Lewis, N. K. (1998). Landslide-driven distribution of aspen and steppe on Kathal Mountain, Alaska. *Journal of Arid Environments*, **38**, 421–435.

Li, B., Zeng, T., Ran, J., *et al.* (2017). Characteristics of the early secondary succession after landslides in a broad-leaved deciduous forest in the south Minshan Mountains. *Forest Ecology and Management*, **405**, 238–245.

Li, J. H., Fang, X. W., Jia, J. J., & Wang, G. (2007). Effect of legume species introduction to early abandoned field on vegetation development. *Plant Ecology*, **191**, 1–9.

Li, M., Liu, A., Zou, C., Xu, W., Shimizu, H., & Wang, K. (2012). An overview of the "Three-North" shelterbelt project in China. *Forestry Studies in China*, **14**, 70–79.

Li, S. P., Cadotte, M. W., Meiners, S. J., Pu, Z. C., Fukami, T., & Jiang, L. (2016). Convergence and divergence in a long-term old-field succession: The importance of spatial scale and species abundance. *Ecology Letters*, **19**, 1101–1109.

Li, S. Q., Yang, B. S., & Wu, D. M. (2008). Community succession analysis of naturally colonized plants on coal gob piles in Shanxi mining areas, China. *Water Air and Soil Pollution*, **193**, 211–228.

Li, W. J., Zuo, X. A., & Knops, J. M. H. (2013). Different fire frequency impacts over 27 years on vegetation succession in an infertile old-field grassland. *Rangeland Ecology & Management*, **66**, 267–273.

Li, X., Zhang, Z., Tan, H., Gao, Y., Liu, L., & Wang, X. (2014). Ecological restoration and recovery in the wind-blown sand hazard areas of northern China: Relationship between soil water and carrying capacity for vegetation in the Tengger Desert. *Science China – Life Sciences*, **57**, 539–548.

Lichter J. (1998). Primary succession and forest development on coastal Lake Michigan sand dunes. *Ecological Monographs*, **68**, 487–510.

Lichter, J. (2000). Colonization constraints during primary succession on coastal Lake Michigan sand dunes. *Journal of Ecology*, **88**, 825–839.

Lienard, J., Florescu, I., & Strigul, N. (2015). An appraisal of the classic forest succession paradigm with the shade tolerance index. *PLoS ONE*, **10**, e0117138.

Likens, G. E. (2013). The Hubbard Brook Ecosystem Study: Celebrating 50 years. *Bulletin of the Ecological Society of America*, **94**, 336–337.

Lin, W.-T., Chou, W.-C., & Lin, C.-Y. (2008). Earthquake-induced landslide hazard and vegetation recovery assessment using remotely sensed data and a neural network-based classifier: A case study in central Taiwan. *Natural Hazards*, **47**, 331–347.

Lin, W.-T., Lin, C.-Y., & Chou, W.-C. (2006). Assessment of vegetation recovery and soil erosion at landslides caused by a catastrophic earthquake: A case study in central Taiwan. *Ecological Engineering*, **28**, 79–89.

Lindenmayer, D. B., Burton, P. J., & Franklin, J. F. (2008). *Salvage Logging and Its Ecological Consequences*. Washington, DC: Island Press.

Lindenmayer, D. B., Likens, G. E., Krebs, C. J., & Hobbs, R. J. (2010). Improved probability of detection of ecological "surprises." *Proceedings of the National Academy of Sciences of the United States of America*, **107**, 21957–21962.

Lindig-Cisneros, R., Galindo-Vallejo, S., & Lara-Cabrera, S. (2006). Vegetation of tephra deposits 50 years after the end of the eruption of the Parícutin Volcano, Mexico. *Southwestern Naturalist*, **51**, 455–461.

Lindsey, A. A., Petty, R. O., Sterling, D. K., & Van Asdall, W. (1961). Vegetation and environment along the Wabash and Tippecanoe Rivers. *Ecological Monographs*, **31**, 105–156.

Lithgow, D., Martínez, M. L., Gallego-Fernández, J. B., *et al.* (2013). Linking restoration ecology with coastal dune restoration. *Geomorphology*, **199**, 214–224.

Little, P. J., Richardson, J. S., & Younes, A. (2013). Channel and landscape dynamics in the alluvial forest mosaic of the Carmanah River valley, British Columbia, Canada. *Geomorphology*, **202**, 86–100.

Liu, B., Zhao, W., Liu, Z., *et al.* (2015). Changes in species diversity, aboveground biomass, and vegetation cover along an afforestation successional gradient in a semiarid desert steppe of China. *Ecological Engineering*, **81**, 301–311.

Lloret, F. & Vila, M. (2003). Diversity patterns of plant functional types in relation to fire regime and previous land use in Mediterranean woodlands. *Journal of Vegetation Science*, **14**, 387–398.

Lodge, D. J. & Cantrell, S. (1995). Fungal communities in wet tropical forests: Variation in time and space. *Canadian Journal of Botany*, **73**, 1391–1398.

Lodge, D. J., Scatena, F. N., Asbury, C. E., & Sánchez, M. J. (1991). Fine litterfall and related nutrient inputs resulting from Hurricane Hugo in subtropical wet and lower montane rainforests in Puerto Rico. *Biotropica*, **23**, 336–342.

Lohier, T., Jabot, F., Wiegelt, A., Schmid, B., & Deffuant, G. (2016). Predicting stochastic community dynamics in grasslands under the assumption of competitive symmetry. *Journal of Theoretical Biology*, **399**, 53–61.

Loidi, J. & Fernández-Gonzáles, F. (2012). Potential natural vegetation: Reburying or reboring? *Journal of Vegetation Science*, **23**, 596–604.

Lomolino, M. V., Riddle, B. R., & Brown, J. H. (2006). *Biogeography*. Sunderland, MA: Sinauer.

Londo, G. (1974). Successive mapping of dune slack vegetation. *Vegetatio*, **29**, 51–61.

Lorimer, C. G. (1980). Age structure and disturbance history of a southern Appalachian virgin forest. *Ecology*, **61**, 1169–1184.

Lucas, K. L. & Carter, G. A. (2013). Change in distribution and composition of vegetated habitats on Horn Island, Mississippi, northern Gulf of Mexico, in the initial five years following Hurricane Katrina. *Geomorphology*, **199**, 129–137.

Lucas, R. M., Honzák, M., Do Amaral, I., Curran, P. J., & Foody, G. M. (2002). Forest regeneration on abandoned clearances in central Amazonia. *International Journal of Remote Sensing*, **23**, 965–988.

Lugo, A. E. (2008). Visible and invisible effects of hurricanes on forest ecosystems: An international review. *Austral Ecology*, **33**, 368–398.

Lugo, A. E. & Heartsill Scalley, T. (2014). Research in the Luquillo Experimental Forest has advanced understanding of tropical forests and resolved management issues. In D. C. Hayes, S. Stout, R. Crawford, & A. Hoover, eds., *USDA Forest Service Experimental Forests and Ranges*, pp. 435–461. New York: Springer.

Lugo, A. E. & Scatena, F. N. (1996). Background and catastrophic tree mortality in tropical moist, wet, and rain forests. *Biotropica*, **28**, 585–599.

Lugo, A. E., Applefield, M., Pool, D. J., & McDonald, R. B. (1983). The impact of Hurricane David on the forests of Dominica. *Canadian Journal of Forest Research*, **13**, 201–211.

Luken, J. O. (1990). *Directing Ecological Succession*. London: Chapman & Hall.

Luken, J. O. & Fonda, R. W. (1983). Nitrogen accumulation in a chronosequences of red alder communities along the Hoh River, Olympic National Park, Washington. *Canadian Journal of Forest Research*, **13**, 1228–1237.

Lundgren, L. (1978). Studies of soil and vegetation development on fresh landslide scars in the Mgeta Valley, Western Ulugura Mountains, Tanzania. *Geografiska Annaler*, **60A**, 91–127.

Luo, Y., Zhao, X., Li, Y., & Wang, T. (2017). Effects of foliage litter of a pioneer shrub (*Artemisia halodendron*) on germination from the soil seedbank in a semi-arid grassland in China. *Journal of Plant Research*, **130**, 1013–1021.

Luviano, N., Villa-Galaviz, E., Boege, K., Zaldívar-Riverón, A., & del-Val, E. (2018). Hurricane impacts on plant-herbivore networks along a successional chronosequences in a tropical dry forest. *Forest Ecology and Management*, **426**, 158–163.

Lytle, D. A. & Merritt, D. M. (2004). Hydrologic regimes and riparian forests: A structured population model for cottonwood. *Ecology*, **85**, 2493–2503.

Mabry, C. & Korsgren, T. (1998). A permanent plot study of vegetation and vegetation-site factors fifty-three years following disturbance in central New England, U.S.A. *Écoscience*, **5**, 232–240.

MacArthur, R. H. & Wilson, E. O. (1967). *The Theory of Island Biogeography*. Princeton, NJ: Princeton University Press.

Maekawa, M. & Nakagoshi, N. (1997). Riparian landscape changes over a period of 46 years, on the Azusa River in central Japan. *Landscape and Urban Planning*, **37**, 37–43.

Magnússon, B. & Magnússon, S. H. (2000). Vegetation succession on Surtsey, Iceland, during 1990–1998 under the influence of breeding gulls. *Surtsey Research*, **11**, 9–20.

Mahoney, J. & Rood, S. (1998). Streamflow requirements for cottonwood seedling recruitment: An integrative model. *Wetlands*, **18**, 634–645.

Major, K. C., Nosko, P., Kuehne, C., Campbell, D., & Bauhus, J. (2013). Regeneration dynamics of non-native northern red oak (*Quercus rubra* L.) populations as influenced by environmental factors: A case study in managed hardwood forests of southwestern Germany. *Forest Ecology and Management*, **291**, 144–153.

Makoto, K. & Wilson, S. D. (2019). When and where does dispersal limitation matter in primary succession? *Journal of Ecology*, **107**, 559–565.

Malanson, G. P. (1993). *Riparian Landscapes*. Cambridge: Cambridge University Press.

Mallik, A. U. (2003). Conifer regeneration problems in boreal and temperate forests with ericaceous understory: Role of disturbance, seedbed limitation, and keystone species change. *Critical Reviews in Plant Sciences*, **22**, 341–366.

Mallik, A. U., Bloom, R. G., & Whisenant, S. G. (2010). Seedbed filter controls post-fire succession. *Basic and Applied Ecology*, **11**, 170–181.

Mann, D. H., Fastier, C. L., Rowland, E. L., & Bigelow, N. H. (1995). Spruce succession, disturbance, and geomorphology on the Tanana River floodplain, Alaska. *Écoscience*, **2**, 184–199.

Mantilla-Contreras, J., Schirmel, J., & Zerbe, S. (2012). Influence of soil and microclimate on species composition and grass encroachment in heath succession. *Journal of Plant Ecology*, **5**, 249–259.

Marcante, S., Winkler, E., & Erschbamer, B. (2009). Population dynamics along a primary succession gradient: Do alpine species fit into demographic succession theory? *Annals of Botany*, **103**, 1129–1143.

Maren, I. E., Janovský, Z., Spindelbock, J. P., Daws, M. I., Kaland, P. E., & Vandvik, V. (2010). Prescribed burning of northern heathlands: *Calluna vulgaris* germination cues and seed-bank dynamics. *Plant Ecology*, **207**, 245–256.

Margalef, R. (1958). Temporal succession and spatial heterogeneity in phytoplankton. In A. A. Buzzati-Traverso, ed., *Perspectives in Marine Biology*, pp. 323–349. Berkeley: University of California Press.

Margalef, R. (1968). *Perspectives in Ecological Theory*. Chicago: University of Chicago Press.

Mark, A. F., Dickinson, K. J. M., & Fife, A. J. (1989). Forest succession on landslides in the Fiord Ecological Region, southwestern New Zealand. *New Zealand Journal of Botany*, **27**, 369–390.

Mark, A. F., Scott, G. A. M., Sanderson, F. R., & James, P. W. (1964). Forest succession on landslides above Lake Thomson, Fiordland. *New Zealand Journal of Botany*, **2**, 60–89.

Markowicz, A., Wozniak, G., Borymski, S., Piotrowska-Seget, Z., & Chmura, D. (2015). Links in the functional diversity between soil microorganisms and plant communities during natural succession in coal mine spoil heaps. *Ecological Research*, **30**, 1005–1014.

Marler, T. E. & del Moral, R. (2011). Primary succession along an elevation gradient 15 years after the eruption of Mount Pinatubo, Luzon, Philippines. *Pacific Science*, **65**, 157–173.

Marler, T. E. & del Moral, R. (2013). Primary succession in Mount Pinatubo: Habitat availability and ordination analysis. *Communicative and Integrative Biology*, **6**, e25924.

Marozas, V., Grigaitis, V., & Brazaitis, G. (2005). Edge effect on ground vegetation in clear-cut edges of pine-dominated forests. *Scandinavian Journal of Forest Research*, **20**, 43–48.

Marrs, R. H. (2002). Manipulating the chemical environment of the soil. In M. R. Perrow & A. J. Davy, eds., *Handbook of Ecological Restoration*, Vol. 1, pp. 155–183. Cambridge: Cambridge University Press.

Marrs, R. H. & Bradshaw, A. D. (1993). Primary succession on man-made wastes: The importance of resource acquisition. In J. Miles & D. H. Walton, eds., *Primary Succession on Land*, pp. 221–248. Oxford: Blackwell.

Martínez, M. L. (2003). Facilitation of seedling establishment by an endemic shrub in tropical coastal sand dunes. *Plant Ecology*, **168**, 333–345.

Martínez-Duro, E., Ferrandis, P., Escudero, A., Luzuriaga, A. L., & Herranz, J. M. (2010). Secondary old-field succession in an ecosystem with restrictive soils: Does time from abandonment matter? *Applied Vegetation Science*, **13**, 234–248.

Martínez-Ramos, M. & Soto-Castro, A. (1993). Seed rain and advanced regeneration in a tropical rain forest. *Vegetatio*, **107/108**, 299–318.

Martínez-Ruiz, C. & Marrs, R. (2007). Some factors affecting successional change on uranium mine wastes: Insights for ecological restoration. *Applied Vegetation Science*, **10**, 333–325.

Martín-Sanz, R. C., Fernández-Santos, B., & Martínez-Ruiz, C. (2015). Early dynamics of natural revegetation on roadcuts of the Salamanca province (CW Spain). *Ecological Engineering*, **75**, 223–231.

Matlack, G. R. (1993). Microenvironment variation within and among forest edge sites in the eastern United States. *Bilogical Conservation*, **66**, 185–194.

Matsamura, T. & Takeda, Y. (2010). Relationship between species richness and spatial and temporal distance from seed source in semi-natural grassland. *Applied Vegetation Science*, **13**, 336–345.

Matt, F., Almeida, K., Arguero, A., & Reudenbach, C. (2008). Seed dispersal by birds, bats, and wind. In E. Beck, J. Bendix, I. Kottke, F. Makeschin, & R. Monsandl, eds., *Gradients in a Tropical Mountain Ecosystem of Ecuador: Ecological Studies*, Ecological Studies Volume 198, pp. 157–165. Berlin: Springer Press.

Matthews, J. A. (1992). *The Ecology of Recently Deglaciated Terrain: A Geographical Approach to Glacier Forelands and Primary Succession*. Cambridge: Cambridge University Press.

Matthews, J. A. (1999). Disturbance regimes and ecosystem recovery on recently-deglaciated surfaces. In L. R. Walker, ed., *Ecosystems of Disturbed Ground, Ecosystems of the World 16*, pp. 17–37. Amsterdam: Elsevier.

Matthews, J. A. & Whittaker, R. J. (1987). Vegetation succession on the Storbreen Glacier Foreland, Jotunheimen, Norway: A review. *Arctic and Alpine Research*, **19**, 385–395.

Maza-Villalobos, S., Poorter, L., & Martínez-Ramos, M. (2013). Effects of ENSO and temporal rainfall variation on the dynamics of successional communities in old-field succession of a tropical dry forest. *PLoS ONE*, **8**, e82040.

McCoy, S., Jaffre, T., Rigault, F., & Ash, J. E. (1999). Fire and succession in the ultramafic maquis of New Caledonia. *Journal of Biogeography*, **26**, 579–594.

McDonald, M. A. & Healey, J.R. (2000). Nutrient cycling in secondary forests in the Blue Mountains of Jamaica. *Forest Ecology and Management*, **139**, 257–278.

McDonald, P. M. & Reynolds, P. E. (1999). Plant community development after 28 years in small group-selection openings. *Usda Forest Service Pacific Southwest Research Station Research Paper*, **241**, 1–17.

McDowell, W. M., Sánchez, C. G., Asbury, C. E., & Ramos Pérez, C. R. (1990). Influence of sea salt aerosols and long range transport on precipitation chemistry at El Verde, Puerto Rico. *Atmospheric Environment*, **24A**, 2813–2821.

McIntosh, R. P. (1985). *The Background of Ecology*. Cambridge: Cambridge University Press.

McIntosh, R. P. (1999). The succession of succession: A lexical chronology. *Bulletin of the Ecological Society of America*, **80**, 256–265.

McKee, S. E., Aust, W. M., Seiler, J. R., Strahm, B. D., & Schilling, E. B. (2012). Long-term site productivity of a tupelo-cypress swamp 24 years after harvesting disturbances. *Forest Ecology and Management*, **265**, 172–180.

McKenzie, D., Miller, C., & Falk, D. A., eds. (2011). *The Landscape Ecology of Fire*. New York: Springer.

McKernan, C., Cooper, D. J., & Schweiger, E. W. (2018). Glacial loss and its effect on riparian vegetation of alpine streams. *Freshwater Biology*, **63**, 518–529.

McLauchlan, K. K., Higuera, P. E., Gavin, D. G., et al. (2014). Reconstructing disturbance and their biogeochemical consequences over multiple timescales. *BioScience*, **64**, 105–116.

McLendon, T., Naumburg, E., & Martin, D. W. (2012). Secondary succession following cultivation in an arid ecosystem: The Owens Valley, California. *Journal of Arid Environments*, **82**, 136–146.

Mei, W. & Xie, S.-P. (2016). Intensification of landfalling typhoons over the northwest Pacific since the late 1970s. *Nature Geoscience*, **9**, 753–757.

Meiners, S. J., Cadenasso, M. L., & Pickett, S. T. A. (2007). Succession on the Piedmont of New Jersey and its implications for ecological restoration. In V. A. Cramer & R. J. Hobbs, eds., *Old Fields: Dynamics and Restoration of Abandoned Farmlands*, pp. 145–161. Washington, DC: Island Press.

Meiners, S. J., Pickett, S. T. A., & Cadenasso, M. L. (2002). Exotic plant invasions over 40 years of old field successions: Community patterns and associations. *Ecography*, **25**, 215–223.

Meiners, S. J., Pickett, S. T. A., & Cadenasso, M. L. (2015b). *An Integrative Approach to Successional Dynamics: Tempo and Mode of Vegetation Change*. New York: Springer.

Meiners, S. J., Cadotte, M. W., Fridley, J. D., Pickett, S. T. A., & Walker, L. R. (2015a). Is successional research nearing its climax? New approaches for understanding dynamic communities. *Functional Ecology*, **29**, 154–164.

Meira-Neto, J. A. A., Clemente, A., Oliveira, G., Nunes, A., & Correia, O. (2011). Post-fire and post-quarry rehabilitation successions in Mediterranean-like ecosystems: Implications for ecological restoration. *Ecological Engineering*, **37**, 1132–1139.

Meitzen, K., Phillips, J. N., Perkins, T., Manning, A., & Julian, J. P. (2018). Catastrophic flood disturbance and a community's response to plant resilience in the heart of the Texas Hill Country. *Geomorphology*, **305**, special issue SI, 20–32.

Meli, P., Holl, K. D., Rey Benayas, J. M., et al. (2017). A global review of past land use, climate, and active vs. passive restoration effects on forest recovery. *PLoS ONE*, **12**, e0171368.

Menges, E. S. & Waller, D. M. (1983). Plant strategies in relation to elevation and light in floodplain herbs. *The American Naturalist*, **122**, 454–473.

Mentis, M. T. (2006). Restoring native grassland on land disturbed by coal mining on the Eastern Highveld of South Africa. *South African Journal of Science*, **102**, 193–197.

Mentis, M. T. & Ellery, W. N. (1998). Environmental effects of mining coastal dunes: Conjectures and refutations. *South African Journal of Science*, **94**, 215–222.

Merrens, E. J. & Peart, D. R. (1992). Effects of hurricane damage on individual growth and stand structure in a hardwood forest in New Hampshire, USA. *Journal of Ecology*, **80**, 787–795.

Messer, A. C. (1988). Regional variation in rates of pedogenesis and the influence of climatic factors on moraine chronosequences, southern Norway. *Arctic and Alpine Research*, **20**, 31–39.

Michalová, Z., Morrissey, R. C., Wohlgemuth, T., Bače, R., Fleischer, P., & Svoboda, M. (2017). Salvage-logging after windstorm leads to structural and functional homogenization of understory layer and delayed spruce tree recovery in Tatra Mts., Slovakia. *Forests*, **8**, 88. doi: 10.3390/f8030088.

Miles, D. W. R. & Swanson, F. J. (1986). Vegetation composition on recent landslides in the Cascade Mountains of western Oregon. *Canadian Journal of Forest Research*, **16**, 739–744.

Miles, D. W. R., Swanson, F. J., & Youngberg, C. T. (1984). Effect of landslide erosion on subsequent Douglas-fir growth and stocking levels in the Western Cascades, Oregon. *Soil Science Society of American Journal*, **48**, 667–671.

Miles, J. (1979). *Vegetation Dynamics*. London: Chapman & Hall.

Miles, J. & Walton, D. W. H. (1993). *Primary Succession on Land*. Oxford: Blackwell.

Miller, T. E., Gornish, E. S., & Buckley, H. L. (2010). Climate and coastal dune vegetation: Disturbance, recovery, and succession. *Plant Ecology*, **206**, 97–104.

Millett, J. & Edmondson, S. (2013). The impact of 36 years of grazing management on vegetation dynamics in dune slacks. *Journal of Applied Ecology*, **50**, 1367–1376.

Milner, A. M., Fastie, C. L., Chapin III, F. S., *et al.* (2007). Interactions and linkages among ecosystems during landscape evolution. *BioScience*, **57**, 237–247.

Mistry, J. (2000). *World Savannas: Ecology and Human Use*. New York: Routledge.

Mittelbach, G. G. & Schemske, D. W. (2015). Ecological and evolutionary perspectives on community assembly. *Trends in Ecology and Evolution*, **30**, 241–247.

Miyanishi, K. & Johnson, E. A. (2007). Coastal dune succession and the reality of dune processes. In E. A. Johnson & K. Miyanishi, eds., *Plant Disturbance Ecology: The Process and the Response*, pp. 249–282. Amsterdam: Academic Press.

Mizuno, K. & Fujita, T. (2014). Vegetation succession on Mt. Kenya in relation to glacial fluctuation and global warming. *Journal of Vegetation Science*, **25**, 559–570.

Moktan, M. R., Gratzer, G., Richards, W. H., Tek Bahadur, R., Dukpa, D., & Tenzin, K. (2009). Regeneration of mixed conifer forests under group tree selection harvest management in western Bhutan Himalayas. *Forest Ecology and Management*, **257**, 2121–2132.

Møller, A. P., Barnier, F., & Mousseau, T. A. (2012). Ecosystem effects 25 years after Chernobyl: Pollinators, fruit set and recruitment. *Oecologia*, **170**, 1155–1165.

Molnár, Z. & Botta-Dukát, Z. (1998). Improved space-for-time substitution for hypothesis generation: Secondary grasslands with documented site history in SE-Hungary. *Phytocoenologia*, **28**, 1–29.

Monokrousos, N., Boutsis, G., & Diamantopoulos, J. D. (2014). Development of soil chemical and biological properties in the initial stages of post-mining deposition sites. *Environmental Monitoring and Assessment*, **186**, 9065–9074.

Montoni, M. V. F., Honaine, M. F., & del Rio, J. L. (2014). An assessment of spontaneous vegetation recovery in aggregate quarries in coastal sand dunes in Buenos Aires Province, Argentina. *Environmental Management*, **54**, 180–193.

Moola, F. M. & Vasseur, L. (2004). Recovery of late-seral vascular plants in a chronosequence of post-clearcut forest stands in coastal Nova Scotia, Canada. *Plant Ecology*, **172**, 183–197.

Mooney, H. A., Mack, R., McNeely, J. A., Neville, L. E., Schei, P. J., & Waage, K. (2005). *Invasive Alien Species: A New Synthesis*. Washington, DC: Island Press.

Mora, J. L., Armas-Herrera, C. M., Guerra, J. A., Rodríguez-Rodríguez, A., & Arbelo, C. D. (2012). Factors affecting vegetation and soil recovery in the Mediterranean woodland of the Canary Islands (Spain). *Journal of Arid Environments*, **87**, 58–66.

Moravec, J. (1969). Succession of plant communities and soil development. *Folia Geobtanica et Phytotaxonomica*, **4**, 133–164.

Moreau, M., Mercier, D., Laffly, D., & Roussel, E. (2008). Impacts of recent paraglacial dynamics on plant colonization: A case study on Midtre Lovenbreen foreland, Spitsbergen (79 degrees N). *Geomorphology*, **95**, 48–60.

Moreno-Casasola, P. (1986). Sand movement as a factor in the distribution of plant communities in a coastal dune system. *Vegetatio*, **65**, 67–76.

Moreno-de las Heras, M., Nicolau, J. M., & Espigares, T. (2008). Vegetation succession in reclaimed coal-mining slopes in a Mediterranean-dry environment. *Ecological Engineering*, **34**, 168–178.

Mori, A. S., Osono, T., Uchida, M., & Kanda, H. (2008). Changes in the structure and heterogeneity of vegetation and microsite environments with the chronosequence of primary succession on a glacier foreland in Ellesmere Island, High Arctic, Canada. *Ecological Research*, **23**, 363–370.

Mori, A. S., Uchida, M., & Kanda, H. (2013). Non-stochastic colonization by pioneer plants after deglaciation in a polar oasis of the Canadian High Arctic. *Polar Science*, **7**, 278–287.

Morris, L. R. & Leger, E. A. (2016). Secondary succession in the sagebrush semi-desert 66 years after fire in the Great Basin, USA. *Natural Areas Journal*, **36**, 187–193.

Morris, L. R., Monaco, T. A., & Sheley, R. L. (2011). Land-use legacies and vegetation recovery 90 years after cultivation in Great Basin sagebrush ecosystems. *Rangeland Ecology & Management*, **64**, 488–497.

Morris, M. R. & Stanford, J. A. (2011). Floodplain succession and soil nitrogen accumulation on a salmon river in southwestern Kamchatka. *Ecological Monographs*, **81**, 43–61.

Morrison, D. A., Cary, G. J., Pengelly, S. M., et al. (1995). Effects of fire frequency on plant-species composition of sandstone communities in the Sydney Region: Inter-fire interval and time-since fire. *Australian Journal of Ecology*, **20**, 239–247.

Mota, J. F., Sola, A. J., Jiménez-Sánchez, M. L., Pérez-Garcia, F. J., & Merlo, M. E. (2004). Gypsicolous flora, conservation and restoration of quarries in the southeast of the Iberian Peninsula. *Biodiversity and Conservation*, **13**, 1797–1808.

Mote, P. W. & Kaser, G. (2007). The shrinking glaciers of Kilimanjaro: Can global warming be blamed? *American Scientist*, **95**, 318–325.

Motzkin, G., Wilson, P., Foster, D. R., & Allen, A. (1999). Vegetation patterns in heterogeneous landscapes: The importance of history and environment. *Journal of Vegetation Science*, **10**, 903–920.

Mouw, J. E. B., Chaffin, J. L., Whited, D. C., Hauer, F. R., Matson, P. L., & Stanford, J. A. (2013). Recruitment and successional dynamics diversify the shifting habitat mosaic of an Alaskan floodplain. *River Research and Applications*, **29**, 671–685.

Mudrák, O., Doležal, J., & Frouz, J. (2016). Initial species composition predicts the progress in the spontaneous succession on mine sites. *Ecological Engineering*, **95**, 665–670.

Muñoz Vallés, S., Gallego-Fernández, J. B., & Cambrollé, J. (2013). The biological flora of coastal dunes and wetlands: *Retama monosperma* (L.) Boiss. *Journal of Coastal Research*, **29**, 1101–1110.

Muñoz-Mas, R., Garófano-Gómez, V., Andrés-Doménech, I., *et al.* (2017). Exploring the key drivers of riparian woodland successional pathways across three European river reaches. *Ecohydrology*, **10**, e1888.

Muñoz-Reinoso, J. C. (2018). Doñana mobile dunes: What is the vegetation pattern telling us? *Journal of Coastal Conservation*, **22**, 605–614.

Murphy, H. T. & Metcalfe, D. J. (2016). The perfect storm: Weed invasion and intense storms in tropical forests. *Austral Ecology*, **41**, 864–874.

Murphy, H. T., Metcalfe, D. J., Bradford, M. G., *et al.* (2008). Recruitment dynamics of invasive species in rainforest habitats following Cyclone Larry. *Austral Ecology*, **33**, 495–502.

Mylliemngap, W., Nath, D., & Barik, S. (2016). Changes in vegetation and nitrogen mineralization during recovery of a montane subtropical broadleaved forest in North-eastern India following anthropogenic disturbance. *Ecological Research*, **31**, 21–38.

Myster, R. W. (1994). Landslide insects show small differences between an island (Puerto Rico) and the mainland (Costa Rica). *Acta Científica*, **8**, 105–113.

Myster, R. W. (1997). Seed predation, disease and germination on landslides in Neotropical lower montane wet forest. *Journal of Vegetation Science*, **8**, 55–64.

Myster, R. W. (2002). Foliar pathogen and insect herbivore effects on two landslide tree species in Puerto Rico. *Forest Ecology and Management*, **169**, 231–242.

Myster, R. W. & Fernández, D. S. (1995). Spatial gradients and patch structure on two Puerto Rican landslides. *Biotropica*, **27**, 149–159.

Myster, R. W. & Sarmiento, F. O. (1998). Seed inputs to microsite patch recovery on two tropandean landslides in Ecuador. *Restoration Ecology*, **6**, 35–43.

Myster, R. W. & Walker, L. R. (1997). Plant successional pathways on Puerto Rican landslides. *Journal of Tropical Ecology*, **13**, 165–173.

Myster, R. W., Thomlinson, J. R., & Larsen, M. C. (1997). Predicting landslide vegetation in patches on landscape gradients in Puerto Rico. *Landscape Ecology*, **12**, 299–307.

Nadeau, L. B. & Corns, I. G. W. (2002). Post-fire vegetation of the Montane natural subregion of Jasper National Park. *Forest Ecology and Management*, **163**, 165–183.

Nagashima, K., Yoshida, S., & Hosaka, T. (2009). Patterns and factors in early-stage vegetation recovery at abandoned plantation clearcut sites in Oita, Japan: Possible indicators for evaluating vegetation status. *Journal of Forest Research*, **14**, 135–146.

Nagy, L. & Grabherr, G. (2009). *The Biology of Alpine Habitats*. Oxford: Oxford University Press.

Naiman, R. J. & Rogers, K. H. (1997). Large animals and system-level characteristics in river corridors. *BioScience*, **47**, 521–529.

Nakamura, F., Shin, N., & Inahara, S. (2007). Shifting mosaic in maintaining diversity of floodplain tree species in the northern temperate zone of Japan. *Forest Ecology and Management*, **241**, 28–38.

Nakamura, F., Yajima, T., & Kikuchi, S. (1997). Structure and composition of riparian forests with special reference to geomorphic site conditions along the Tokachi River, northern Japan. *Plant Ecology*, **133**, 209–219.

Nakamura, T. (1984). Vegetational recovery of landslide scars in the upper reaches of the Oi River, Central Japan. *Journal of the Japanese Forestry Society*, **66**, 328–332.

Nakamura, T. (1985). Forest succession in the subalpine region of Mt. Fuji, Japan. *Vegetatio*, **64**, 15–27.

Nakashizuka, T., Iida, S., Suzuki, W., & Tanimoto, T. (1993). Seed dispersal and vegetation development on a debris avalanche on the Ontake volcano, Central Japan. *Journal of Vegetation Science*, **4**, 537–542.

Nanson, G. C. & Beach, H. F. (1977). Forest succession and sedimentation on a meandering-river floodplain, northeast British Columbia, Canada. *Journal of Biogeography*, **4**, 229–251.

Nara, K. & Hogetsu, T. (2004). Ectomycorrhizal fungi on established shrubs facilitate subsequent seedling establishment of successional plant species. *Ecology*, **85**, 1700–1707.

Naveh, Z. & Lieberman, A. S. (1984). *Landscape Ecology: Theory and Application*. New York: Springer.

Nechaev, A. P. (1967). Seed regeneration of willows on the pebble-bed shoals of the Bureya River. *Lesovedenie*, **1**, 54–64. (Original title: Semennoe vozobnovlenie ivovych na galechnikach reki Bohrei.)

Neeman, G. & Izhaki, I. (1996). Colonization in an abandoned East-Mediterranean vineyard. *Journal of Vegetation Science*, **7**, 465–472.

Nelson, Z. J., Weisberg, P. J., & Kitchen, S. G. (2014). Influence of climate and environment on post-fire recovery of mountain big sagebrush. *International Journal of Wildland Fire*, **23**, 131–142.

Nemet, E., Ruprecht, E., Galle, R., & Marko, B. (2016). Abandonment of crop lands leads to different recovery patterns for ant and plant communities in Eastern Europe. *Community Ecology*, **17**, 79–87.

Neto, C., Cardigos, P., Oliveira, S. C., & Zêzere, J. L. (2017). Floristic and vegetation successional processes within landslides in a Mediterranean environment. *Science of the Total Environment*, **574**, 969–981.

Newbold, T., Hudson, L. N., Hill, S. L. L., *et al.* (2015). Global effects of land use on local terrestrial biodiversity. *Nature*, **520**, 45–50.

Nguyen-Xuan, T., Bergeron, Y., Simard, D., Fyles, J. W., & Pare, D. (2000). The importance of forest floor disturbance in the early regeneration patterns of the boreal forest of western and central Quebec: A wildfire versus logging comparison. *Canadian Journal of Forest Research*, **30**, 1353–1364.

Nikolic, N., Bocker, R., & Nikolic, M. (2016). Long-term passive restoration following fluvial deposition of sulphidic copper tailings: Nature filters out the solutions. *Environmental Science and Pollution Research*, **23**, 13672–13680.

Nikolic, N., Kostic, L., & Nikolic, M. (2018). To dam or not to dam? Abolishment of further flooding impedes the natural revegetation processes after long-term fluvial deposition of copper tailings. *Land Degradation and Development*, **29**, 1915–1924.

Nilsson, C., Ekblad, A., Dynesius, M., *et al.* (1994). A comparison of species richness and traits of riparian plants between a main river channel and its tributaries. *Journal of Ecology*, **82**, 281–295.

Ninot, J. M., Herrero, P., Ferré, A., & Guardia, R. (2001). Effects of reclamation measures on plant colonization on lignite waste in the eastern Pyrenees, Spain. *Applied Vegetation Science*, **4**, 29–34.

Nishi, H. & Tsuyuzaki, S. (2004). Seed dispersal and seedling establishment of *Rhus trichocarpa* promoted by a crow (*Corvus macrorhynchos*) on a volcano in Japan. *Ecography*, **27**, 311–322.

Nishimura, A., Tsuyuzaki, S., & Haraguchi, A. (2009). A chronosequence approach for detecting revegetation patterns after sphagnum-peat mining, northern Japan. *Ecological Research*, **24**, 237–246.

Noble, I. R. & Slatyer, R. O. (1980). The use of vital attributes to predict successional changes in plant-communities subject to recurrent disturbances. *Vegetatio*, **43**, 5–21.

Norby, R. J. & Zak, D. R. (2011). Ecological lessons from free-air CO_2 enrichment (FACE) experiments. *Annual Review of Ecology and Systematics*, **42**, 181–203.

Norden, N., Angarita, H. A., Bongers, F., *et al.* (2015). Successional dynamics in Neotropical forests are as uncertain as they are predictable. *Proceedings of the National Academy of Science of the United States of America*, **112**, 8013–8018.

Nossov, D. R., Hollingsworth, T. N., Ruess, R. W., & Kielland, K. (2011). Development of *Alnus tenuifolia* stands on an Alaskan floodplain: Patterns of recruitment, disease and succession. *Journal of Ecology*, **99**, 621–633.

Novák, J. & Prach, K. (2003). Vegetation succession in basalt quarries: Pattern over a landscape scale. *Applied Vegetation Science*, **6**, 111–116.

Novák, J. & Prach, K. (2010). Artificial sowing of endangered dry grassland species into disused basalt quarries. *Flora*, **205**, 179–183.

Nurtjahya, E., Setiadi, D., Guhardja, E., Muhadiono, & Setiadi, Y. (2009). Succession on tin-mined land in Bangka Island. *Blumea*, **54**, 131–138.

Nyland, R. D. (2016). *Silviculture: Concepts and Applications*, 3rd ed. Long Grove, IL: Waveland Press.

Nylén, T. & Luoto, M. (2015). Primary succession, disturbance and productivity drive complex species richness patterns on land uplift beaches. *Journal of Vegetation Science*, **26**, 267–277.

Nylén, T., Le Roux, P. C., & Luoto, M. (2013). Biotic interactions drive species occurrences and richness in dynamic beach environments. *Plant Ecology*, **214**, 1455–1466.

Obase, K., Tamai, Y., Yajima, T., & Miyamoto, T. (2008). Mycorrhizal colonization status of plant species established in an exposed area following the 2000 eruption of Mt. Usu, Hokkaido, Japan. *Landscape and Ecological Engineering*, **4**, 57–61.

Oberbauer, S. F., Whelan, K. R. T., & Koptur, S. (1996). Effects of Hurricane Andrew on epiphyte communities within cypress domes of Everglades National Park. *Ecology*, **77**, 964–967.

O'Donnell, J., Fryirs, K. A., & Leishman, M. R. (2016). Seed banks as a source of vegetation regeneration to support the recovery of degraded rivers:

A comparison of river reaches of varying condition. *Science of the Total Environment*, **542**, 591–602.

Odum, E. P. (1953). *Fundamentals of Ecology*. Philadelphia: Saunders.

Odum, E. P. (1969). The strategy of ecosystem development. *Science*, **164**, 262–270.

Odum, H. T. & Pinkerton, R. C. (1955). Time's speed regulator: The optimum efficiency for maximum power output in physical and biological systems. *American Scientist*, **43**, 331–343.

Ohl, C. & Bussman, R. (2004). Recolonisation of natural landslides in tropical mountain forests of Southern Ecuador. *Feddes Repertorium*, **115**, 248–264.

Ohsawa, M. (1984). Differentiation of vegetation zones and species strategies in the subalpine region of Mt. Fuji. *Vegetatio*, **57**, 15–52.

Olff, H., Huisman, J., & Van Tooren, B. F. (1993). Species dynamics and nutrient accumulation during early primary succession in coastal sand dunes. *Journal of Ecology*, **81**, 693–706.

Oliveira-Filho, A. T., Vilela, E. A., Gavilanes, M. L., & Carvalho, D. A. (1994). Effect of flooding regime and understorey bamboos on the physiognomy and tree species composition of a tropical semideciduous forest in southeastern Brazil. *Vegetatio*, **113**, 99–124.

Olson, J. S. (1958). Rates of succession and soil changes on southern Lake Michigan sand dunes. *Botanical Gazette*, **119**, 125–170.

Olsson, B. A. & Staaf, H. (1995). Influence of harvesting intensity of logging residues on ground vegetation in coniferous forests. *Journal of Applied Ecology*, **32**, 640–654.

Oosting, H. J. (1948). *The Study of Plant Communities*. San Francisco: Freeman.

Orwig, D. A. & Abrams, M. D. (1994). Land-use history (1720–1992), composition, and dynamics of oak pine forests within the Piedmont and coastal-plain of northern Virginia. *Canadian Journal of Forest Research*, **24**, 1216–1225.

Osbornová, J., Kovářová, M., Lepš, J., & Prach, K., eds. (1990). *Succession in Abandoned Fields: Studies in Central Bohemia, Czechoslovakia*. Dordrecht: Kluwer.

Osipov, S. V., Cherdantseva, V. Y., Galanina, I. A., & Yakubov, V. V. (2008). Species composition and ecologo-phytocenotic spectra of vascular plants, mosses, and lichens on gold-mining sites in the taiga zone of the lower Amur River basin, the Russian Far East. *Contemporary Problems of Ecology*, **1**, 425–439.

Osono, T., Mori, A. S., Uchida, M., & Kanda, H. (2016). Accumulation of carbon and nitrogen in vegetation and soils of deglaciated area in Ellesmere Island, high-Arctic Canada. *Polar Science*, **10**, 288–296.

Öster, M., Ask, K., Cousins, S. A. O., & Eriksson, O. (2009). Dispersal and establishment limitation reduced the potential for successful restoration of semi-natural grassland communities on former arable fields. *Journal of Applied Ecology*, **46**, 1266–1274.

Otto, R., Krüsi, B. O., Burga, C. A., & Fernández-Palacios, J. M. (2006). Old-field succession along a precipitation gradient in the semi-arid coastal region of Tenerife. *Journal of Arid Environments*, **65**, 156–178.

Overbeck, G. F., Miller, S. C., Pillar, V. D., & Pfadenhauer, J. (2005). Fine-scale post-fire dynamics in southern Brazilian subtropical grassland. *Journal of Vegetation Science*, **16**, 655–664.

Pabst, R. J. & Spies, T. A. (2001). Ten years of vegetation succession on a debris-flow deposit in Oregon. *Journal of the American Water Association*, **37**, 1693–1708.

Paine, R. T. (1969). A note on trophic complexity and community stability. *The American Naturalist*, **103**, 91–93.

Paine, R. T., Tegner, M. J., & Johnson, E. A. (1998). Compounded perturbations yield ecological surprises. *Ecosystems*, **1**, 535–545.

Pakeman, R. J., Alexander, J., Beaton, J., et al. (2015). Species composition of coastal dune vegetation in Scotland has proved resistant to climate change over a third of a century. *Global Change Biology*, **21**, 3738–3747.

Palmer, M. W., McAlister, S. D., Arévalo, J. R., & DeCoster, J. K. (2000). Changes in the understory during 14 years following catastrophic windthrow in two Minnesota forests. *Journal of Vegetation Science*, **11**, 841–854.

Pandey, A. N. & Singh, J. S. (1985). Mechanisms of ecosystem recovery: A case study from Kumaun Himalaya. *Recreation and Revegetation Research*, **3**, 271–292.

Papanastasis, V. P. (2007). Land abandonment and old field dynamics in Greece. In V. A. Cramer & R. J. Hobbs, eds., *Old Field Dynamics and Restoration of Abandoned Farmland*, pp. 225–246. Washington, DC: Island Press.

Parendes, L. A. & Jones, J. A. (2000). Role of light availability and dispersal in exotic plant invasion along roads and streams in the H. J. Andrews Experimental Forest, Oregon. *Conservation Biology*, **14**, 64–75.

Parker, D. E., Wilson, H., Jones, P. D., Christy, J. R., & Folland, C. K. (1996). The impacts of Mount Pinatubo on world-wide temperatures. *International Journal of Climatology*, **16**, 487–497.

Parker, V. T. (1997). The scale of successional models and restoration objectives. *Restoration Ecology*, **5**, 301–306.

Parker-Nance, T., Talbot, M. M. B., & Bate, G. C. (1991). Vegetation and geomorphic age in the Alexandria coastal dunefield, eastern Cape, South Africa. *South African Journal of Science*, **87**, 252–259.

Párraga-Aguado, I., Querejeta, J. I., González-Alcaraz, M. N., Jiménez-Cárceles, F. J., & Conesa, H. M. (2014). Usefulness of pioneer vegetation for the phyto-management of metal(loid)s enriched tailings: Grasses vs. shrubs vs. trees. *Journal of Environmental Management*, **133**, 51–58.

Pärtel, M., Szava-Kovats, R., & Zobel, M. (2011). Dark diversity: Shedding light on absent species. *Trends in Ecology and Evolution*, **26**, 124–128.

Partomihardjo, T., Mirmanto, E., & Whittaker, R. J. (1992). Anak Krakatau's vegetation and flora circa 1991, with observations on a decade of development and change. *GeoJournal*, **28**, 233–248.

Paschke, M. W., McLendon, T., & Redente, E. F. (2000). Nitrogen availability and old-field succession in a shortgrass steppe. *Ecosystems*, **3**, 144–158.

Pätzold, S., Hejcman, M., Barej, J., & Schellberg, J. (2013). Soil phosphorus fractions after seven decades of fertilizer application in the Rengen Grassland Experiment. *Journal of Plant Nutrition and Soil Science*, **176**, 910–920.

Pausas, J. G. & Lavorel, S. (2003). A hierarchical deductive approach for functional types in disturbed ecosystems. *Journal of Vegetation Science*, **14**, 409–416.

Pearce, A. J. & O'Loughlin, C. L. (1985). Landsliding during a M 7.7 earthquake: Influence of geology and topography. *Geology*, **13**, 855–858.

Pegman, A. P. McK. & Rapson, G. L. (2005). Plant succession and dune dynamics on actively prograding dunes, Whatipu Beach, northern New Zealand. *New Zealand Journal of Botany*, **43**, 223–244.

Peh, K. S.-H., Corlett, R. T., & Bergeron Y., eds. (2015). *Routledge Handbook of Forest Ecology*. Boca Raton, FL: Routledge/CRC Press.

Peloquin, R. L. & Hiebert, R. D. (1999). The effects of black locust (*Robinia pseudoacacia* L.) on species diversity and composition of black oak savanna/ woodland communities. *Natural Areas Journal*, **19**, 121–131.

Peltzer, D. A., Bellingham, P. J, Kurokawa, H., Walker, L. R., Wardle, D. A., & Yeates, G. W. (2009). Punching above their weight: Low-biomass non-native plant species alter soil properties during primary succession. *Oikos*, **118**, 1001–1014.

Peltzer, D. A., Wardle, D. A., Allison, V. J., *et al.* (2010). Understanding ecosystem retrogression. *Ecological Monographs*, **80**, 509–529.

Pennanen, T., Strömmer, R., Markkola, A., & Fritze, H. (2001). Microbial and plant community structure across a primary succession gradient. *Scandinavian Journal of Forest Research*, **16**, 37–43.

Pensa, M., Sellin, A., Luud, A., & Valgma, I. (2004). An analysis of vegetation restoration on opencast oil shale mines in Estonia. *Restoration Ecology*, **12**, 200–206.

Perera, A. H., Buse, L. J., & Weber, M. G., eds. (2007). *Emulating Natural Forest Landscape Disturbances: Concepts and Applications*. New York: Columbia University Press.

Perla, R. I. & Martinelli, M., Jr. (1976). *Avalanche Handbook*, and: Washington, DC: U.S. Department of Agriculture, Forest Service, Agriculture Handbook 489, Washington, DC.

Perren, B. B., Massa, C., Bichet, V., *et al.* (2012). A paleoecological perspective on 1450 years of human impacts from a lake in southern Greenland. *Holocene*, **22**, 1025–1034.

Perrow, M. R. & Davy, A. J., eds. (2002). *Handbook of Ecological Restoration*. Vol. 2: Restoration in Practice. Cambridge: Cambridge University Press.

Perryman, S. A. M., Castells-Brooke, N. I. D., Glendining, M. J., *et al.* (2018). The electronic Rothamsted Archive (e-RA), an online resource for data from the Rothamsted long-term experiments. *Scientific Data*, **5**, article number 180072.

Peterken, G. F. 1996. *Natural Woodland: Ecology and Conservation in Northern Temperate Regions*. Cambridge: Cambridge University Press.

Peterson, G. D. & Heemskerk, M. (2001). Deforestation and forest regeneration following small-scale gold mining in the Amazon: The case of Suriname. *Environmental Conservation*, **28**, 117–126.

Pettit, N. E. & Naiman, R. J. (2007). Fire in the riparian zone: Characteristics and ecological consequences. *Ecosystems*, **10**, 673–687.

Pickett, S. T. A. (1976). Succession: An evolutionary perspective. *The American Naturalist*, **110**, 107–119.

Pickett, S. T. A. (1989). Space for time substitutions as an alternative to long-term studies. In G. E. Likens, ed., *Long Term Studies in Ecology*, pp. 110–135. New York: Springer.

Pickett, S. T. A., Collins, S. L., & Armesto, J. J. (1987a). Models, mechanisms and pathways of succession. *The Botanical Review*, **53**, 335–371.

Pickett, S. T. A., Collins, S. L., & Armesto, J. J. (1987b). A hierarchical consideration of causes and mechanisms of succession. *Vegetatio*, **69**, 109–114.

Pickett, S. T. A. & White, P. S., eds. (1985). *The Ecology of Natural Disturbance and Patch Dynamics*. New York: Academic Press.

Piekarska-Stachowiak, A., Szary, M., Ziemer, B., Besenyei, L., & Wozniak, G. (2014). An application of the plant functional group concept to restoration practice on coal mine spoil heaps. *Ecological Research*, **29**, 843–853.

Pietsch, W. H. O. (1996). Recolonization and development of vegetation on mine spoils following brown coal mining in Lusatia. *Water Air and Soil Pollution*, **91**, 1–15.

Piiroinen, T., Valtonen, A., & Roininen, H. (2017). Vertebrate herbivores are the main cause of seedling mortality in a logged African rainforest: Implications for forest restoration. *Restoration Ecology*, **25**, 442–452.

Pimm, S. L. (1984). The complexity and stability of ecosystems. *Nature*, **307**, 321.

Platt, W. J. & Connell, J. H. (2003). Natural disturbances and directional replacement of species. *Ecological Monographs*, **73**, 507–522.

Plotkin, A. B., Schoonmaker, P., Leon, B., & Foster, D. (2017). Microtopography and ecology of pit-mound structures in second-growth versus old-growth forests. *Forest Ecology and Management*, **404**, 14–23.

Poschlod, P. (2017). *Geschichte der Kulturlandschaft*. Stuttgart: Ulmer.

Poschlod, P., Kleyer, M., Jackel, A.-K., Dannemann, A., & Tackenberg, O. (2003). BIOPOP – A database of plant traits and internet application for nature conservation. *Folia Geobotanica*, **38**, 263–271.

Poulson, T. L. (1999). Autogenic, allogenic, and individualistic mechanisms of dune succession at Miller, Indiana. *Natural Areas Journal*, **19**, 172–176.

Powers, J. S., Becknell, J. M., Irving, J., & Perez-Aviles, D. (2009). Diversity and structure of regenerating tropical dry forests in Costa Rica: Geographic patterns and environmental drivers. *Forest Ecology and Management*, **258**, 959–970.

Prach, K. (1985). Succession of vegetation in abandoned fields in Finland. *Annales Botanici Fennici*, **22**, 307–314.

Prach, K. (1994). Vegetation succession on river gravel bars across the northwestern Himalayas, India. *Arctic and Alpine Research*, **26**, 349–353.

Prach K. (2015). Mining site restoration by spontaneous processes in the Czech Republic. *Cornerstone*, **4**, 40–43.

Prach, K. & Hobbs, R. J. (2008). Spontaneous succession versus technical reclamation in the restoration of disturbed sites. *Restoration Ecology*, **16**, 363–366.

Prach, K. & Pyšek, P. (2001). Using spontaneous succession for restoration of human-disturbed habitats: Experience from Central Europe. *Ecological Engineering*, **17**, 55–62.

Prach, K. & Rachlewicz, G. (2012). Succession of vascular plants in front of retreating glaciers in central Spitsbergen. *Polish Polar Research*, **33**, 319–328.

Prach, K. & Řehounková, K. (2006). Vegetation succession over broad geographical scales: Which factors determine the patterns? *Preslia*, **78**, 469–480.

Prach, K. & Tolvanen, A. (2016). How can we restore biodiversity and ecosystem services in mining and industrial sites? *Environmental Science and Pollution Research*, **23**, 13587–13590.

Prach, K. & Walker, L. R. (2011). Four opportunities for studies of ecological succession. *Trends in Ecology and Evolution*, **26**, 119–123.

Prach, K. & Walker, W. R. (2019). Differences between primary and secondary plant succession among biomes of the world. *Journal Ecology*, **107**, 510–516.

Prach, K., Chenoweth, J., & del Moral, R. (2019). Spontaneous and assisted restoration of vegetation on the bottom of a former water reservoir, the Elwha River, Olympic National Park, WA, USA. *Restoration Ecology*, **27**, 592–599.

Prach, K., Jírová, A., & Doležal, J. (2014a). Pattern of succession in old-field vegetation at a regional scale. *Preslia*, **86**, 119–130.

Prach, K., Pyšek, P., & Řehounková, K. (2014c). Role of substrate and landscape context in early succession: An experimental approach. *Perspectives in Plant Evolution and Systematics*, **16**, 174–179.

Prach, K., Pyšek, P., & Šmilauer, P. (1993). On the rate of succession. *Oikos*, **66**, 343–346.

Prach, K., Pyšek, P., & Šmilauer, P. (1997). Changes in species traits during succession: A search for pattern. *Oikos*, **79**, 201–205.

Prach, K., Pyšek, P., & Šmilauer, P. (1999). Prediction of vegetation succession in human-disturbed habitats using an expert system. *Restoration Ecology*, **7**, 15–23.

Prach, K., Marrs, R., Pyšek, P., & van Diggelen, R. (2007). Manipulation of succession. In L. R. Walker, J. Walker, & R. J. Hobbs, eds., *Linking Restoration and Ecological Succession*, pp. 121–149. New York: Springer.

Prach, K., Petřík, P., Brož, Z., & Song, J.-S. (2014b). Vegetation succession on river sediments along the Nakdong River, South Korea. *Folia Geobotanica*, **49**, 507–519.

Prach, K., Šebelíková, L., Řehounková, K., & del Moral, R. (2019). Possibilities and limitations of passive restoration of heavily disturbed sites. *Landscape Research*, https://doi.org/10.1080 /01426397.2019.1593335.

Prach, K., Tichý, L., Vítovcová, K., & Řehounková, K. (2017). Participation of the Czech flora in succession at disturbed sites: Quantifying species' colonization ability. *Preslia*, **89**, 87–100.

Prach, K., Bartha, S., Joyce, C. H. B., Pyšek, P., van Diggelen, R., & Wiegleb, G. (2001). The role of spontaneous vegetation succession in ecosystem restoration: A perspective. *Applied Vegetation Science*, **4**, 111–114.

Prach, K., Karešová, P., Jírová, A., Dvořáková, H., Konvalinková, P., & Řehounková, K. (2015). Do not neglect surroundings in restoration of disturbed sites. *Restoration Ecology*, **23**, 310–314.

Prach, K., Lencová, K., Řehounková, K., *et al.* (2013). Spontaneous vegetation succession at different central European mining sites: A comparison across seres. *Environmental Science and Pollution Research*, **20**, 7680–7685.

Prach, K., Řehounková, K., Lencová, K., *et al.* (2014d). Vegetation succession in restoration of disturbed sites in Central Europe: The direction of succession and species richness across 19 seres. *Applied Vegetation Science*, **17**, 193–200.

Prach, K., Tichý, L., Lencová, K., et al. (2016). Does succession run towards potential natural vegetation? An analysis across seres. *Journal of Vegetation Science*, **27**, 515–523.

Prather, C. (2014). Divergent responses of leaf herbivory to simulated hurricane effects in a rainforest understory. *Forest Ecology and Management*, **332**, 87–92.

Privett, S. D. J., Cowling, R. M., & Taylor, H. C. (2001). Thirty years of change in the fynbos vegetation of the Cape of Good Hope Nature Reserve, South Africa. *Bothalia*, **31**, 99–115.

Prober, S. M., Thiele, K. R., Lunt, I. D., & Koen, T. B. (2005). Restoring ecological function in temperate grassy woodlands: Manipulating soil nutrients, exotic annuals and native perennial grasses through carbon supplements and spring burns. *Journal of Applied Ecology*, **42**, 1073–1085.

Provoost, S., Jones, M., Laurence, M., & Edmondson, S. E. (2011). Changes in landscape and vegetation of coastal dunes in northwest Europe: A review. *Journal of Coastal Conservation*, **15**, 207–226.

Pueyo, Y. & Alados, C. L. (2007). Effects of fragmentation, abiotic factors and land use on vegetation recovery in a semi-arid Mediterranean area. *Basic and Applied Ecology*, **8**, 158–170.

Purdie, R. W. & Slatyer, R. O. (1976). Vegetation succession after fire in sclerophyll woodland communities in southeastern Australia. *Australian Journal of Ecology*, **1**, 223–236.

Putz, F. E. & Brokaw, N. V. L. (1989). Sprouting of broken trees on Barro Colorado Island, Panama. *Ecology*, **70**, 508–512.

Putz, F. E. & Chan, H. T. (1986). Tree growth, dynamics, and productivity in a mature mangrove forest in Malaysia. *Forest Ecology and Management*, **17**, 211–230.

Putz, F. E., Coley, P. D., Lu, K., Montalvo, A., & Aiello, A. (1983). Uprooting and snapping of trees: Structural determinants and ecological consequences. *Canadian Journal of Forest Research*, **13**, 1011–1020.

Pyšek, P. & Richardson, D. M. (2006). Plant invasions: Merging the concepts of species invasiveness and community invasibility. *Progress in Physical Geography*, **30**, 409–431.

Pyšek, P., Davis, M. A., Daehler, C. C., & Thompson, K. (2004). Plant invasions and vegetation succession: Closing the gap. *Bulletin of the Ecological Society of America*, **85**, 105–109.

Pyšek, P., Sádlo, J., Mandák, B., & Jarošík, V. (2003). Czech alien flora and the historical pattern of its formation: What came first to central Europe? *Oecologia*, **135**, 122–130.

Pyšek, P., Pergl, J., Ess, F., et al. (2017). Naturalized alien flora of the world: Species diversity, taxonomic and phylogenetic patterns, geographic distribution and global hotspots of plant invasion. *Preslia*, **89**, 203–274.

R Development Core Team (2015). *R: A language and Environment for Statistical Computing*. Vienna, Austria: R Foundation for Statistical Computing (www.R-project.org/).

Raevel, V., Violle, C., & Munoz, F. (2012). Mechanisms of ecological succession: Insights from plant functional strategies. *Oikos*, **121**, 1761–1770.

Raharimalala, O., Buttler, A., Ramohavelo, C. D., Razanaka, S., Sorg, J. P., & Gobat, J. M. (2010). Soil-vegetation patterns in secondary slash and burn successions in Central Menabe, Madagascar. *Agriculture Ecosystems & Environment*, **139**, 150–158.

Raich, J. W., Russell, A. E., & Vitousek, P. M. (1997). Primary productivity and ecosystem development along an elevational gradient on Mauna Loa, Hawaii. *Ecology*, **78**, 707–721.

Raich, J. W., Russell, A. E., Crews, T. E., Farrington, H., & Vitousek, P. M. (1996). Both nitrogen and phosphorus limit plant production on young Hawaiian lava flows. *Biogeochemistry*, **32**, 1–14.

Ramankutty, N. & Foley, J. A. (1999). Estimating historical changes in global land cover: Croplands from 1700 to 1992. *Global Biogeochemical Cycles*, **13**, 997–1027.

Randelovic, D., Cvetkovic, V., Mihailovic, N., & Jovanovic, S. (2014). Relation between edaphic factors and vegetation development on copper mine wastes: A case study from Bor (Serbia, SE Europe). *Environmental Management*, **53**, 800–812.

Raup, H. M. (1971). The vegetational relations of weathering, frost action and patterned ground processes. *Meddelelser om Grønland*, **194**, 1–92.

Raus, Th. (1988). Vascular plant colonization and vegetation development on sea-born volcanic islands in the Aegean (Greece). *Vegetatio*, **77**, 139–147.

Rawat, G. S. (2005). Vegetation dynamics and management of *Rhinoceros* habitat in Duars of West Bengal: An ecological review. *National Academy of Science Letters – India*, **28**, 177–184.

Rebele, F. & Lehmann, C. (2002). Restoration of a landfill site in Berlin, Germany by spontaneous and directed succession. *Restoration Ecology*, **10**, 340–347.

Rebollo, S., Pérez-Camacho, L., Valencia, J., & Gómez-Sal, A. (2003). Vole mound effects and disturbance rate in a Mediterranean plant community under different grazing and irrigation regimes. *Plant Ecology*, **169**, 227–243.

Reddy, V. S. & Singh, J. S. (1993). Changes in vegetation and soil during succession following landslide disturbance in the central Himalaya. *Journal of Environmental Management*, **39**, 235–250.

Rees, D. C. & Juday, G. P. (2002). Plant species diversity on logged versus burned sites in central Alaska. *Forest Ecology and Management*, **155**, 291–302.

Řehounková, K. & Prach, K. (2006). Spontaneous vegetation succession in disused gravel-sand pits: Role of local site and landscape factors. *Journal of Vegetation Science*, **17**, 583–590.

Řehounková, K. & Prach, K. (2008). Spontaneous vegetation succession in gravel-sand pits: A potential for restoration. *Restoration Ecology*, **16**, 305–312.

Řehounková, K. & Prach, K. (2010). Life-history traits and habitat preferences of colonizing plant species in long-term spontaneous succession in abandoned gravel-sand pits. *Basic and Applied Ecology*, **11**, 45–53.

Řehounková, K., Lencová, K., & Prach, K. (2018). Spontaneous establishment of woodland during succession in a variety of central European disturbed sites. *Ecological Engineering*, **111**, 94–99.

Řehounková, K., Lencová, K., & Prach, K. (in press). Threatened vascular plant species in spontaneously revegetated post-mining sites: Paradise lost or paradise regained? *Restoration Ecology*, **27**, doi.org/10.1111/rec.13027.

Řehounková, K., Řehounek, J., & Prach, K., eds. (2012). *Near-Natural Restoration vs. Technical Reclamation of Mining Sites in the Czech Republic*. České Budějovice: USB (available at www.restoration-ecology.eu).

Řehounková, K., Čížek, L., Řehounek, J., et al. (2016). Additional disturbances as a beneficial tool for restoration of post-mining sites: A multi-taxa approach. *Environmental Science and Pollution Research*, **23**, 13745–13753.

Reice, S. R. (2003). *The Silver Lining: The Benefits of Natural Disasters*. Princeton, NJ: Princeton University Press.

Reich, P. B., Bakken, P., Carlson, D., Frelich, L. E., Friedman, S. K., & Grigal, D. F. (2001). Influence of logging, fire, and forest type on biodiversity and productivity in southern boreal forests. *Ecology*, **82**, 2731–2748.

Reid, W. V. & Miller, K. R. (1989). *Keeping Options Alive: The Scientific Basis for Conserving Biodiversity*. Washington, DC: World Resources Institute.

Reinecke, M. K., Pigot, A. L., & King, J. M. (2008). Spontaneous succession of riparian fynbos: Is unassisted recovery a viable restoration strategy? *South African Journal of Botany*, **73**, 412–420.

Reiners, W. A., Worley, I. A., & Lawrence, D. B. (1971). Plant diversity in a chronosequence at Glacier Bay, Alaska. *Ecology*, **52**, 55–69.

Reinhart, K. O., Wilson, G. W. T., & Rinella, M. J. (2012). Predicting plant responses to mycorrhizae: Integrating evolutionary history and plant traits. *Ecology Letters*, **15**, 689–695.

Rejmánek, M. (1989). Invasibility of plant communities. In J. A. Drake, H. A. Mooney, F. di Castri, R. H. Groves, & F. J. Kruger, eds., *Biological Invasions: A Global Perspective*, pp. 369–388. Chichester, UK: Wiley.

Rejmánek, M. (1999). Holocene invasions: Finally the resolution ecologists were waiting for! *Trends in Ecology and Evolution*, **14**, 8–10.

Rejmánek, M. (2000). Invasive plants: Approaches and predictions. *Austral Ecology*, **25**, 497–506.

Rejmánek, M. & Rosén, E. (1992). Influence of colonizing shrubs on species–area relationships in alvar plant communities *Journal of Vegetation Science*, **3**, 625–630.

Rejmánek, M. & Van Katwyk, K. P. (2005). Old-field succession: A bibliographic review (1901–1991). www.botanika.prf.jcu.cz/suspa/pdf/BiblioOF.pdg.

Rejmánek, M., Haagerová, R., & Haager, J. (1982). Progress of plant succession on the Parícutin Volcano: 25 years after activity ceased. *The American Midland Naturalist*, **108**, 194–201.

Rejmánek, M., Sasser, C. E., & Gosselink, J. G. (1987). Modeling of vegetation dynamics in the Mississippi River deltaic plain. *Vegetatio*, **69**, 133–140.

Renard, S. M., Gauthier, S., Fenton, N. J., Lafleur, B., & Bergeron, Y. (2016). Prescribed burning after clearcut limits paludification in black spruce boreal forest. *Forest Ecology and Management*, **359**, 147–155.

Restrepo, C. & Alvarez, N. (2006). Landslides and their contribution to land-cover changes in the Mountains of Mexico and Central America. *Biotropica*, **38**, 446–457.

Restrepo, C. & Vitousek, P. M. (2001). Landslides, alien species, and the diversity of a Hawaiian montane mesic ecosystem. *Biotropica*, **33**, 409–420.

Restrepo, C., Vitousek, P., & Neville, P. (2003). Landslides significantly alter land cover and the distribution of biomass: An example from the Ninole ridges of Hawai'i. *Plant Ecology*, **166**, 131–143.

360 · References

Rhind, P., Jones, R., & Jones, L. (2013). The impact of dune stabilization on the conservation status of sand dune systems in Wales. In M. L. Martínez, J. B. Gallego-Fernández, & P. A. Hesp, eds., *Restoration of Coastal Dunes*, pp. 125–144. New York: Springer.

Ribeiro, M. B. N., Bruna, E. M., & Mantovani, W. (2010). Influence of post-clearing treatment on the recovery of herbaceous plant communities in Amazonian secondary forests. *Restoration Ecology*, **18**, 50–58.

Richardson, S. J., Holdaway, R. J., & Carswell, F. E. (2014). Evidence for arrested successional processes after fire in the Waikare River catchment, Te Urewera. *New Zealand Journal of Ecology*, **38**, 221–229.

Ricklefs, R. E. (2000). *The Economy of Nature*. New York: Freeman.

Riedel, S. M. & Epstein, H. E. (2005). Edge effects on vegetation and soils in a Virginia old-field. *Plant and Soil*, **270**, 13–22.

Riege, D. A. & del Moral, R. (2004). Differential tree colonization of old fields in a temperate rain forest. *American Midland Naturalist*, **151**, 251–264.

Rizzo, B. & Wiken, E. (1992). Assessing the sensitivity of Canada's ecosystems to climate change. *Climatic Change*, **21**, 37–55.

Robert, E. C., Rochefort, L., & Garneau, M. (1999). Natural revegetation of two block-cut mined peatlands in eastern Canada. *Canadian Journal of Botany*, **77**, 447–459.

Roberts, M. R. (2004). Response of the herbaceous layer to natural disturbance in North American forests. *Canadian Journal of Botany*, **82**, 1273–1283.

Robertson, K. M. (2006). Distributions of tree species along point bars of 10 rivers in the southeastern US Coastal Plain. *Journal of Biogeography*, **33**, 121–132.

Robledano-Aymerich, F., Romero-Díaz, A., Belmonte-Serrato, F., Zapata-Pérez, V. M., Martínez-Hernández, C., & Martínez-López, V. (2014). Ecogeomorphological consequences of land abandonment in semiarid Mediterranean areas: Integrated assessment of physical evolution and biodiversity. *Agriculture Ecosystems & Environment*, **197**, 222–242.

Rocha, M., Santos, C. C., Damasceno, G. A., Pott, V. J., & Pott, A. (2015). Effect of fire on a monodominant floating mat of *Cyperus giganteus* Vahl in a neotropical wetland. *Brazilian Journal of Biology*, **75**, 114–124.

Rogers, B. M., Soja, A. J., Goulden, M. L., & Randerson, J. T. (2015). Influence of tree species on continental differences in boreal fires and climate feedbacks. *Nature Geoscience*, **8**, 228–234.

Rohani, S., Dullo, B., Woudwijk, W., de Hoop, P., Kooijman, A., & Grootjans, A. P. (2014). Accumulation rates of soil organic matter in wet dune slacks on the Dutch Wadden Sea islands. *Plant and Soil*, **380**, 181–191.

Rola, K., Osyczka, P., Nobis, M., & Drozd, P. (2015). How do soil factors determine vegetation structure and species richness in post-smelting dumps? *Ecological Engineering*, **75**, 332–342.

Rolim, S. G., Machado, R. E., & Pillar, V. D. (2017). Divergence in a Neotropical forest during 33 years of succession following clear-cutting. *Journal of Vegetation Science*, **28**, 495–503.

Romano, S. P. (2010). Our current understanding of the Upper Mississippi River System floodplain forest. *Hydrobiologia*, **640**, 115–124.

Romme, W. H., Whitby, T. G., Tinker, D. B., & Turner, M. G. (2016). Deterministic and stochastic processes lead to divergence in plant communities 25 years after the 1988 Yellowstone fires. *Ecological Monographs*, **86**, 327–351.

Rondina, L., Berbel, A., Cristye, T. B., *et al.* (2019). Plants of distinct successional stages have different strategies for nutrient acquisition in an Atlantic rain forest ecosystem. *International Journal of Plant Science*, **180**, 186–199.

Rood, S. B. (2006). Unusual disturbance: Forest change following a catastrophic debris flow in the Canadian Rocky Mountains. *Canadian Journal of Forest Research*, **36**, 2204–2215.

Rood, S. B. & Mahoney, J. M. (2000). Revised instream flow regulation enables cottonwood recruitment along the St. Mary River, Alberta, Canada. *Rivers*, **7**, 109–125.

Rood, S. B., Samuelson, G. M., Braatne, J. H., Gourley, C. R., Hughes, F. M. R., & Mahoney, J. M. (2005). Managing river flows to restore floodplain forests. *Frontiers in Ecology and the Environment*, **3**, 193–201.

Rosenberg, D. K., Noon, B. R., & Meslow, E. C. (1997). Biological corridors: Form, function, and efficacy. *BioScience*, **47**, 677–687.

Rothstein, D. E., Vitousek, P. M., & Simmons, B. L. (2004). An exotic tree alters decomposition and nutrient cycling in a Hawaiian montane forest. *Ecosystems*, **7**, 805–814.

Roubíčková, A., Mudrák, O., & Frouz, J. (2012). The effect of belowground herbivory by wireworms (Coleoptera: Elateridae) on performance of *Calamagrostis epigejos* (L.) Roth in post-mining sites. *European Journal of Soil Biology*, **50**, 51–55.

Roux, E. R. & Warren, M. (1963). Plant succession on abandoned fields in central Oklahoma and in Transvaal Highveld. *Ecology*, **44**, 576–583.

Roy-Bolduc, A., Laliberté, E., Boudreau, S., & Hijri, M. (2016). Strong linkage between plant and soil fungal communities along a successional coastal dune system. *FEMS Microbiology Ecology*, **92**, fiw156.

Royo, A. A., Heartsill Scalley, T., Moya, S., & Scatena, F. N. (2011). Non-arborescent vegetation trajectories following repeated hurricane disturbance: Ephemeral versus enduring responses. *Ecosphere*, **2**, article 77.

Royo, A. A., Peterson, C. J., Stanovick, J. S., & Carson, W. P. (2016). Evaluating the ecological impacts of salvage logging: Can natural and anthropogenic disturbances promote coexistence? *Ecology*, **97**, 1566–1582.

Rudgers, J. A. & Maron, J. L. (2003). Facilitation between coastal dune shrubs: A non-nitrogen fixing shrub facilitates establishment of a nitrogen-fixer. *Oikos*, **102**, 75–84.

Rufaut, C. G. & Craw, D. (2010). Geoecology of ecosystem recovery at an inactive coal mine site, New Zealand. *Environmental Earth Sciences*, **60**, 1425–1437.

Ruocco, M., Bertoni, D., Sarti, G., & Ciccarelli, D. (2014). Mediterranean coastal dune systems: Which abiotic factors have the most influence on plant communities? *Estuarine Coastal and Shelf Science*, **149**, 213–222.

Ruokolainen, L. & Salo, K. (2009). The effect of fire intensity on vegetation succession on a sub-xeric heath during ten years after wildfire. *Annales Botanici Fennici*, **46**, 30–42.

Ruprecht, E. (2005). Secondary succession in old-fields in the Transylvanian Lowland (Romania). *Preslia*, **77**, 145–157.

Ruprecht, E. (2006). Successfully recovered grassland: A promising example from Romanian old-fields. *Restoration Ecology*, **14**, 473–480.

Ruskule, A., Nikodemus, O., Kasparinskis, R., Prižavoite, D., Bojāre, D., & Brūmelis, G. (2016). Soil-vegetation interactions in abandoned farmland within the temperate region of Europe. *New Forests*, **47**, 587–605.

Russell, A. E. & Vitousek, P. M. (1997). Decomposition and potential nitrogen fixation in *Dicranopteris linearis* litter on Mauna Loa, Hawaii. *Journal of Tropical Ecology*, **13**, 579–594.

Russell, A. E., Raich, J. W., & Vitousek, P. M. (1998). The ecology of the climbing fern *Dicranopteris linearis* on windward Mauna Loa, Hawaii. *Journal of Ecology*, **86**, 765–779.

Rydgren, K., Halvorsen, R., Odland, A., & Skjerdal, G. (2011). Restoration of alpine spoil heaps: Successional rates predict vegetation recovery in 50 years. *Ecological Engineering*, **37**, 294–301.

Rydgren, K., Halvorsen, R., Töpper, J. P., Auestad, I., Hamre, L. N., Jongejans, E., & Sulavik, J. (2018). Advancing restoration ecology: A new approach to predict time to recovery. *Journal of Applied Ecology*, **56**, 225–234.

Rydlová, J. & Vosátka, M. (2001). Associations of dominant plant species with arbuscular mycorrhizal fungi during vegetation development on coal mine spoil banks. *Folia Geobotanica*, **36**, 85–97.

Saccone, P., Pagès, J.-P., Girel, J., Burn, J.-J., & Michalet, R. (2010). *Acer negundo* invasion along a successional gradient: Early direct facilitation by native pioneers and late indirect facilitation by conspecifics. *New Phytologist*, **187**, 831–842.

Safford, H. D., Rejmánek, M., & Hadač, E. (2001). Species pools and the "humpback" model of plant species diversity: An empirical analysis at a relevant spatial scale. *Oikos*, **95**, 282–290.

Sakai, A., Sakai, T., Kuramoto, S., & Sato, S. (2010). Soil seed banks in a mature Hinoki (*Chamaecyparis obtusa* Endl.) plantation and initial process of secondary succession after clearcutting in southwestern Japan. *Journal of Forest Research*, **15**, 316–327.

Sakio, H. (1997). Effects of natural disturbance on the regeneration of riparian forests in Chibichu Mountains, central Japan. *Plant Ecology*, **132**, 181–185.

Sams, M. A., Lai, H. R., Bonser, S. P., *et al.* (2017). Landscape context explains changes in the functional diversity of regenerating forests better than climate or species richness. *Global Ecology and Biogeography*, **26**, 1165–1176.

Samuels, C. L. & Drake, J. A. (1997). Divergent perspectives on community convergence. *Trends in Ecology and Evolution*, **12**, 427–432.

Santana, V. M., Baeza, M. J., Marrs, R. H., & Vallejo, V. R. (2010). Old-field secondary succession in SE Spain: Can fire divert it? *Plant Ecology*, **211**, 337–349.

Sarkar, A., Asaeda, T., Wang, Q., & Rashid, Md. H. (2016). Arbuscular mycorrhizal association for growth and nutrients assimilation of *Phragmites japonica* and *Polygonum cuspidatum* plants growth on river bank soil. *Communications in Soil Science and Plant Analysis*, **47**, 87–100.

Sarmiento, L., Llambi, L. D., Escalona, A., & Marquez, N. (2003). Vegetation patterns, regeneration rates and divergence in an old-field succession of the high tropical Andes. *Plant Ecology*, **166**, 63–74.

Sarneel, J. M., Kardol, P., & Nilsson, C. (2016). The importance of priority effects for riparian plant community dynamics. *Journal of Vegetation Science*, **27**, 658–667.

Sax, D. F. (2001). Latitudinal gradients and geographic ranges of exotic species: Implications for biogeography. *Journal of Biogeography*, **28**, 139–150.

Scatena, F. N., Moya, S., Estrada, C., & Chinea, J. D. (1996). The first five years in the reorganization of aboveground biomass and nutrient use following Hurricane Hugo in the Bisley Experimental Watersheds, Luquillo Experimental Forest, Puerto Rico. *Biotropica*, **28**, 424–440.

Schaffhauser, A., Curt, T., Vela, E., & Tatoni, T. (2012). Recurrent fires and environment shape the vegetation in *Quercus suber* L. woodlands and maquis. *Comptes Rendus Biologies*, **335**, 424–434.

Schimel, D. (2013). *Climate and Ecosystems*. Princeton, NJ: Princeton University Press.

Schimel, J. P., Cates, R. G., & Ruess, R. (1998). The role of balsam poplar secondary chemicals in controlling soil nutrient dynamics through succession in the Alaskan taiga. *Biogeochemistry*, **42**, 221–234.

Schipper, L. A., Degens, B. P., Sparlling, G. P., & Duncan, L. (2001). Changes in microbial heterotrophic diversity along five plant successional sequences. *Soil Biology and Biochemistry*, **33**, 2093–2103.

Schmidt, W. & Brubach, M. (1993). Plant-distribution patterns during early succession on an artifical protosoil *Journal of Vegetation Science*, **4**, 247–254.

Schnitzler, A., Hale, B. W., & Alsum, E. (2005). Biodiversity of floodplain forests in Europe and eastern North America: A comparative study of the Rhine and the Mississippi Valleys. *Biodiversity and Conservation*, **14**, 97–117.

Schoenfelder, A. C., Bishop, J. G., Martinson, H. M., & Fagan, W. F. (2010). Resource use efficiency and community effects of invasive *Hypochaeris radicata* (Asteraceae) during primary succession. *American Journal of Botany*, **97**, 1772–1792.

Schroeder, T. A., Cohen, W. B., & Yang, Z. Q. (2007). Patterns of forest regrowth following clearcutting in western Oregon as determined from a Landsat timeseries. *Forest Ecology and Management*, **243**, 259–273.

Schuler, T. M. & Gillespie, A. R. (2000). Temporal patterns of woody species diversity in a central Appalachian forest from 1856 to 1997. *Journal of the Torrey Botanical Society*, **127**, 149–161.

Schulze, E. D., Wirth, C., Mollicone, D., & Ziegler, W. (2005). Succession after stand replacing disturbances by fire, wind throw, and insects in the dark Taiga of Central Siberia. *Oecologia*, **146**, 77–88.

Schulze, E. D., Bouriaud, L., Bussler, H., *et al.* (2014). Opinion Paper: Forest management and biodiversity. *Web Ecology*, **14**, 3–10.

Schumacher, A. (1997). Die Vegetationsentwicklung auf dem Bergrutsch am Hirschkopf (Baden-Württemberg): Sukzession auf Kalkschutt und Mergelrohböden (Vegetation development on the Hirschkopf landslide: Succession on raw calcareous and marly soils). *Forstwissenschaftliches Centralblatt*, **116**, 232–242.

Schuster, R. L. & Highland, L. M. (2007). Overview of the effects of mass wasting on the natural environment. *Environmental & Engineering Geoscience*, **13**, 25–44.

Schwilk, D. W., Keeley, J. E., & Bond, W. J. (1997). The intermediate disturbance hypothesis does not explain fire and diversity pattern in fynbos. *Plant Ecology*, **132**, 77–84.

Sciandrello, S., Tomaselli, G., & Minissale, P. (2015). The role of natural vegetation in the analysis of the spatio-temporal changes of coastal dune system: A case study in Sicily. *Journal of Coastal Conservation*, **19**, 199–212.

Scott, A. J. & Morgan, J. W. (2012). Early life-history stages drive community reassembly in Australian old-fields. *Journal of Vegetation Science*, **23**, 721–731.

Šebelíková, L., Řehounková, K., & Prach, K. (2016). Spontaneous revegetation vs. forestry reclamation in post-mining sand pits. *Environmental Science and Pollution Research*, **23**, 13598–13605.

Šebelíková, L., Csicsek, G., Kirmer, A., *et al.* (2019). Succession vs. reclamation – Vegetation development in coal mining spoil heaps across Central Europe. *Land Degradation and Development*, **10**, 153–164.

Sedláková, I. & Chytrý, M. (1999). Regeneration patterns in a Central European dry heathland: Effects of burning, sod-cutting and cutting. *Plant Ecology*, **143**, 77–87.

Seiwa, K., Miwa, Y., Akasaka, S., *et al.* (2013). Landslide-facilitated species diversity in a beech-dominant forest. *Ecological Research*, **28**, 29–41.

SER (2004). *The SER International Primer on Ecological Restoration*. Tuscon, AZ: Society for Ecological Restoration International.

Serong, M. & Lill, A. (2008). The timing and nature of floristic and structural changes during secondary succession in wet forests. *Australian Journal of Botany*, **56**, 220–231.

Settele, J., Margules, C., Poschlod, P., & Henle, R., eds. (1996). *Species Survival in Fragmented Landscapes*. Dordrecht: Kluwer.

Sewerniak, P. & Jankowski, M. (2017). Topographically-controlled site conditions drive vegetation pattern on inland dunes in Poland. *Acta Oecologica-International Journal of Ecology*, **82**, 52–60.

Shaffer, G. P., Sasser, C. E., Gosselink, J. G., & Rejmánek, M. (1992). Vegetation dynamics in the emerging Atchafalaya Delta, Louisiana, USA. *Journal of Ecology*, **80**, 677–687.

Shafroth, P. B., Friedman, J. M., Auble, G. T., Scott, M. L., & Braatne, J. H. (2002). Potential responses of riparian vegetation to dam removal: Dam removal generally causes changes to aspects of the physical environment that influence the establishment and growth of riparian vegetation. *BioScience*, **52**, 703–712.

Shanahan, M., Harrison, R. D., Yamuna, R., Boen, W., & Thornton, I. W. B. (2001). Colonization of an island volcano, Long Island, Papua New Guinea, and an emergent island, Motmot, in its caldera lake. V. Colonization by figs (*Ficus* spp.), their dispersers and pollinators. *Journal of Biogeography*, **28**, 1365–1377.

Sharpe, J. M. & Shiels, A. B. (2014). Understory fern community structure, growth and spore production responses to a large-scale hurricane experiment in a Puerto Rico rainforest. *Forest Ecology and Management*, **332**, 75–86.

Shenoy, A., Kielland, K., & Johnstone, J. F. (2013). Effects of fire severity on plant nutrient uptake reinforce alternate pathways of succession in boreal forests. *Plant Ecology*, **214**, 587–596.

Shields, L. M. & Crispin, J. (1956). Vascular vegetation of a recent volcanic area in New Mexico. *Ecology*, **37**, 341–351.

Shiels, A. B. (2002). Bird perches and soil amendments as revegetation techniques for landslides in Puerto Rico. MS thesis, Department of Biological Sciences, University of Nevada, Las Vegas, NV.

Shiels, A. B. & Walker, L. R. (2003). Bird perches increase forest seeds on Puerto Rican landslides. *Restoration Ecology*, **11**, 457–465.

Shiels, A. B. & Walker, L. R. (2013). Landslides cause spatial and temporal gradients at multiple scales in the Luquillo Mountains, Puerto Rico. In *Ecological Gradient Analyses in a Tropical Ecosystem*, eds. G. González, M. Willig, and R. Waide. *Ecological Bulletins*, **54**, 211–221.

Shiels, A. B., González, G., & Willig, M. R. (2014). Responses to canopy loss and debris deposition in a tropical forest ecosystem: Synthesis from an experimental manipulation simulating effects of hurricane disturbance. *Forest Ecology and Management*, **332**, 124–133.

Shiels, A. B., Walker, L. R., & Thompson, D. B. (2006). Organic matter inputs create variable resource patches on Puerto Rican landslides. *Plant Ecology*, **195**, 165–178.

Shiels, A. B., Gonzalez, G., Lodge, D. J., Willig, M. R., & Zimmerman, J. K. (2015). Cascading effects of canopy opening and debris deposition from a large-scale hurricane experiment in a tropical rain forest. *BioScience*, **65**, 871–881.

Shiels, A. B., West, C. A., Weiss, L., Klawinski, P. D., & Walker, L. R. (2008). Soil factors predict initial plant colonization on Puerto Rican landslides. *Plant Ecology*, **195**, 165–178.

Shiels, A. B., Zimmerman, J. K., García-Montiel, D. C., et al. (2010). Plant responses to simulated hurricane impacts in a subtropical wet forest, Puerto Rico. *Journal of Ecology*, **98**, 659–673.

Shimizu, Y. (2005). A vegetation change during a 20-year period following two continuous disturbances (mass-dieback of pine trees and typhoon damage) in the *Pinus-Schima* secondary forest on Chichijima in the Ogasawara (Bonin) Islands: Which won, advanced saplings or new seedlings? *Ecological Research*, **20**, 708–725.

Shimokawa, E. (1984). A natural process of recovery of vegetation on landslide scars and landslide periodicity in forested drainage basins. In C. L. O'Laughlin & A. J. Pierce, eds., *Symposium on Effects of Forest Land Use on Erosion and Slope Stability*, pp. 99–107. Honolulu: University of Hawaii, Honolulu, East-West Center.

Shooner, S., Chisholm, C., & Davies, T. J. (2015). The phylogenetics of succession can guide restoration: An example from abandoned mine sites in the subarctic. *Journal of Applied Ecology*, **52**, 1509–1517.

Shugart, H. H. & West, D. C. (1980). Forest succession models. *BioScience*, **30**, 308–313.

Shugart, H. H., Leemans, R., & Bonan, G. B., eds. (1992). *A Systems Analysis of the Global Boreal Forest*. Cambridge: Cambridge University Press.

Shumway, S. W. (2000). Facilitative effects of a sand dune shrub on species growing beneath the shrub canopy. *Oecologia*, **124**, 138–148.

Sidle, R. C. & Ochiai, H. (2006). *Landslides: Processes, Prediction, and Land Use*. Water Resources Monograph Series, Volume 18. Washington, DC: American Geophysical Union.

Sikes, B. A., Maherali, H. Z., & Klironomos, J. N. (2012). Arbuscular mycorrhizal fungal communities change among three stages of primary sand dune succession but do not alter plant growth. *Oikos*, **121**, 1791–1800.

Silva, J. S., Catry, F. X., Moreira, F., Lopes, T., Forte, T., & Bugalho, M. N. (2014). Effects of deer on the post-fire recovery of a Mediterranean plant community in Central Portugal. *Journal of Forest Research*, **19**, 276–284.

Silva, L. C. R., Correa, R. S., Doane, T. A., Pereira, E. I. P., & Horwath, W. R. (2013). Unprecedented carbon accumulation in mined soils: The synergistic effect of resource input and plant species invasion. *Ecological Applications*, **23**, 1345–1356.

Silva, L. C. R., Hoffmann, W. A., Rossatto, D. R., Haridasan, M., Franco, A. C., & Horwath, W. R. (2013). Can savannas become forests? A coupled analysis of nutrient stocks and fire thresholds in central Brazil. *Plant and Soil*, **373**, 829–842.

Silver, W. & Vogt, K. (1993). Fine root dynamics following single and multiple disturbances in a subtropical wet forest ecosystem. *Journal of Ecology*, **81**, 729–738.

Silver, W. L., Scatena, F. N., Johnson, A. H., Siccama, T. G., & Watt, F. (1996). At what temporal scales does disturbance affect belowground nutrient pools? *Biotropica*, **28**, 441–457.

Sklenář, P., Kovář, P., Palice, Z., Stančík, D., & Soldán, Z. (2010). Primary succession of high-altitude Andean vegetation on lahars of Volcán Cotopaxi, Ecuador. *Phytocoenologia*, **40**, 15–28.

Sklenička, P. & Molnárová, K. (2010). Visual perception of habitats adopted for post-mining landscape rehabilitation. *Environmental Management*, **46**, 424–435.

Skłodowski, J. W., Buszyniewicz, J., & Domański, M. (2014). Spontaniczne odnowienie drzewostanu zaburzonego huraganem w lipcu 2002 roku [Spontaneous regeneration of a stand disturbed by a hurricane in July 2002]. *Sylwan*, **158**, 499–508.

Skousen, J. G., Johnson, C. D., & Garbutt, K. (1994). Natural revegetation of 15 abandoned mine land sites in West-Virginia. *Journal of Environmental Quality*, **23**, 1224–1230.

Slocum, M. G., Aide, T. M., Zimmerman, J. K., & Navarro, L. (2004). Natural regeneration of subtropical montane forest after clearing fern thickets in the Dominican Republic. *Journal of Tropical Ecology*, **20**, 483–486.

Smale, M. C. (1990). Ecological role of buddleia (*Buddleja davidii*) in streambeds in Te Urewera National Park. *New Zealand Journal of Ecology*, **14**, 1–6.

Smale, M. C., McLeod, M., & Smale, P. N. (1997). Vegetation and soil recovery on shallow landslide scars in Tertiary hill country, East Cape region, New Zealand. *New Zealand Journal of Ecology*, **21**, 31–41.

Small, C. & Naumann, T. (2001). The global distribution of human population and recent volcanism. Global Environmental Change Part B. *Environmental Hazards*, **3**, 93–109.

Smirnova, E., Bergeron, Y., & Brais, S. (2008). Influence of fire intensity on structure and composition of jack pine stands in the boreal forest of Quebec: Live trees, understory vegetation and dead wood dynamics. *Forest Ecology and Management*, **255**, 2916–2927.

Smith, G. F., Nicholas, N. S., & Zedaker, S. M. (1997). Succession dynamics in a maritime forest following Hurricane Hugo and fuel reduction burns. *Forest Ecology and Management*, **95**, 275–283.

Smith, R. & Olff, H. (1998). Woody species colonisation in relation to habitat productivity. *Plant Ecology*, **139**, 203–209.

Smith, R. B., Commandeur, P. R., & Ryan, M. W. (1986). Soils, vegetation, and forest growth on landslides and surrounding logged and old-growth areas on the Queen Charlotte Islands. Land Management Report Number 41. British Columbia Ministry of Forests, Victoria.

Smith, S. M. & Lee, W. G. (1984). Vegetation and soil development on a Holocene river terrace sequence, Arawata Valley, South Westland, New Zealand. *New Zealand Journal of Science*, **27**, 187–196.

Smuts, J. C. (1926). *Holism and Evolution*. New York: MacMillan.

Sojneková, M. & Chytrý, M. (2015). From arable land to species-rich semi-natural grasslands: Succession in abandoned fields in a dry region of central Europe. *Ecological Engineering*, **77**, 373–381.

Sommerville, P., Mark, A. F., & Wilson, J. B. (1982). Plant succession on moraines of the upper Dart Valley, southern South Island, New Zealand. *New Zealand Journal of Botany*, **20**, 227–244.

Somodi, I., Molnár, Zs., Czúcz, B., et al. (2017). Implementation and application of multiple potential natural vegetation models: A case study of Hungary. *Journal of Vegetation Science*, **28**, 1260–1269.

Soussana, J.-F., Maire, V., Gross, N., et al. (2012). Gemini: A grassland model simulating the role of plant traits for community dynamics and ecosystem functioning. Parameterization and evaluation. *Ecological Modelling*, **231**, 134–145.

Southon, G. E., Field, C., Caporn, S., Britton, A., & Power, S. (2013). Nitrogen deposition reduces plant diversity and alters ecosystem functioning: Field-scale evidence from a nationwide survey of UK heathlands. *PLoS ONE*, **8**, 59031.

Sparrius, L. B., Kooijman, A. M., Riksen, M. P. J. M., & Sevink, J. (2013). Effect of geomorphology and nitrogen deposition on rate of vegetation succession in inland drift sands. *Applied Vegetation Science*, **16**, 379–389.

Spellman, B. T. & Wurtz, T. L. (2011). Invasive sweetclover (*Melilotus alba*) impacts native seedling recruitment along floodplains of interior Alaska. *Biological Invasions*, **13**, 1779–1790.

Spellman, K. V., Mulder, C. P. H., & Hollingsworth, T. N. (2014). Susceptibility of burned black spruce (*Picea mariana*) forests to non-native plant invasions in interior Alaska. *Biological Invasions*, **16**, 1879–1895.

Stadler, J., Trefflich, A., Brandl, R., & Klotz, S. (2007). Spontaneous regeneration of dry grasslands on set-aside fields. *Biodiversity and Conservation*, **16**, 621–630.

Standish, R. J., Cramer, V. A., Wild, S. L., & Hobbs, R. J. (2007). Seed dispersal and recruitment limitation are barriers to native recolonization of old-fields in western Australia. *Journal of Applied Ecology*, **44**, 435–445.

St. John, M. G., Bellingham, P. J., Walker, L. R., et al. (2012). Loss of a dominant nitrogen-fixing shrub in primary succession: Consequences for plant and below-ground communities. *Journal of Ecology*, **100**, 1074–1084.

Stokes, A., Lucas, A., & Jouneau, L. (2007). Plant biomechanical strategies in response to frequent disturbance: Uprooting of *Phyllostachys nidularia* (Poaceae) growing on landslide-prone slopes in Sichuan, China. *American Journal of Botany*, **94**, 1129–1136.

Stokes, A., Atger, C., Bengough, A. G., Fourcaud, T., & Sidle, R. C. (2009). Desirable plant root traits for protecting natural and engineered slopes against landslides. *Plant and Soil*, **324**, 1–30.

Stokes, A., Douglas, G. B., Thierry, F., et al. (2014). Ecological mitigation of hillslope instability: Ten key issues facing researchers and practitioners. *Plant Soil*, **377**, 1–23.

Stover, M. E. & Marks, P. L. (1998). Successional vegetation on abandoned cultivated and pastured land in Tompkins County, New York. *Journal of the Torrey Botanical Society*, **125**, 150–164.

Stromberg, J. C., Lite, S. J., Marler, R., et al. (2007). Altered stream-flow regimes and invasive species: The *Tamarix* case. *Global Ecology and Biogeography*, **16**, 381–393.

Stromberg, M. R. & Griffin, J. R. (1996). Long-term patterns in coastal California grasslands in relation to cultivation, gophers, and grazing. *Ecological Applications*, **6**, 1189–1211.

Strong, W. L. (2009). *Populus tremuloides* Michx. postfire stand dynamics in the northern boreal-cordilleran ecoclimatic region of central Yukon Territory, Canada. *Forest Ecology and Management*, **258**, 1110–1120.

Stubbs, W. J. & Wilson, J. B. (2004). Evidence for limiting similarity in a sand dune community. *Journal of Ecology*, **92**, 557–567.

Sturm, M., Racine, C., & Tape, K. (2001). Increasing shrub abundance in the Arctic. *Nature*, **411**, 546–547.

Suárez, E., Orndahl, K., & Godwin, K. (2015). Lava flows and moraines as corridors for early plant colonization of glacier forefronts on tropical volcanoes. *Biotropica*, **47**, 645–649.

Suazo-Ortuño, I., Urbina-Cardona, J. N., Lara-Uribe, N., et al. (2018). Impact of a hurricane on the herpetofaunal assemblages of a successional chronosequence in a tropical dry forest. *Biotropica*, **50**, 649–663.

Sugg, P. M. & Edwards, J. S. (1998). Pioneer aeolian community development on pyroclastic flows after the eruption of Mount St. Helens, Washington, U.S.A. *Arctic and Alpine Research*, **30**, 400–407.

Sulieman, H. M. (2014). Natural regeneration potential of abandoned agricultural land in the southern Gadarif Region, Sudan: Implications for conservation. *African Journal of Ecology*, **52**, 217–227.

Svoboda, J. & Henry, G. H. R. (1987). Succession in marginal arctic environments. *Arctic and Alpine Research*, **19**, 373–384.

Swanson, F. J., Kratz, T. K., Caine, N., & Woodmansee, R. G. (1988). Landform effects on ecosystem patterns and processes. *BioScience*, **38**, 92–98.

Swanson, M. E., Franklin, J. F., Beschtaet, R. L., Crisafulli, Ch. M., & DellaSala, D. A. (2011). The forgotten stage of forest succession: Early-successional ecosystems on forest sites. *Frontiers in Ecology and the Environment*, **9**, 117–125.

Syers, J. K. & Walker, T. W. (1969). Phosphorus transformations in a chronosequences of soils developed on wind-blown sand in New Zealand. *Journal of Soil Science*, **20**, 57–64.

Sykes, M. T. & Wilson, J. B. (1989). The effect of salinity on the growth of some New Zealand sand dune species. *Acta Botanica Neerlandica*, **38**, 173–182.

Syphard, A. D., Radeloff, V. C., Hawbaker, T. J., & Stewart, S. I. (2009). Conservation threats due to human-caused increases in fire frequency in Mediterranean-climate ecosystems. *Conservation Biology*, **23**, 758–769.

Szarek-Lukaszewska, G. (2009). Vegetation of reclaimed and spontaneously vegetated Zn-Pb mine wastes in Southern Poland. *Polish Journal of Environmental Studies*, **18**, 717–733.

Tagawa, H. (1964). A study of the volcanic vegetation in Sakurajima, south-west Japan. I. Dynamics of the vegetation. *Memoirs of the Faculty of Science, Kyushu University, Series E (Biology)*, **3**, 166–228.

Tagawa, H., Suzuki, E., Partomikhardio, T., & Suriadarma, A. (1985). Vegetation and succession on the Krakatau Islands, Indonesia. *Vegetatio*, **60**, 131–145.

Takenaka, A., Washitani, I., Kuramoto, N., & Inoue, K. (1996). Life history and demographic features of *Aster kantoensis*, an endangered local endemic of floodplains. *Biological Conservation*, **78**, 345–352.

Takeuchi, K. & Shimano, K. (2009). Vegetation succession at the abandoned Ogushi sulfur mine, central Japan. *Landscape and Ecological Engineering*, **5**, 33–44.

Talbot, S. S., Talbot, S. L., & Walker, L. R. (2010). Post-eruption legacy effects and their implications for long-term recovery of the vegetation on Kasatochi Island, Alaska. *Arctic, Antarctic & Alpine Research*, **42**, 285–296.

Tang, C. Q., Zhao, M. H., Li, X. S., Ohsawa, M., & Ou, X. K. (2010). Secondary succession of plant communities in a subtropical mountainous region of SW China. *Ecological Research*, **25**, 149–161.

Tanner, E. V. J. & Bellingham, P. J. (2006). Less diverse forest is more resistant to hurricane disturbance: Evidence from montane rain forests in Jamaica. *Journal of Ecology*, **94**, 1003–1010.

Tárrega, R., Luiscalabuig, E., & Alonso, I. (1995). Comparison of the regeneration after burning, cutting and plowing in a *Cistus ladanifer* shrubland. *Vegetatio*, **120**, 59–67.

Tatoni, T. & Roche, P. (1994). Comparison of old-field and forest revegetation dynamics in Provence. *Journal of Vegetation Science*, **5**, 295–302.

Tatoni, T., Magnin, F., Bonin, G., & Vaudour, J. (1994). Secondary succession on abandoned cultivation terraces in Provence. 1. Vegetation and soil. *Acta Oecologica-International Journal of Ecology*, **15**, 431–447.

Tavşanoğlu, C. & Gürkan, B. (2014). Long-term post-fire dynamics of co-occurring woody species in *Pinus brutia* forests: The role of regeneration mode. *Plant Ecology*, **215**, 355–365.

Taylor, A. R. & Chen, H. Y. H. (2011). Multiple successional pathways of boreal forest stands in central Canada. *Ecography*, **34**, 208–219.

Taylor, B. W. (1957). Plant succession on recent volcanoes in Papua. *Journal of Ecology*, **45**, 233–243.

Teixeira, L. H., Weisser, W., & Ganade, G. (2016). Facilitation and sand burial affect plant survival during restoration of a tropical coastal sand dune degraded by tourist cars. *Restoration Ecology*, **24**, 390–397.

Temperton, V. M., Hobbs, R. J., Nuttle T., & Halle, S., eds. (2004). *Assembly Rules and Restoration Ecology: Bridging the Gap between Theory and Practice*. Washington, DC: Island Press.

Tepley, A. J., Swanson, F. J., & Spies, T. A. (2014). Post-fire tree establishment and early cohort development in conifer forests of the western Cascades of Oregon, USA. *Ecosphere*, **5**, article 80.

Teramoto, Y., Shimokawa, E., Ezaki, T., Chun, K.-W., Kim, S.-W., & Lee, Y.-T. (2017). Influence of volcanic activity on vegetation succession and growth environment on the hillslope of Sakurajima Volcano in southern Kyushu, Japan. *Journal of Forest Research*, **28**, 309–317.

Terborgh, J. & Petren, K. (1991). Development of habitat structure through succession in an Amazonian floodplain forest. In S. S. Bell, E. D. McCoy, & H. R. Mushinsky, eds., *Habitat Structure: The Physical Environment of Objects in Space*, pp. 28–46. London: Routledge, Chapman & Hall.

Terborgh, J., Nuñez, N. H., Loayza, P. A., & Valverde, F. C. (2017). Gaps contribute tree diversity to a tropical floodplain forest. *Ecology*, **98**, 2895–2903.

Terwei, A., Zerbe, S., Zeileis, A., *et al.* (2013). Which are the factors controlling tree seedling establishment in North Italian floodplain forests invaded by non-native tree species? *Forest Ecology and Management*, **304**, 192–203.

Teste, F. P. & Laliberté, E. (2019). Plasticity in root symbioses following shifts in soil nutrient availability during long-term ecosystem development. *Journal of Ecology*, **107**, 633–649.

Tezuka, Y. (1961). Development of vegetation in relation to soil formation in the volcanic island of Oshima, Izu, Japan. *Japanese Journal of Botany*, **17**, 371–402.

Thevs, N., Zerbe, S., Peper, J., & Succow, M. (2008). Vegetation and vegetation dynamics in the Tarim River floodplain of continental-arid Xinjiang, NW China. *Phytocoenologia*, **38**, 65–84.

Thomas, D. N., Fogg, G. E., Convey, P., *et al.* (2008). *The Biology of Polar Regions*. Oxford: Oxford University Press.

Thompson, K., Bakker, J. P., & Bekker, R. M. (1996). *The Soil Seed Banks of North West Europe: Methodology, Density and Longevity*. Cambridge: Cambridge University Press.

Thoreau, H. D. (1860). *Succession of Forest Trees. Massachusetts Board of Agriculture Eighth Annual Report*. Boston: Wm. White Printer. Not seen but cited in McIntosh (1999).

Thornton, I. (1996). *Krakatau: The Destruction and Reassembly of an Island Ecosystem*. Cambridge, MA: Harvard University Press.

Thornton, I. W. B., Cooks, S., Edwards, J. S., *et al.* (2001). Colonization of an island volcano, Long Island, Papua New Guinea, an emergent island, Motmot, in its caldera lake. VII. Overview and discussion. *Journal of Biogeography*, **28**, 1389–1410.

Thrall, P. H., Hochberg, M. E., Burdon, J. J., & Bever, J. D. (2007). Coevolution of symbiotic mutualists and parasites in a community context. *Trends in Ecology and Evolution*, **22**, 120–126.

Thuiller, W., Albert, C., Araujo, M. B., *et al.* (2008). Predicting global change impacts on plant species' distributions: Future challenges. *Perspectives in Plant Ecology, Evolution and Systematics*, **9**, 137–152.

Tilman, D. (1988). *Plant Strategies and the Dynamics and Structure of Plant Communities*. Princeton, NJ: Princeton University Press.

Timoney, K. P., Peterson, G., & Wein, R. (1997). Vegetation development of boreal riparian plant communities after flooding, fire, and logging, Peace River, Canada. *Forest Ecology and Management*, **93**, 101–120.

Tischew, S., Baasch, A., Grunert, H., & Kirmer, A. (2014). How to develop native plant communities in heavily altered ecosystems: Examples from large-scale surface mining in Germany. *Applied Vegetation Science*, **17**, 288–301.

Tisdale, E. W., Fosberg, M. A., & Poulton, C. E. (1966). Vegetation and soil development on a recently glaciated area near Mount Robson, British Columbia. *Ecology*, **47**, 517–523.

Tissier, E. J., McLoughlin, P. D., Sheard, J. W., & Johnstone, J. F. (2013). Distribution of vegetation along environmental gradients on Sable Island, Nova Scotia. *Écoscience*, **20**, 361–372.

Titus, J. H. (2009). Nitrogen-fixers *Alnus* and *Lupinus* influence soil characteristics but not colonization by later successional species in primary succession on Mount St. Helens. *Plant Ecology*, **203**, 289–301.

Titus, J. H. & Bishop, J. (2014). Propagule limitation and competition with nitrogen fixers limit conifer colonization during primary succession. *Journal of Vegetation Science*, **25**, 990–1003.

Titus, J. H. & del Moral, R. (1998). Vesicular-arbuscular mycorrhizae influence Mount St. Helens pioneer species in greenhouse experiments. *Oikos*, **81**, 495–510.

Titus, J. H. & Tsuyuzaki, S. (2003a). Distribution of plants in relation to microsites on recent volcanic substrates on Mount Koma, Hokkaido, Japan. *Ecological Research*, **18**, 91–98.

Titus, J. H. & Tsuyuzaki, S. (2003b). Influence of a non-native invasive tree on primary succession at Mt. Kona, Hokkaido, Japan. *Plant Ecology*, **169**, 307–315.

Titus, J. H., del Moral, R., & Gamiet, S. (1998). The distribution of vesicular-arbuscular mycorrhizae on Mount St. Helens, Washington. *Madroño*, **45**, 162–170.

Titus, J. H., Titus, P. J., & del Moral, R. (1999). Wetland development in primary and secondary successional substrates fourteen years after the eruption of Mount St. Helens, Washington, USA. *Northwest Science*, **73**, 186–204.

Tiwari, A. K., Mehta, J. S., Goel, O. P., & Singh, J. S. (1986). Geo-forestry of landslide-affected areas in a part of Central Himalaya. *Environmental Conservation*, **13**, 299–309.

Tobias, M. M. (2015). California foredune plant biogeomorphology. *Physical Geography*, **36**, 19–33.

Tognetti, P. M., Chaneton, E. J., Omacini, M., Trebino, H. J., & Leon, R. J. C. (2010). Exotic vs. native plant dominance over 20 years of old-field succession on set-aside farmland in Argentina. *Biological Conservation*, **143**, 2494–2503.

Toh, I., Gillespie, M., & Lamb, D. (1999). The role of isolated trees in facilitating tree seedling recruitment at a degraded sub-tropical rainforest site. *Restoration Ecology*, **7**, 288–297.

Török, P., Kelemen, A., Valkó, O., Deák, B., Lukács, B., & Tóthmérész, B. (2011). Lucerne-dominated fields recover native grass diversity without intensive management actions. *Journal of Applied Ecology*, **48**, 257–264.

Tovilla-Hernández, C., de la Lanza, G. E., & Orihuela-Belmonte, D. E. (2001). Impact of logging on a mangrove swamp in South Mexico: Cost/benefit analysis. *Revista de Biología Tropical*, **49**, 571–580.

Trabaud, L. & Campant, C. (1991). Problem of naturally colonizing the Salzmann Pine, *Pinus nigra* Arn. ssp. *Salzmannii* (Dunal) Franco after fire. *Biological Conservation*, **58**, 329–343.

Trefilova, O. V. & Efimov, D. Y. (2015). Changes in the vegetation cover and soils under natural overgrowth of felled areas in fir forests of the Yenisei Ridge. *Eurasian Soil Science*, **48**, 792–801.

Triisberg, T., Karofeld, E., Liira, J., Orru, M., Ramst, R., & Paal, J. (2014). Microtopography and the properties of residual peat are convenient indicators for restoration planning of abandoned extracted peatlands. *Restoration Ecology*, **22**, 31–39.

Tropek, R., Hejda, M., Kadlec, R., et al. (2013). Local and landscape factors affecting communities of plants and diurnal Lepidoptera in black coal spoil heaps: Implications for restoration management. *Ecological Engineering*, **57**, 252–260.

Tropek, R., Kadlec, T., Karešová, P., et al. (2010). Spontaneous succession in limestone quarries as an effective restoration tool for endangered arthropods and plants. *Journal of Applied Ecology*, **47**, 139–147.

Tsuyuzaki, S. (1989). Analysis of revegetation dynamics on the Volcano Usu, Northern Japan, deforested by 1977–1978 eruptions. *American Journal of Botany*, **68**, 1468–1477.

Tsuyuzaki, S. (1994). Fate of plants from buried seeds on Volcano Usu, Japan, after the 1977–1978 eruptions. *American Journal of Botany*, **81**, 395–399.

Tsuyuzaki, S. (1995). Vegetation recovery patterns in early volcanic succession. *Journal of Plant Research*, **108**, 241–248.

Tsuyuzaki, S. (2009). Causes of plant community divergence in the early stages of volcanic succession. *Journal of Vegetation Science*, **20**, 959–969.

Tsuyuzaki, S. & del Moral, R. (1995). Species attributes in early primary succession on volcanoes. *Journal of Vegetation Science*, **6**, 517–522.

Tsuyuzaki, S. & Haruki, M. (1996). Tree regeneration patterns on Mount Usu, northern Japan, since the 1977–78 eruptions. *Vegetatio*, **126**, 191–198.

Tsvuura, Z. & Lawes, M. J. (2016). Light availability drives tree seedling success in a subtropical coastal dune forest in South Africa. *South African Journal of Botany*, **104**, 91–97.

Tu, M., Titus, J. H., del Moral, R., & Tsuyuzaki, S. (1998). Composition and dynamics of wetland seed banks on Mount St. Helens, Washington, USA. *Folia Geobotanica*, **33**, 3–16.

Tucker, C. J., Dregne, H. E., & Newcomb, W. W. (1991). Expansion and contraction of the Sahara Desert from 1980 to 1990. *Science*, **253**, 299–300.

Tulande-M., E., Barrera-Cataño, J. I., Alonso-Malaver, C. E., Moranted-Ariza, C., & Basto, S. (2018). Soil macrofauna in areas with different ages after *Pinus patula* clearcutting. *Universitas Scientiarum*, **23**, 383–417.

Tullus, T., Tullus, A., Roosaluste, E., Kaasik, A., Lutter, R., & Tullus, H. (2013). Understorey vegetation in young naturally regenerated and planted birch (*Betula* spp.) stands on abandoned agricultural land. *New Forests*, **44**, 591–611.

Türkmen, N. & Düzenli, A. (2005). Changes in floristic composition of *Quercus coccifera* macchia after fire in the Qukurova region (Turkey). *Annales Botanici Fennici*, **42**, 453–460.

Turner, B. L., Zemunik, G., Laliberté, E., Drake, J. J., Jones, F. A., & Saltonstall, K. (2019). Contrasting patterns of plant and microbial diversity during long-term ecosystem development. *Journal of Ecology*, **107**, 606–621.

Turner, T. R., Duke, S. D., Fransen, B. R., *et al.* (2010). Landslide densities associated with rainfall, stand age, and topography on forested landscaped, southwestern Washington, USA. *Forest Ecology and Management*, **259**, 2233–2247.

Tyler, G. (2008). The ground beetle fauna (Coleoptera: Carabidae) of abandoned fields, as related to plant cover, previous management and succession stage. *Biodiversity and Conservation*, **17**, 155–172.

Tzanopoulos, J., Mitchley, J., & Pantis, J. D. (2007). Vegetation dynamics in abandoned crop fields on a Mediterranean island: Development of succession model and estimation of disturbance thresholds. *Agriculture Ecosystems & Environment*, **120**, 370–376.

Tzeng, H.-Y., Wang, W., Tseng, Y.-H., Chiu, C.-A., Kuo, C.-C., & Tsai, S.-T. (2018). Tree mortality in response to typhoon-induced floods and mudslides is determined by tree species, size, and position in a riparian Formosan gum forest in subtropical Taiwan. *PLoS ONE*, **13**, Article Number e0190832.

Uesaka, S. & Tsuyuzaki, S. (2004). Differential establishment and survival of species in deciduous and evergreen shrub patches and on bare ground, Mt. Koma, Hokkaido, Japan. *Plant Ecology*, **175**, 165–177.

Uhe, G. (1988). The composition of the plant communities inhabiting the volcanic ejecta of Yasour "Tanna" New Hebrides. *Tropical Ecology*, **29**, 48–54.

Ujházy, K., Fanta, J., & Prach, K. (2011). Two centuries of vegetation succession in an inland sand dune area, central Netherlands. *Applied Vegetation Science*, **14**, 316–325.

Uliassi, D. D. & Ruess, R. W. (2002). Limitations to symbiotic nitrogen fixation in primary succession on the Tanana River floodplain. *Ecology*, **83**, 88–103.

Uriarte, M., Rivera, L. W., Zimmerman, J. K., Aide, T. M., Power, A. G., & Flecker, A. S. (2004). Effects of land use history on hurricane damage and recovery in a neotropical forests. *Plant Ecology*, **174**, 49–58.

Uriarte, M., Canham, Ch. D., Thompson, J., et al. (2009). Natural disturbance and human land use as determinants of tropical forest dynamics: Results from a forest simulator. Ecological Monographs, **79**, 423–443.

Uriarte, M., Clark, J. S., Zimmerman, J. K., et al. (2012). Multidimensional trade-offs in species responses to disturbance: Implications for diversity in a subtropical forest. Ecology, **93**, 191–205.

USGS (2017). www2.usgs.gov/faq/categories/9840/2554 (accessed April 14, 2017).

Usher, M. B. (1992). Statistical models of succession. In D. C. Glenn-Lewin, R. K Peet, & T. T. Veblen, eds., Plant Succession: Theory and Prediction, pp. 215–248. London: Chapman & Hall.

Valdez-Hernández, M., Sánchez, O., Islebee, G. A., Snook, L. K., & Negreros-Castillo, P. (2014). Recovery and early succession after experimental disturbance in a seasonally dry tropical forest in Mexico. Forest Ecology and Management, **334**, 331–343.

van Andel, J. & Aronson, J. (2012). Restoration Ecology: The New Frontier, 2nd ed. London: Wiley-Blackwell.

van Andel, T. (2001). Floristic composition and diversity of mixed primary and secondary forests in northwest Guyana. Biodiversity and Conservation, **10**, 1645–1682.

Van Auken, O. W. & Bush, J. K. (1985). Secondary succession on terraces of the San Antonio River. Bulletin of the Torrey Botanical Club, **112**, 158–166.

Van Bloem, S. J., Murphy, P. G., Lugo, A. E., et al. (2005). The influence of hurricane winds on Caribbean dry forest structure and nutrient pools. Biotropica, **27**, 571–583.

Van Breugel, M., Craven, D., Lai, H. R., Baillon, M., Turner, B. L., & Hall, J. S. (2019). Soil nutrients and dispersal limitation shape compositional variation in secondary tropical forests across multiple scales. Journal of Ecology, **107**, 566–581.

Van Cleve, K. & Viereck, L. A. (1981). Forest succession in relation to nutrient cycles in the boreal forest of Alaska. In D. C. West, H. H. Shugart, & D. B. Botkin, eds., Forest Succession, pp. 185–211. New York: Springer.

Van Cleve, K., Viereck, L. A., & Schlentner, R. L. (1971). Accumulation of nitrogen in alder (Alnus) ecosystems near Fairbanks, Alaska. Arctic and Alpine Research, **3**, 101–114.

Van Cleve, K., Yarie, J., Viereck, L. A., & Dyrness, C. T. (1993). Conclusions on the role of salt-affected soils in primary succession on the Tanana River floodplain, interior Alaska. Canadian Journal of Forest Research, **23**, 1015–1018.

van Coller, A. L., Rogers, K. H., & Heritage, G. L. (2000). Riparian vegetation-environment relationships: Complimentarity of gradients versus patch hierarch approaches. Journal of Vegetation Science, **11**, 337–350.

van der Biest, K., De Nocker, L., Provoost, S., Boerema, A., Staes, J., & Meire, P. (2017). Dune dynamics safeguard ecosystem services. Ocean and Coastal Management, **149**, 148–158.

Van der Burght, L., Stoffel, M., & Bigler, C. (2012). Analysis and modeling of tree succession on a recent rockslide deposit. Plant Ecology, **213**, 35–46.

van der Ent, A., van Vugt, R., & Wellinga, S. (2015). Ecology of *Paphiopedilum rothschildianum* at the type locality in Kinabalu Park (Sabah, Malaysia). *Biodiversity and Conservation*, **24**, 1641–1656.

van der Maarel, E. (1998). Coastal dunes: Pattern and process, zonation and succession. In E. van der Maarel, ed., *Dry Coastal Ecosystems: Ecosystems of the World 2C*, pp. 505–517. The Hague: Elsevier.

van der Maarel, E., Boot, R., van Dorp, D., & Rijntjes, J. (1985). Vegetation succession on the dunes near Oostvoorne, The Netherlands: A comparison of the vegetation in 1959 and 1980. *Vegetatio*, **58**, 137–187.

van der Merwe, H. & van Rooyen, M. W. (2011). Life form and species diversity on abandoned croplands, Roggeveld, South Africa. *African Journal of Range & Forage Science*, **28**, 99–110.

van der Putten, W. H., Dijk, C. V., & Peters, B. A. M. (1993). Plant-specific soil-borne diseases contribute to succession in foredune vegetation. *Nature*, **362**, 53–56.

van der Putten, W. H., Bardgett, R. D., Bever, J. D., *et al.* (2013). Plant-soil feedbacks: The past, the present and future challenges. *Journal of Ecology*, **101**, 265–276.

van der Putten, W. H., Mortimer, S. R., Hedlund, K., *et al.* (2000). Plant species diversity as a driver of early succession in abandoned fields: A multi-site approach. *Oecologia*, **124**, 91–99.

van der Valk, A. G. (1992). Establishment, colonization and persistence. In D. C. Glenn-Lewin, R. K. Peet, & T. T. Veblen, eds., *Plant Succession: Theory and Prediction*, pp. 60–102. London: Chapman & Hall.

van der Valk, A. G. & Davis, C. B. (1978). The role of seed banks in the vegetation dynamics of prairie glacial marshes. *Ecology*, **59**, 322–335.

van de Voorde, T. F. J., van der Putten, W. H., & Bezemer, T. M. (2012). The importance of plant-soil interactions, soil nutrients, and plant life history traits for the temporal dynamics of *Jacobaea vulgaris* in a chronosequence of old-fields. *Oikos*, **121**, 1251–1262.

Van Eynde, E., Dondeyne, S., Isabirye, M., Deckers, J., & Poesen, J. (2017). Impact of landslides on soil characteristics for estimating their age. *Catena*, **157**, 173–179.

Van Gemerden, B. S., Shu, G. N., & Olff, H. (2003). Recovery of conservation values in Central African rain forest after logging and shifting cultivation. *Biodiversity and Conservation*, **12**, 1553–1570.

van Moorleghem, C. & de la Peña, E. (2016). Aphid herbivory as a potential driver of primary succession in coastal dunes. *Arthropod-Plant Interactions*, **10**, 89–100.

Van Pelt, R., O'Keefe, T. C., Latterell, J. J., & Naiman, R. J. (2006). Riparian forest stand development along the Queets River in Olympic National Park, Washington. *Ecological Monographs*, **76**, 277–298.

Vandermeer, J., Brenner, A., & Granzow de la Cerda, I. (1998). Growth rates of tree height six years after hurricane damage at four localities in eastern Nicaragua. *Biotropica*, **30**, 502–509.

Vandermeer, J., Granzow de la Cerda, I., Boucher, D., Perfecto, I., & Ruiz, J. (2000). Hurricane disturbance and tropical tree species diversity. *Science*, **290**, 788–791.

Varnes, D. J. (1958). *Special Report 29: Landslides and Engineering Practice*. Washington, DC: National Academy of Sciences, Transportation Research Board.

Vavrus, S., Ruddiman, W. F., & Kutzbach, J. E. (2008). Climate model tests of the anthropogenic influence on greenhouse-induced climate change: The role of early human agriculture, industrialization, and vegetation feedbacks. *Quaternary Science Reviews*, **27**, 1410–1425.

Vázquez-Yanes, C. & Smith, H. (1982). Phytochrome control of seed germination in the tropical rain forest pioneer trees *Cecropia obtusifolia* and *Piper auritum* and its ecological significance. *New Phytologist*, **92**, 477–485.

Vazquez-Yanes, C., Orozco-Segovia, A., Rincón, E., *et al.* (1990). Light beneath the litter in a tropical forest: Effect on seed germination. *Ecology*, **71**, 1952–1958.

Veblen, T. T. & Ashton, D. H. (1978). Catastrophic influences on the vegetation of the Valdivian Andes, Chile. *Vegetatio*, **36**, 149–167.

Veblen, T. T., Ashton, D. H., Schlegel, F. M., & Veblen, A. T. (1977). Plant succession in a timberline depressed by volcanism in south-central Chile. *Journal of Biogeography*, **4**, 275–294.

Veblen, T. T., Ashton, D. H., Rubulis, S., Lorenz, D. C., & Cortes, M. (1989). *Nothofagus* stand development on in-transit moraines, Casa Pangue Glacier, Chile. *Arctic and Alpine Research*, **21**, 144–155.

Veblen, T. T., Hadley, K. S., Nel, E. M., Kitzberger, T., Reid, M., & Villalba, R. (1994). Disturbance regime and disturbance interactions in a Rocky Mountain subalpine forest. *Journal of Ecology*, **82**, 125–135.

Velázquez, E. & Gómez-Sal, A. (2007). Environmental control of early succession in a landslide on a dry tropical ecosystem (Casita Volcano, Nicaragua). *Biotropica*, **35**, 601–609.

Velázquez, E. & Gómez-Sal, A. (2008). Landslide early succession in a neotropical dry forest. *Plant Ecology*, **199**, 295–308.

Velázquez, E. & Gómez-Sal, A. (2009a). Different growth strategies in the tropical pioneer tree *Trema micrantha* during succession on a large landslide on Casita Volcano, Nicaragua. *Journal of Tropical Ecology*, **25**, 249–260.

Velázquez, E. & Gómez-Sal, A. (2009b). Changes in the herbaceous communities on the landslide of the Casita Volcano, Nicaragua, during early succession. *Folia Geobotanica*, **44**, 1–18.

Velázquez, E., De la Cruz, M., & Gómez-Sal, A. (2014). Changes in spatial point patterns of pioneer woody plants across a large tropical landslide. *Acta Oecologica*, **61**, 9–18.

Velle, L. G. & Vandvik, V. (2014). Succession after prescribed burning in coastal *Calluna* heathlands along a 340-km latitudinal gradient. *Journal of Vegetation Science*, **25**, 546–558.

Vesipa, R., Camporeale, C., & Ridolfi, L. (2017). Effect of river flow fluctuations on riparian vegetation dynamics: Processes and models. *Advances in Water Resources*, **110**, 29–50.

Vetaas, O. R. (1994). Primary succession of plant assemblages on a glacier foreland – Bodalsbreen, southern Norway. *Journal of Biogeography*, **21**, 297–308.

Viereck, L. A. (1966). Plant succession and soil development on gravel outwash of the Muldrow Glacier, Alaska. *Ecological Monographs*, **36**, 181–199.

Viereck, L. A. (1970). Forest succession and soil development adjacent to the Chena River in interior Alaska. *Arctic and Alpine Research*, **2**, 1–26.

Viereck, L. A., Van Cleve, K., Adams, P. C., & Schlentner, R. E. (1993). Climate of the Tanana River floodplain near Fairbanks, Alaska. *Canadian Journal of Forest Research*, **23**, 899–913.

Vindušková, O. & Frouz, J. (2013). Soil carbon accumulation after open-cast coal and oil shale mining in Northern Hemisphere: A quantitative review. *Environmental Earth Sciences*, **69**, 1685–1698.

Vitousek, P. M. (1999). Nutrient limitation to nitrogen fixation in young volcanic sites. *Ecosystems*, **2**, 505–510.

Vitousek, P. M. (2004). *Nutrient Cycling and Limitation: Hawai'i as a Model System*. Princeton, NJ: Princeton University Press.

Vitousek, P. M. & Farrington, H. (1997). Nutrient limitation and soil development: Experimental test of a biogeochemical theory. *Biogeochemistry*, **37**, 63–75.

Vitousek, P. M. & Hobbie, S. (2000). Heterotrophic nitrogen fixation in decomposing litter: Patterns and regulation. *Ecology*, **81**, 2366–2376.

Vitousek, P. M. & Walker, L. R. (1987). Colonization, succession and resource availability: Ecosystem-level interactions. In A. J. Gray, M. J. Crawley, & P. J. Edwards, eds., *Colonization, Succession and Stability*, pp. 207–223. Oxford: Blackwell.

Vitousek, P. M. & Walker, L. R. (1989). Biological invasion by *Myrica faya* in Hawaii: Plant demography, nitrogen fixation, and ecosystem effects. *Ecological Monographs*, **59**, 247–265.

Vitousek, P. M., Porder, S., Houlton, B. Z., & Chadwick, O. A. (2010). Terrestrial phosphorus limitation: Mechanisms, implications, and nitrogen-phosphorus interactions. *Ecological Applications*, **20**, 5–15.

Vitousek, P. M., Walker, L. R., Whiteaker, L. D., Mueller-Dombois, D., & Matson, P. A. (1987). Biological invasion by *Myrica faya* alters primary succession in Hawaii. *Science*, **238**, 802–804.

Vitousek, P. M., Aber, J. D., Howarth, R. W., *et al.* (1997). Human alteration of the global nitrogen cycle: Sources and consequences. *Ecological Applications*, **7**, 737–750.

Vogt, K. A., Vogt, D. J., Boon, P., *et al.* (1996). Litter dynamics along stream, riparian and upslope areas following Hurricane Hugo, Luquillo Experimental Forest, Puerto Rico. *Biotropica*, **28**, 458–470.

Wali, M. K. (1999). Ecological succession and the rehabilitation of disturbed terrestrial ecosystems. *Plant and Soil*, **213**, 195–220.

Walker, J. & Reddell, P. (2007). Retrogressive succession and restoration on old landscapes. In L. R. Walker, J. Walker, & R. J. Hobbs, eds., *Linking Restoration and Ecological Succession*, pp. 69–89. New York: Springer.

Walker, J., Lees, B., Olley, J., & Thompson, C. (2018). Dating the Cooloola coastal dunes of South-Eastern Queensland, Australia. *Marine Geology*, **398**, 73–85.

Walker, J., Thompson, C. H., Fergus, I. F., & Tunstall, B. R. (1981). Plant succession and soil development in coastal sand dunes of subtropical eastern Australia. In D. C. West, H. H. Shugart, & D. B. Botkin, eds., *Forest Succession: Concepts and Applications*, pp. 107–131. New York: Springer.

Walker, L. R. (1989). Soil nitrogen changes during primary succession on a floodplain in Alaska, USA. *Arctic and Alpine Research*, **21**, 341–349.

Walker, L. R. (1991). Tree damage and recovery from Hurricane Hugo in Luquillo Experimental Forest, Puerto Rico. *Biotropica*, **23**, 379–385.

Walker, L. R. (1993). Nitrogen fixers and species replacements in primary succession. In J. Miles & D. W. H. Walton, eds., *Primary Succession on Land*, pp. 249–272. Oxford: Blackwell.

Walker, L. R. (1994). Effects of fern thickets on woodland development on landslides in Puerto Rico. *Journal of Vegetation Science*, **5**, 525–532.

Walker, L. R. (1995). How unique is primary plant succession at Glacier Bay? In D. R. Engstrom, ed., *Proceedings of the Third Glacier Bay Science Symposium, 1993*, pp. 137–146. Anchorage, AK: National Park Service.

Walker, L. R. (1999b). Patterns and processes in primary succession. In L. R. Walker, ed., *Ecosystems of Disturbed Ground, Ecosystems of the World 16*, pp. 585–610. Amsterdam: Elsevier.

Walker, L. R. (2000). Seedling and sapling dynamics of treefall pits in Puerto Rico. *Biotropica*, **32**, 262–275.

Walker, L. R. (2011). Integration of the study of natural and anthropogenic disturbances using severity gradients. *Austral Ecology*, **36**, 916–922.

Walker, L. R. (2012). *The Biology of Disturbed Habitats*. Oxford: Oxford University Press.

Walker, L. R. & Bellingham, P. J. (2011). *Island Environments in a Changing World*. Cambridge: Cambridge University Press.

Walker, L. R. & Boneta, W. (1995). Plant and soil responses to fire on a fern-covered landslide in Puerto Rico. *Journal of Tropical Ecology*, **11**, 473–479.

Walker, L. R. & Chapin, F. S. III. (1987). Interactions among processes controlling successional change. *Oikos*, **50**, 131–135.

Walker, L. R. & del Moral, R. (2003). *Primary Succession and Ecosystem Rehabilitation*. Cambridge: Cambridge University Press.

Walker, L. R. & Neris, L. E. (1993). Posthurricane seed rain dynamics in Puerto Rico. *Biotropica*, **25**, 408–418.

Walker, L. R. & Sharpe, J. M. (2010). Ferns, disturbance and succession. In K. Mehltreter, L. R. Walker, & J. M. Sharpe, eds., *Fern Ecology*, pp. 177–219. Cambridge: Cambridge University Press.

Walker, L. R. & Shiels, A. B. (2008). Post-disturbance erosion impacts carbon fluxes and plant succession on recent tropical landslides. *Plant and Soil*, **313**, 205–216.

Walker, L. R. & Shiels, A. B. (2013). *Landslide Ecology*. Cambridge: Cambridge University Press.

Walker, L. R. & Vitousek, P. M. (1991). An invader alters germination and growth of a native dominant tree in Hawai'i. *Ecology*, **72**, 1449–1455.

Walker, L. R. & Wardle, D. A. (2014). Plant succession as an integrator of contrasting ecological time scale. *Trends in Ecology and Evolution*, **29**, 504–510.

Walker, L. R., Bellingham, P. B., & Peltzer, D. A. (2006). Plant characteristics are poor predictors of microsite colonization during the first two years of primary succession. *Journal of Vegetation Science*, **17**, 397–406.

Walker, L. R., Zasada, J. C., & Chapin, F. S. III. (1986). The role of life history processes in primary succession on an Alaskan floodplain. *Ecology*, **67**, 1243–1253.

Walker, L. R., Lodge, D. J., Guzmán-Grajales, S. M., & Fetcher, N. (2003). Species-specific seedling responses to hurricane disturbance in a Puerto Rican forest. *Biotropica*, **35**, 472–485.

Walker, L. R., Wardle, D. A., Bardgett, R. D., & Clarkson, B. D. (2010b). The use of chronosequences in studies of ecological succession and soil development. *Journal of Ecology*, **98**, 725–736.

Walker, L. R., Zimmerman, J. K., Lodge, D. J., & Guzmán-Grajales, S. (1996b). An altitudinal comparison of growth and species composition in hurricane-damaged forests in Puerto Rico. *Journal of Ecology*, **84**, 877–889.

Walker, L. R., Landau, F. H., Velázquez, E., Shiels, A. B., & Sparrow, A. (2010a). Early successional woody plants facilitate and ferns inhibit forest development on Puerto Rican landslides. *Journal of Ecology*, **98**, 625–635.

Walker, L. R., Voltzow, J., Ackerman, J. D., Fernández, D. S., & Fetcher, N. (1992). Immediate impact of Hurricane Hugo on a Puerto Rican rain forest. *Ecology*, **73**, 691–694.

Walker, L. R., Zarin, D. J., Fetcher, N., Myster, R. W., & Johnson, A. H. (1996). Ecosystem development and plant succession on landslides in the Caribbean. *Biotropica*, **28**, 566–576.

Walker, L. R., Shiels, A. B., Bellingham, P. J., *et al.* (2013a). Changes in abiotic influences on seed plants and ferns during 18 years of primary succession on Puerto Rican landslides. *Journal of Ecology*, **101**, 650–661.

Walker, L. R., Sikes, D. S., DeGange, A. R., *et al.* (2013b). Biological legacies: Direct early ecosystem recovery and food web reorganization after a volcanic eruption in Alaska. *Écoscience*, **20**, 240–251.

Walker, L. R., ed. (1999a). *Ecosystems of Disturbed Ground. Ecosystems of the World 16.* Amsterdam: Elsevier.

Walker, L. R., Walker, J., & Hobbs, R. J., eds. (2007). *Linking Restoration and Ecological Succession.* New York: Springer.

Walker, L. R., Brokaw, N. V. L., Lodge, D. J., & Waide, R. B., eds. (1991). Ecosystem, plant and animal responses to hurricanes in the Caribbean. *Biotropica*, **23**, 313–521.

Walker, L. R., Silver, W. L., Willig, M. R., & Zimmerman, J. K., eds. (1996a). Long term responses of Caribbean ecosystems to disturbance. *Biotropica*, **28**, 414–614.

Walker, T. W. & Syers, J. K. (1976). The fate of phosphorus during pedogenesis. *Geoderma*, **15**, 1–19.

Walter, H. 1970. *Vegetationszonen und Klima.* Stuttgart: Verlag Eugen Ulmer.

Wang, N., Jiao, J. Y., Jia, Y. F., Bai, W. J., & Zhang, Z. G. (2010). Germinable soil seed banks and the restoration potential of abandoned cropland on the Chinese Hilly-Gullied Loess Plateau. *Environmental Management*, **46**, 367–377.

Wang, Y.-C., Ooi, M. K. J., Ren, G.-H., *et al.* (2015). Species shifts in above-ground vegetation and the soil seed bank in the inter-dune lowlands of an active dune field in Inner Mongolia, China. *Basic and Applied Ecology*, **16**, 490–499.

Ward, D. (2016). *The Biology of Deserts.* 2nd ed. Oxford: Oxford University Press.

Wardle, D. A., Walker, L. R., & Bardgett, R. D. (2004). Ecosystem properties and forest decline in contrasting long-term chronosequences. *Science*, **305**, 509–513.

Wardle, D. A., Jonsson, M., Bansal, S., Bardgett, R. D., Gundale, M. J., & Metcalfe, D. B. (2012). Linking vegetation change, carbon sequestration and biodiversity: Insights from island ecosytems in a long-term natural experiment. *Journal of Ecology*, **100**, 16–30.

Wardle, P. 1979. Primary succession in Westland National Park and its vicinity, New Zealand. *New Zealand Journal of Botany*, **18**, 221–232.

Warming, E. (1895). *Plantesamfund: Grundträk af den Ökologiska Plantegeografi*. Copenhagen: Philipsen.

Warming, E. (1909). *Oecology of Plants: An Introduction to the Study of Plant Communities*. Oxford: Clarendon Press.

Warren, D. R., Keeton, W. S., Kiffney, P. M., Kaylor, M. J., Bechtold, H. A., & Magee, J. (2016). Changing forests-changing streams: Riparian forest stand development and ecosystem function in temperate headwaters. *Ecosphere*, **7**, e01435.

Wassenaar, T. D., van Aarde, R. J., Pimm, S. L., & Ferreira, S. M. (2005). Community convergence in disturbed subtropical dune forests. *Ecology*, **86**, 655–666.

Watts, A. C. & Kobziar, L. N. (2013). Smoldering combustion and ground fires: Ecological effects and multi-scale significance. *Fire Ecology*, **9**, 124–132.

Weaver, P. L. (1989). Forest changes after hurricanes in Puerto Rico's Luquillo Mountains. *Interciencia*, **14**, 181–192.

Webb, L. J. (1958). Cyclones as an ecological factor in tropical lowland rain forest, North Queensland. *Australian Journal of Botany*, **6**, 220–230.

Webb, S. L. (1999). Disturbance by wind in temperate-zone forests. In L. R. Walker, ed., *Ecosystems of Disturbed Ground. Ecosystems of the World 16*, pp. 187–222. Amsterdam: Elsevier.

Webb, S. L. & Scanga, S. E. (2001). Windstorm disturbance without patch dynamics: Twelve years of change in a Minnesota forest. *Ecology*, **82**, 893–897.

Webster, P. J., Holland, G. J., Curry, J. A., & Chang, H.-R. (2005). Changes in tropical cyclone number, duration, and intensity in a warming environment. *Science*, **309**, 1844–1846.

Weiher, E., Clarke, G. D. P., & Keddy, P. A. (1998). Community assembly rules, morphological dispersion, and the coexistence of plant species. *Oikos*, **81**, 309–322.

Weiher, E. & Keddy, P. A., eds. (1999). *Ecological Assembly Rules: Perspectives, Advances, Retreats*. Cambridge: Cambridge University Press.

Welc, M., Frossard, E., Egli, S., Bünemann, E. K., & Jansa, J. (2014). Rhizosphere fungal assemblages and soil enzymatic activities in a 110-years alpine chronosequence. *Soil Biology & Biochemistry*, **74**, 21–30.

Wen, S., Fetcher, N., & Zimmerman, J. K. (2008). Acclimation of tropical tree species to hurricane disturbance: Ontogenetic differences. *Tree Physiology*, **28**, 935–946.

Werdin-Pfisterer, N. R., Kielland, K., & Boone, R. D. (2012). Buried organic horizon represent amino acid reservoirs in boreal forest soils. *Soil Biology and Biochemistry*, **55**, 122–131.

Whelan, P. & Bach, A. J. (2017). Retreating glaciers, incipient soils, emerging forests: 100 years of landscape change on Mount Baker, Washington, USA. *Annals of the American Association of Geographers*, **107**, 336–349.

Whelan, R. J. (1994). *The Ecology of Fire*. Cambridge: Cambridge University Press.

Whigham, D. F., Olmsted, I., Cabrera Cano, E., & Harmon, M. E. (1991). The impact of Hurricane Gilbert on trees, litter fall, and woody debris in a dry tropical forest in the northeastern Yucatan Peninsula. *Biotropica*, **23**, 434–441.

Whisenant, S. G. (1999). *Repairing Damaged Wildlands*. Cambridge: Cambridge University Press.

Whisenant, S. G., Thurow, T. L., & Maranz, S. J. (1995). Initiating autogenic restoration on shallow semiarid sites. *Restoration Ecology*, **3**, 61–67.

White, P. S. & Jentsch, A. (2001). The search for generality in studies of disturbance and ecosystem dynamics. *Progress in Botany*, **62**, 399–450.

White, P. S. & Jentsch, A. (2004). Disturbance, succession, and community assembly in terrestrial plant communities. In V. M. Temperton, R. J. Hobbs, T. Nuttle, & S. Halle, eds., *Assembly Rules and Restoration Ecology: Bridging the Gap between Theory and Practice*, pp. 342–366. Washington, DC: Island Press.

Whitfeld, T. J. S., Kress, W. J., Erickson, D. L., & Weiblen, G. D. (2012). Change in community phylogenetic structure during tropical forest succession: Evidence from New Guinea. *Ecography*, **35**, 821–830.

Whitford, W. (2002). *Ecology of Desert Systems*. New York: Academic Press.

Whitmore, T. C. (1974). Change with time and the role of cyclones in tropical rain forest on Kolombangara, Solomon Islands. Institute Paper No. 46, Commonwealth Forestry Institute, University of Oxford.

Whitmore, T. C. (1989). Changes over twenty-one years in the Kolombangara rain forests. *Journal of Ecology*, **77**, 469–483.

Whitmore, T. C. (1998). *An Introduction to Tropical Rain Forests*. Oxford: Oxford University Press.

Whittaker, R. H. (1975). *Communities and Ecosystems*. New York: MacMillan.

Whittaker, R. H. (1953). A consideration of climax theory: The climax as a population and a pattern. *Ecological Monographs*, **23**, 41–78.

Whittaker, R. J. & Bush, M. B. (1993). Dispersal and establishment of tropical forest assemblages, Krakatau, Indonesia. In J. Miles & D. W. H. Walton, eds., *Primary Succession on Land*, pp. 147–160, Oxford: Blackwell.

Whittaker, R. J. & Jones, S. H. (1994). The role of frugivorous bats and birds in the rebuilding of a tropical forest ecosystem, Krakatau, Indonesia. *Journal of Biogeography*, **21**, 689–702.

Whittaker, R. J. & Turner, B. D. (1994). Dispersal, fruit utilization and seed predation of *Dysoxylum gaudichaudianum* in early successional rainforest, Krakatau, Indonesia. *Journal of Tropical Ecology*, **10**, 167–181.

Whittaker, R. J., Bush, M. B., & Richards, K. (1989). Plant recolonization and vegetation succession on the Krakatau Islands, Indonesia. *Ecological Monographs*, **59**, 59–123.

Whittaker, R. J., Jones, S. H., & Partomihardjo, T. (1997). The rebuilding of an isolated rain forest assemblage, how disharmonic is the flora of Krakatau? *Biodiversity and Conservation*, **6**, 1671–1696.

Whittaker, R. J., Walden, J., & Hill, J. (1992). Post-1883 ash fall on Panjang and Sertung and its ecological impact. *GeoJournal*, **28**, 153–171.

Widenfalk, O. & Weslien, J. (2009). Plant species richness in managed boreal forests: Effects of stand succession and thinning. *Forest Ecology and Management*, **257**, 1386–1394.

Wiegleb, G. & Felinks, B. (2001). Predictability of early stages of primary succession in post-mining landscapes of Lower Lusatia, Germany. *Applied Vegetation Science*, **4**, 5–18.

Wieland, L. M., Mesquita, R. C. G., Bobrowiec, P. E. D., Bentos, T. V., & Williamson, G. B. (2011). Seed rain and advance regeneration in secondary succession in the Brazilian Amazon. *Tropical Conservation Science*, **4**, 300–316.

Wielgolaski, F. E., ed. (1997). *Polar and Alpine Tundra: Ecosystems of the World 3*. Amsterdam: Elsevier.

Williams, B. K. (2011). Adaptive management of natural resources: Framework and issues. *Journal of Environmental Management*, **92**, 1346–1353.

Willig, M. R., Kaufman, D. M., & Stevens, R. D. (2003). Latitudinal gradients of biodiversity: Pattern, process, scale, and synthesis. *Annual Review of Ecology and Systematics*, **34**, 273–309.

Wilmshurst, J. M. & McGlone, M. S. (1996). Forest disturbance in the central North Island, New Zealand, following the 1850 BP Taupo eruption. *The Holocene*, **6**, 399–411.

Wilsey, B. (2018). *The Biology of Grasslands*. Oxford: Oxford University Press.

Wilson, J. B. (1994). Who makes the assembly rules? *Journal of Vegetation Science*, **2**, 289–290.

Wilson, J. B. & Agnew, A. D. Q. (1992). Positive-feedback switches in plant communities. *Advances in Ecological Research*, **23**, 263–336.

Wilson, J. B., Peet, R. K., Dengler, J., & Pärtel, M. (2012). Plant species richness: The world records. *Journal of Vegetation Science*, **23**, 796–802.

Wilson, R. E. (1970). Succession in stands of Populus deltoids along the Missouri River in southeastern South Dakota. *The American Midland Naturalist*, **83**, 330–342.

Wilson, S. D. & Tilman, D. (2002). Quadratic variation in old-field species richness along gradients of disturbance and nitrogen. *Ecology*, **83**, 492–504.

Wiser, S. K., Allen, R. B., & Platt, K. H. (1997). Mountain beech forest succession after a fire at Mount Thomas Forest, Canterbury, New Zealand. *New Zealand Journal of Botany*, **35**, 505–515.

Wittmann, F. & Parolin, P. (2005). Aboveground roots in Amazonian floodplain trees. *Biotropica*, **37**, 609–619.

Woch, M. W., Kapusta, P., & Stefanowicz, A. M. (2016). Variation in dry grassland communities along a heavy metals gradient. *Ecotoxicology*, **25**, 80–90.

Wohlgemuth, T., Jentsch, A., & Seidl, R. (2019). *Störungsökologie*. Bern, Switzerland: UBT.

Wolkovich, E. M., Cook, B. I., McLauchlan, K. K., & Davies, T. J. (2014). Temporal ecology in the Anthropocene. *Ecology Letters*, **17**, 1365–1379.

Wong, N. K., Morgan, J. W., & Dorrough, J. (2010). A conceptual model of plant community changes following cessation of cultivation in semi-arid grassland. *Applied Vegetation Science*, **13**, 389–402.

Wood, T. W. W. (1970). Wind damage in the forest of Western Samoa. *The Malayan Forester*, **23**, 92–99.

Woodley, J. D., Chornesky, E. A., Clifford, P. A., *et al.* (1981). Hurricane Allen's impact on Jamaican coral reefs. *Science*, **214**, 749–755.

Worley, I. A. (1973). The "black crust" phenomena in upper Glacier Bay, Alaska. *Northwest Science*, **47**, 20–29.

Woziwoda, B. & Kopec, D. (2014). Afforestation or natural succession? Looking for the best way to manage abandoned cut-over peatlands for biodiversity conservation. *Ecological Engineering*, **63**, 143–152.

Wozniak, G., Chmura, D., Blonska, A., Tokarska-Guzik, B., & Sierka, E. (2011). Applicability of functional groups concept in analysis of spatiotemporal vegetation changes on manmade habitats. *Polish Journal of Environmental Studies*, **20**, 623–631.

Wright, A., Schnitzer, S., Dickie, I., *et al.* (2013). Complex facilitation and competition in a temperate grassland: Loss of plant diversity and elevated CO_2 have divergent and opposite effects on oak establishment. *Oecologia*, **171**, 449–458.

Wright, J. P. & Fridley, J. D. (2010). Biogeographic synthesis of secondary succession rates in eastern North America. *Journal of Biogeography*, **37**, 1584–1596.

Wright, R. A. & Mueller-Dombois, D. (1988). Relationships among shrub population structure, species associations, seedling root form and early volcanic succession, Hawaii. In M. J. A. Werger, P. J. M. van der Aart, H. J. During, & J. T. A. Verhoeven, eds., *Plant Form and Vegetation Structure*, pp. 87–104. The Hague: SPB Academic Publishing.

Wu, G. L., Zhao, L. P., Wang, D., & Shi, Z. H. (2014). Effects of time-since-fire on vegetation composition and structures in semi-arid perennial grassland on the Loess Plateau, China. *Clean-Soil Air Water*, **42**, 98–103.

Wu, G., Jiang, S., Liu, W., Zhao, C., & Li, J. (2016). Competition between *Populus euphratica* and *Tamarix ramosissima* seedlings under simulated high groundwater availability. *Journal of Arid Land*, **2**, 293–303.

Wynn-Williams, D. D. (1993). Microbial processes and initial stabilization of fellfield soil. In J. Miles & D. W. H. Walton, eds., *Primary Succession on Land*, pp. 17–32. Oxford: Blackwell.

Xi, H., Feng, Q., Zhang, L., *et al.* (2016). Effects of water and salinity on plant species composition and community succession in Ejina Desert Oasis, northwest China. *Environmental Earth Sciences*, **75**, 138. doi: 10.1007/s12665-015-4823-7.

Xue, S., Zhu, F., Kong, X., *et al.* (2016). A review of the characterization and revegetation of bauxite residues (red mud). *Environmental Science Pollution Research*, **23**, 1120–1132.

Yamamoto, S.-I. (1995). Natural disturbance and tree species coexistence in an old-growth beech-dwarf bamboo forest, southwestern Japan. *Journal of Vegetation Science*, **6**, 875–886.

Yamanaka, T. & Okabe, H. (2006). Distribution of *Frankia*, ectomycorrhizal fungi, and bacteria in soil after the eruption of Miyake-Jima (Izu Islands, Japan) in 2000. *Journal of Forest Research*, **11**, 21–26.

Yanagawa, A., Sasaki, T., Jamsran, U., Okuro, T., & Takeuchi, K. (2016). Factors limiting vegetation recovery processes after cessation of cropping in a semiarid grassland in Mongolia. *Journal of Arid Environments*, **131**, 1–5.

Yang, Q.-W., Liu, S.-J., Hu, C.-H., *et al.* (2016). Ecological species groups and interspecific association of vegetation in natural recovery process at Xiejiadian landslide after 2008 Wenchuan earthquake. *Journal of Mountain Science*, **13**, 1609–1620.

Yannelli, F. A., Tabeni, S., Mastrantonio, L. E., & Vezzani, N. (2014). Assessing degradation of abandoned farmlands for conservation of the Monte Desert biome in Argentina. *Environmental Management*, **53**, 231–239.

Yao, J., He, X. Y., Wang, A. Z., *et al.* (2012). Influence of forest management regimes on forest dynamics in the upstream region of the Hun River in Northeastern China. *PLoS ONE*, **7**(6), e39058.

Yap, S. L., Davies, S. J., & Condit, R. (2016). Dynamic response of a Philippine dipterocarp forest to typhoon disturbance. *Journal of Vegetation Science*, **27**, 133–143.

Yates, C. J., Hopper, S. D., Brown, A., & van Leeuwen, S. (2003). Impact of two wildfires on endemic granite outcrop vegetation in Western Australia. *Journal of Vegetation Science*, **14**, 185–194.

Yoshida, T. & Noguchi, M. (2008). Vulnerability to strong winds for major tree species in a northern Japanese mixed forest: Analyses of historical data. *Ecological Research*, **24**, 909–919.

Young, D. R., Erickson, D. L., & Semones, S. W. (1994). Salinity and the small-scale distribution of three barrier island shrubs. *Canadian Journal of Botany*, **72**, 1365–1372.

Young, I. W. R., Naguit, C., Halwas, S. J., Renault, S., & Markham, J. H. (2013). Natural revegetation of a boreal gold mine tailings pond. *Restoration Ecology*, **21**, 498–505.

Young, T. P., Chase, J. M., & Huddleston, R. T. (2001). Community succession and assembly comparing contrasting and combining paradigms in the context of ecological restoration. *Ecological Restoration*, **19**, 5–18.

Zarin, D. J. & Johnson, A. H. (1995a). Base saturation, nutrient cation, and organic matter increases during early pedogenesis on landslide scars in the Luquillo Experimental Forest, Puerto Rico. *Geoderma*, **65**, 317–330.

Zarin, D. J. & Johnson, A. H. (1995b). Nutrient accumulation during primary succession in a montane tropical forest, Puerto Rico. *Soil Science Society of America Journal*, **59**, 1444–1452.

Zhang, J.-Y. & Wu, Y.-X. (2014). Changes in diversity and importance of clonal plants during sand dune succession in northeastern China. *Ecological Research*, **29**, 393–399.

Zhao, D., Allen, B., & Sharitz, R. (2006). Twelve year response of old-growth southeastern bottomland hardwood forests to disturbance from Hurricane Hugo. *Canadian Journal of Forest Research*, **36**, 3136–3147.

Zhu, W. Z., Cheng, S., Cai, X. H., He, F., & Wang, J. X. (2009). Changes in plant species diversity along a chronosequence of vegetation restoration in the humid evergreen broad-leaved forest in the Rainy Zone of West China. *Ecological Research*, **24**, 315–325.

Zimmerman, J. K., Aide, T. M., & Lugo, A. E. (2007). Implications of land use history for natural forest regeneration and restoration strategies in Puerto Rico. In V. A. Cramer & R. J. Hobbs, eds., *Old Field Dynamics and Restoration of Abandoned Farmland*, pp. 51–74. Washington, DC: Island Press.

Zimmerman, J. K., Willig, M. R., Walker, L. R., & Silver, W. L. (1996). Introduction: Disturbance and Caribbean ecosystems. *Biotropica*, **28**, 414–423.

Zimmerman, J. K., Aide, T. M., Rosario, M., Serrano, M., & Herrera, L. (1995). Effects of land management and a recent hurricane on forest structure and composition in the Luquillo Experimental Forest, Puerto Rico. *Forest Ecology and Management*, **77**, 65–76.

Zimmerman, J. K., Everham, E. M. III, Waide, R. B., Lodge, D. J., Taylor, C. M., & Brokaw, N. V. L. (1994). Responses of tree species to hurricane winds in sub-tropical wet forest in Puerto Rico: Implications for tropical tree life histories. *Journal of Ecology*, **82**, 911–922.

Zobel, D. B. & Antos, J. A. (1991). Growth and development of natural seedlings of *Abies* and *Tsuga* in old-growth forest. *Journal of Ecology*, **79**, 985–998.

Zobel, D. B. & Antos, J. A. (2009). Species properties and recovery from disturbance: Forest herbs buried by volcanic tephra. *Journal of Vegetation Science*, **20**, 650–662.

Zobel, D. B. & Antos, J. A. (2016). Flowering patterns of understory herbs 30 years after disturbance of subalpine old-growth forests by tephra from Mount St. Helens. *International Journal of Plant Sciences*, **177**, 145–156.

Zobel, M. (1997). The relative of species pools in determining plant species richness: An alternative explanation of species coexistence? *Trends in Ecology and Evolution*, **12**, 266–269.

Zobel, M., van der Maarel, E., & Dupré, C. (1998). Species pool: The concept, its determination and significance for community restoration. *Applied Vegetation Science*, **1**, 55–66.

Index

The page numbers in italics refer to figures or tables